Installing and Configuring Windows Server 2016 (Hands-on Lab Manual Guide)

Copyright © 2018 ProTechGurus

All rights reserved.

Contents

Copyright 8

About This Book 8

Audience and Candidates Prerequisites 8

Disclaimer 8

What's New in Windows Server 2016? 9

    Host Guardian Service 9

    Multipoint Services 9

    Windows Server Essentials Experience 9

    Setup and Boot Event Collections 9

    SMB Bandwidth Limit 9

    Windows Biometric Framework 9

    BitLocker Network Unlock 10

What's new in Windows Server 2016 Hyper-V 11

    Host Resource Protection 11

    Hot Add and Remove Network Adapters and Memory 11

    Linux Secure Boot 11

    Nested Virtualization 11

    Windows PowerShell Direct 12

    Discrete Device Assignment 12

    Shielded Virtual Machines 12

    Hyper-V Containers 12

What's new in DNS in Windows Server 2016 13

    DNS Policies 13

    In which scenarios, the DNS policies can help you? 13

    Response Rate Limiting 13

    DNS-based Authentication of Named Entities 13

    Supports Unknown Records 14

    Supports IPv6 Root Hints 14

Working with Windows Server 2016 Desktop Experience 15

    Start button 15

    Task Manager 16

    Task View 17

Setup Your Virtual Lab 19
    Preparing Virtual Lab Setup 19
    Task 1: Installing VMware Workstation on the Host Machine 21
    Task 2: Installing and Configuring the DC1 Virtual Machine 22
    Task 3: Configuring the DC1 Virtual Machine 27
    Task 4: Promoting the DC1 Virtual Machine as a Domain Controller 28
    Task 5: Installing and Configuring the SERVER1 Virtual Machine 32
    Task 6: Installing and Configuring the CLIENT1 Virtual Machine 33
    Task 7: Installing and Configuring the ROUTER Virtual Machine 34
    Task 8: Creating and Configuring the SERVER2 Virtual Machine 37
    Task 9: Creating Snapshots of Virtual Machines 38

Exercise 1: Installing and Configuring Windows Server Core Machine 39
    Task 1: Installing Windows Server Core Machine. 39
    Task 2: Configuring the Windows Server 2016 Core Machine. 41
    Task 3: Adding CORE1 to Domain 44

Exercise 2: Managing Servers Remotely 46
    Task 1: Creating and Managing the Server Group 46
    Task 2: Deploying Roles and Features on CORE1 Machine 47
    Task 3: Managing Services on the CORE1 Machine. 49

Exercise 3: Using Windows PowerShell to Manage Servers 52
    Task 1: Using the Windows PowerShell to Connect Remotely to Servers and View Information 52
    Task 2: Using Windows PowerShell to Manage Roles and Features Remotely 53

Exercise 4: Installing and Configuring Domain Controllers 55
    Task 1: Adding the AD DS Role on a Member Server 55
    Task 2: Configuring SERVER1 Server as a Domain Controller 57
    Task 3: Configuring SERVER1 as a Global Catalog Server 59

Exercise 5: Installing and Configuring Read-Only Domain Controller (RODC) 61
    Task 1: Preparing DC1 to Deploy RODC 61
    Task 2: Installing RODC Domain Controller 62
    Task 3: Verifying RODC Configuration 66
    Task 4: Securing Accounts If an RODC is Stolen 69

Exercise 6: Installing a Domain Controller by Using IFM 72

Task 1: Generating a IFM Data File..72

Task 2: Adding the AD DS Role to the Member Server 72

Task 3: Configuring SERVER1 as a New Domain Controller Using the IFM Data File........74

Exercise 7: Managing Organizational Units and Groups in AD DS....................................77

Task 1: Managing Organizational Units and Groups 77

Task 2: Delegating the Permissions 80

Task 3: Configuring Home Folders for User Accounts 82

Task 4: Testing and Verifying the Home Folders and Delegated Permissions.................86

Task 5: Resetting the Computer Accounts 88

Task 6: Examining the Behavior when a User Logins on Client. 89

Task 7: Rejoining the Domain to Reconnect the Computer Account 89

Exercise 8: Using Windows PowerShell to Create User Accounts and Groups 92

Task 1: Creating a User Account Using Windows PowerShell 92

Task 2: Creating Groups Using Windows PowerShell..92

Task 3: Exporting User Accounts Using the ldifde Tool 93

Exercise 9: Installing and Configuring the DHCP Server Role 94

Task 1: Installing the DHCP Server Role 94

Task 2: Configuring the DHCP Scope 95

Task 3: Configuring DHCP Client..100

Task 4: Configuring DHCP Reservation 101

Exercise 10: Configuring IPAM with DHCP 105

Task 1: Installing IPAM Feature on SERVER1..105

Task 2: Configuring IPAM Server 105

Task 3: Verifying IPAM Configuration..111

Exercise 11: Installing and Configuring DNS..113

Task 1: Configuring SERVER1 as a Domain Controller without Installing the DNS Server Role 113

Task 2: Creating and Configuring the Myzone.local Zone on DC1...................................115

Task 3: Adding the DNS Server Role on the SERVER1 118

Task 4: Verifying Replication of the mcsalab.local Zone 119

Task 5: Configuring DNS Forwarder 121

Task 6: Managing the DNS Cache 123

Exercise 12: Installing and Configuring Windows Deployment Services (WDS)................126

Prerequisites to Configure WDS Server 126

Task 01: Installing WDS Server Role 126

Task 02: Configure WDS Server 127

Task 03: Adding Install Image to WDS Server 129

Task 04: Adding Boot Image to WDS Server 130

Task 05: Installing Windows OS using WDS 131

Exercise 13: Implementing LAN Routing 132

Task 1: Installing the LAN Routing Feature on ROUTER 132

Task 2: Configuring the LAN Routing Service on ROUTER 133

Task 3: Testing the Connectivity between DC1 and SERVER2 Servers 135

Exercise 14: Configuring IPv6 Addressing 138

Task 1: Disabling IPv6 Address on DC1 138

Task 2: Disabling IPv4 Address on SERVER2 141

Task 3: Configuring an IPv6 Network on ROUTER 142

Task 4: Verifying IPv6 Address on SERVER2 143

Exercise 15: Installing and Configuring Remote Access VPN Server 144

Task 1: Installing Remote Access Service Role 144

Task 2: Configure VPN 145

Task 3: Creating VPN User 149

Task 4: Connecting VPN Client to VPN Server 150

Exercise 16: Installing and Configuring Disk Storage 156

Task 1: Adding New Virtual Disks to DC1 156

Task 2: Initializing the Added Disks 158

Task 3: Creating and Formatting Simple Volumes 160

Task 4: Shrinking the Volumes 162

Task 5: Extending the Volumes 163

Exercise 17: Configuring a Redundant Storage Space 165

Task 1: Creating a Storage Pool 165

Task 2: Creating a Mirrored Virtual Disk 167

Task 3: Creating a File in to Mirrored Volume1 171

Task 4: Removing a Physical Drive 171

Task 5: Verifying the File Availability 172

Exercise 18: Implementing File Sharing 174

Task 1: Creating the Folder Structure for the New Share 174

Task 2: Configuring NTFS Permissions on the Folder Structure 175

Task 3: Sharing the Folder 178

Task 4: Accessing the Shared Folder 180

Task 5: Enabling Access-based Enumeration 180

Task 6: Testing the Access-based Enumeration Configuration 181

Exercise 19: Implementing Shadow Copies 183

Task 1: Configuring Shadow Copies 183

Task 2: Recovering a Deleted File Using Shadow Copy 184

Exercise 20: Implementing Network Printing 186

Task 1: Installing the Print and Document Services Server Role 186

Task 2: Installing a New Printer 186

Task 3: Configuring Printer Pooling 188

Task 4: Connecting a Printer on a Client 190

Exercise 21: Implementing Group Policy Objects 192

Task 1: Creating a New GPO 192

Task 2: Configuring the Internet Explorer GPO 193

Task 3: Creating a Domain User to Test the GPO 195

Task 4: Testing the Internet Explorer GPO 195

Task 5: Configuring Security Filtering to Exempt a User from the Internet Explorer GPO
 196

Task 6: Testing the Internet Explorer GPO 198

Exercise 22: Implementing AppLocker and Firewall Using Group Policy 200

Task 1: Restricting an Application Using AppLocker 200

Task 2: Configuring Windows Firewall Rules Using Group Policy 206

Exercise 23: Installing and Configuring Network Load Balancing 211

Task 1: Installing the Network Load Balancing Feature on NLB nodes 211

Task 2: Configuring A Network Load Balance Cluster 212

Task 3: Configuring Default Website to Test the NLB Configuration 218

Task 4: Verifying NLB Cluster 219

Copyright

The author holds all the rights of publishing and reproducing to this book. The content of this book cannot be reproduced or copied in any form or by any means or reproduced without the prior written permission of the author.

About This Book

MCSA Windows Server 2016 certification is in the beta state that contains three exams: 740, 741, and 742. This book is mainly covers the topics of MCSA Windows Server 2016 740 exam.
This book contains the virtual lab setup guide and the lab exercises for installing and configuring Windows Server 2016. You can create the virtual lab infrastructure on your own system and you can easily perform all the lab exercises mentioned in this book. Candidate having the basic knowledge of Windows operating systems and networking fundamentals can perform all the lab exercises without (or least) the need of a trainer or faculty. This book mainly covers the initial implementation and configuration of core services, such as AD DS, networking services.

Audience and Candidates Prerequisites

This book is intended for the candidates who have basic operating system knowledge, and want to gain the hands-on practice skills and knowledge necessary to implement the core infrastructure services. In addition, this book is also helpful for the candidate who are looking for certification in the Windows Server 2016 platform.
The candidates should have the basic knowledge of the networking fundamentals, Windows-based operating systems, and virtualization platforms to perform the hands-on practices.

Disclaimer

We made almost every effort to avoid errors or omissions in this guide. However, errors may slink in. Any mistake, error or discrepancy noted by the readers are requested to share with us, which will be highly appreciable. The contents and images in this guide could include technical inaccuracies or typographical errors. Author(s) or publisher makes no representations about the accuracy of the information contained in the guide. All product and company names are trademarks™ or registered® trademarks mentioned in this book (such as Microsoft, VMware, VirtualBox) of their respective holders. Use of them does not imply any affiliation with or endorsement by them.

What's New in Windows Server 2016?

In Windows Server 2016, there are many new roles and features have been added. Some of the major new roles and features are:

- Host Guardian Service
- Multipoint Services
- Windows Server Essentials Experience
- Setup and Boot Event Collections
- SMB Bandwidth Limit
- Windows Biometric Framework
- BitLocker Network Unlock

Host Guardian Service

The Host Guardian Service (HGS) is a server role introduced in Windows Server 2016. It provides the Attestation and Key Protection services that allow Guarded Hosts to run shielded virtual machines. The Attestation service validates guarded host identity and configuration. The Key Protection service allows transport keys to enable guarded hosts to unlock and run shielded virtual machines.

Multipoint Services

It allows multiple users to simultaneously share one computer and each user has their own independent and familiar Windows experience.

Windows Server Essentials Experience

This is a role service that sets up the IT infrastructure and offers powerful functions, such as "PC backups" that helps organizations' to protect data, and "Remote Web Access" that helps access business information from anywhere, virtually. It also helps you to simply and rapidly connect to cloud-based applications and services to extend the functionality of the servers.

Setup and Boot Event Collections

It is a feature that enables the collection and logging of setup and boot events from other computers on the network.

SMB Bandwidth Limit

This feature provides a mechanism to track SMB traffic per category and allows you to limit the amount of traffic allowed for a given category. It is commonly used to limit the bandwidth used by live migration over SMB.

Windows Biometric Framework

This feature allows fingerprint devices to be used to identify and verify identities and to sign in to Windows.

BitLocker Network Unlock

This feature enables a network-based key protector to be used to automatically unlock

BitLocker-protected operating system drives in domain-joined computers, when the computer is restarted.

What's new in Windows Server 2016 Hyper-V

We have already discussed about the major new features of Windows Server 2016. Here we will describe what's new in Windows Server 2016 Hyper-V. There are various new features and improvements have been added to the Hyper-V server role in Windows Server 2016. Some of the major new features of Windows Server 2016 Hyper-V are listed below:

Host Resource Protection

When you run multiple applications on a Hyper-V virtual machine, the virtual machine starts to consume more resources of the Hyper-V host. If the Hyper-V host does not have much of resources, the performance of Hyper-V host will be degraded. Host resource protection feature helps you to overcome these issues. It allows you to enforce a virtual machine to use only the amount of resources for that it is allowed. So the virtual machine cannot use the excessive resources of the host machine. Thus preventing from degrading the performance of the host or other virtual machines.

Hot Add and Remove Network Adapters and Memory

How swapping is a technique that allows you to add or remove components to a system or device while the device or system is running. In Windows Server 2016 Hyper-V, you can now add or remove a network adapter without shutting down the virtual machine. However, this applies only to the Generation 2 virtual machines. In addition, now, in Windows Server 2016 Hyper-V role, you can also modify the amount of virtual memory for a virtual machine while the virtual machine being used.

Linux Secure Boot

Secure boot is a trending security feature in nowadays. It prevents the systems from the malicious users who try to take control of the system by inserting a code or script that works even before the system or machine boots. With the help of Windows Server 2016 Hyper-V, now, you can enable secure boot for the latest Linux-based virtual machine. Secure Boot is supported on the following Linux platforms and versions:

1. Ubuntu 14.04 and later

2. SUSE Linux Enterprise Server 12 and later

3. Red Hat Enterprise Linux 7.0 and later

4. CentOS 7.0 and later

Nested Virtualization

Nested virtualization allows you to run a Hypervisor inside a Hypervisor. Means, you can run a virtual machine inside a virtual machine. This was initially supported by VMware platform. But, now with Hyper-V in Windows Server 2016, you can install and use Hyper-V role on a virtual machine that is already running on the Hyper-V host. Nested virtualization is especially useful in the development, training, and testing environments. In order to use nested virtualization, the Hyper-V must have at least 4 GB of RAM and the Intel VT-x supported processor.

Note: Currently, only Intel processors support the Nested virtualization.

Windows PowerShell Direct

In the previous version Windows servers, the virtual machines are typically managed by using the VMConnect and Remote Desktop Protocol (RDP). However, RDP requires a proper network connection and Windows Firewall configuration. With the introduction of Hyper-V in Windows Server 2016, a new method has been introduced to manage Hyper-V virtual machine called "Windows PowerShell Direct". By using this feature, you can directly run the PowerShell cmdlets on virtual machines from the Hyper-V host. More importantly, you don't need to setup networking or configure Windows Firewall.

Discrete Device Assignment

This feature enables Hyper-V virtual machines to directly and exclusively access to some PCIe devices. Logically, it acts in the same manner as a physical machine access the PCIe devices. Thus resulting the faster access the host resources.

Shielded Virtual Machines

With the more and more use and rapid growth of the Cloud technologies, data security becoming a major concern for the companies who want to deploy their virtual machines on the vendor's Cloud. On the Public Cloud platform, a cloud service provider typically hosts the virtual machines of various customers. What would happen if somehow a customer get access (or copy) the virtual machines' Virtual Hard Disk (VHD or VHDX) files of another customer's VHDs? The copied VHDs can be imported and used on the other compatible Hyper-V hosts. Now, I think you got the idea behind introducing the Shielded Virtual Machine feature.

Here, comes a new security feature called "Shielded Virtual Machine" for Windows Server 2016 Hyper-V hosts. Shielded virtual machines make it tougher for unintended Hyper-V administrators and malware on the host to access, interfere with, or steal data from a shielded virtual machine. For this, first, you need to encrypt the virtual machine. Once the virtual machine is encrypted using the Shielded virtual machine, it can run only on the authorized Hyper-V hosts. The authorized Hyper-V hosts are determined by a server called Host Guardian Server.

Hyper-V Containers

Hyper-V containers are the light-weight form of virtual machines. Each Hyper-V container allows you to run many isolated applications on a single system. The most important things behind the popularity of containers are their fast to build, highly scalable, and portable behaviors.

What's new in DNS in Windows Server 2016

Windows Server 2016 is almost ready to be launched. The expected release date for Windows Server 2016 is the first quarter in 2017. There are various new features and enhancement (improvements) have been introduced with Windows Server 2016. Here, we are going to discuss what is new in DNS server in Windows Server 2016.

The following are some of the key features and functions that are available within DNS Server in Windows Server 2016.

Note: This article is based on Windows Server 2016 technical preview 5 version.

DNS Policies

You can configure DNS policies to define how a DNS server answers to DNS queries. DNS responses can be based on client IP address (location), time of the day, and several other parameters.

In which scenarios, the DNS policies can help you?

The following are some of the common scenarios where DNS policies can be helpful:

Application high availability: DNS clients can be redirected to the best-suited endpoint for a specific application.

Traffic management: Now, DNS server helps to utilize bandwidth in the better manner. In order to reduce the bandwidth consumption, DNS clients can be redirected to the nearest datacenter.

Split-Brain DNS: DNS records are split into different Zone Scopes. The DNS clients receive an answer depending on whether they are internal or external clients.

Protection from malicious users: Malicious IP addresses and FQDNs can be blocked to prevent from performing DNS queries. In addition, malicious DNS clients can be redirected to a specific network zone (where they can be managed) instead of the system they are trying to access.

Time and day based redirection: This allows you to redirect specific DNS clients to specific datacenters during the specific time of the day.

Response Rate Limiting

You can enable response rate limiting on your DNS servers. Doing this allows you to avoid the possibility of malicious systems using your DNS servers to initiate a Denial of Service (DoS) attack from a DNS client.

DNS-based Authentication of Named Entities

With the DNS in Windows Server 2016, you can use Transport Layer Security Authentication (TLSA) records to prevent Man-In-The-Middle (MITM) attacks.

Supports Unknown Records

With the DNS in Windows Server 2016, you can add records which are not explicitly supported by the Windows DNS server. This is done by using the unknown record feature.

Supports IPv6 Root Hints

Now, DNS server in Windows Server 2016 supports the native IPv6 root hints. It helps to perform the Internet name resolution using the IPv6 root servers. What's new in DNS Server in Windows Server 2016

Along with the above-mentioned new features of DNS Server in Windows Server 2016, there are various new Windows PowerShell cmdlets have been added. These new cmdlets allow you to configure and manage the DNS server in Windows Server 2016 with more flexibility and CLI control.

Working with Windows Server 2016 Desktop Experience

GUI interface of Windows Server 2016 is almost has similar functions as used in windows Server 2012 R2. However, there are some new feature have been added to make the user experience more interesting. Some of the basic GUI features are:
- Start button
- Task Manager
- Task View

Start button

1. Sign in to **DC1** and click the **Start** button. It will show you the various options, such as **Server Manager**, **Settings**, **PowerShell**, and **Calculator** that can be accessed directly.

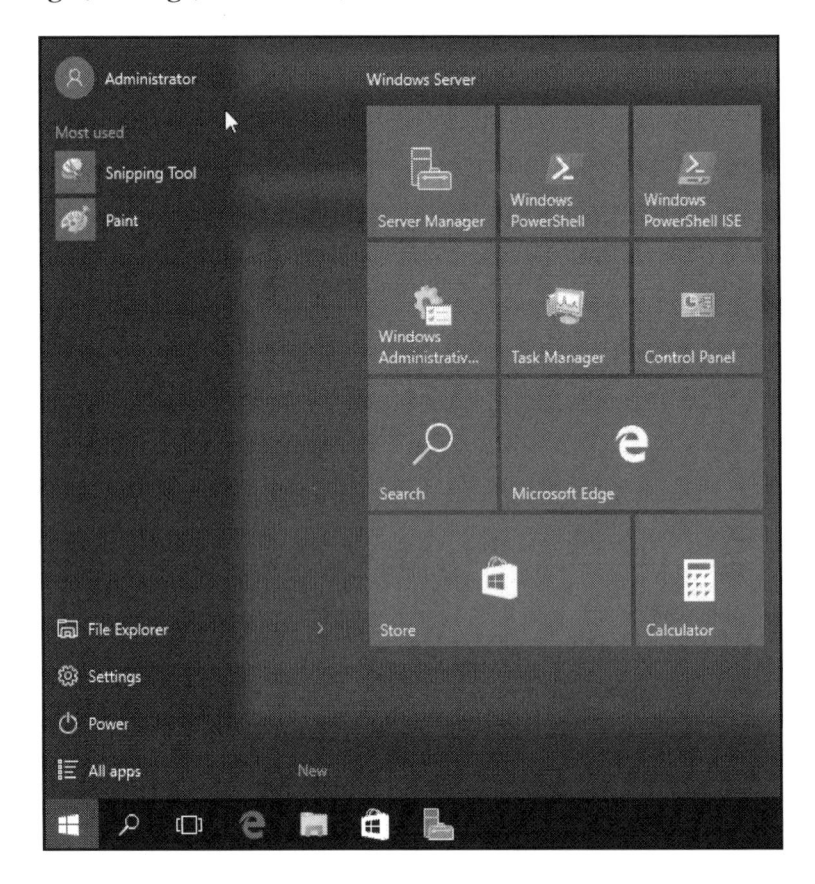

2. If you right-click the **Start** button, it will show you few more options, as shown in the following figure.

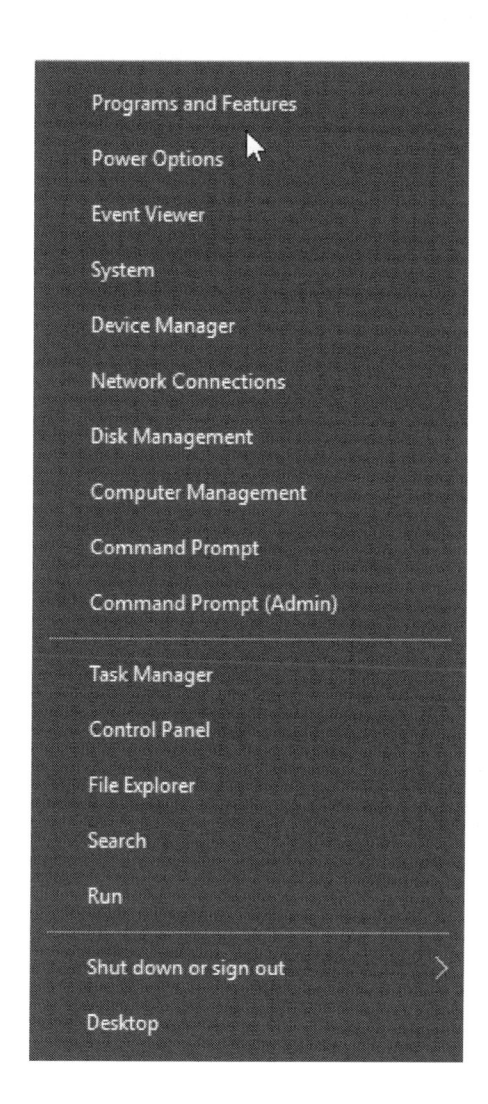

```
Programs and Features

Power Options

Event Viewer

System

Device Manager

Network Connections

Disk Management

Computer Management

Command Prompt

Command Prompt (Admin)

Task Manager

Control Panel

File Explorer

Search

Run

Shut down or sign out          >

Desktop
```

Task Manager

The Task Manager in Windows Server 2016 is much similar to the Task Manager that has been used in Windows Server 2012 R2.

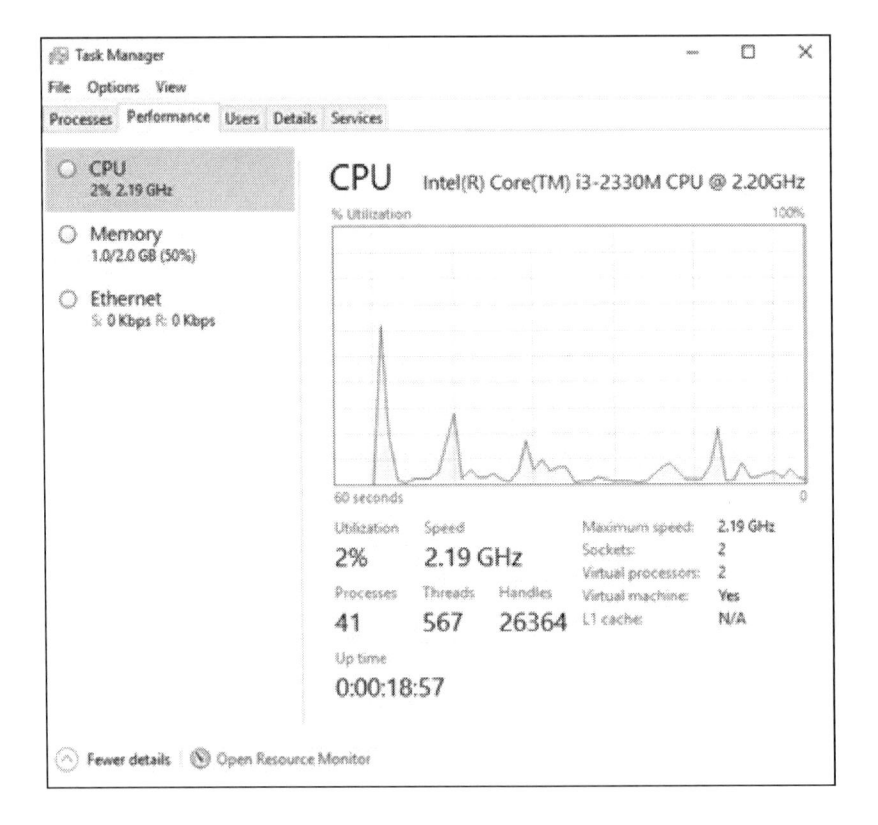

Task View

Task View allows you to view and switch between different active windows. This feature was not available in Windows Server 2012 R2.

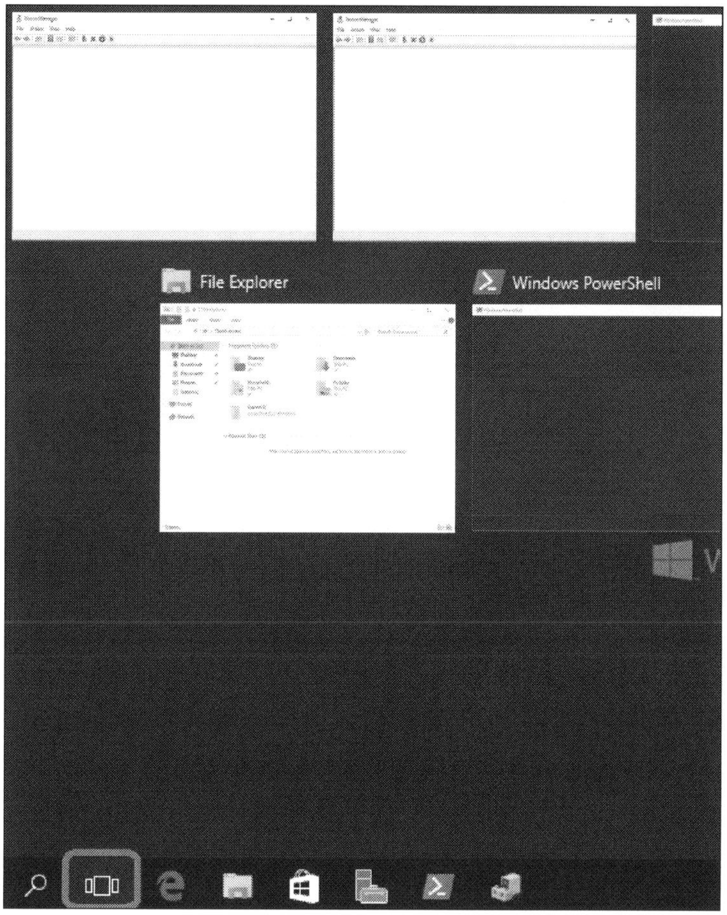
File Explorer
Windows PowerShell

Setup Your Virtual Lab

All the lab exercises mentioned in this book will be tested and performed using VMware Workstation/Player platform. Alternatively, you can also use VirtualBox or Hyper-V platform. You can visit the following links for the if you want to know more about VirtualBox and VMware platform:

- http://protechgurus.com/getting-started-virtualbox-step-by-step-guide/
- http://protechgurus.com/category/vmware/

The virtual machines that will be used throughout this book are listed in the following table.

S. No.	VM Name	Operating System
1	Core	Windows Server 2016
2	DC1	Windows Server 2016
3	SERVER1	Windows Server 2016
4	CLIENT1	Windows 8.1/10
5	ROUTER1	Windows Server 2016
6	SERVER2	Windows Server 2016

To prepare the virtual machines mentioned in the preceding table, you need ISO images. You can download the evaluation ISO images (Windows Server 2016 (Technical Preview) and Windows 8.1/10) from the Microsoft download center.

Each virtual machine will act as a separate machine with the unique GUID, SID, and IP address. The following table lists the IP addresses and roles of the respective VMs.

S. No.	VM Name	IP Address	Role
1	DC1	10.0.0.100	Domain controller of the mcsalab.local domain.
2	SERVER1	10.0.0.101	Member server of the mcsalab.local domain.
3	CLIENT1	10.0.0.102	Client machine of the mcsalab.local domain.
4	ROUTER1	Internal Subnet: 10.0.0.1 External Subnet: 192.168.0.1	Router server to perform the LAN routing.
5	SERVER2	192.168.0.2	Workgroup server in the external subnet.
6	Core1	Depends on your choice	Server Core machine

Preparing Virtual Lab Setup

To create the virtual machines, you need to perform the following tasks on the host machine:
1. Install VMware Workstation or Player.
2. Install and configure the DC1 virtual machine
3. Install and configure the SERVER1 virtual machine
4. Install and configure the CLIENT1 virtual machine

5. Install and configure the ROUTER1 virtual machine
6. Install and configure the SERVER2 virtual machine

Task 1: Installing VMware Workstation on the Host Machine

To Install VMware Workstation or VMware Player, first you need to download it. Once it is downloaded, just double-click the setup file, and follow the simple steps to complete the installation process.

Use the following link to download the VMware Workstation for creating the lab setup for this exercise.

If you are not much familiar with the VMware Workstation or Player, you can read the following step by step guide and you can be familiar with the VMware Workstation/Player in just a one day.

- https://getbook.at/vmware-guide

Task 2: Installing and Configuring the DC1 Virtual Machine

To install and configure the DC1 virtual machine, you need to perform the following steps:
1. Make sure that the **VMware** console is active.
2. Select **File** and then select **New Virtual Machine**.
3. On the **New Virtual Machine Wizard**, click **Next**.

4. On the **Guest Operating System Installation** page, select the **Installer disc image file (iso):** radio button, browse the location of the Server 2016 ISO image file, and then click **Next**.

Note: If you use the VMware platform that automatically detects the version of the Windows server, you may asked to set the following settings:

1.Product key

2.Operating system edition

3.Administrator password

Otherwise, you may skip it.

5. On the **Select a Guest Operating System** page, select the highest supported version of Windows server (in this case Windows Server 2012 but it will still support Windows Server 2016), and then click **Next**.

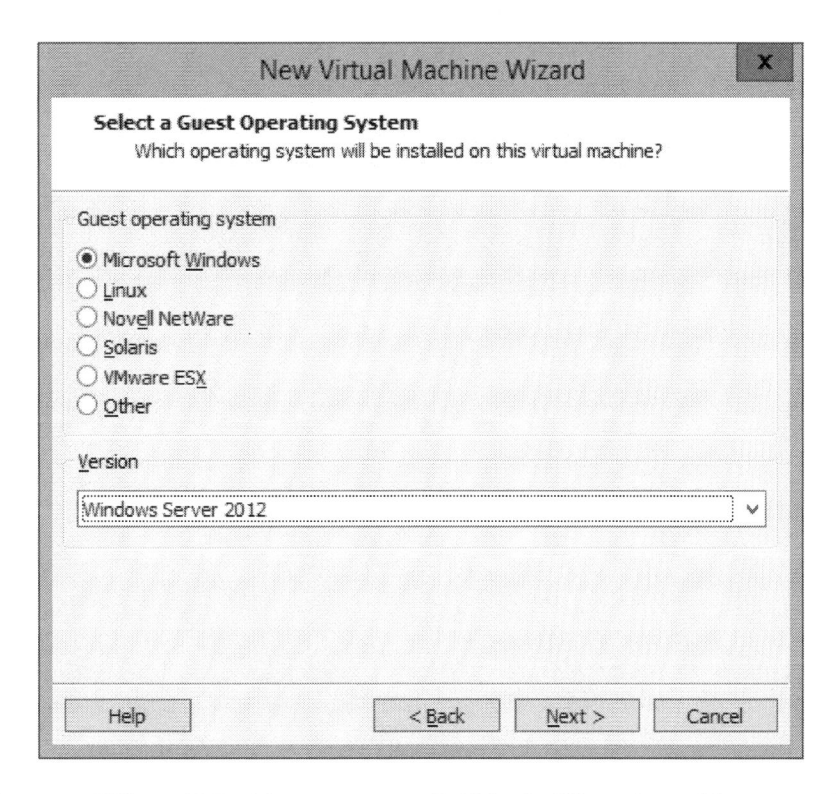

6. On the **Name and Virtual Machine** page, type **DC1** in the **Virtual machine name** field.
7. In the **Location** field, navigate the location where you want to save the virtual machine, such as **H:\VMs\2k16\DC1**, and then click **Next**.

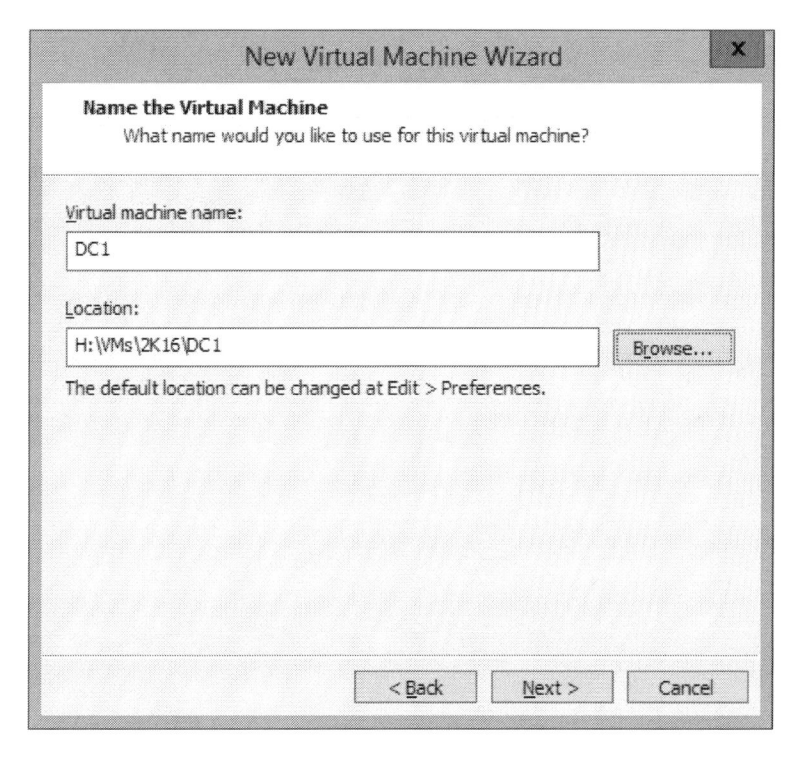

8. On the **Specify Disk Capacity** page, select **Store virtual disk as a single file**, optionally you can also set the disk size as well, and then click **Next**.

9. On the **Ready to Create Virtual Machine** page, click **Customize Hardware**.
10. On the **Hardware** window, select **Network Adapter** in the left pane. Select the **Host only** radio button, and then click **Close**.

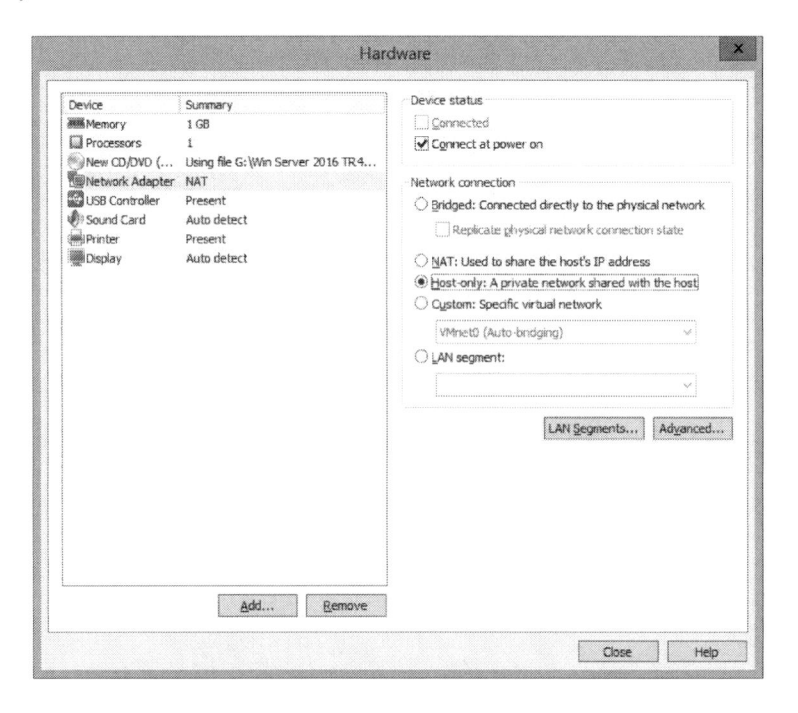

11. Click **Finish**.
12. On the **VMware** console, power on the **DC1** virtual machine.
13. On the **Windows Setup** page, click **Next**, and then click **Install Now**.

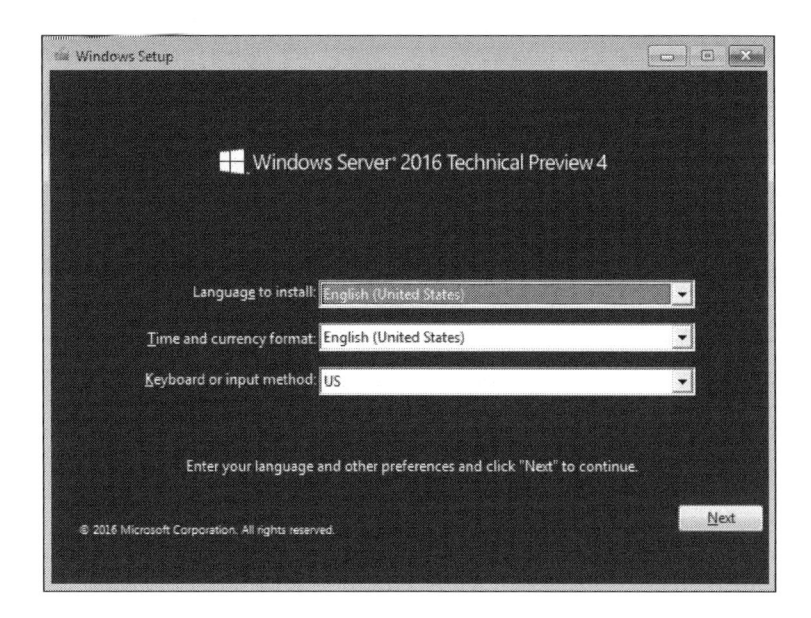

14. On the **Select the operating system you want to install** page, select the **Windows Server 2016 Desktop Experience**, and then click **Next**.

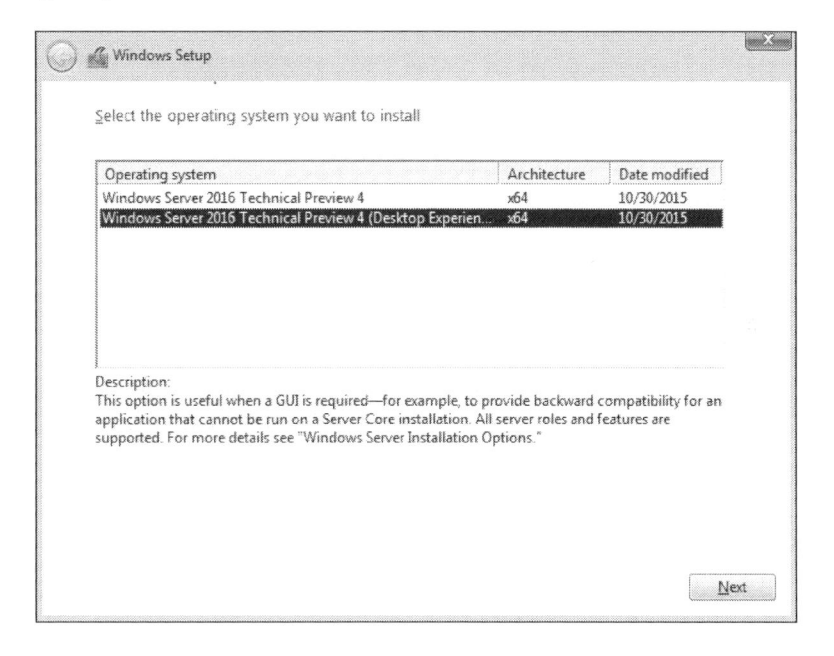

15. On the **License terms** page, select the **I accept the license terms** check box, and then click **Next**.
16. On the **Which type of installation do you want page**, select the **Custom** option, and then click **Next**.
17. On the **Where do you want to install Windows** page, click **Next**.

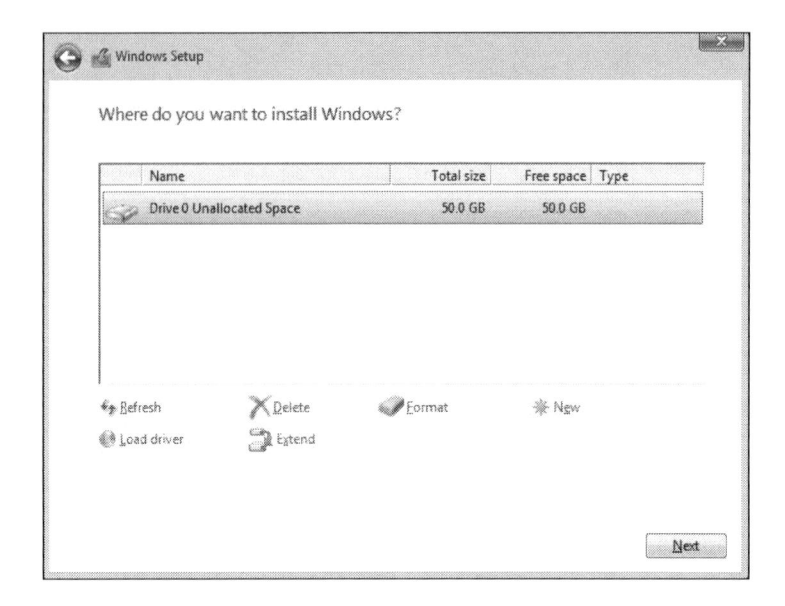

18. The Installation process will begin, after 10-15 minutes the **Customize settings** screen will display.
19. Set Administrator password as **Password@123**.

Task 3: Configuring the DC1 Virtual Machine
1. Sign in to **DC1** with the **Administrator** account.
2. Open the **System Properties** (sysdm.cpl) and set the computer name as **DC1**.

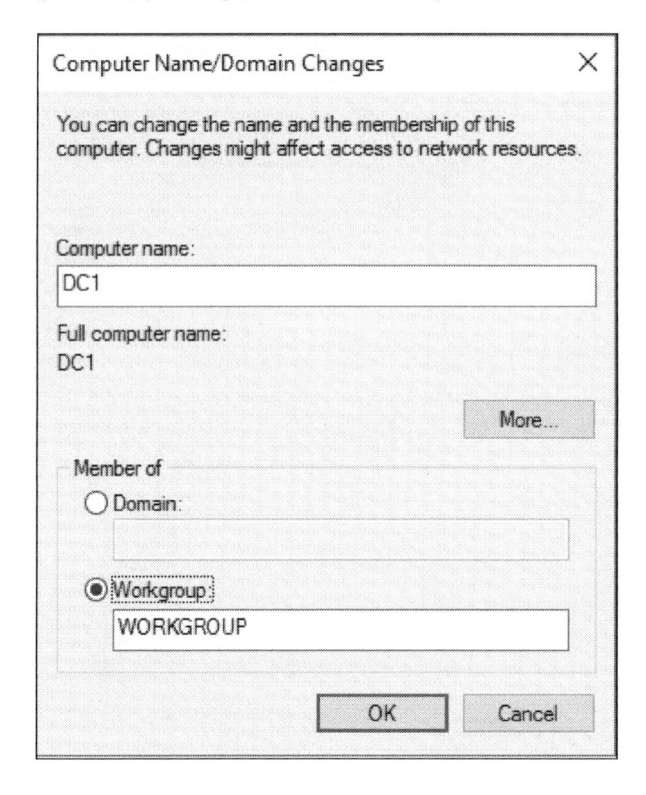

3. Restart and sign in to the system with the **Administrator** account. After some time, the **Server Manager** console will display.

4. Open the **Run** dialog box, type **ncpa.cpl**, and then press **Enter**.
5. Select and right-click the active network adapter, and then select **Properties**.
6. Set the following TCP/IP settings:
    - IP address: **10.0.0.100**.
    - Subnet mask: **255.0.0.0**.
    - Default gateway: **10.0.0.1**.
    - Preferred DNS server: **10.0.0.100**.

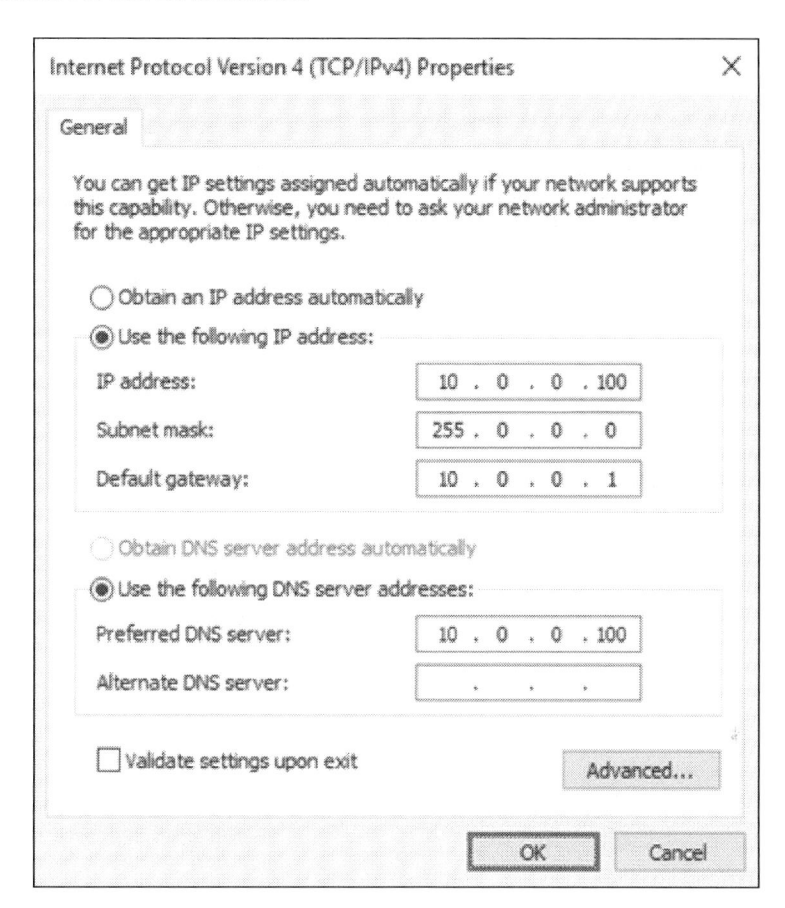

7. Close the **Network Connections** console.

Task 4: Promoting the DC1 Virtual Machine as a Domain Controller

To promote the DC1 virtual machine as a domain controller, you need to perform the following steps:
1. Open the **Server Manager** console.
2. Click the **Add roles and features** link.
3. On the **Before you begin** page, click **Next**.
4. On the **Select installation type** page, click **Next**.
5. On the **Select destination server** page, click **Next**.
6. On the **Select server roles** page, select the **Active Directory Domain Services** check box, as shown in the following figure.

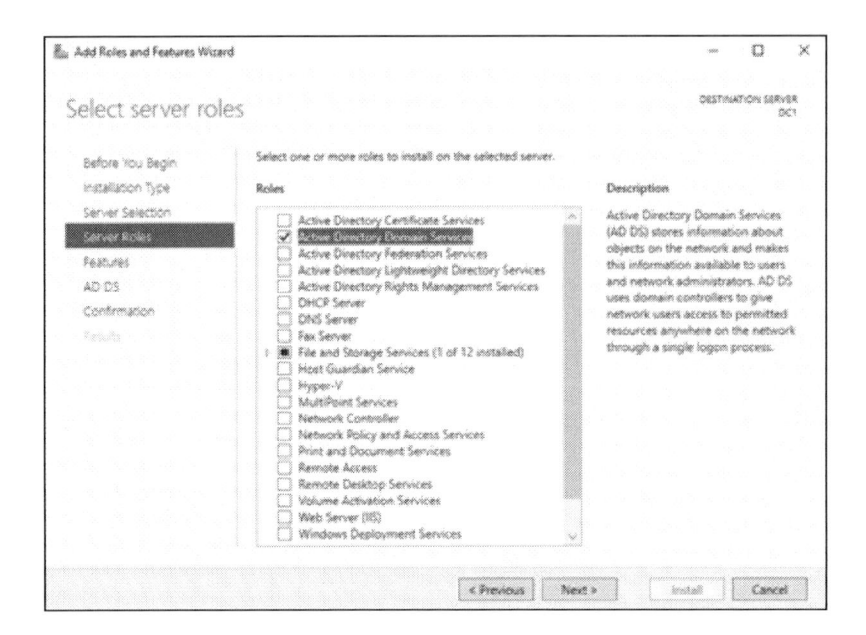

7. Accept the default selections through rest of the wizard and complete the installation process.
8. Click **Close**, once the installation succeeds on **DC1**.
9. On the **Server Manager** console, click the **Notifications** icon.
10. Click the **Promote this server to a domain controller** link, as shown in the following figure.

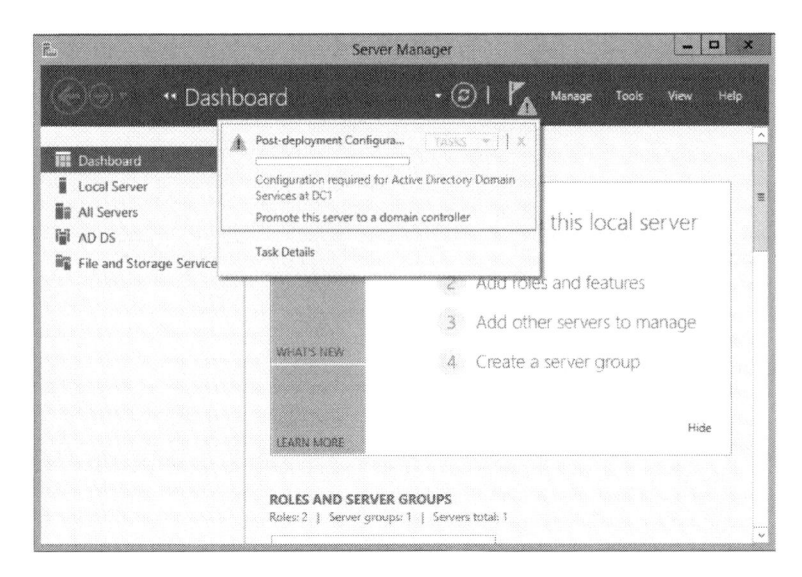

11. On the **Deployment Configuration** page, select the **Add a new forest** radio button.
12. In the **Root domain name** text box, type **mcsalab.local,** as shown in the following figure, and then click **Next**.

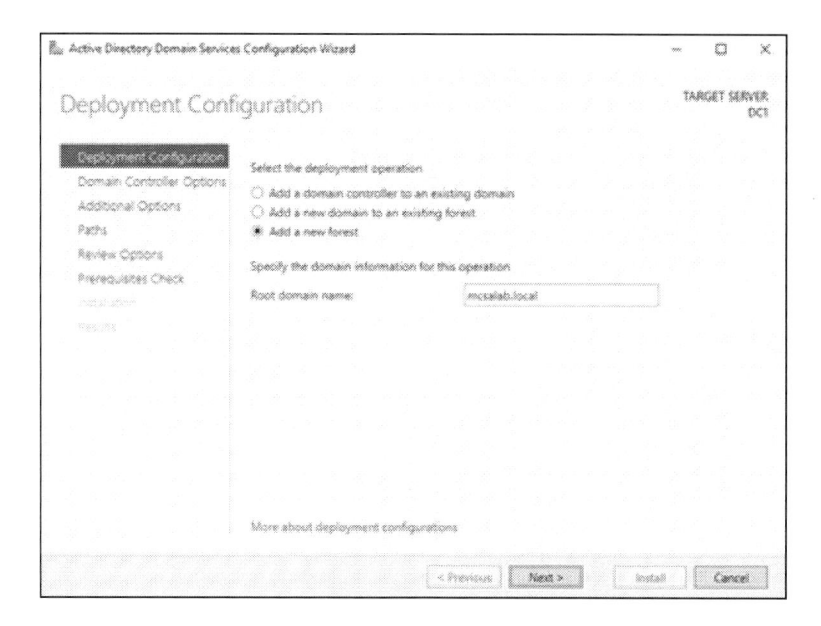

13. On the **Domain Controller Options** page, make sure that the **Domain Name System (DNS) server** check box is selected, as shown in the following figure.

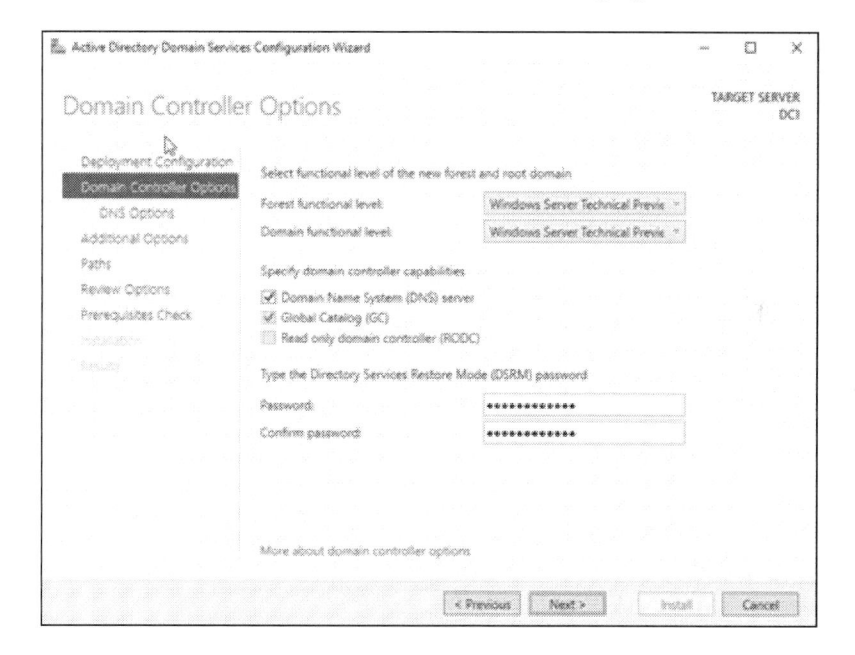

14. In the **Password** and **Confirm password** text boxes, type the **Password@123**, and then click **Next**.
15. On the **DNS Options** page and then click **Next**.
16. On the **Additional Options** page, click **Next**.
17. On the **Paths** page, as shown in the following figure, review the default location for the AD DS database file, and then click **Next**.

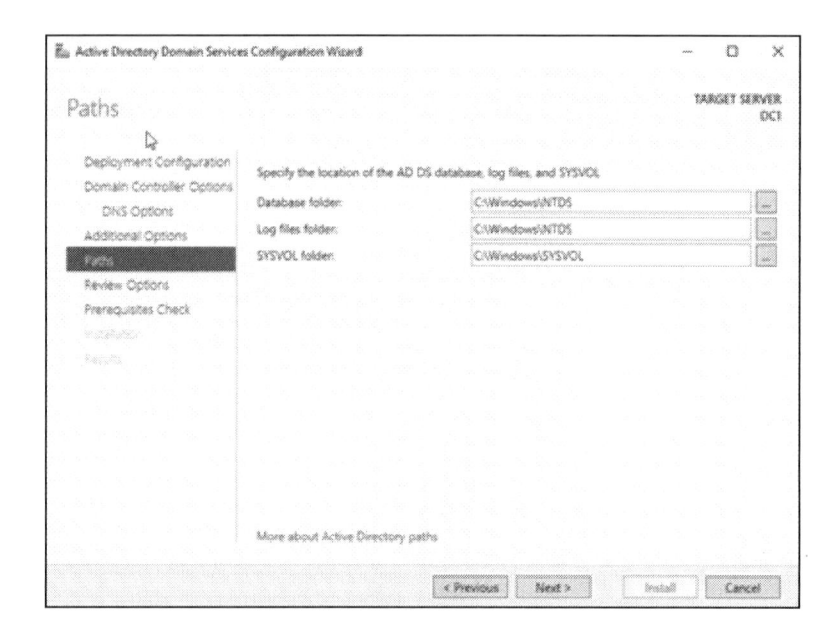

18. On the **Review Options** page, click **Next**.
19. On the **Prerequisites Check** page, as shown in the following figure, review the prerequisites, and then click **Install**.

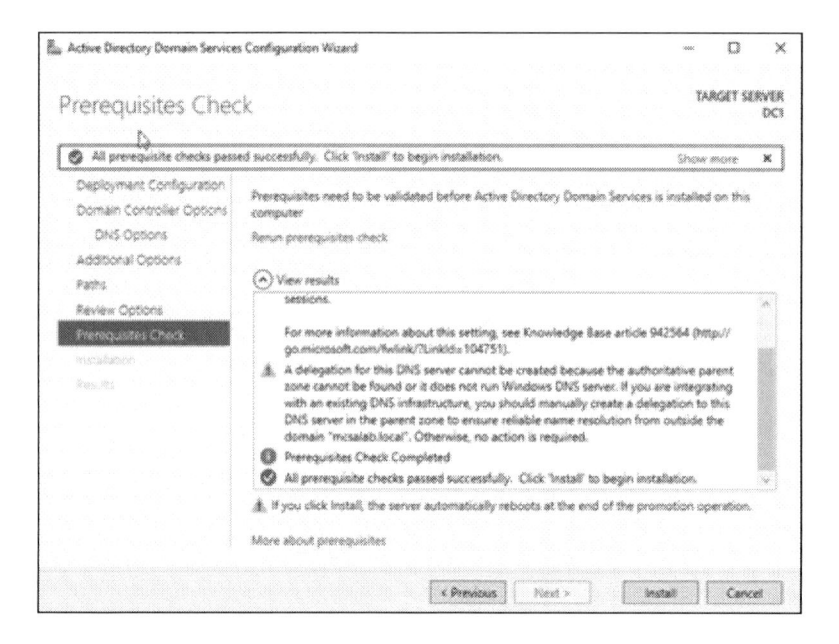

20. After some time, the system will restart automatically, sign in to **DC1** with the **MCSALAB\Administrator** account.
21. Do not shut down the **DC1** virtual machine.

Task 5: Installing and Configuring the SERVER1 Virtual Machine

To install and configure the **SERVER1** virtual machine, you can follow the simple steps as you used to install and configure the **DC1** virtual machine.

1. During the installing **SERVER1** virtual machine, make sure that you use the following settings and options:
   - Virtual machine name: **SERVER1**.
   - Operating system version: **Windows Server 2016**.
   - Memory: **2048 MB**
   - Hard disk size: **50 GB**
   - Network Adapter: Host only (click Customize Hardware before clicking the Finish button.)
   - Password: **Password@123**
2. Once you installed the **SERVER1** virtual machine with the preceding settings, configure the following TCP/IP settings:
   - IP address: **10.0.0.101**
   - Subnet mask: **255.0.0.0**
   - Default gateway: **10.0.0.1**
   - Preferred DNS server: **10.0.0.100**
3. Once you configured the preceding TCP/IP settings, open the **System Properties** dialog box and click **Change**.
4. On the **Computer Name/Domain Changes** dialog box, in the **Computer name** text box, type **SERVER1**.
5. Select the **Domain** radio button, in the **Member of** section, and then type **mcsalab.local**, and then click **OK**.
6. On the **Windows Security** dialog box, provide the credentials of the **DC1** server, and restart the **SERVER1** virtual machine.
7. Sign in to **SERVER1** with the Administrator account.
8. Shut down the **SERVER1** virtual machine.

Task 6: Installing and Configuring the CLIENT1 Virtual Machine

To install and configure the **CLIENT1** virtual machine, you can follow the simple steps as you used to install and configure the **DC1** virtual machine.

1. During the installing **CLIENT1** virtual machine, make sure that you use the following settings and options:
   - Virtual machine name: **CLIENT1**.
   - Operating system version: **Windows 8.1/10**.
   - Memory: **1024 MB**
   - Hard disk size: **50 GB**
   - Network Adapter: **Host only** (click Customize Hardware before clicking the Finish button.)
   - Password: **Password@123**
2. Once you installed the **CLIENT1** virtual machine with the preceding settings, configure the following TCP/IP settings:
   - IP address: **10.0.0.102**
   - Subnet mask: **255.0.0.0**
   - Default gateway: **10.0.0.1**
   - Preferred DNS server: **10.0.0.100**
3. Once you configured the preceding TCP/IP settings, open the **System Properties** dialog box, and click **Change**.
4. On the **Computer Name/Domain Changes** dialog box, in the **Computer name** text box, type **CLIENT1**.
5. Select the **Domain** radio button in the **Member of** section, type **mcsalab.local**, and then click **OK**.
6. On the **Windows Security** dialog box, provide the credentials of the **DC1** server, and restart the **CLIENT1** virtual machine.
7. Sign in to **CLIENT1** with the Administrator account.
8. Shut down the **CLIENT1** virtual machine.

Task 7: Installing and Configuring the ROUTER Virtual Machine

To install and configure the **ROUTER** virtual machine, you can follow the simple steps as you used to install and configure the **DC1** virtual machine.

1. During the creating **ROUTER** virtual machine, make sure that you use the following settings and options:
   - Virtual machine name: **ROUTER**.
   - Operating system version: **Windows Server 2016**.
   - Memory: **1024 MB**
   - Hard disk size: **50 GB**
   - Network Adapter: **Host only**
2. Once you created the **ROUTER** virtual machine with the preceding settings, select the **ROUTER** virtual machine, click **Edit virtual machine settings**, as shown in the following figure.

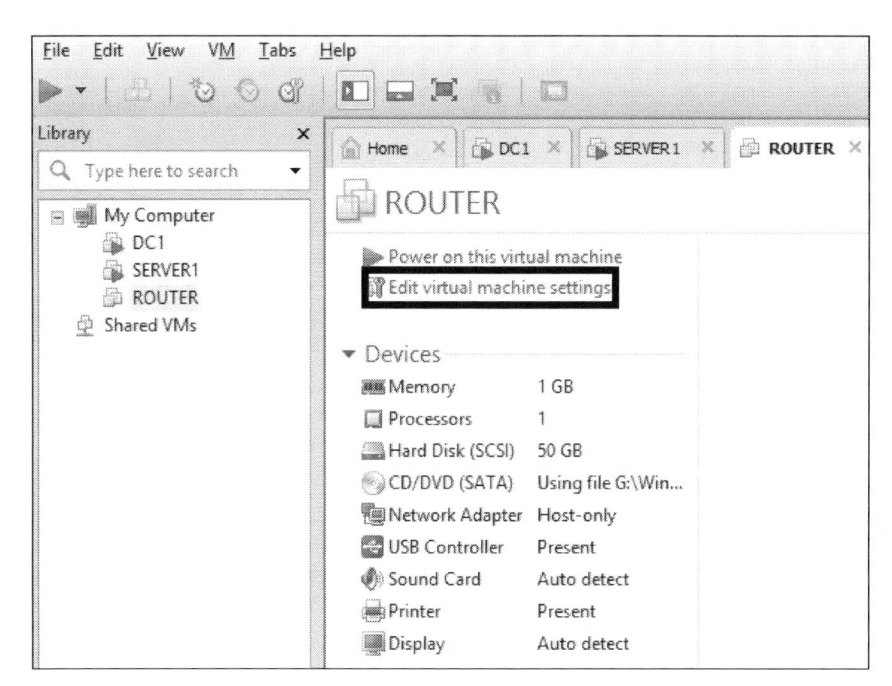

3. On the **Virtual Machine Settings** dialog box, click **Add**.
4. On the **Add Hardware Wizard**, select **Network Adapter**, and then click **Next**.

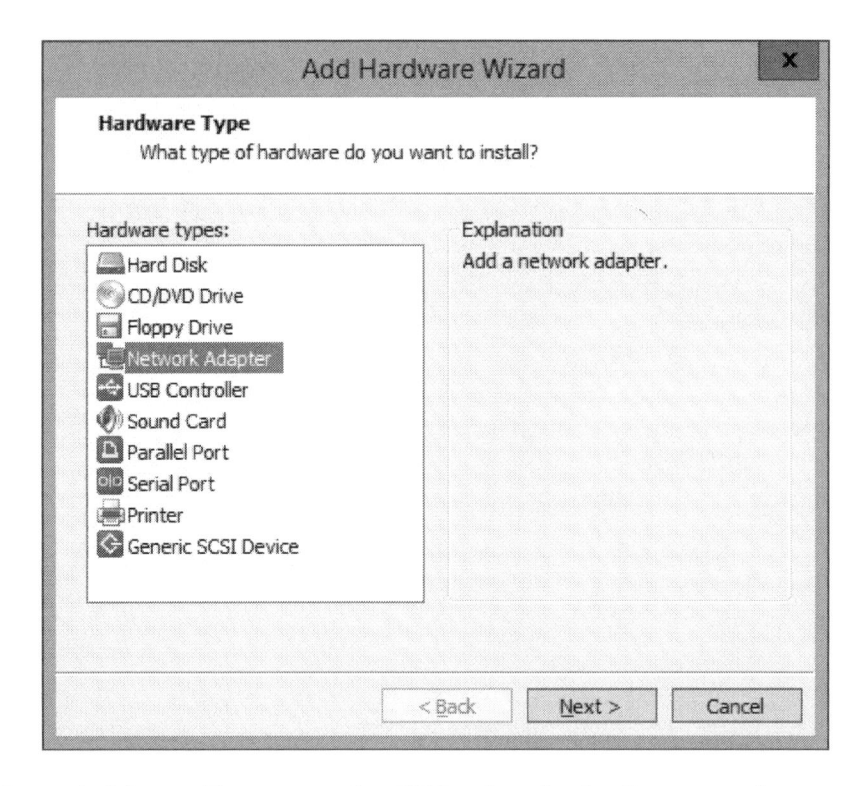

5. On the **Network Adapter Type** page, select **VMnet2** under the **Custom** option.

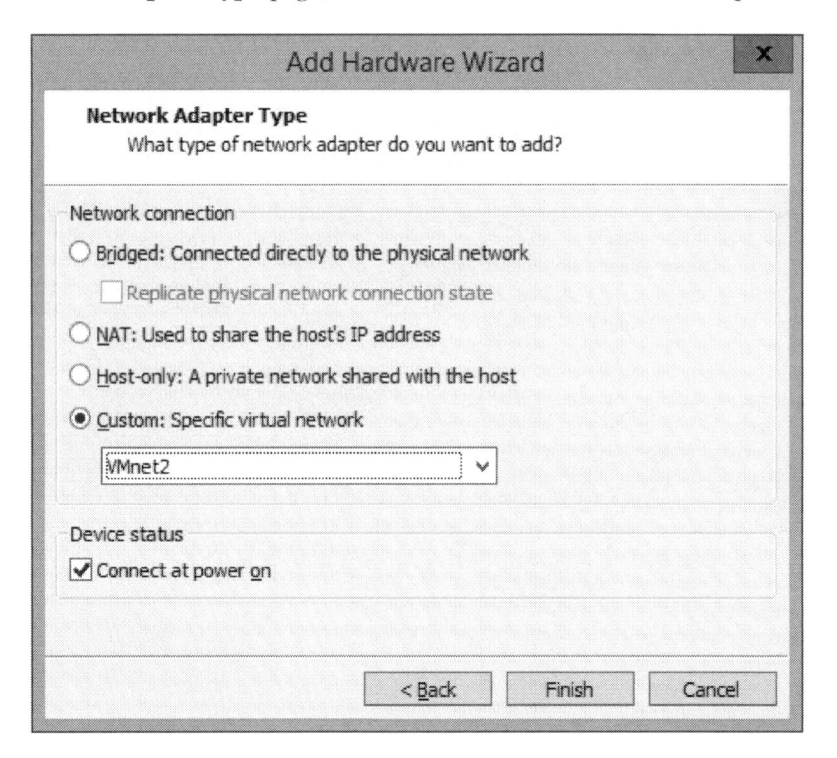

6. Click **Finish** and then click **OK**.
7. Power on the **ROUTER** virtual machine.
8. Follow the simple steps to install the **ROUTER** virtual machine. Use **Password@123** as Administrator password.
9. Once you installed the **ROUTER** virtual machine with the preceding settings, configure the

following TCP/IP settings on the first network adapter (connected to the **Host only** network):
- IP address: **10.0.0.1**
- Subnet mask: **255.0.0.0**
- Preferred DNS server: **10.0.0.100**

10. Configure the following TCP/IP settings on the second network adapter (connected to the **VMnet2** network):
    - IP address: **192.168.0.1**
    - Subnet mask: **255.255.255.0**

11. Once you configured the preceding TCP/IP settings, open the **System Properties** dialog box, set the computer name as **ROUTER**, and restart the **ROUTER** virtual machine.
12. Open the **Command Prompt** window, type **ping 10.0.0.100**, and then press **Enter**.
13. You should be able to communicate (ping) with the **DC1** server.

Note: If you are unable to communicate with the DC1 server, you may need to interchange the TCP/IP settings of the network adapters.

---

14. Do not shut down the **ROUTER1** virtual machine.

Task 8: Creating and Configuring the SERVER2 Virtual Machine

To install and configure the **SERVER2** virtual machine, you can follow the simple steps as you used to install and configure the **DC1** virtual machine.

1. During the installing **SERVER2** virtual machine, make sure that you use the following settings and options:
   - Virtual machine name: **SERVER2**.
   - Operating system version: **Windows Server 2016**.
   - Memory: **1024 MB**
   - Hard disk size: **50 GB**
   - Network Adapter: **VMnet2**
   - Password: **Password@123**
2. Once you installed the **SERVER2** virtual machine with the preceding settings, configure the following TCP/IP settings:
   - IP address: **192.168.0.2**
   - Subnet mask: **255.255.255.0**
   - Default gateway: **192.168.0.1**
   - Preferred DNS server: **10.0.0.100**
3. Once you configured the preceding TCP/IP settings, open the **System Properties** dialog box, set the computer name as **SERVER2**, and restart the **SERVER2** virtual machine.
4. Sign in to **SERVER2** with the Administrator account.
5. Shut down the **SERVER2** virtual machine.
6. Shut down the **DC1** virtual machine.

Task 9: Creating Snapshots of Virtual Machines

Once you installed and configured all the virtual machines, you need to create the snapshots/checkpoints for each virtual machine. Snapshot will help you to revert a virtual machine to its previously used state (at the point when you had created it).

To create a snapshot, you need to perform the following tasks:
1. Make sure that the all virtual machines are turned off.
2. Select and right-click any virtual machine, select **Snapshot**, and then select **Take snapshot**. After few seconds, the snapshot will be created.
3. Using the preceding method, create snapshots of all the virtual machines.

Exercise 1: Installing and Configuring Windows Server Core Machine

In this exercise, you will install and configure a Windows Server core machine. The installation process for the server core option and full GUI option is almost identical. However, server core option requires less hardware resources and it is more secure than the full GUI option. In this exercise, you will use the following virtual machines:
- DC1
- CORE1

To install and configure the Windows Server core machine, you need to perform the following tasks:

Task 1: Installing Windows Server Core Machine.
1. Create a virtual machine with the following settings:
2. During the creating the virtual machine, make sure that you use the following settings and options:
    - Virtual machine name: **CORE1**.
    - Operating system version: **Windows Server 2016**.
    - Memory: **512 MB**
    - Hard disk size: **20 GB**
    - Network Adapter: **Host only**
    - Password: **Password@123**

3. Once the virtual machine is created, power on the CORE1 virtual machine.
4. After some time, the **Windows Setup** screen will display.
5. Click **Next** and then click **Install now**.
6. If the Activate Windows screen is displayed, click I don't have a product key link.

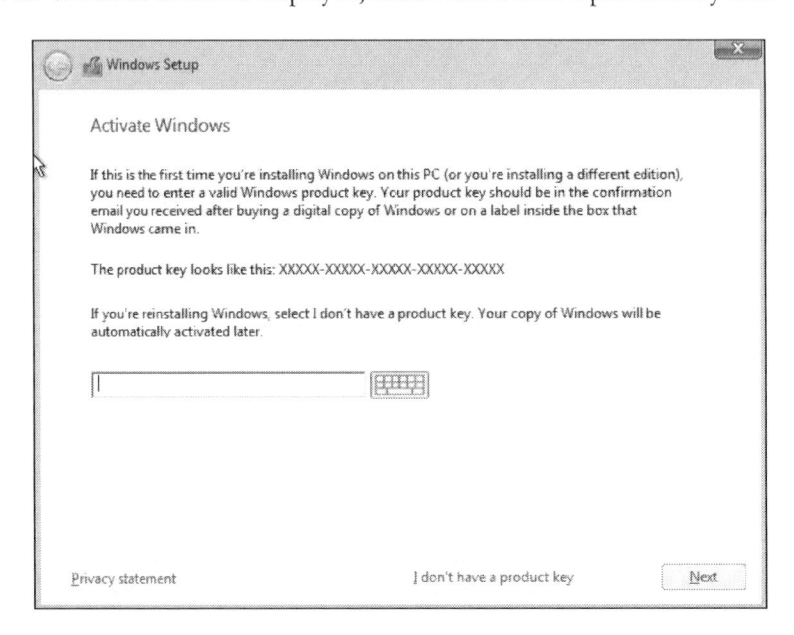

7. On the **Select the operating system you want to install** page, select **Windows Server**

2016 Technical Preview 4, and then click **Next**.

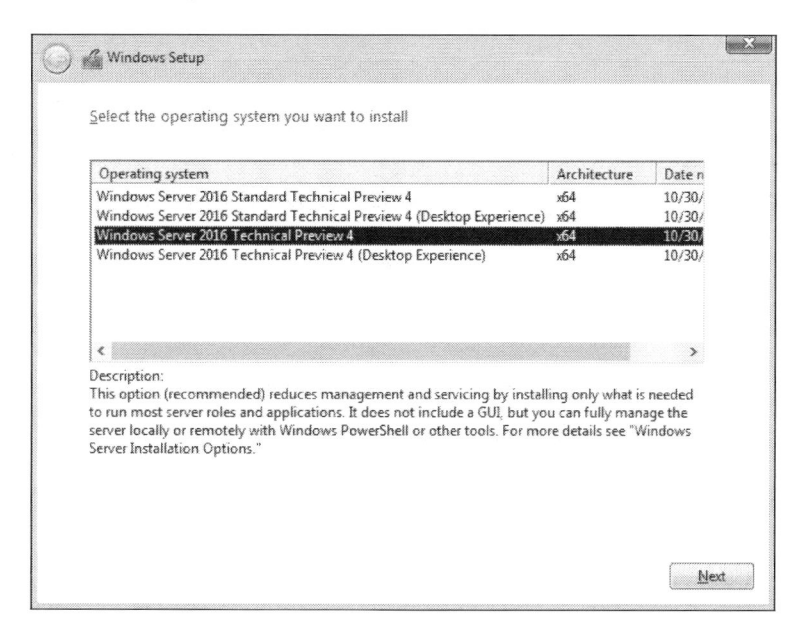

8. On the **License terms** page, select the **I accept the license terms** check box, and then click **Next**.
9. On the **Which type of installation do you want?** page, click **Custom: Install Windows only (advanced)**, as shown in the following figure.

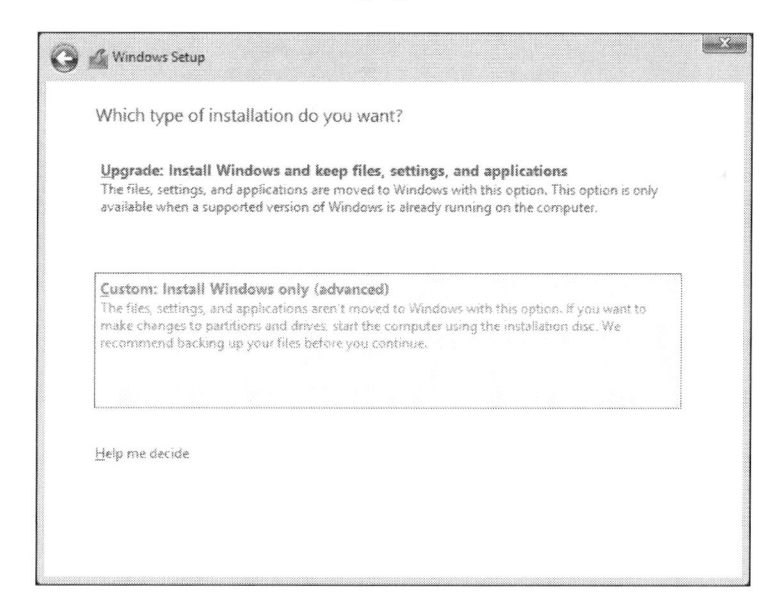

10. On the **Where do you want to install Windows?** page, click **Next**.
11. The installation process will start.
12. After some time, the sign in screen will display, and you will be asked to change the Administrator password.

13. Set the Administrator password as **Password@123**.

Task 2: Configuring the Windows Server 2016 Core Machine.

To configure the Windows Server 2016 core machine, you need to perform the following steps:
1. Sign in to **CORE1** with the Administrator account.
2. On the **Command Prompt** window, type **sconfig.cmd**, and then press **Enter**. The **Server Configuration** options will display, as shown in the following figure.

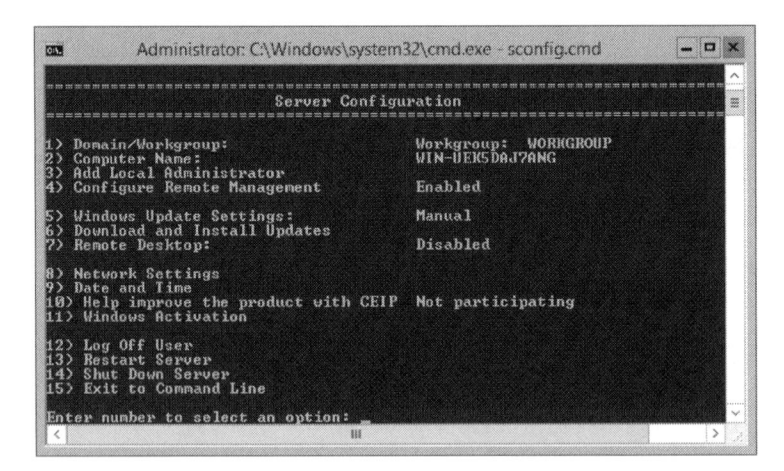

3. To change the system **Date and Time**, type **9**, and then press **Enter**.
4. On the **Date and Time** dialog box, as shown in the following figure, click **Change time zone**.

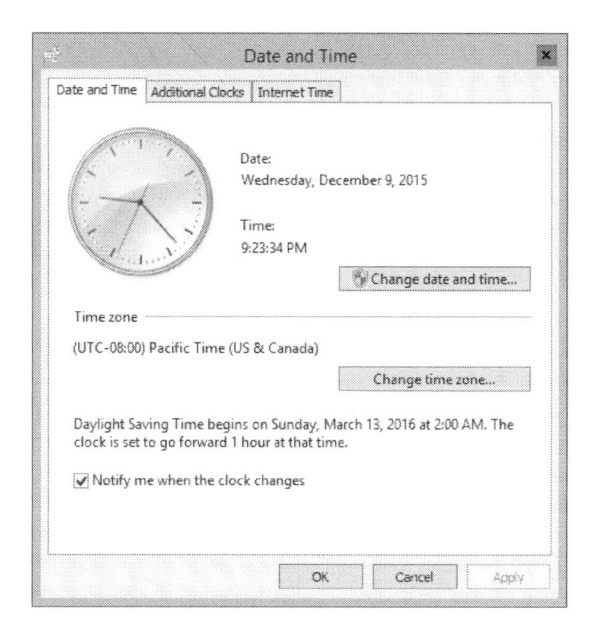

5. Select the desired time zone, and then click **OK**.
6. In the **Date and Time** dialog box, click **Change Date and Time**, and verify the date and time, and then click **OK**.
7. On the **Command Prompt** window, type **8**, and then press **Enter to configure Network Settings**.
8. Type the index number (in our example it is 10) of the network adapter, as shown in the following figure, and then press **Enter**.

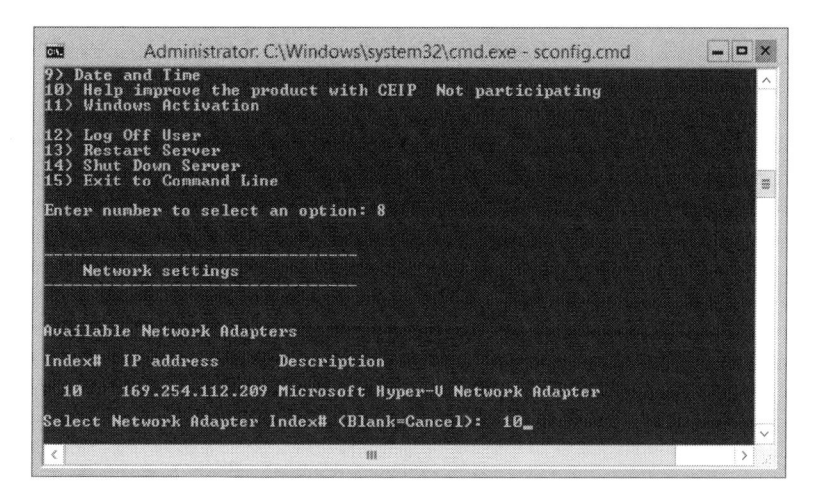

9. On the **Network Adapter Settings** page, type **1**, to set the **Network Adapter Address**, as shown in the following figure, and then press **Enter**.

10. To set static IP address, type **S**, as shown in the following figure, and then press **Enter**.

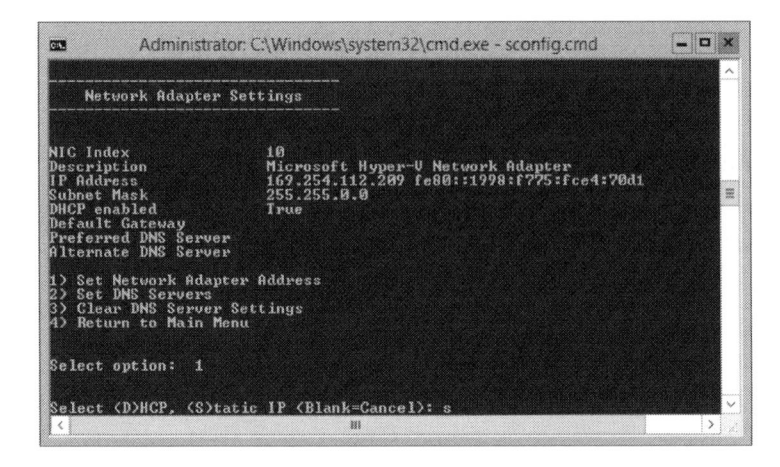

11. At the **Enter static IP address**: prompt, type **10.0.0.103**, and then press **Enter**.
12. At the **Enter subnet mask**: prompt, accept the default value, and then press **Enter**.
13. At the **Enter default gateway**: prompt, type **10.0.0.1**, and then press **Enter**, as shown in the following figure.

14. On the **Network Adapter Settings** option, type **2**, to configure the DNS server address, and then press **Enter**.
15. At the **Enter new preferred DNS server** prompt, type **10.0.0.100**, and then press **Enter**.

16. On the **Network Settings** message box, as shown in the following figure, click **OK**.

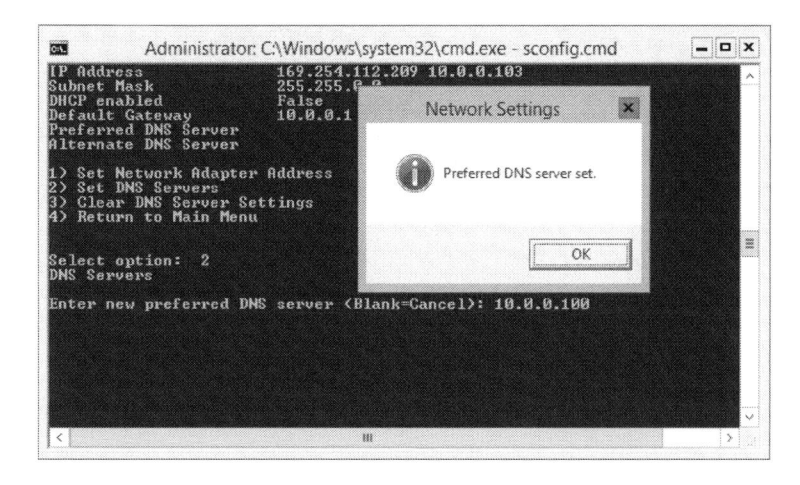

17. Press **Enter** to not configure an alternate DNS server address.
18. At the **Select option:** prompt, type **4**, and then press **Enter** to return to the main menu.
19. At the **Enter number to select an option:** prompt, type **15**, and then press **Enter** to exit the **sconfig.cmd** utility.
20. On the **Command Prompt** window, type ping **dc1.mcsalab.local** to verify the connectivity between **DC1** and **CORE1**.

Task 3: Adding CORE1 to Domain

1. On the **Command Prompt** window, type **sconfig.cmd**, and then press **Enter**.
2. At the **Enter number to select an option:** prompt, type **2**, and then press **Enter**.
3. At the **Enter a new computer name:** prompt, type **CORE1**, and then press **Enter**.
4. On the **Restart** dialog box, click **Yes**.

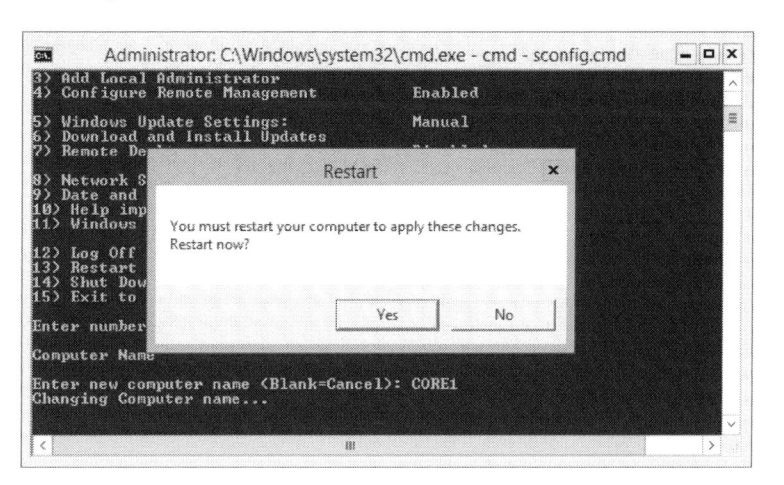

5. The system will restart and after some time the **Sign in** screen will display.
6. Sign in to **CORE1** with the Administrator account.
7. On the **Command Prompt** window, type **hostname**, and then press **Enter** to verify the computer's name.
8. On the **Command Prompt** window, type **sconfig.cmd**, and then press **Enter**.
9. Type **1** to change the **Domain/Workgroup** settings, and then press **Enter**.
10. Type **D** to join a domain, and then press **Enter**.
11. At the **Name of domain to join** prompt, type **mcsalab.local**, and then press **Enter**.

12. At the **Specify an authorized domain\user** prompt, type **Administrator**, and then press **Enter**.
13. At the **Type the password associated with the domain user** prompt, type **Password@123**, and then press **Enter**.
14. At the **Change Computer Name** message box, as shown in the following figure, click **No**.

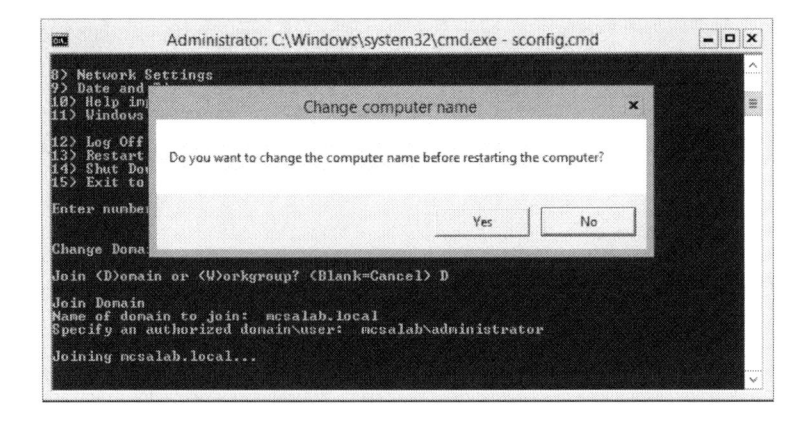

15. On the **Restart** dialog box, click **Yes**. The system will restart. After some time, the sign in screen will display.
16. Sign in to **CORE1** with the MCSALAB\Administrator account.

Results: After completing this exercise, you will have configured a Windows Server 2016 server core machine.

Do not turn off or shut down the DC1 and/or CORE1 virtual machine(s) as these virtual machines will be required to perform the next exercise.

Exercise 2: Managing Servers Remotely

In this exercise, you will manage the server core machine from the remote location. In addition, you will also deploy roles and features on the server core machine. Further, you will manage the services on the server core machine.

Before starting to perform this exercise, make sure that the DC1 and CORE1 virtual machines are running, and you have not reverted them in the previous exercise.

Task 1: Creating and Managing the Server Group

1. Sign in to **DC1** with the MCSALAB\Administrator account.
2. On the **Server Manager** console, make sure that **Dashboard** is selected in the left pane, and then click **Create a server group**.
3. On the **Create Server Group** dialog box, click the **Active Directory** tab, and then click **Find Now**.
4. In the **Server group** name text box, select the **CORE1** and **SERVER1** servers, and then add **CORE1** and **SERVER1** to the server group.
5. In the **Server group** name text box, type **ServerGroup1**, as shown in the following figure.

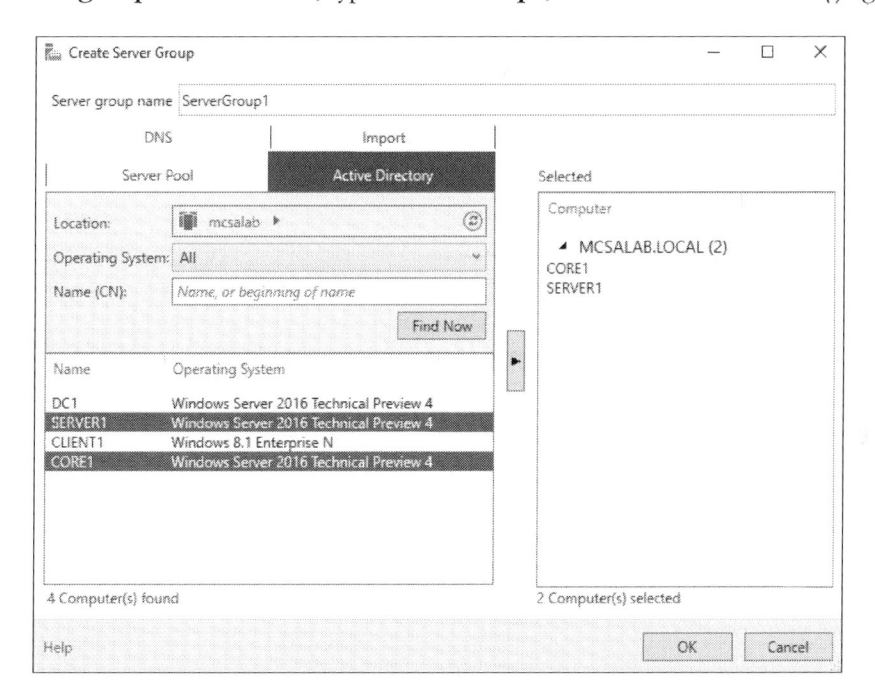

6. Click **OK** to close the **Create Server Group** dialog box.
7. On the **Server Manager** console, select **ServerGroup1** in the left pane. Verify that the both servers are listed in the **Servers** pane, as shown in the following figure.

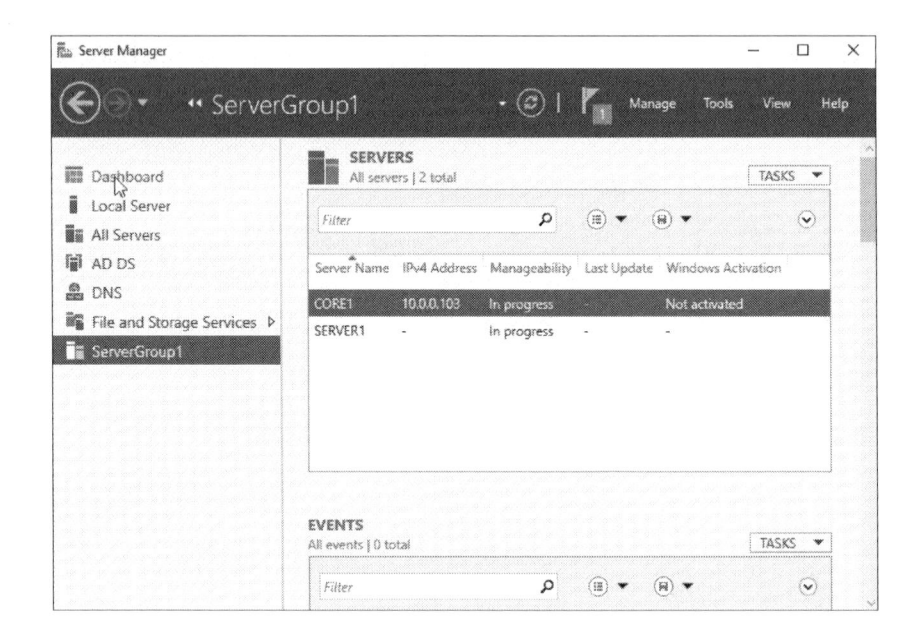

Task 2: Deploying Roles and Features on CORE1 Machine

1. Sign in to **DC1** with the MCSALAB\Administrator account.
2. On the **Server Manager** console, click **ServerGroup1** in the left pane.
3. Scroll to the top of the pane, select and right-click **CORE1**, and then select **Add Roles and Features**, as shown in the following figure.

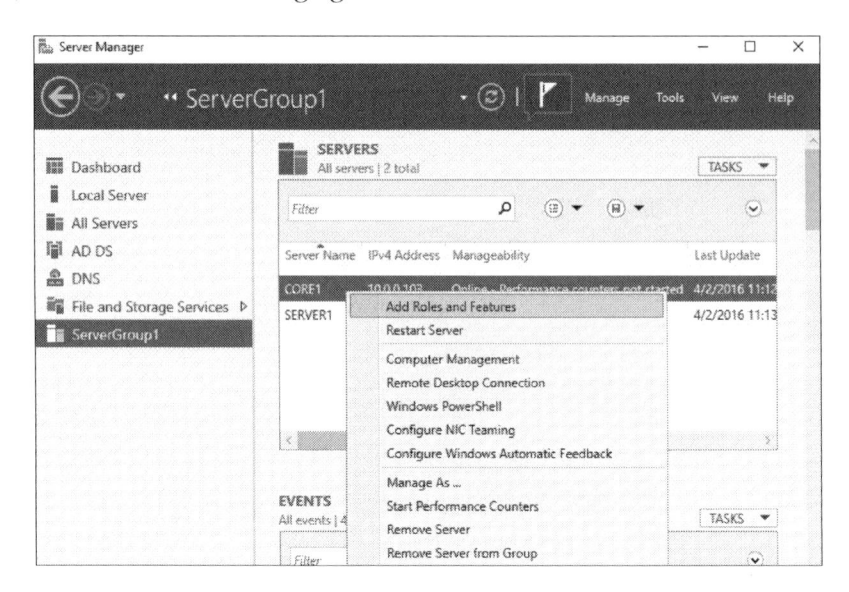

4. On the **Add Roles and Features Wizard**, click **Next**.
5. On the **Select installation type** page, click **Next**.
6. On the **Select destination server** page, make sure that **CORE1.mcsalab.local** is selected, as shown in the following figure, and then click **Next**.

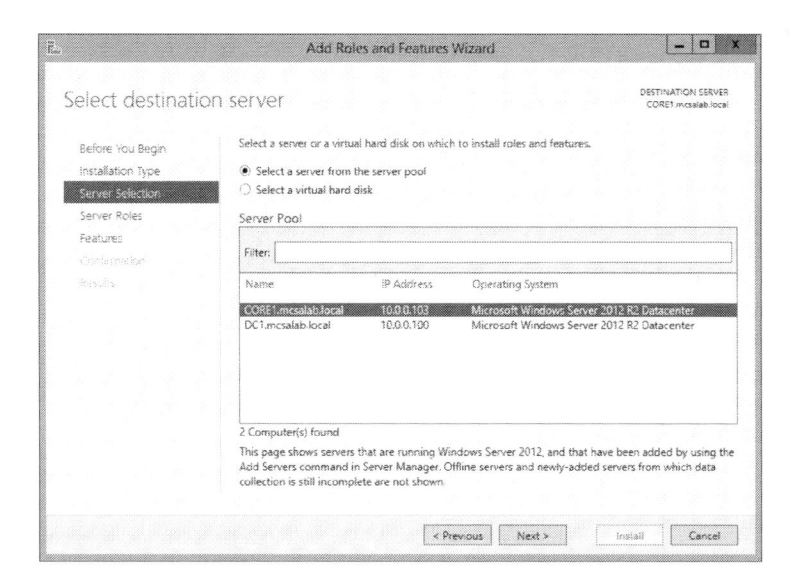

7. On the **Select server roles** page, select the **DHCP Server** check box, as shown in the following figure, and then click **Next**.

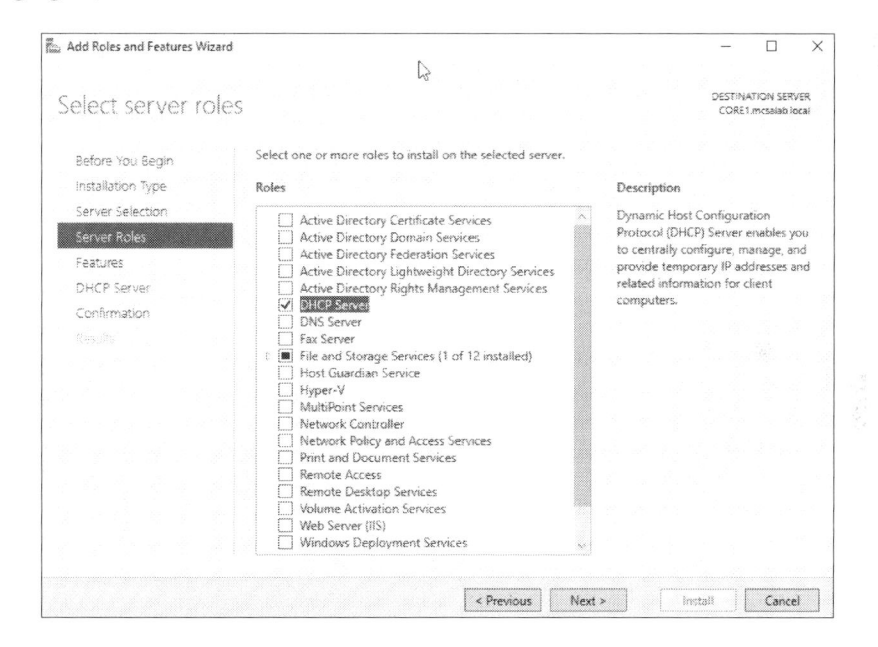

8. On the **Add Roles and Features** dialog box, click **Next**.
9. Click **Next**, until the **Confirm install selections** page is displayed.
10. On the **Confirm installation selections** page, select the **Restart the destination server automatically if required** check box, as shown in the following figure, and then click **Install**.

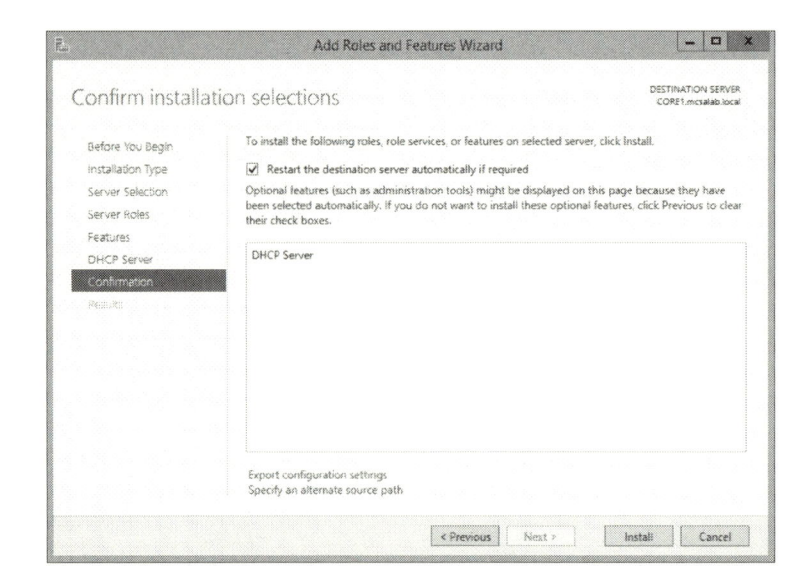

11. Click **Close** to close the **Add Roles and Features Wizard**, once the installation is completed.

Task 3: Managing Services on the CORE1 Machine

1. Switch to as **Other user** and sign in to **CORE1** with the MCSALAB\Administrator account.
2. On the **Command Prompt** window, type the following command, and then press **Enter**, as shown in the following figure.
   ```
   netsh.exe firewall set service remoteadmin enable all
   ```

for labs only better to enable

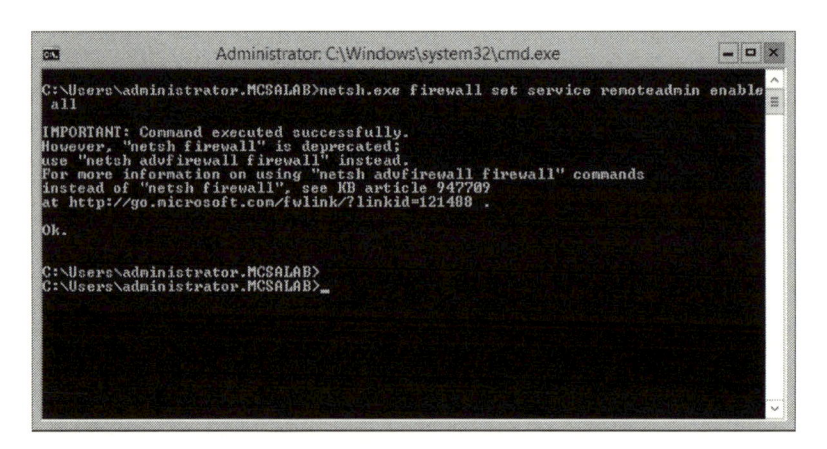

3. Switch back and sign in to **DC1** with the MCSALAB\Administrator account.
4. On the **Server Manager** console, select **ServerGroup1**.
5. Select and right-click **CORE1**, and then click **Computer Management**.
6. On the **Computer Management** console, expand the **Services and Applications** node, and then select **Services**.
7. Select and right-click the **DHCP Server** service, and then click **Properties**, as shown in the following figure.

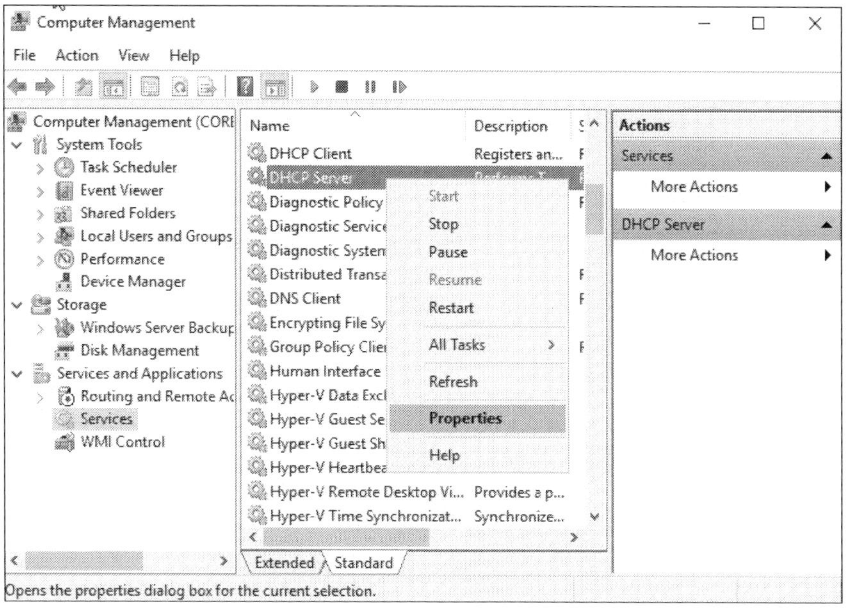

8. On the **Properties** dialog box, on the **General** tab, make sure that the **Startup type** is set to **Automatic**.
9. Select the **Recovery** tab, configure the following settings, as shown in the following figure.
    - First failure: **Restart the Service**
    - Second failure: **Restart the Service**
    - Subsequent failures: **Restart the Computer**
    - Reset fail count after: **1 days**
    - Restart service after: **1 minute**

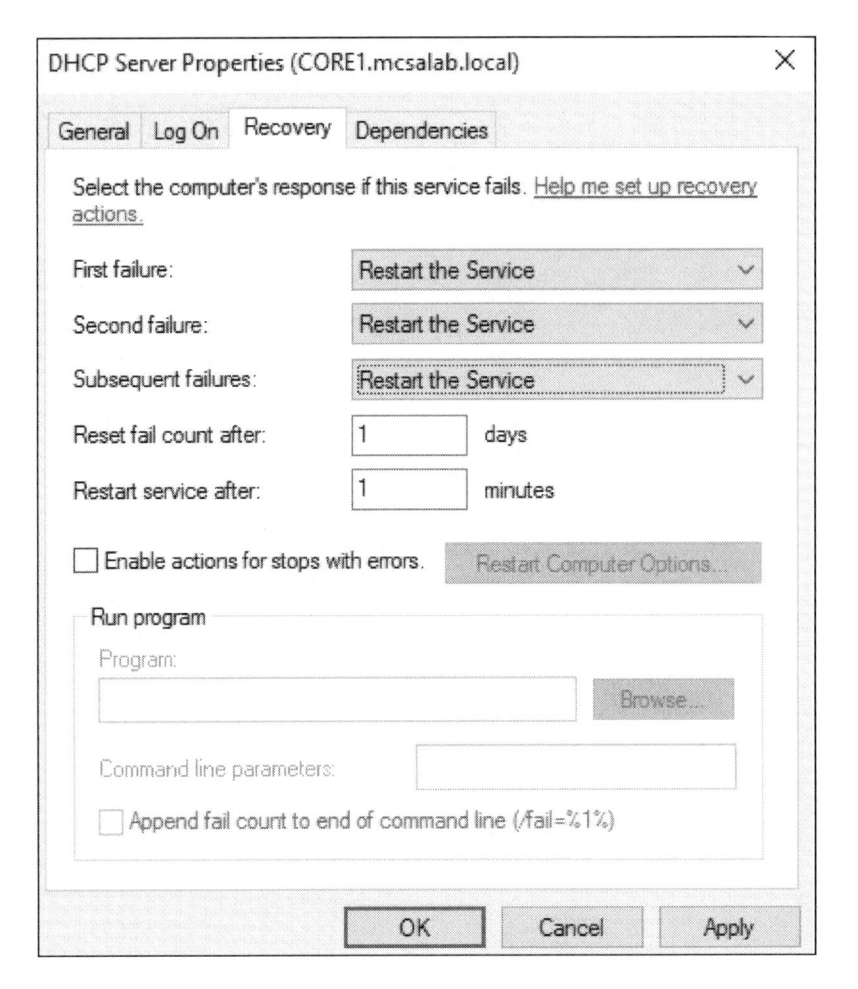

10. On the **Properties** dialog box, click **Restart Computer Options**.
11. On the **Restart Computer Options** dialog box, in the **Restart computer after** box, type **2**, and then click **OK**.
12. Click **OK** to close the **Properties** dialog box.
13. Close the **Computer Management** console.

Results: After completing this exercise, you have created a server group, deployed roles and features, and managed a service remotely.

Shut down and revert the DC1 and CORE1 virtual machines to prepare for the next exercise.

Exercise 3: Using Windows PowerShell to Manage Servers

In this exercise, you will use the Windows PowerShell to manage the Window Server 2016. Windows PowerShell is a command-line interface that is similar to command prompt. It is designed to execute the scripts similar to UNIX/Linux operating systems.

Start the DC1 virtual machine to perform this exercise.

Task 1: Using the Windows PowerShell to Connect Remotely to Servers and View Information

1. Sign in to **DC1** with the MCSALAB\Administrator account.
2. On the **Server Manager** console, select **ServerGroup1**.
3. Select and right-click **CORE1**, and then select **Windows PowerShell**.
4. At the **Windows PowerShell** prompt, type **cd** and then press **Enter**.
5. Type **Import-Module ServerManager**, and then press **Enter**.
6. Type **Get-WindowsFeature** and then press **Enter** to view the installed roles and features on **CORE1**, as shown in the following figure.

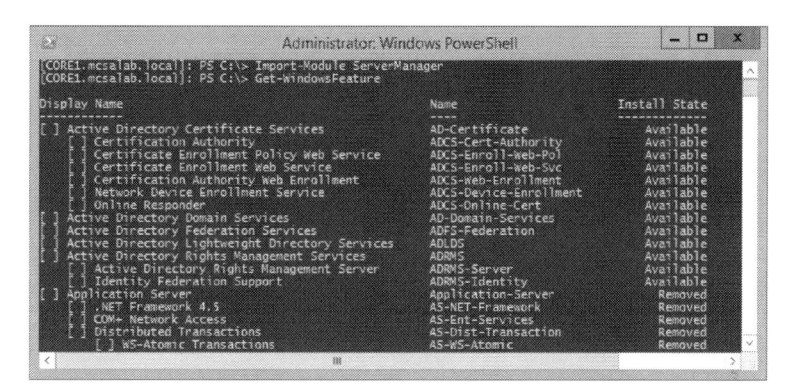

7. Type the following command to view the running services on **CORE1** and then press **Enter**, as shown in the following figure.
   ```
   Get-service | where-object {$_.status -eq "Running"}
   ```

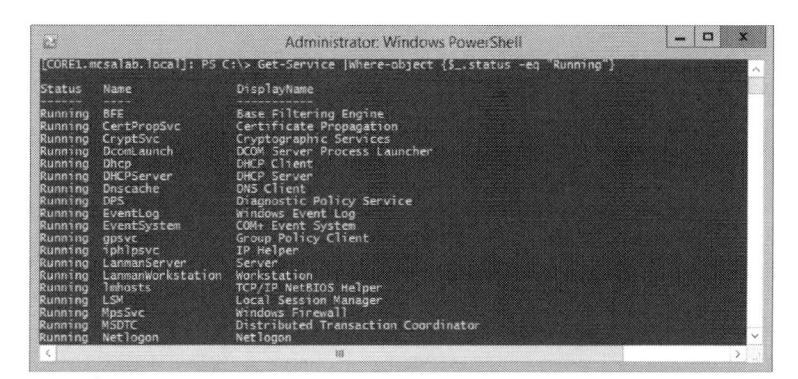

8. Type the following command and then press **Enter** to view a list of processes on **CORE1**, as shown in the following figure.
   ```
   Get-Process
   ```

51

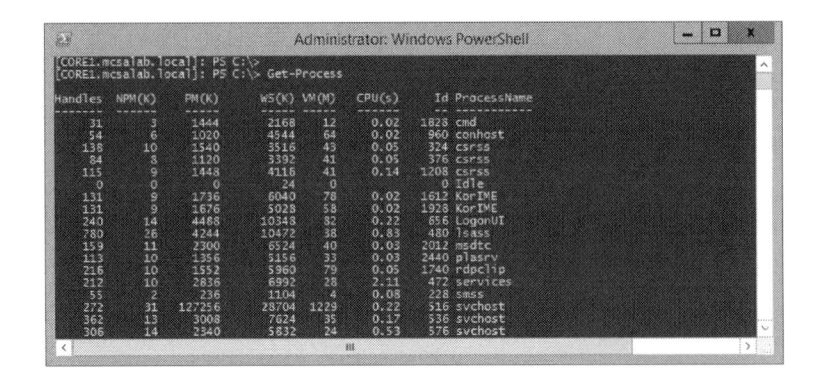

9. Type the following command to view the IP addresses of the **CORE1** machine, and then press **Enter**, as shown in the following figure.
   `Get-NetIPAddress | Format-table`

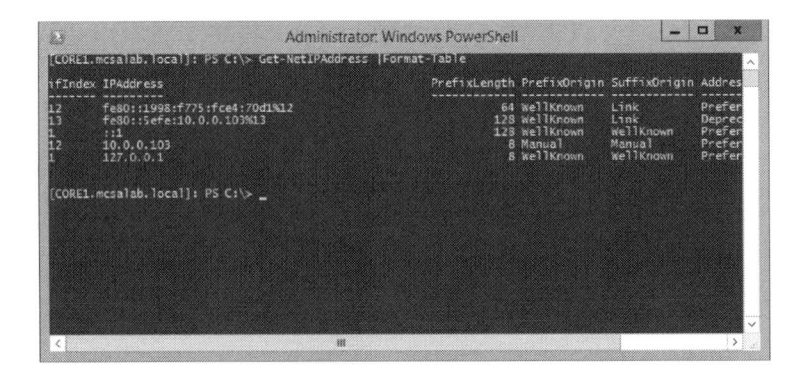

10. Type the following command to view the most recent **5** security logs, and then press **Enter**, as shown in the following figure.
    `Get-EventLog Security -Newest 5`

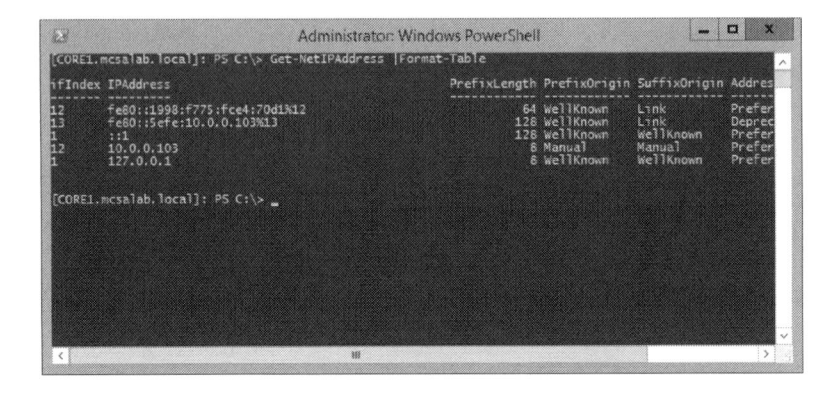

11. Close **Windows PowerShell**.

Task 2: Using Windows PowerShell to Manage Roles and Features Remotely

1. On **DC1**, on the taskbar, click the **Windows PowerShell** icon.
2. At the **Windows PowerShell** prompt, type the following command, and then press **Enter**.
3. **Import-Module ServerManager**

4. To verify that the **WINS Server** feature is not installed on **CORE1**, type the following command, and then press **Enter**, as shown in the following figure.
   ```
   Get-WindowsFeature -ComputerName CORE1
   ```

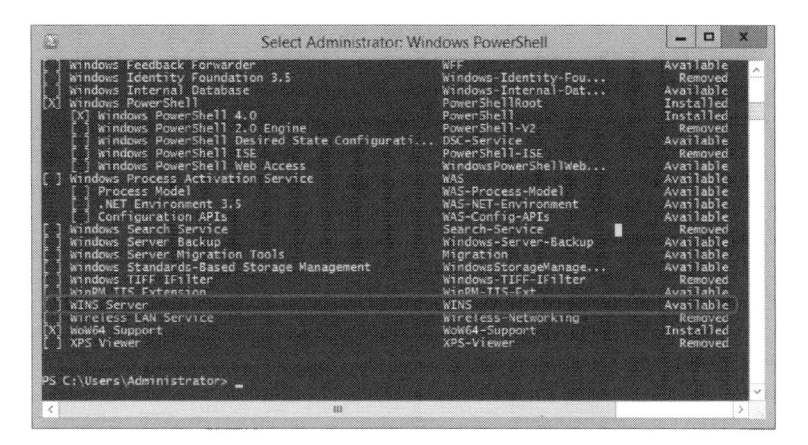

5. To install the **WINS Server** feature on **CORE1**, type the following command, and then press **Enter**, as shown in the following figure.
   ```
   Install-WindowsFeature WINS -ComputerName CORE1
   ```

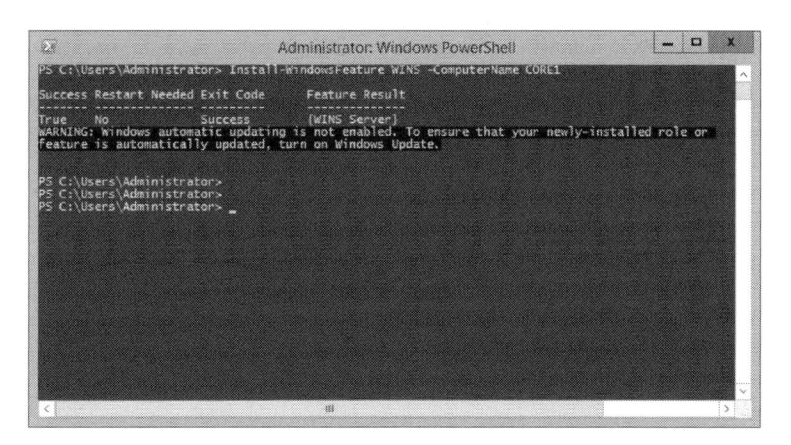

6. Verify that the **Exit Code** status displays as the success text.

Results: After completing this exercise, you have managed the servers using Windows PowerShell.

Shut down and revert the DC1 and CORE1 virtual machines.

Exercise 4: Installing and Configuring Domain Controllers

The system that holds the Active Directory Domain Services role acts as a domain controller. A domain controller is a server that is used to manage and control the clients on a network.

In this exercise, you will learn how to configure a domain controller on Windows Serve 2016. In addition, you will also learn how to configure a server as a Global Catalog server.

Start the DC1 and SERVER1 virtual machines to perform this exercise.

Task 1: Adding the AD DS Role on a Member Server

1. Sign in to **DC1** with the MCSA\Administrator account.
2. On the **Server Manager** console, in the left pane, select and right-click **All Servers**, and then select **Add Servers**.
3. On the **Add Servers** dialog box, in the **Name (CN)** text box, type **SERVER1**, and then click **Find Now**.
4. In the name list area, select **SERVER1**, and then click the arrow to add the server to the **Selected** column, as shown in the following figure.

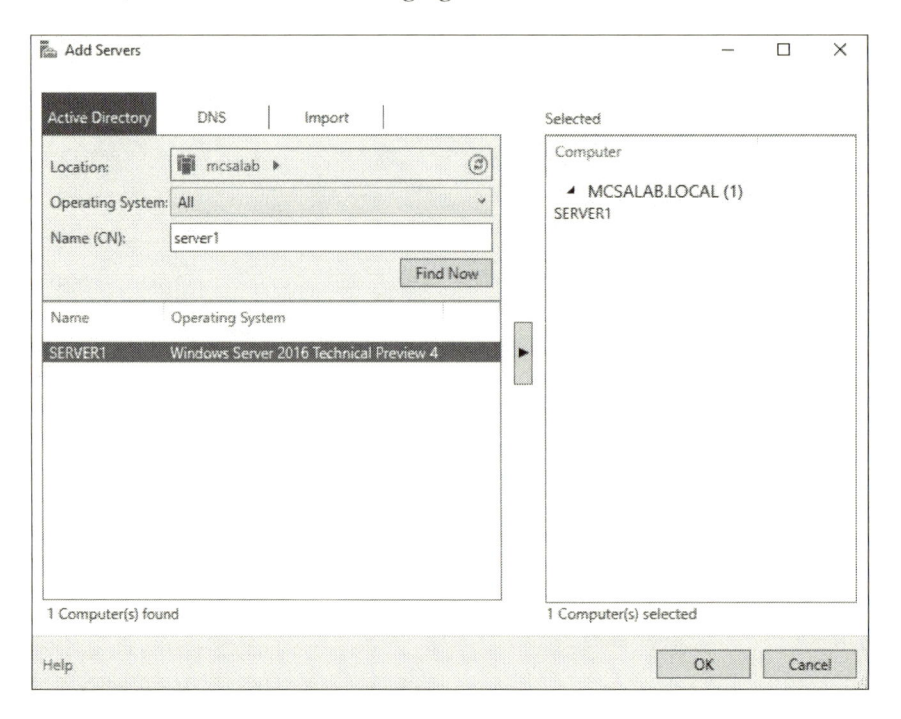

5. Click **OK** to close the **Add Servers** dialog box.
6. On the **Server Manager** console, in the **Servers** pane, wait until the **Manageability** status displays as **Online – Performance counters not started**, as shown in the following figure.

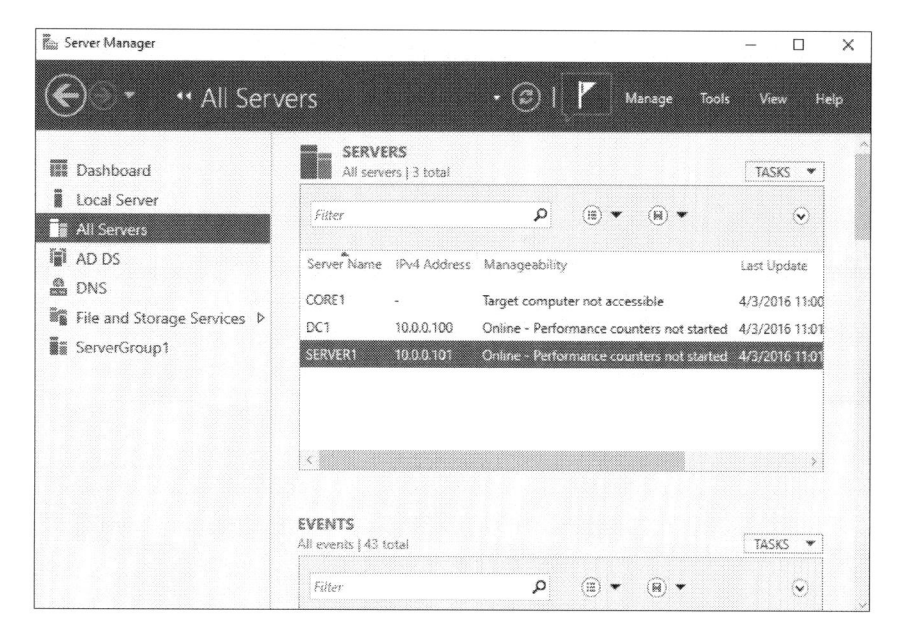

7. Select and right-click **SERVER1**, and then select **Add Roles and Features**.
8. On the **Add Roles and Features Wizard**, click **Next**.
9. On the **Select installation type** page, click **Next**.
10. On the **Select destination server** page, make sure that the **Select a server from the server pool** radio button is selected.
11. In the **Server Pool** area, make sure that **SERVER1.mcsalab.local** is selected, as shown in the following figure, and then click **Next**.

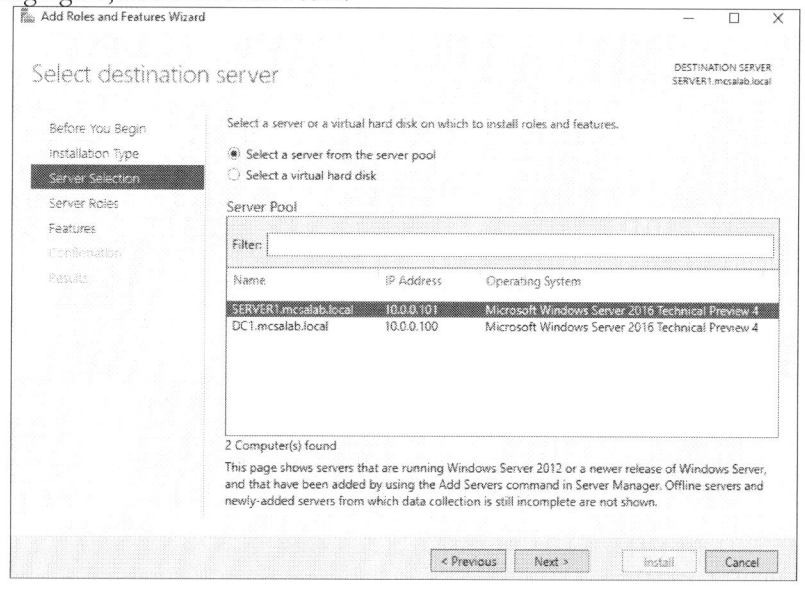

12. On the **Select server** roles page, select the **Active Directory Domain Services** check box.
13. On the **Add Roles and Features** dialog box, click **Add Features**, and then click **Next**.
14. The **Select server roles** page is returned, make sure that the **Active Directory Domain Services** check box is selected, as shown in the following figure, and then click **Next**.

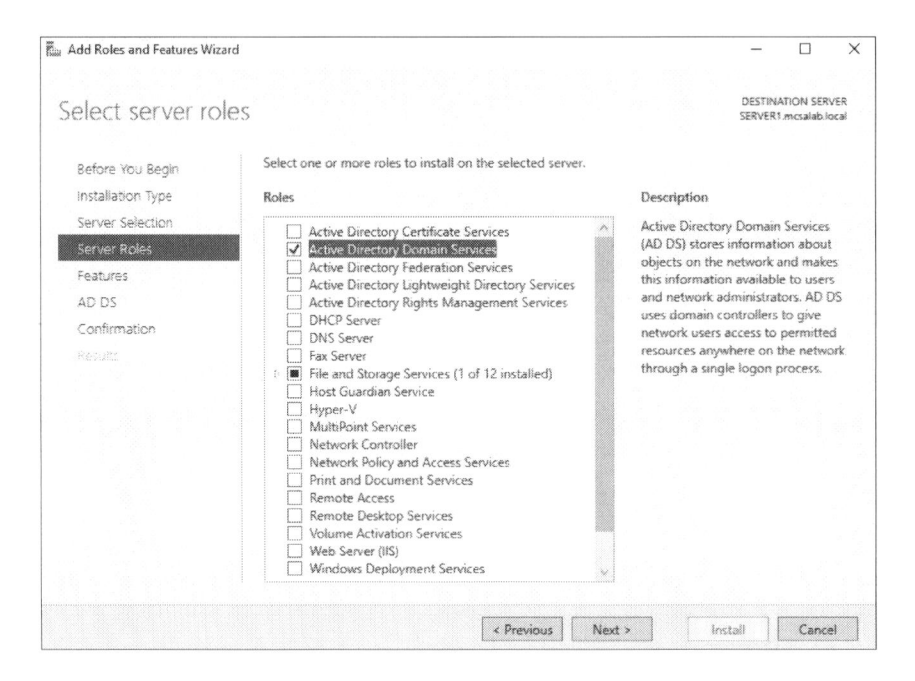

15. Click **Next**, until the **Confirm installation selections** page is displayed.
16. On the **Confirm installation selections** page, select the **Restart the destination server automatically if required** check box, and then click **Install**.
17. The installation process will start. Click **Close** to close the **Add Roles and Features Wizard**, once the installation is completed.

Task 2: Configuring SERVER1 Server as a Domain Controller

1. On **DC1**, on the **Server Manager** console, click the **Notifications** button.
2. On the **Post-deployment Configuration** box, click the **Promote this server to a domain controller** link, as shown in the following figure.

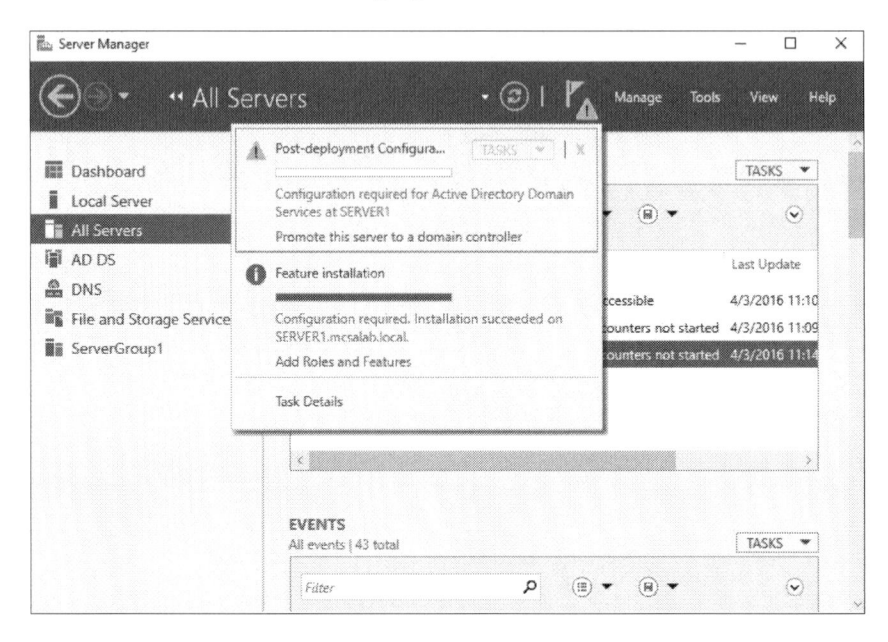

3. On the **Deployment Configuration** page, of the **Active Directory Domain Services Configuration Wizard**, make sure that the **Add a domain controller to an existing**

domain radio button is selected.

4. In the **Domain** text box, make sure that the **mcsalab.local** text is written, as shown in the following figure.

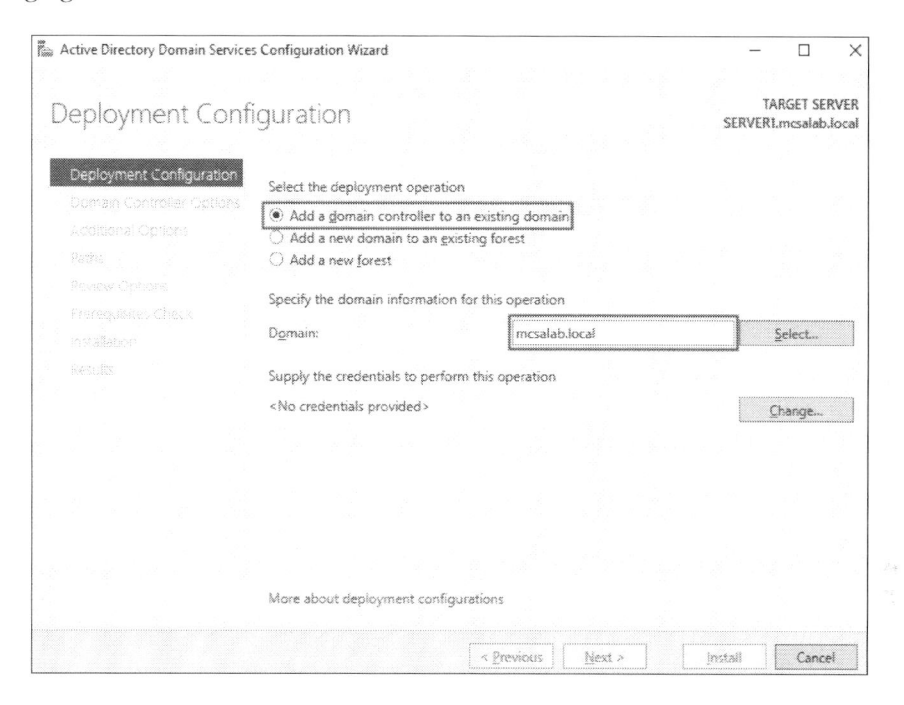

5. In the **Supply the credentials to perform this operation** section, click **Change**.
6. On the **Windows Security** dialog box, in the **Username** text box, type **MCSALAB\Administrator**, in the **Password** box, type **Password@123**, as shown in the following figure.

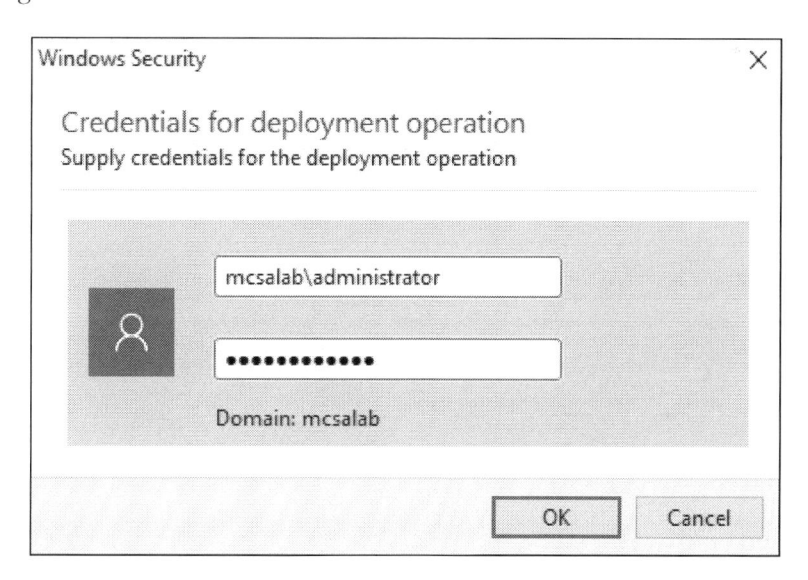

7. Click **OK** and then click **Next**.
8. On the **Domain Controller Options** page, make sure that **Domain Name System (DNS) server** check box is selected, and then clear the **Global Catalog (GC)** check box.
9. In the **Type the Directory Services Restore Mode (DSRM) password** section, type **Password@123**, in the **Password** and **Confirm password** text boxes, as shown in the following figure, and then click **Next**.

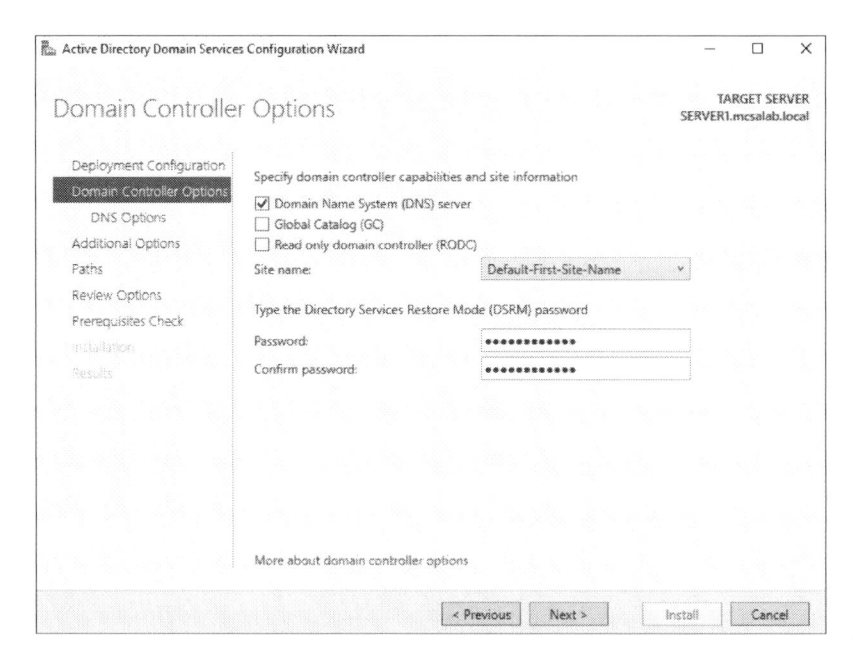

10. Click Next, until the **Prerequisites Check** page is displayed.
11. On the **Prerequisites Check** page, review the warnings, and then click **Install**.
12. The installation process will start, click **Close**, once the installation is completed.
13. The server will restart. Wait for server to restart.

Task 3: Configuring SERVER1 as a Global Catalog Server

1. Switch and sign in to **SERVER1** with the MCSALAB\Administrator account
2. On the **Server Manager** console, click **Tools,** and then click **Active Directory Sites and Services**.
3. On the **Active Directory Sites and Services** console, expand **Sites\Default-First-Site-Name\Servers,** and then click **SERVER1**, as shown in the following figure.

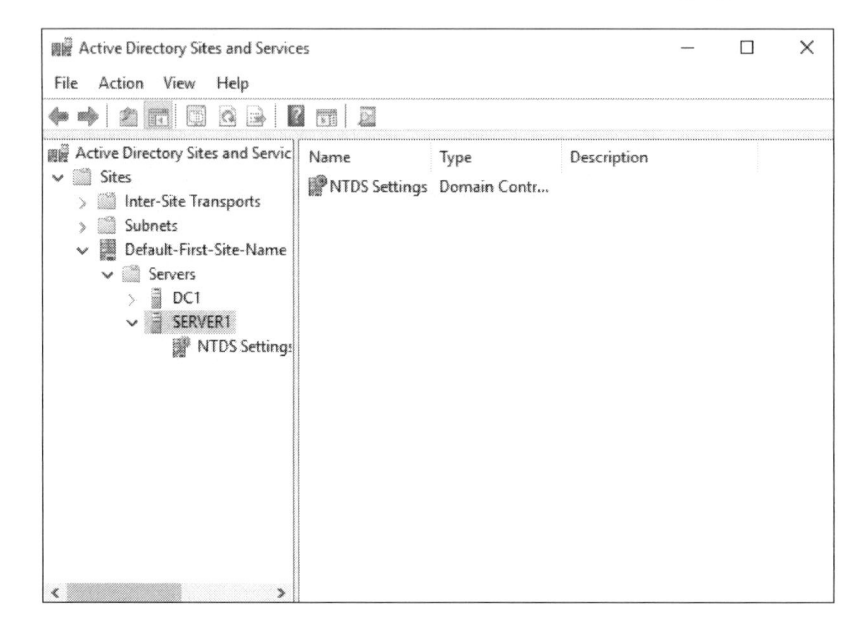

4. In the left pane, select and right-click **NTDS Settings**, and then select **Properties**.

5. On the **NTDS Settings Properties** dialog box, select the **Global Catalog** check box and then click **OK**.

6. Close the **Active Directory Sites and Services** console.

Results: After completing this exercise, you will have explored the Server Manager console and promoted a member server to be a domain controller.

Shut down and revert the DC1 and SERVER1 virtual machines to prepare for the next exercise.

Global Catalog - allows users and applications to find objects in Active Directory. The global catalog contains a partial replica of every naming context in the directory. The replication topology for the global catalog is generated automatically.

stores copies of all AD objects in the forest

Exercise 5: Installing and Configuring Read-Only Domain Controller (RODC)

There are two types of domain controllers: Writable Domain Controllers that have rights to modify and customize the Active Directory database. Second one is Read Only Domain controller that provides the same functionalities as provided by a Writable domain controller. However, neither they can modify Active Directory database, nor they, can store the user's credentials in their database until unless manually allowed by an administrator. Remote branch offices where the physical security is a major concern is the most suitable place to deploy an RODC.

To understand the concept of the RODC, you have to understand the two types of RODC password replication policies. Actually, these are built-in groups that control which user accounts' password can be stored and/or which user accounts' password cannot be stored by an RODC server. These are:

1. Allowed RODC Password Replication Group.
2. Denied RODC Password Replication Group.

By default, the Denied RODC Password Replication Group contains the following members whose passwords are not allowed to be cached by an RODC server:

- Enterprise Domain Controllers
- Enterprise Read-Only Domain Controllers
- Group Policy Creator Owners
- Domain Admins
- Cert Publishers
- Enterprise Admins
- Schema Admins
- Domain-wide krbtgt account
- Account Operators
- Server Operators
- Backup Operators
- Administrators

By default, the Allowed RODC Password Replication Group does not contain any members.

Now, you have the basics of RODC. Here, we are going to install and configure RODC on a server. To perform this lab exercise, ensure that you have reverted the DC1 and SERVER1 virtual machines.

Task 1: Preparing DC1 to Deploy RODC

Before you could deploy the RODC on SERVER1, you have to perform the following tasks on the primary domain controller.

1. Create a user account named RODCAdmin on the Primary server and make it member of Allowed RODC Password Replication Group.

2. Also make it a member of a Server Operators group so it can be logged in locally to the RODC domain controller. Alternatively, you can modify the Default Group Policy to assign allow login locally permission to this user account.

3. After making appropriate changes the RODCAdmin properties should look like the following.

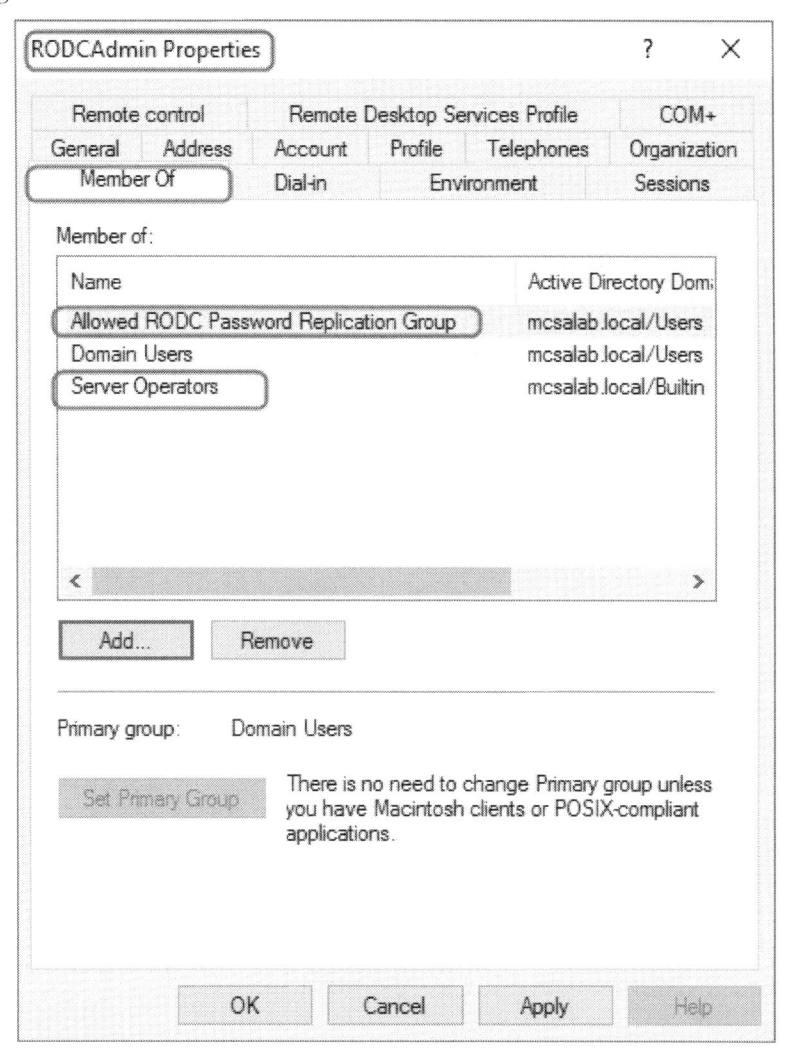

Task 2: Installing RODC Domain Controller

Now you are set to install and configure RODC on SERVER1. To install and configure the RODC server, you need to perform the following steps:

1. Switch on to SERVER1, open the **Server Manager** console and launch the **Add Roles and Features Wizard**.
2. Accept the default selections until the **Select server roles** page displays.
3. Select the **Active Directory Domain Services** check box and complete the Active Directory installation process.

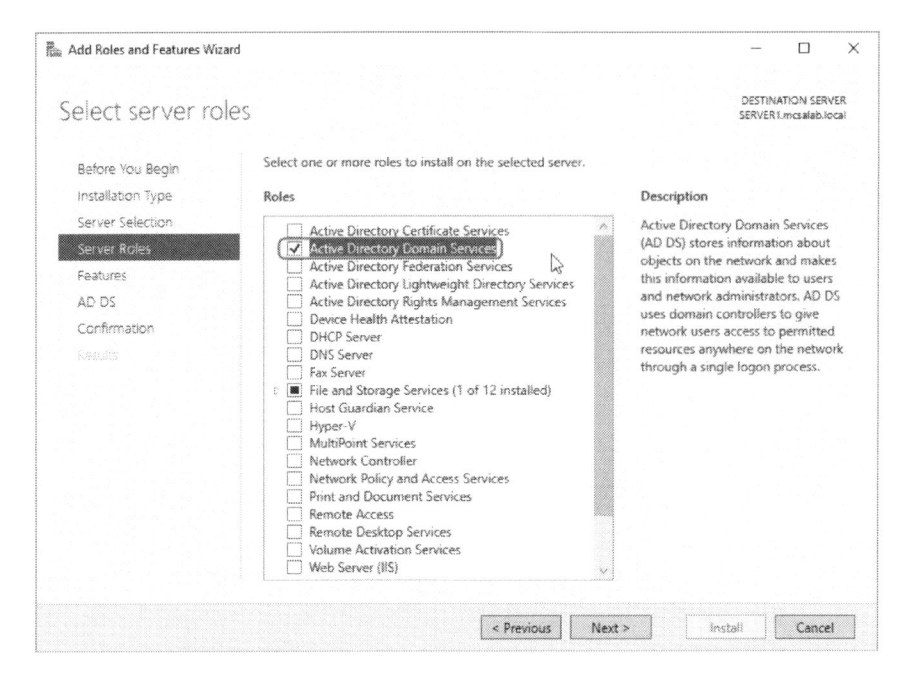

4. On the **Server Manager** console, click the **Promote this server to a domain controller** link.

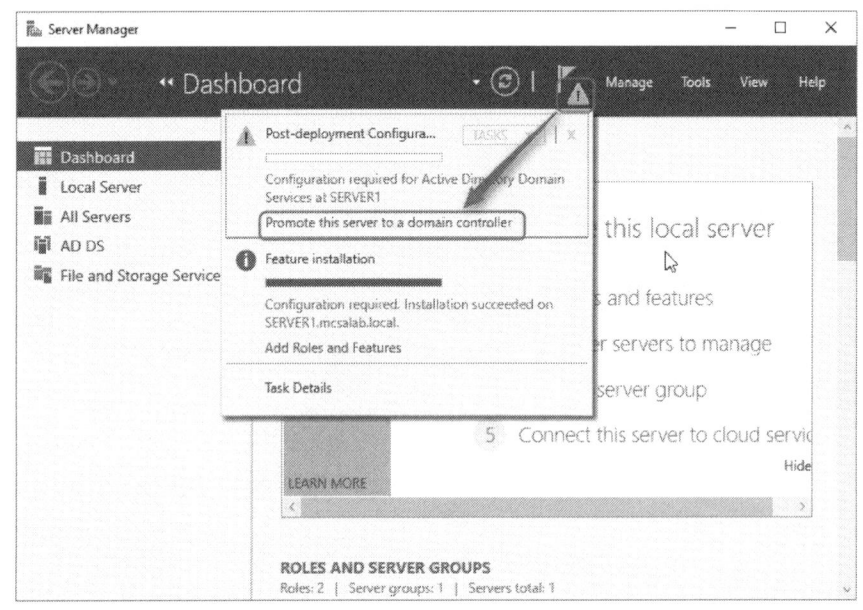

5. On the **Deployment Configuration** page, make sure that the **Add a domain controller to an existing domain** option is selected and then click **Next.**

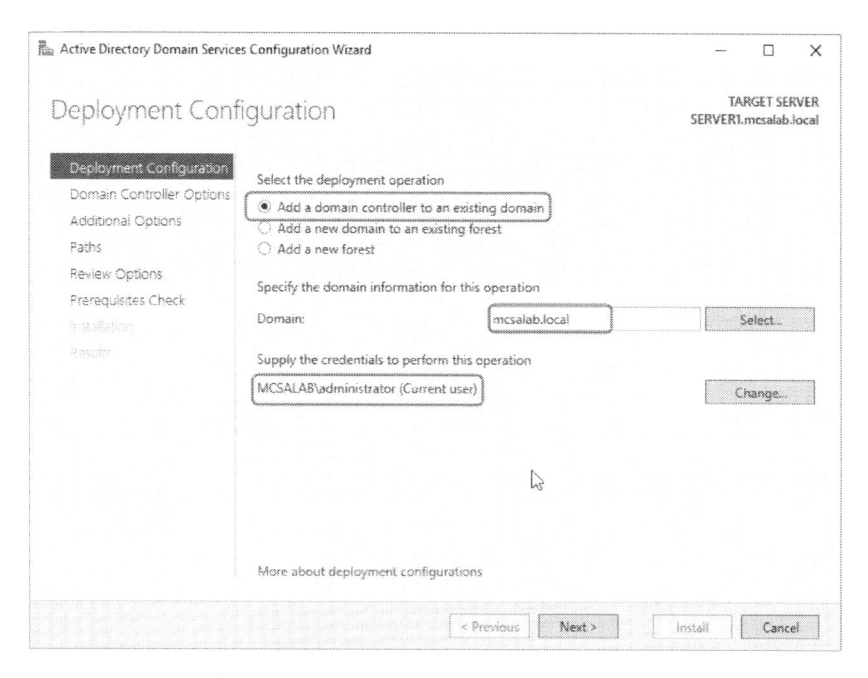

6. On the **Domain Controllers Options** page, select the following check boxes, set the desired DSRM password and then click **Next** to proceed.
   - **Domain Name System (DNS) server**
   - **Global Catalog (GC)**
   - **Read only domain controller (RODC)**

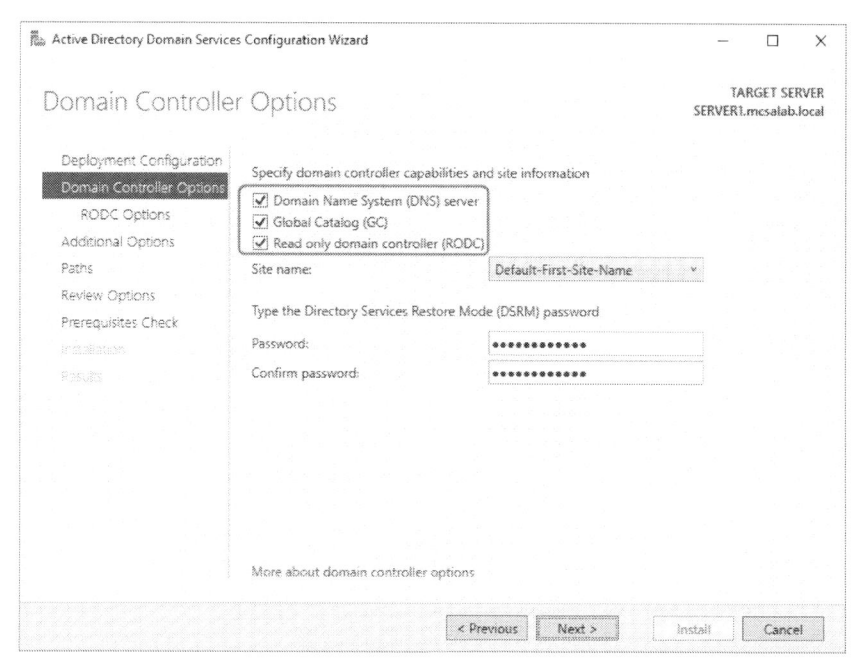

7. On the **RODC Options** page, specify the following options:
   - Delegated Administrator Account: It will be responsible to manage the RODC.
   - Accounts that are allowed to replicate passwords to the RODC.
   - Account that are denied from replicating the passwords to the RODC.

8. For the testing purpose, add **RODCAdmin** as a Delegated administrator account and click **Next** to proceed.

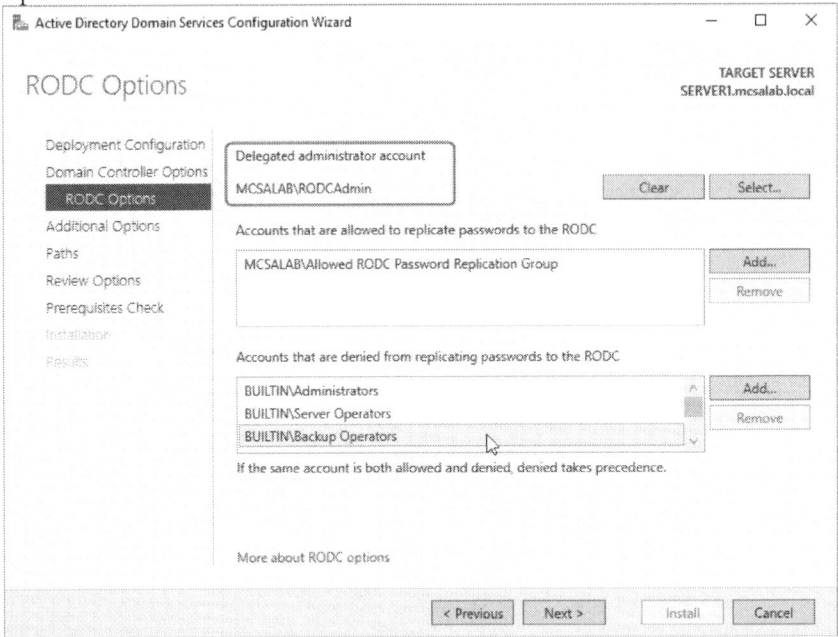

9. On the **Additional Options** page, click **Next**. You can complete the Domain Controller installation using the **Install From Media (IFM)**. We have covered IFM in the next exercise.

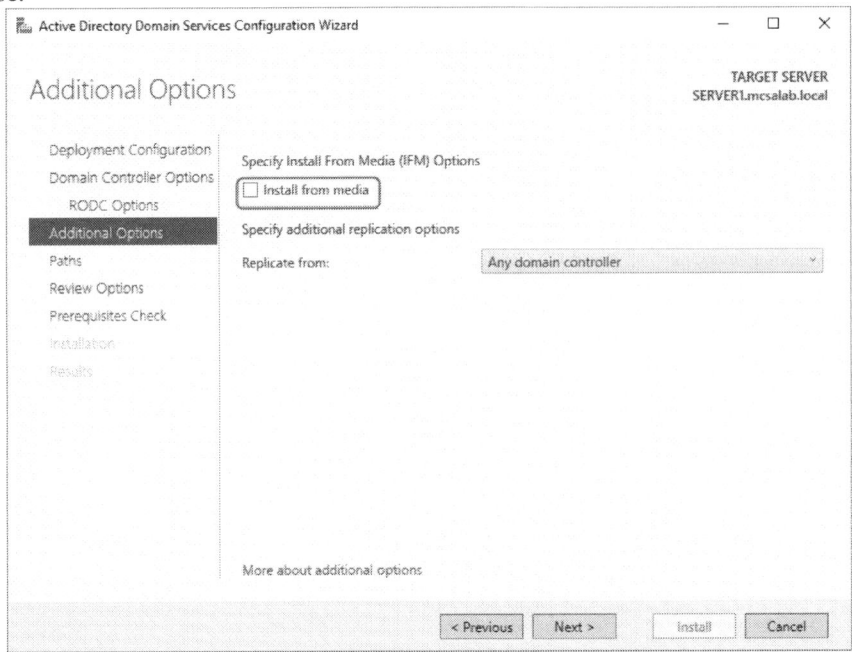

10. On the **Paths** page, click **Next** and proceed to the **Prerequisites Check** page. Verify that all the prerequisites checks passed successfully, click **Install** to begin the installation. You may ignore the prerequisities warnings.

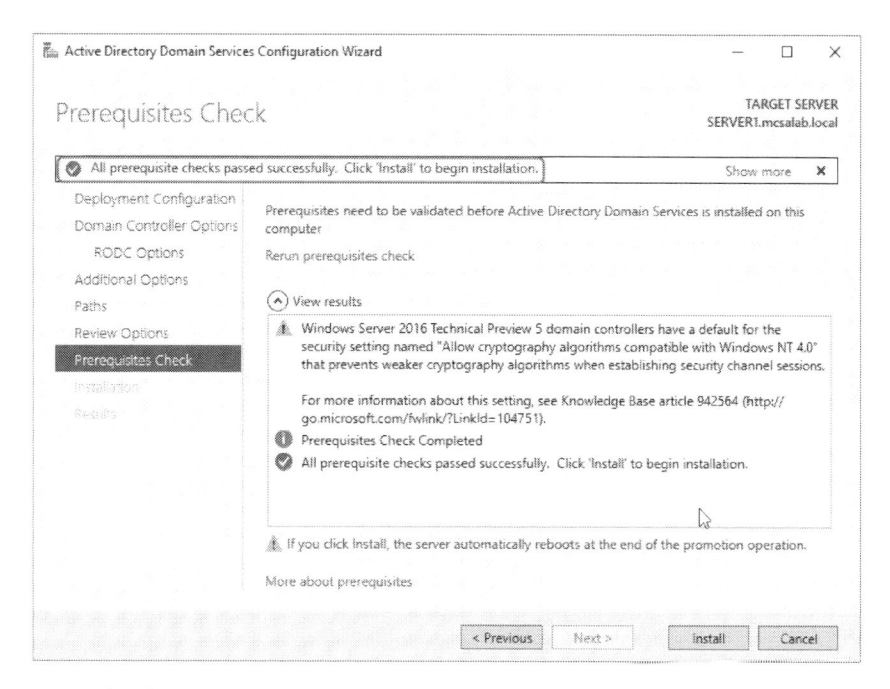

11. The system will reboot once the installation process of RODC completes. Sign in to **MCSALAB\RODCAdmin** delegated administrator account that we have added during the RODC installation.

12. Now, you have successfully installed and configured RODC on SERVER1.

Task 3: Verifying RODC Configuration

In order to verify and test that our RODC server is configured successfully and functioning properly, we will explore some of the RODC verification tasks.

How to view the current credentials that are cached on an RODC?

To view the credentials that are cached on an RODC, you need to perform the following steps on the DC1 primary writable domain controller.

1. Open the **Active Directory Users and Computers** window, expand the **Domain Controllers** node, and then open the **Properties** of your RODC server (SERVER1).
2. Select the **Password Replication Policy** tab and click **Advanced**.

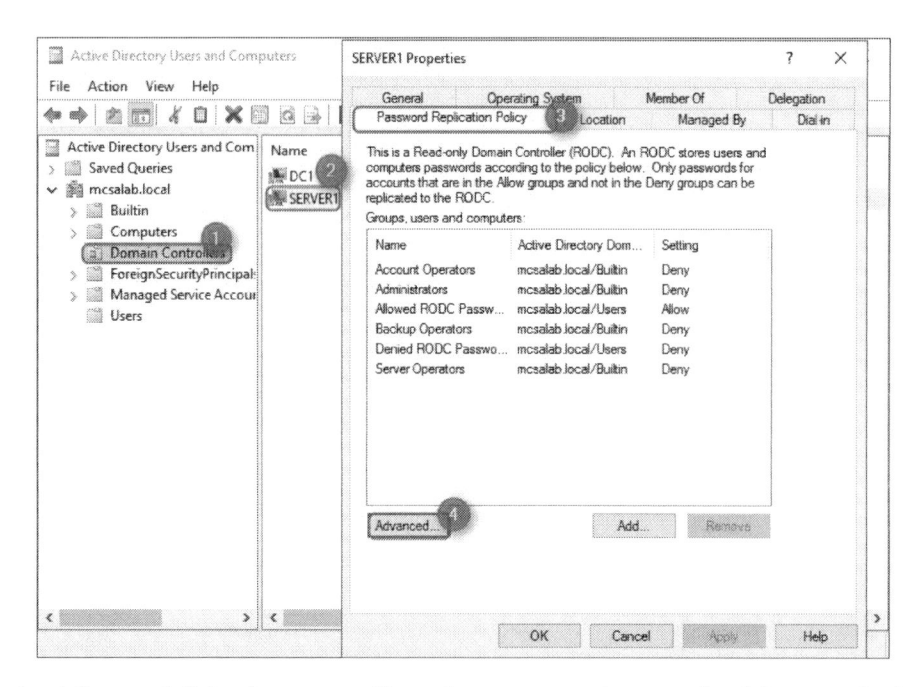

3. On the **Advanced** dialog box, you will see the accounts whose credentials are cached on this RODC.

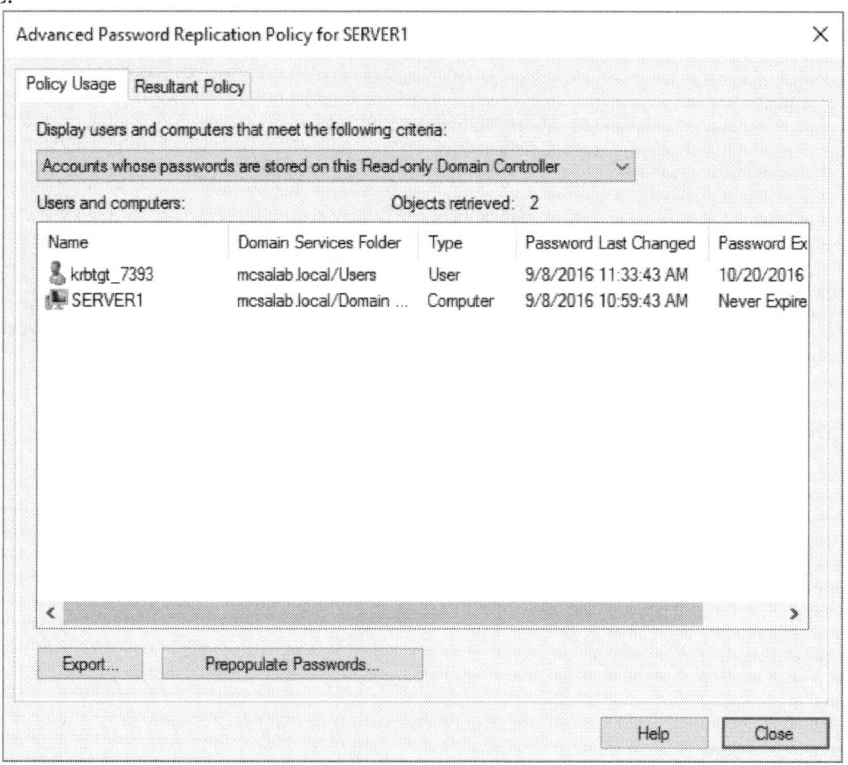

Note: By default, the only credentials that are cached on an RODC are for the computer account of the RODC itself and a krbtgt account.

> *Wait a minute! Where is your RODCAdmin account? Keep following the steps.*

4. To view the **RODCAdmin** account, select the **Accounts that have been authenticated to this Read-Only Domain Controller** option and view the result.

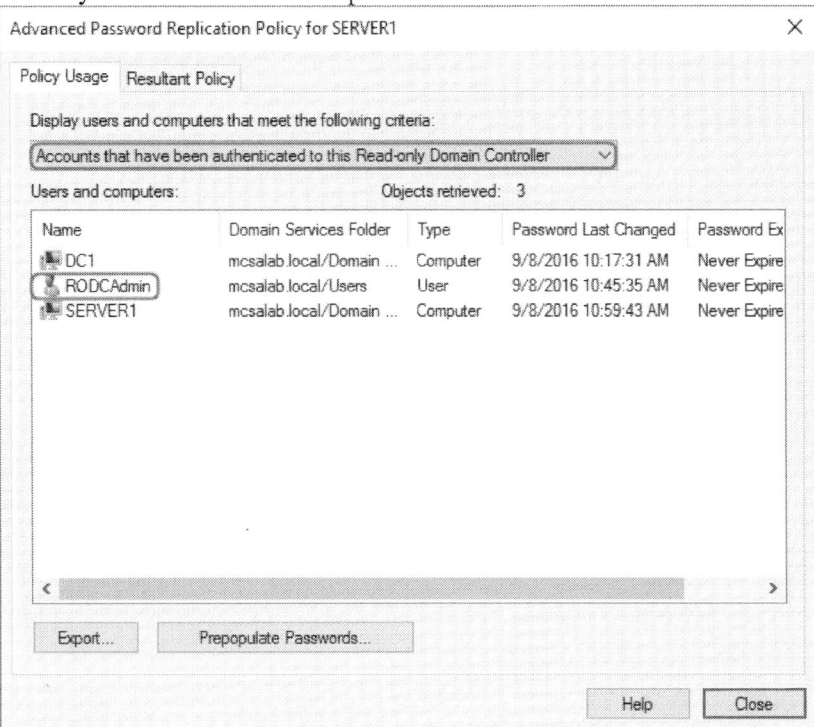

5. To add the specific users, groups, and computers into Allowed list or Denied list, click **Add** and select the desired RODC policy.

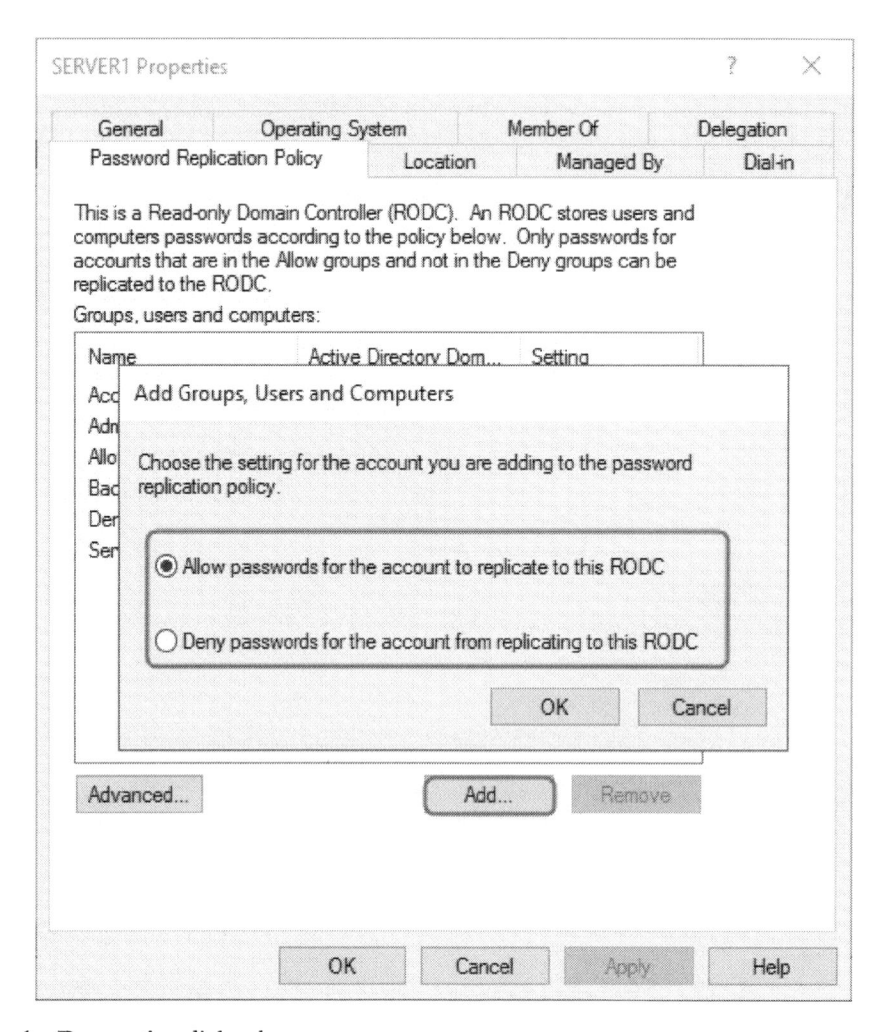

[Screenshot: SERVER1 Properties dialog with Password Replication Policy tab and "Add Groups, Users and Computers" sub-dialog showing options "Allow passwords for the account to replicate to this RODC" (selected) and "Deny passwords for the account from replicating to this RODC".]

6. Close the **Properties** dialog box.

Task 4: Securing Accounts If an RODC is Stolen

To secure accounts and reset the current credentials that are cached on an RODC if the RODC is stolen, you need to perform the following steps:

1. Sign in to **Primary Domain Controller** server (**DC1**) and open the **Active Directory Users and Computers** console.
2. Expand the **Domain Controllers** node.
3. In the details pane, select and right-click the RODC server which has been stolen, and then select **Delete**.

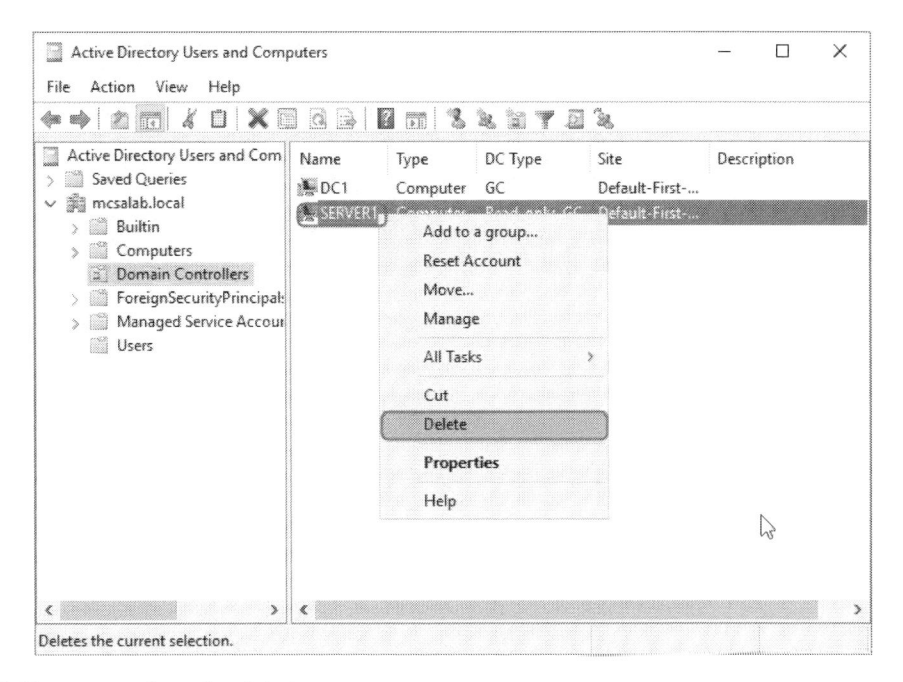

[Screenshot of Active Directory Users and Computers showing a right-click context menu on SERVER1 in the Domain Controllers container, with options including Add to a group..., Reset Account, Move..., Manage, All Tasks, Cut, Delete (highlighted), Properties, and Help.]

4. Click **Yes** to confirm the deletion.
5. In the **Deleting Active Directory Domain Controller** dialog box, read and understand all the available options carefully. Here, you can select the following check boxes depending on your choice and the types of accounts (users or computers) that have been stolen:

    - Reset all passwords for user accounts that were cached on this read-only domain controller.
    - Reset all passwords for computer accounts that were cached on this read-only domain controller.
    - Export the list of accounts that were cached on this read-only domain controller to this file.

6. Specify a file name where the RODC cached credentials will be stored and then click **Delete**. You can refer this file later to reset the credentials of stolen users and computers accounts.

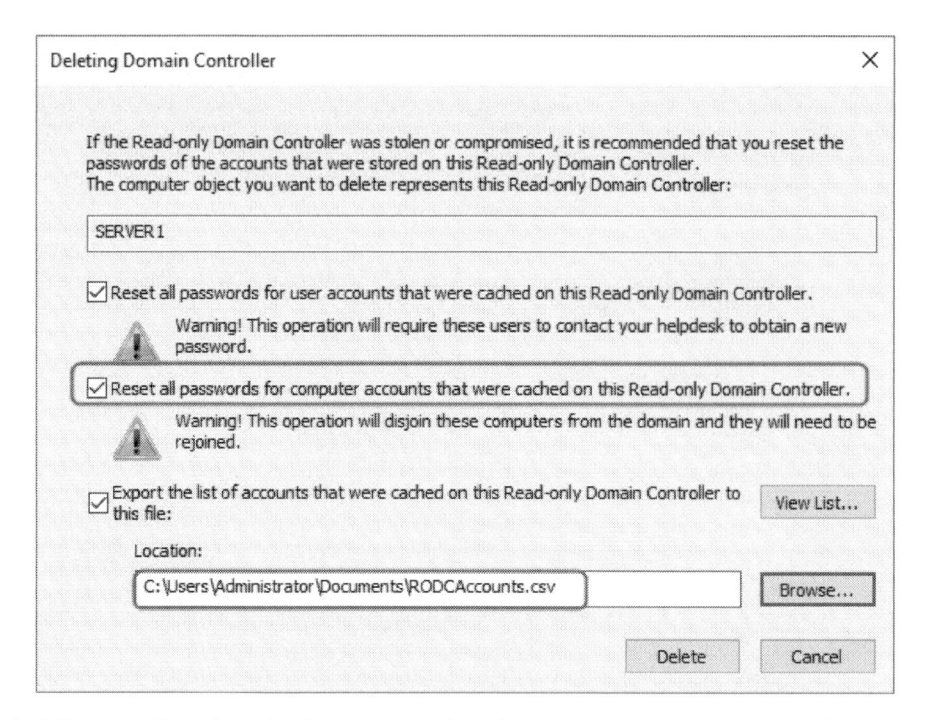

[Dialog box: Deleting Domain Controller]

> If the Read-only Domain Controller was stolen or compromised, it is recommended that you reset the passwords of the accounts that were stored on this Read-only Domain Controller.
> The computer object you want to delete represents this Read-only Domain Controller:
>
> SERVER1
>
> ☑ Reset all passwords for user accounts that were cached on this Read-only Domain Controller.
> ⚠ Warning! This operation will require these users to contact your helpdesk to obtain a new password.
>
> ☑ Reset all passwords for computer accounts that were cached on this Read-only Domain Controller.
> ⚠ Warning! This operation will disjoin these computers from the domain and they will need to be rejoined.
>
> ☑ Export the list of accounts that were cached on this Read-only Domain Controller to this file: [View List...]
> Location:
> C:\Users\Administrator\Documents\RODCAccounts.csv [Browse...]
>
> [Delete] [Cancel]

7. Click **OK** to confirm the selection. Ensure that the RODC server is removed from the **Domain Controllers** node in the **Active Directory Users and Computers** console.
8. That's all you need to secure accounts if the RODC is stolen.

Results: In this lab exercise, you have learned how to install, configure, and deploy RODC Server. Shutdown and revert the DC1 and SERVER1 virtual machines so you can perform the next exercises

---

Exercise 6: Installing a Domain Controller by Using IFM

In this exercise, you will learn how to configure a domain controller using the IFM data file. The Install From Media (IFM) is a feature that allows you to configure a server as a domain controller. This feature helps you to reduce the network bandwidth consumption used during the additional domain controller configuration. IFM allows you to export the Active Directory database file (NTDS) to an external media which can be used to configure an additional domain controller.

Start the DC1 and SERVER1 virtual machines to perform this exercise.

Task 1: Generating a IFM Data File
1. Sign in to **DC1** with the MCSA\Administrator account.
2. Open the **Run** dialog box, in the **Open** text box, type **cmd**, and then press **Enter**.
3. On the **Command Prompt** window, type the following commands, and then press **Enter** after each one, as shown in the following figure.
   ```
   Ntdsutil
   Activate instance ntds
   IFM
   Create sysvol full C:\IFM
   ```

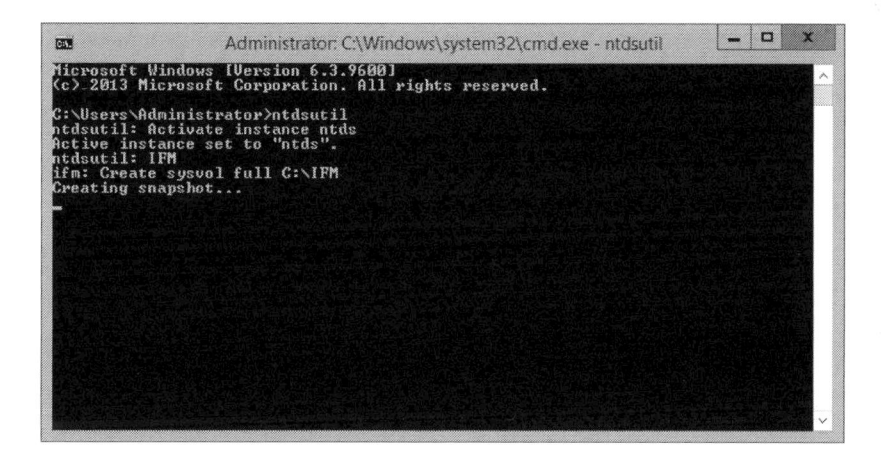

Task 2: Adding the AD DS Role to the Member Server
1. Switch and sign in to **SERVER1** with the MCSALAB\Administrator account.
2. Open the **Command Prompt** window, type the following command, and then press **Enter**, as shown in the following figure.
   ```
   Net use Z: \\DC1\c$\IFM
   ```

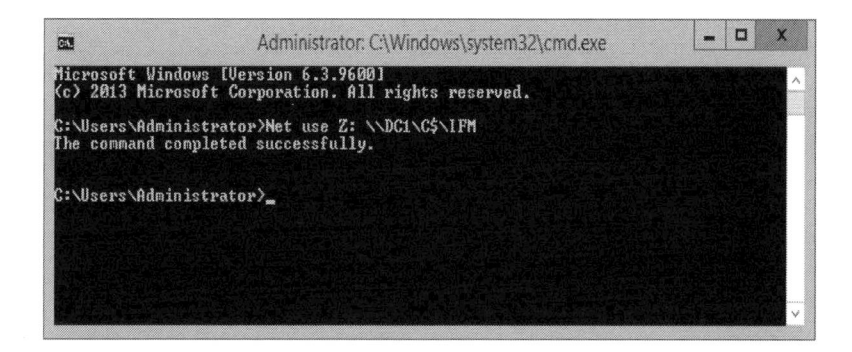

3. Open the **Server Manager** console, if required.
4. In the left pane, select **Local Server**.
5. In the toolbar, click **Manage,** and then click **Add Roles and Features**, as shown in the following figure.

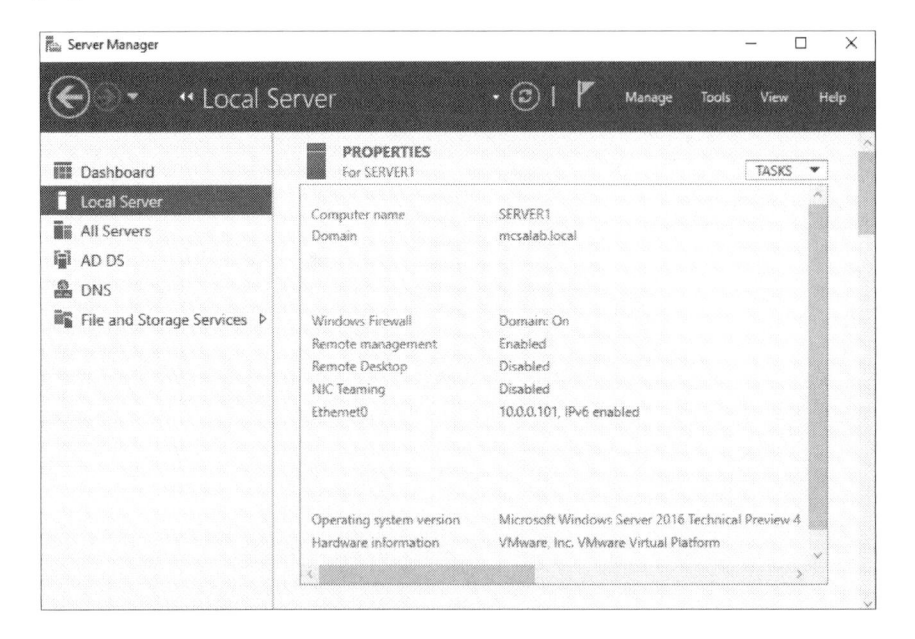

6. On the **Before you begin** page of the **Add Roles and Features Wizard**, click **Next**.
7. On the **Select installation type** page, make sure that the **Role-based or feature-based installation** radio button is selected, and then click **Next**.
8. On the **Select destination server** page, make sure that the **SERVER1** server is selected, and then click **Next**.
9. On the **Select server roles** page, select the **Active Directory Domain Services** check box.
10. On the **Add Roles and Features Wizard** dialog box, click **Add Features**, and then click **Next**.
11. On the **Select Features** page, click **Next**.
12. On the **Active Directory Domain Services** page, click **Next**.
13. On the **Confirm installation selections** page, select the **Restart the destination server automatically if required** check box.
14. On the **Add Roles and Features Wizard** message box, as shown in the following figure, read the message, and then click **Yes**.

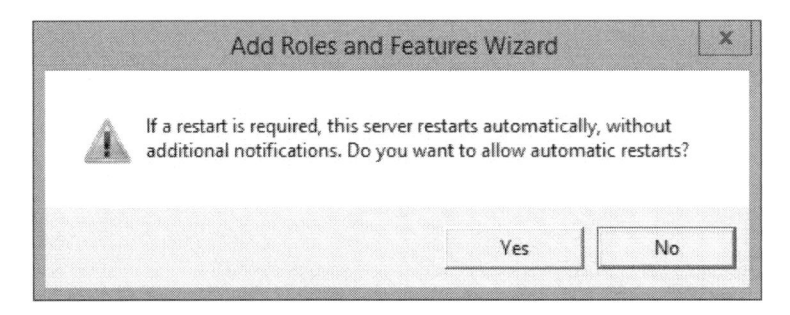

15. On the **Confirm installation selections** page, click **Install**.
16. The installation process will start. Click **Close**, once the installation is completed.

Note: If you see a warning regarding the DNS server delegation, click OK.

Task 3: Configuring SERVER1 as a New Domain Controller Using the IFM Data File

1. On **SERVER1**, open the **Command Prompt** window, if required.
2. On the **Command Prompt** window, type the following commands, and then press **Enter**, as shown in the following figure.
   Robocopy Z: C:\IFM /copyall /s

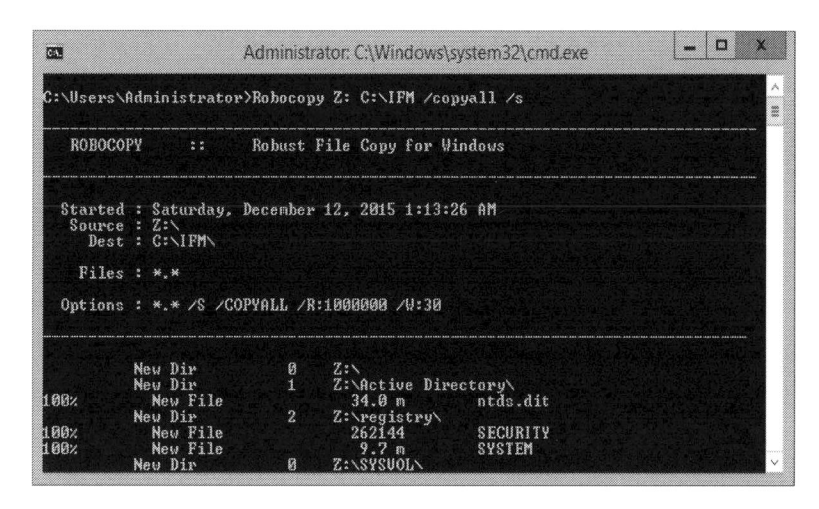

3. Close the **Command Prompt** window, once the copying process is completed.
4. On the **Server Manager** console, click the **Notifications** button.
5. In the **Post-deployment Configuration** box, click the **Promote this server to a domain controller** link.
6. On the **Deployment Configuration** page, make sure that the **Add a domain controller to an existing domain** radio button is selected.
7. Make sure that the **mcsalab.local** text is written in the **Domain** text box, as shown in the following figure.

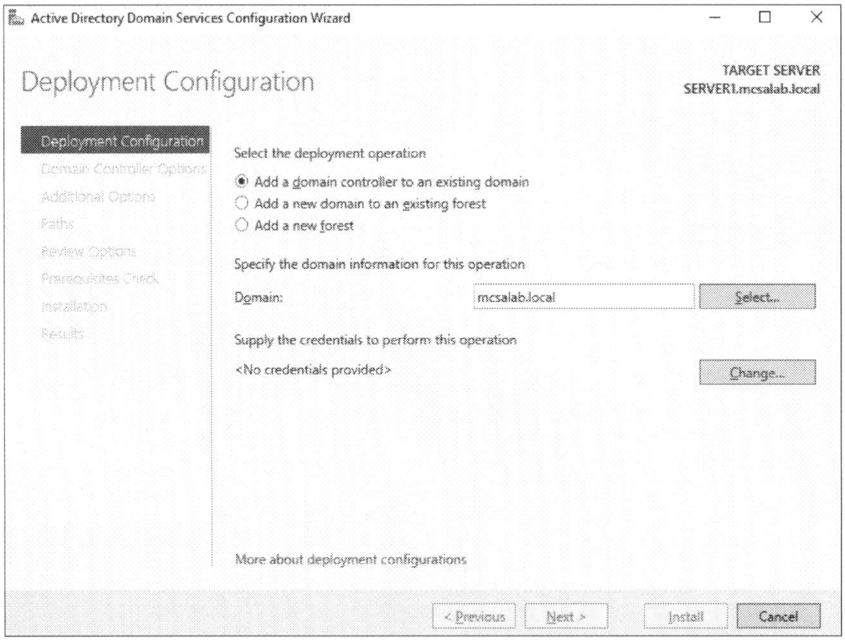
Active Directory Domain Services Configuration Wizard
Deployment Configuration
TARGET SERVER
SERVER1.mcsalab.local
Deployment Configuration
Select the deployment operation
Add a domain controller to an existing domain
Add a new domain to an existing forest
Add a new forest
Specify the domain information for this operation
Domain:
mcsalab.local
Select...
Supply the credentials to perform this operation
<No credentials provided>
Change...
More about deployment configurations
< Previous
Next >
Install
Cancel

8. In the **Supply the credentials to perform this operation** section, click **Change**.

***Note**: If you are already logged in as MCSA\Administrator account, you don't need to change the credentials on this page. If so, move directly to the Domain Controller Options page.*

---

9. On the **Windows Security** dialog box, in the **Username** text box, type **MCSALAB\Administrator**, in the **Password** text box, type **Password@123**.
10. Click **OK**, and then click **Next**.
11. On the **Domain Controller Options** page, make sure that the **Domain Name System (DNS) server** and **Global Catalog (GC)** check boxes are selected.

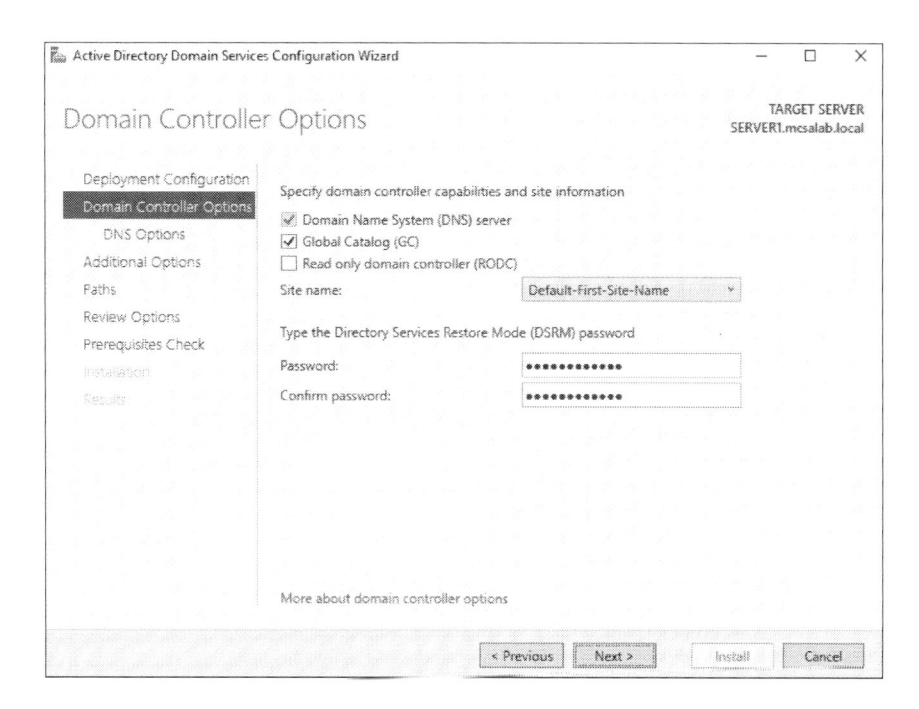

12. Under the **DSRM password** section, type **Password@123** in the **Password** and **Confirm password** text boxes and then click **Next**.
13. On the **DNS Options** page, click **Next**.
14. On the **Additional Options** page, select the **Install from media** check box.
15. In the **Path** text box, type **C:\IFM**, as shown in the following figure.

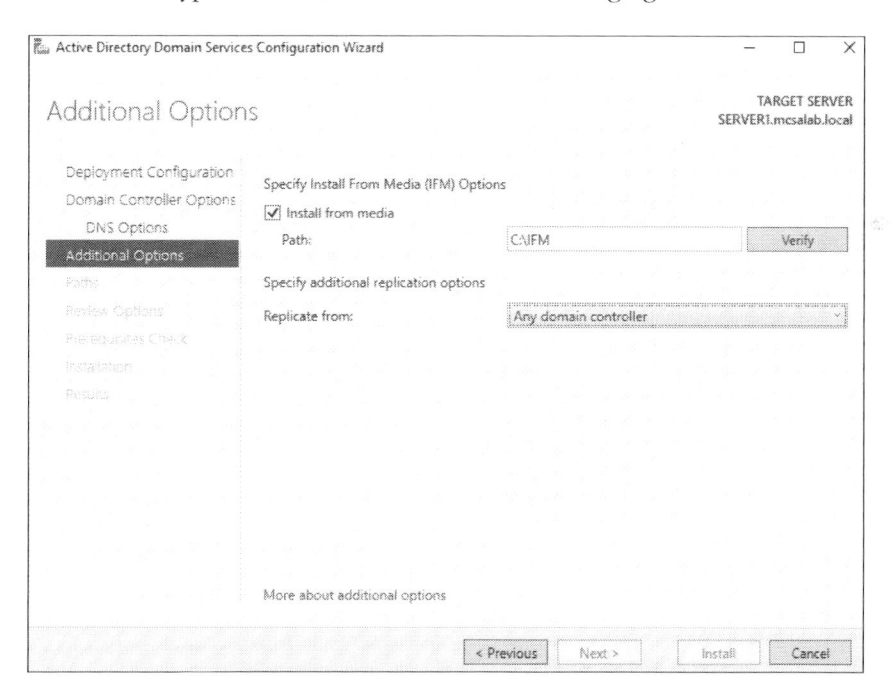

16. Click **Verify**. Once the path has been verified, click **Next**.
17. On the **Paths** page, click **Next**.
18. On the **Review Options** page, click **Next**.
19. On the **Prerequisites Check** page, click **Install**. The installation process will start and the server will restart, once the configuration is completed. Wait for the server to restart.

> **Results**: After completing this exercise, you will have installed an additional domain controller for the branch office by using IFM.

Shut down and revert the DC1 and SERVER1 virtual machines to prepare for the next exercise.

Exercise 7: Managing Organizational Units and Groups in AD DS

Active Directory objects are used to access the various network resources for the various purposes. Once you configured a domain controller, you need to create and manage Active Directory objects, such as OUs, groups, and users. You can delegate the administrative permissions to the Active Directory objects.

In this exercise, you will learn how to create Active Directory objects, how to delegate the permissions, and how to configure home folders. In addition, you will also learn how to reset and rejoin the computer accounts.

Start the DC1 and CLIENT1 virtual machines to perform this exercise.

Task 1: Managing Organizational Units and Groups
1. Sign in to **DC1** with the MCSALAB\Administrator account.
2. On the **Server Manager** console, click **Tools, and then click Active Directory Users and Computers**.
3. On the **Active Directory Users and Computers** console, select and right-click **mcsalab.local**, and then select **New**, and then click **Organizational Unit**, as shown in the following figure.

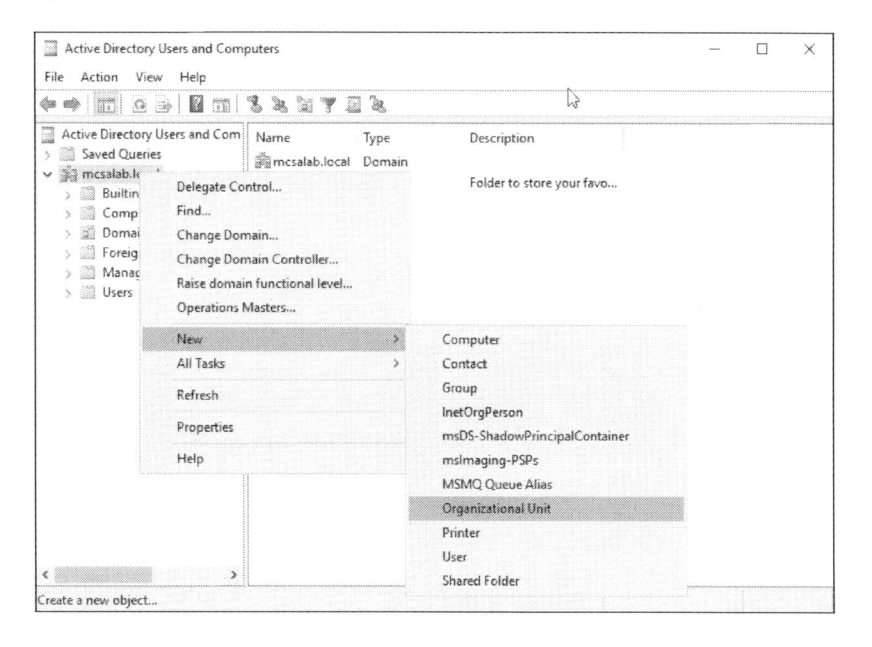

4. On the **New Object – Organizational Unit** dialog box, in the **Name** text box, type **Training**, as shown in the following figure, and then click **OK**.

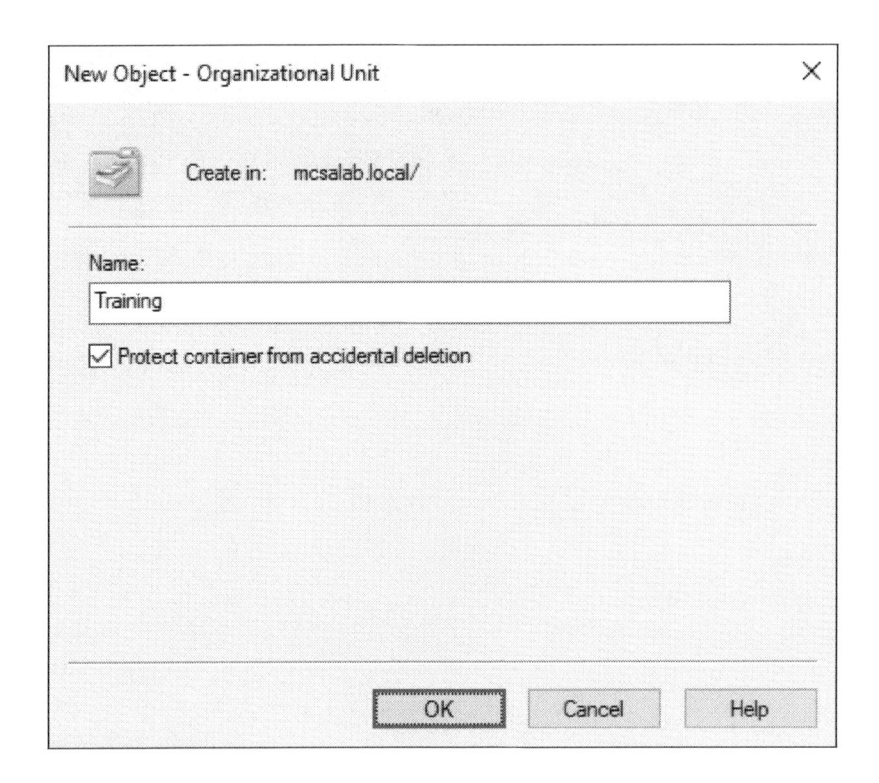

5. Select and right-click the **Training** OU in the left pane, and then select **New**, and then click Group.
6. On the **New Object – Group** dialog box, in the **Group name** text box, type **Students**, as shown in the following figure, and then click **OK**.

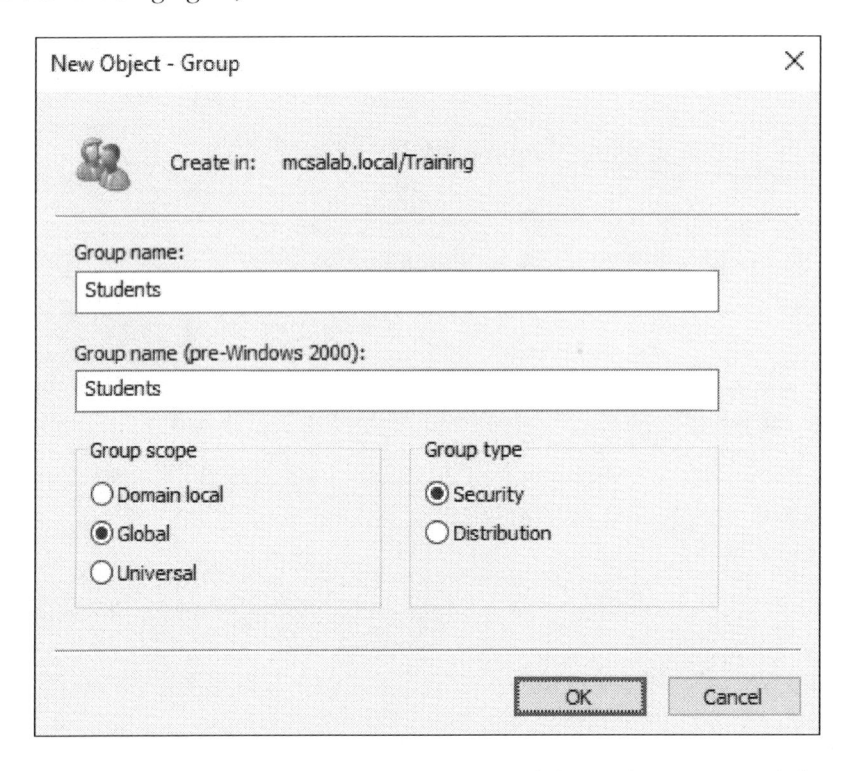

7. Select and right-click **mcsalab.local**, in the left pane, and then select **New**, and then click **Organizational Unit**.

8. On the **New Object – Organizational Unit** dialog box, in the **Name** text box, type **Development**, and then click **OK**.
9. Select and right-click the **Development** OU, and then select **New,** and then click **Group**.
10. On the **New Object – Group** dialog box, in the **Group name** text box, type **Trainers**, and then click **OK**.
11. Select and right-click the **Development** OU, and then select **New**, and then click **Group**.
12. On the **New Object – Group** dialog box, in the **Group name** text box, type **Managers**, and then click **OK**.
13. In the right pane, select and right-click the **Trainers** group, and then select **Move**, as shown in the following figure.

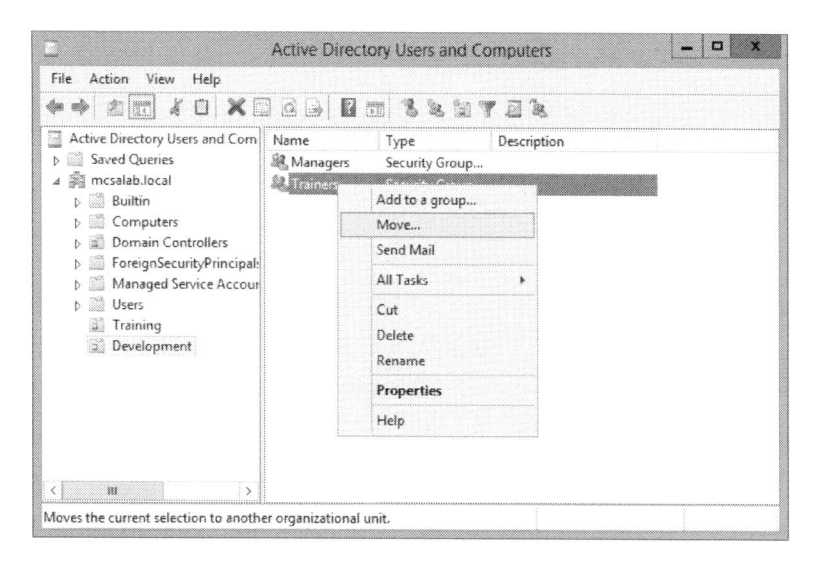

14. On the **Move** dialog box, select the **Training** OU, as shown in the following figure, and then click **OK**.

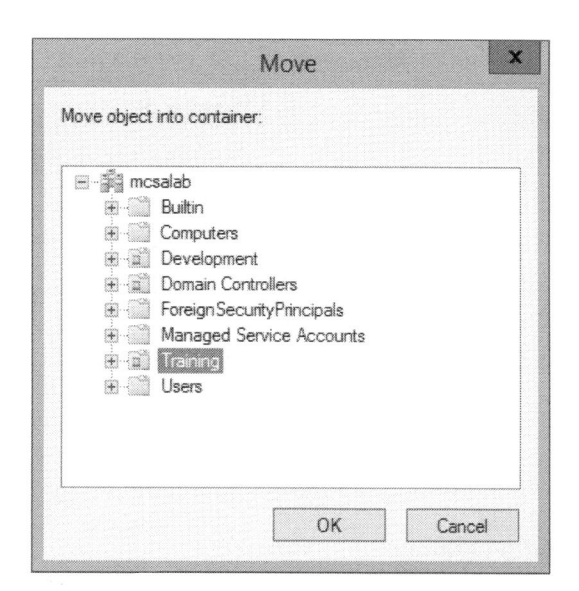

15. In the left pane, select the **Training** OU.
16. In the right pane, select and right-click **Trainers**, and then select **Delete**.
17. On the **Active Directory Domain Services** message box, click **Yes**. Make sure that the **Trainers** group is deleted.

Task 2: Delegating the Permissions

1. Make sure that the **Active Directory Users and Computers** console is active on **DC1**.
2. In the left pane, select and right-click the **Training** OU, and then select **Delegate Control**, as shown in the following figure.

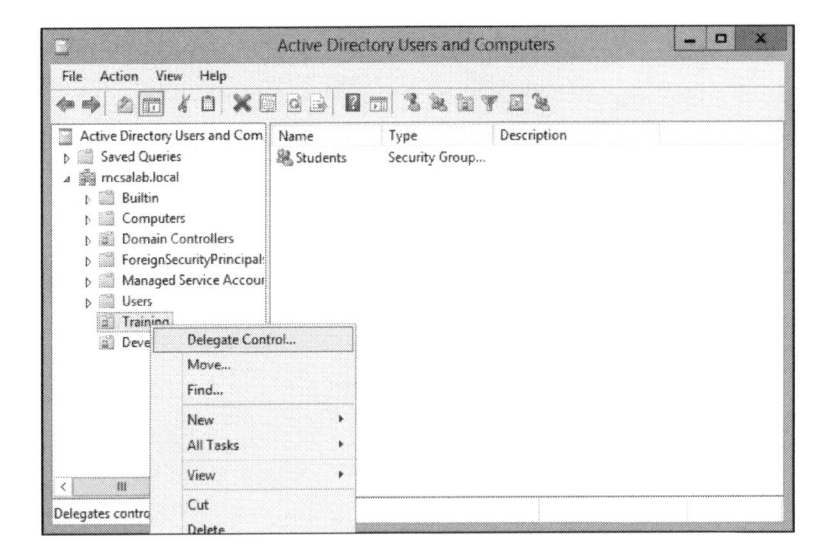

3. On the welcome page of the **Delegation of Control Wizard**, and click **Next**.
4. On the **Users or Groups** page, click **Add**.
5. On the **Select Users, Computers, or Groups** dialog box, in the **Enter the object names to select (examples)** text box, type **Students**, as shown in the following figure, and then click **OK**.

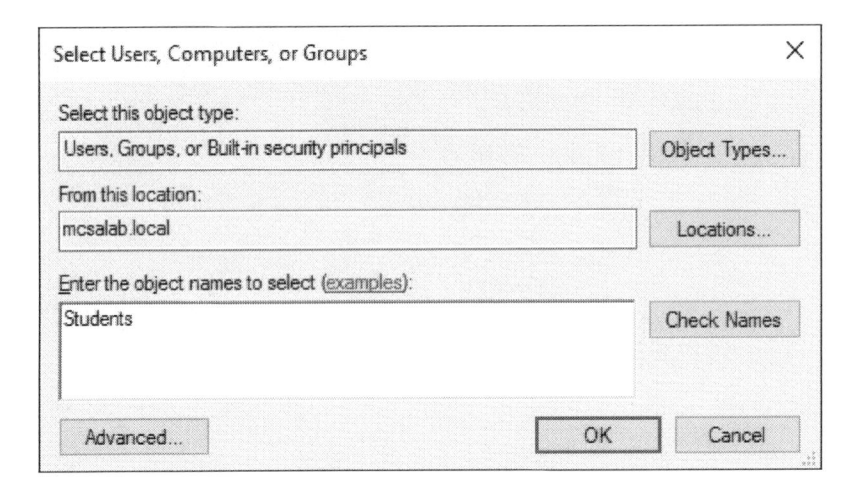

6. On the **Users or Groups** page, click **Next**.
7. On the **Tasks to Delegate** page, make sure that the **Delegate the following common tasks** radio button is selected.
8. Select the **Create, delete, and manage user accounts** check box, as shown in the following figure, and then click **Next**.

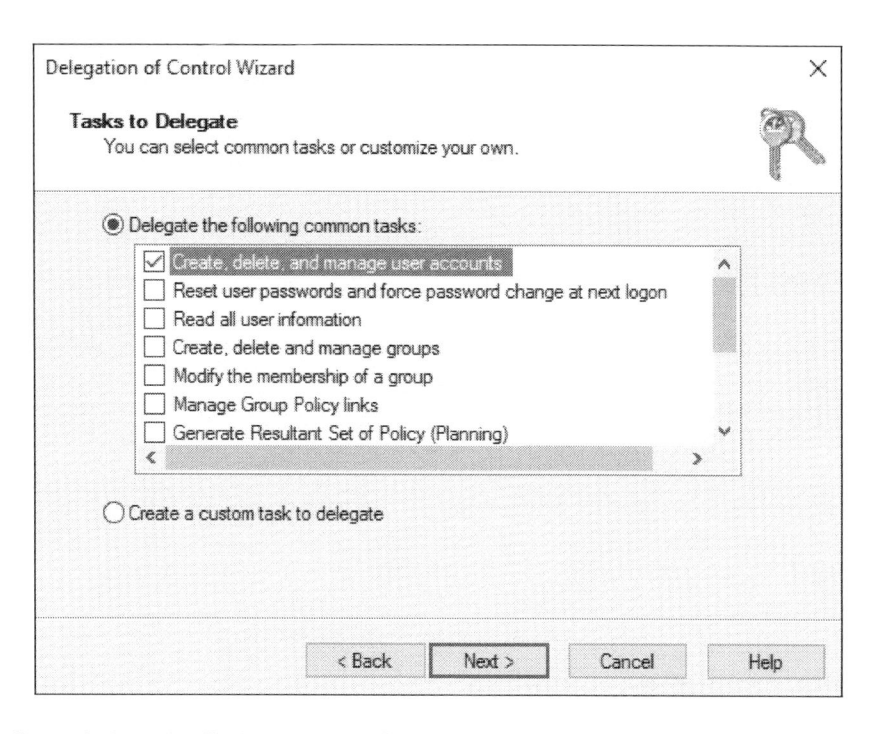

9. On the **Completing the Delegation of Control Wizard** page, click **Finish**.
10. Select and right-click the **Training** OU, and then select **New**, and then click **User**.
11. On the **New Object - User** dialog box, type **Marsh**, in the **First name** and **User logon name** text boxes, as shown in the following figure, and then click **Next**.

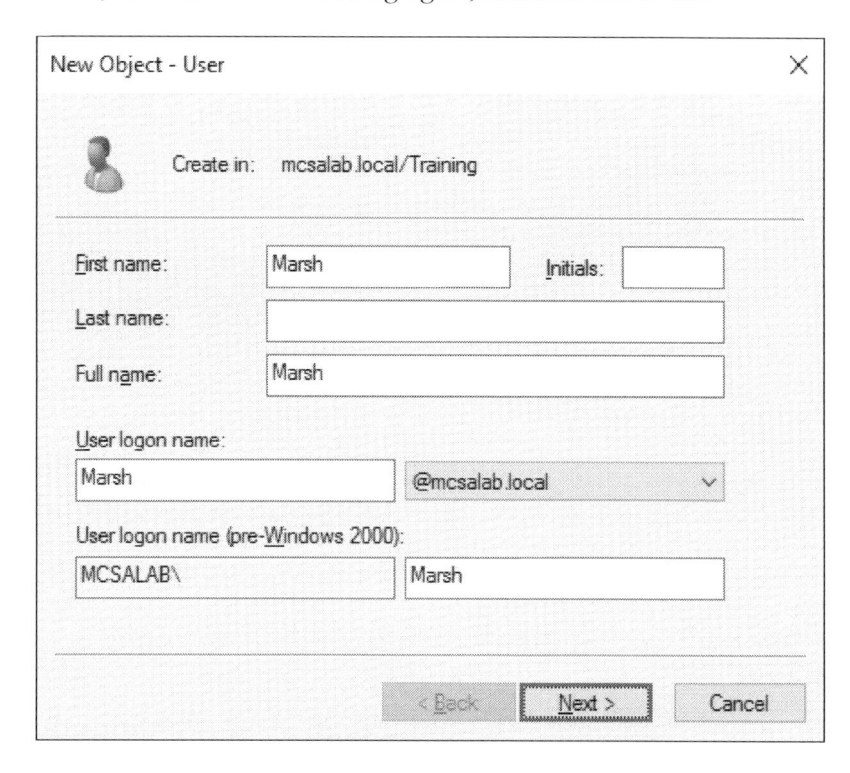

12. In the **Password** and **Confirm password** text boxes, type **Password@123**.
13. Clear the **User must change password at next logon** check box, select the **Password never expires** check box, as shown in the following figure.

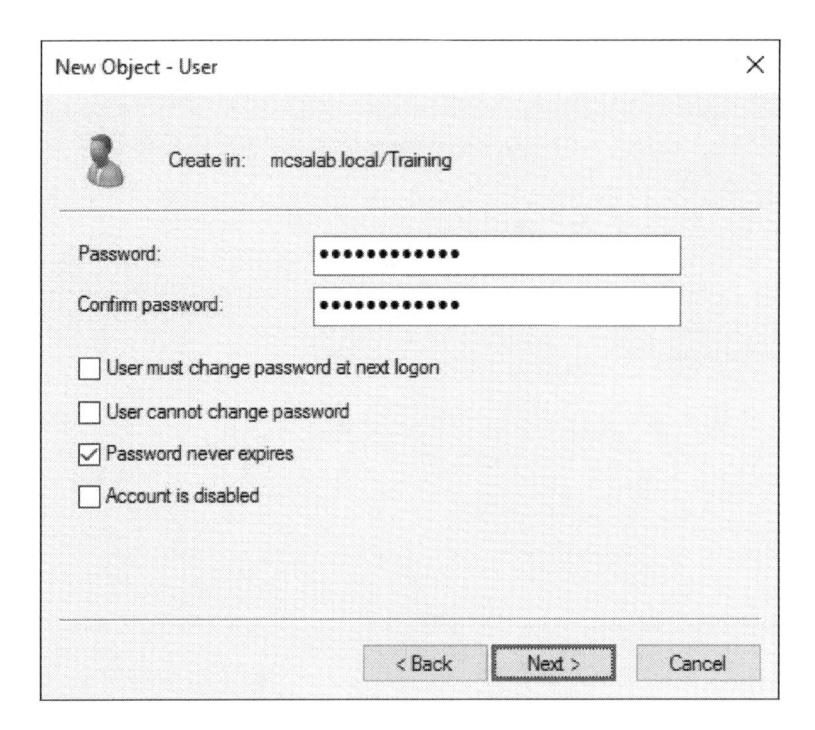

14. Click **Next**, and then click **Finish**.
15. Minimize the **Active Directory Users and Computers** console.

Task 3: Configuring Home Folders for User Accounts

1. On DC1, create a folder named **Marsh Data**, under the **C:\Users\Public** folder, as shown in the following figure.

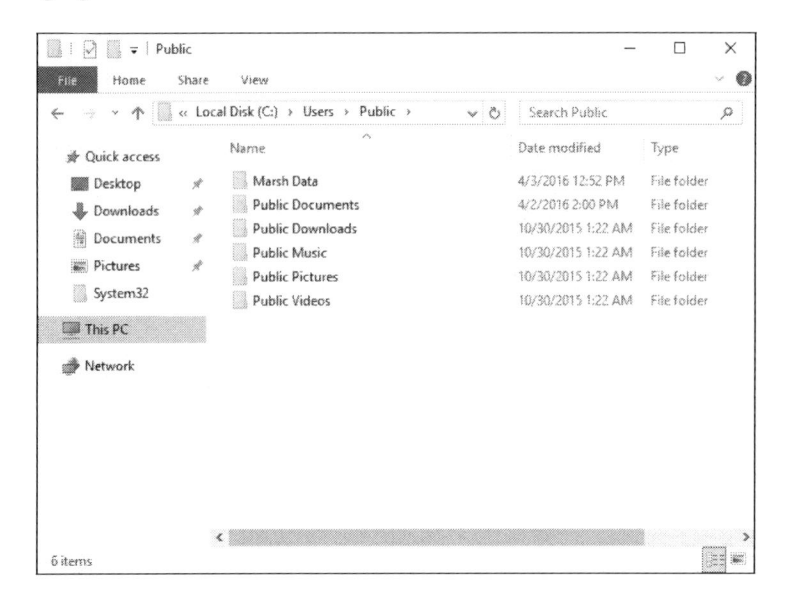

2. Select and right-click the **Marsh Data** folder, and then select **Properties**.
3. On the **Marsh Data Properties** dialog box, select the **Sharing** tab, as shown in the following figure.

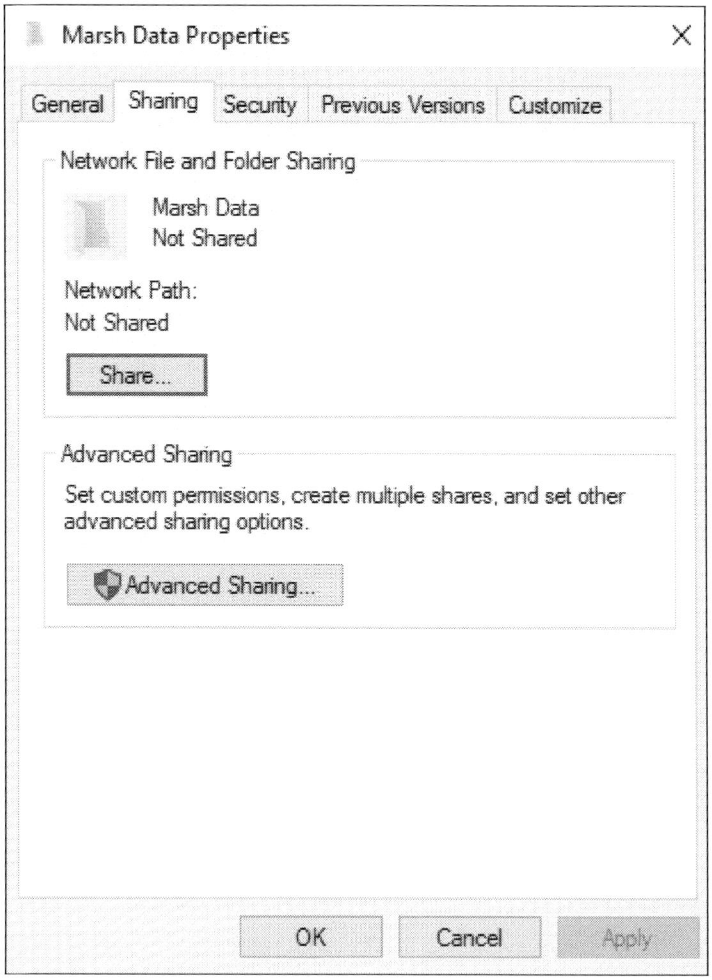

4. Click **Advanced Sharing**.
5. On the **Advanced Sharing** dialog box, select the **Share this folder** check box, as shown in the following figure.

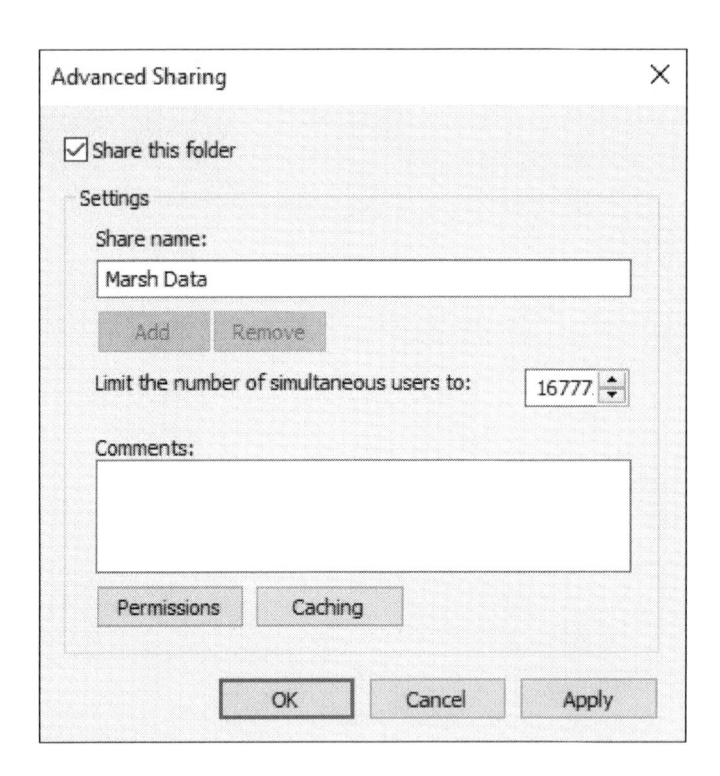

6. Click **Permissions**.
7. On the **Permissions for Marsh Data** dialog box, in the **Permissions for Everyone** section, select the **Full Control** check box, as shown in the following figure.

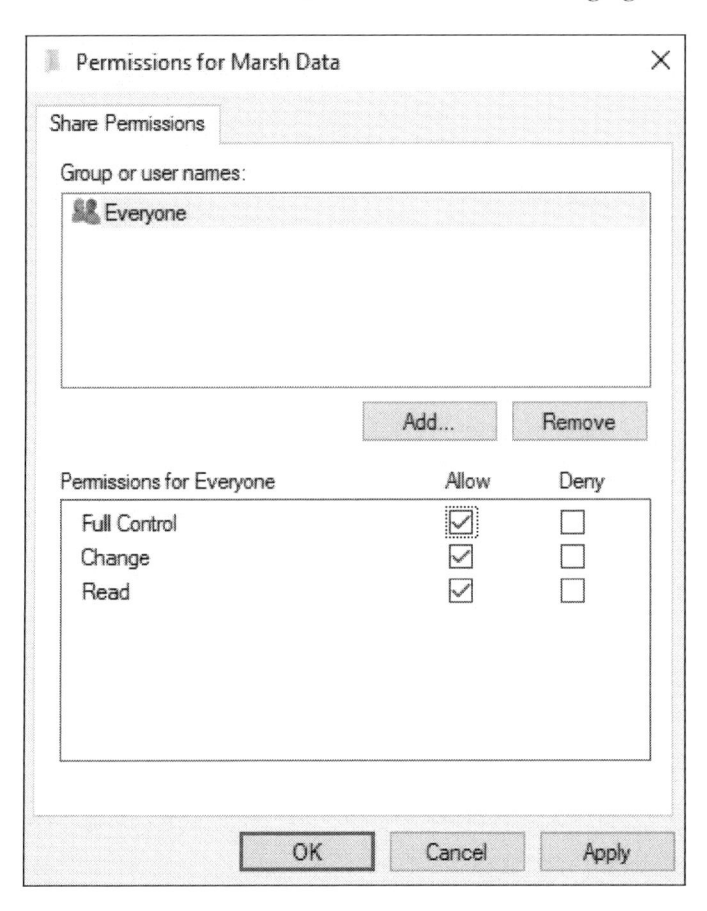

8. Click **Apply**, and then click **OK**.
9. Click **OK** to close **Advanced Sharing** dialog box, and then click **Close**.
10. Close the **Windows Explorer** window.
11. Switch to the **Active Directory Users and Computers** console.
12. Select and right-click the **Marsh** user, and then select **Properties**.
13. On the **Marsh Properties** dialog box, select the **Profile** tab.
14. Under the **Home folder** section, select the **Connect** radio button.
15. In the **To** text box, type **\\DC1\Marsh Data\Marsh**, as shown in the following figure, and then click **Apply**.

Note: By default all the domain users are denied to sign in to the Domain Controller server. In the next steps, we are going to make Marsh as the member of Print Operators group to sign in to Domain Controller to test the exercise. You will learn more about the user rights and permissions in

the upcoming exercises.

16. Select the **Member Of** tab, and then click **Add**.
17. On the **Select Groups** dialog box, in the **Enter the object names to select (example)** text box, type **Print Operators**, as shown in the following figure.

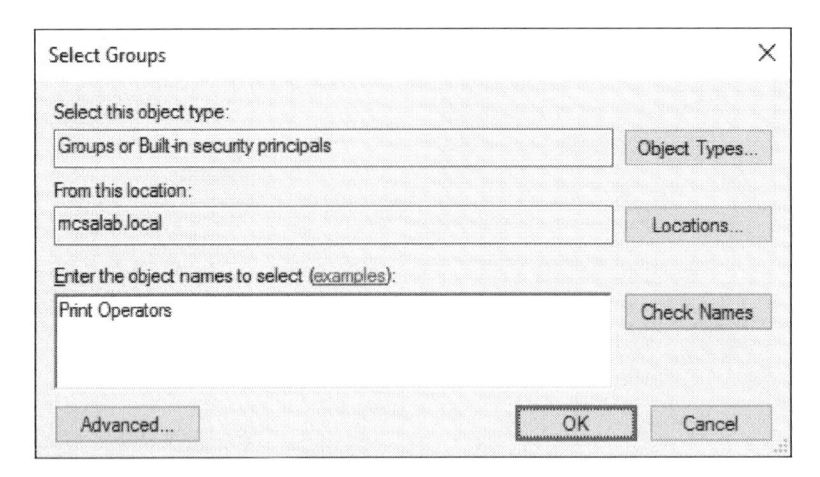

18. Click **Check Names**, and then click **OK**.
19. On the **Member Of** tab, and click again **Add**.
20. On the **Select Groups** dialog box, in the **Enter the object names to select (example)** text box, type **Students**.
21. Click **Check Names**, and then click **OK**.

Note: You have added the Marsh user to Students group to test the delegated permissions.

22. Click **OK** to close the **Marsh Properties** dialog box.
23. Close the **Active Directory Users and Computers** console.

Task 4: Testing and Verifying the Home Folders and Delegated Permissions

1. On **DC1**, open the **Run** dialog box, type **logoff** and then click **OK** to sign out from the **MCSALAB\Administrator** account, as shown in the following figure.

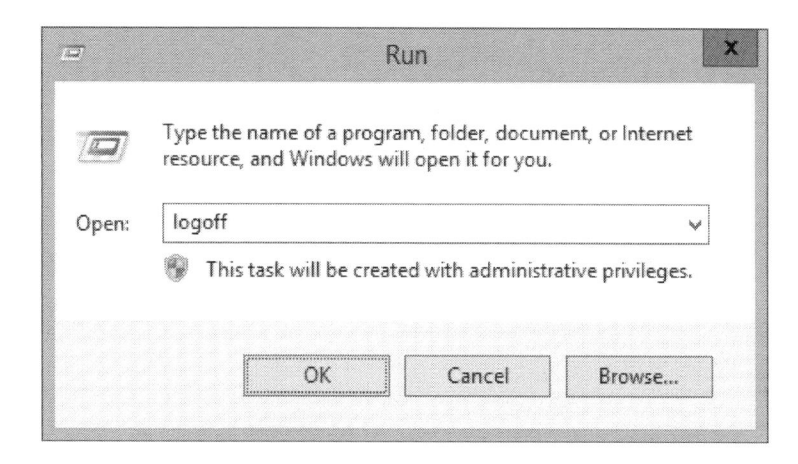

2. Switch to **Other user** and **Sign in** as **Marsh** with the password as **Password@123**, as shown in the following figure.

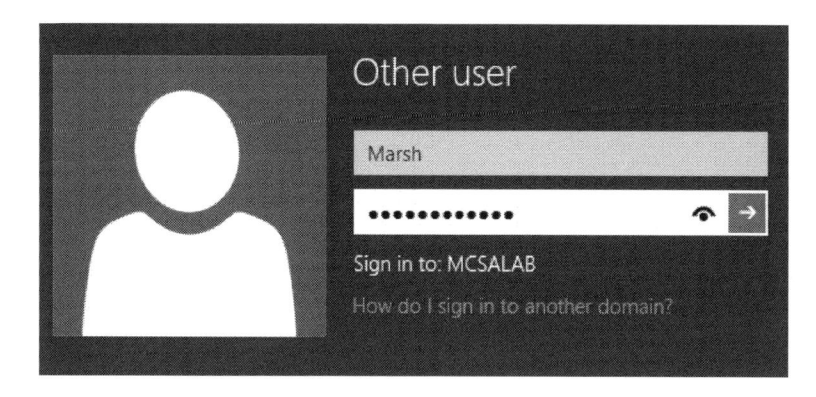

3. Press the **Windows+E** keys to open the **Windows Explorer** window.
4. Verify that drive **Z** is mapped to **(\\DC1\Marsh Data),** as shown in the following figure.

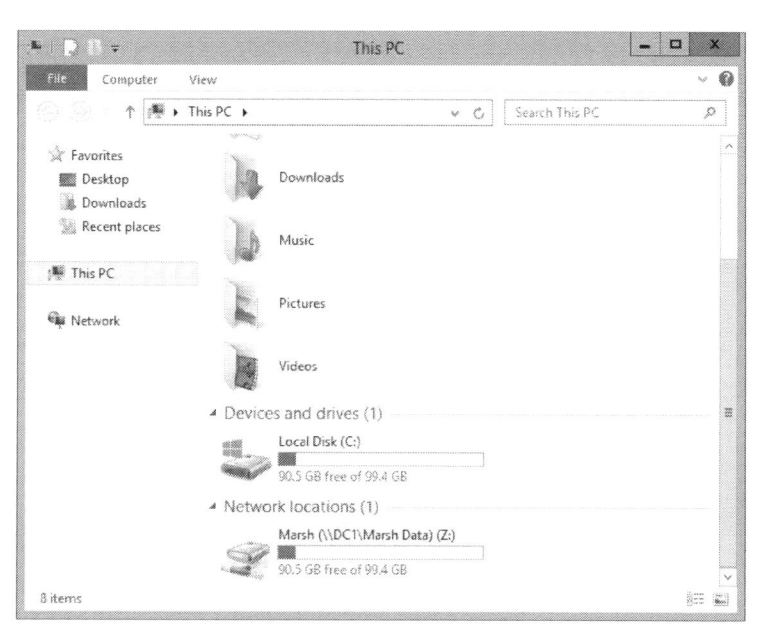

5. Double-click **Marsh (\\DC1\Marsh Data) (Z:)**.

Note: You should be able to access this drive without any errors. If you receive no errors, you have been successful.

6. Close the **Windows Explorer** window.
7. Open the **Run** dialog box, type **dsa.msc**, in the **Open** text box, and then press **Enter**.
8. On the **User Account Control** dialog box, in the **User name** text box, type **Marsh**.
9. In the **Password** text box, type **Password@123**, as shown in the following figure, and then click **Yes**.

10. On the **Active Directory Users and Computers** console, expand **mcsalab.local**.
11. Select and right-click **Training, and then click New**, and then click **User**.
12. On the **New Object – User** dialog box, in the **First name** and **User logon name** text boxes, type **Test User2**, and then click **Next**.
13. In the **Password** and **Confirm password** text boxes, type **Password@123**.
14. Click **Next**, and then click **Finish**.
15. Make sure that the **Test User1** account is created, under the **Training OU**.
16. Select and right-click **Development, and then click New**, and then click **User**.
17. On the **New Object – User** dialog box, in the **First name** and **User logon name** text boxes, type **Test User2**, and then click **Next**.
18. In the **Password** and **Confirm password** text boxes, type **Password@123**, click **Next**, and then click **Finish**.
19. Make sure that you get the following error message.

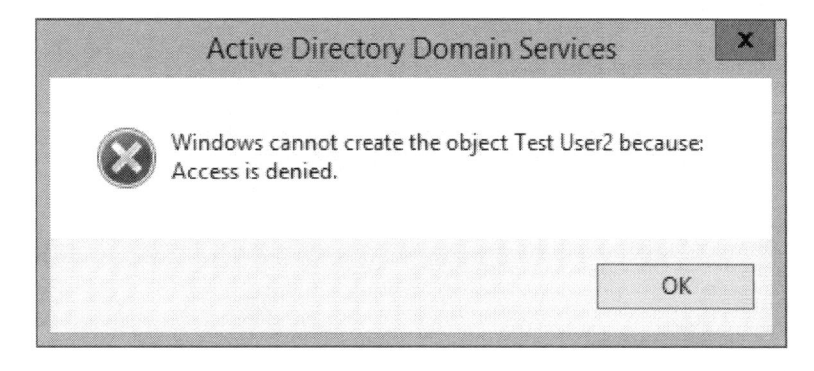

> Active Directory Domain Services
>
> ⊗ Windows cannot create the object Test User2 because:
> Access is denied.
>
> OK

20. Click **OK**, and then click **Cancel**.
21. Close the **Active Directory Users and Computers** console.
22. Sign out from the **Marsh** user.

Task 5: Resetting the Computer Accounts
1. Sign in to **DC1** with the MCSALAB\Marsh account.
2. On the **Server Manager** console, click **Tools, and then click Active Directory Users and Computers**.
3. On the **Active Directory Users and Computers** console, expand **mcsalab.local**.
4. In the left pane, select **Computers**.
5. In the right pane, select and right-click **CLIENT1**, and then click **Reset Account**, as shown in the following figure.

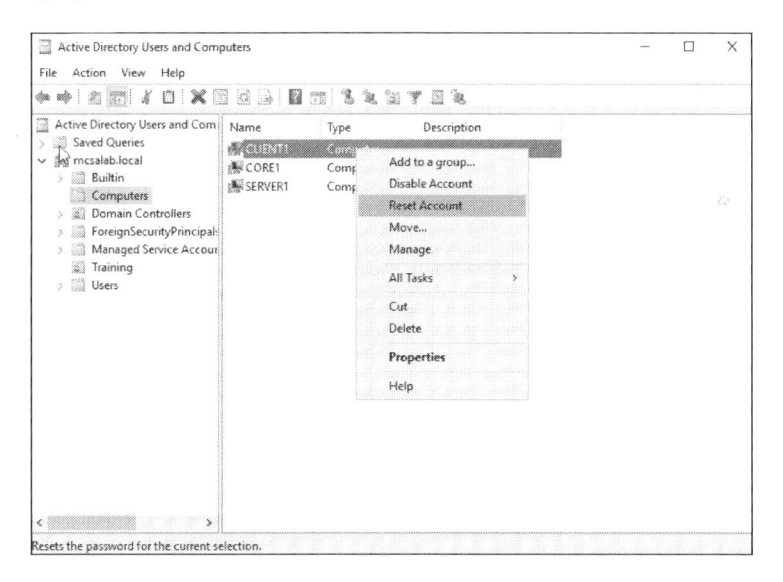

6. On the **Active Directory Domain Services** message box, click **Yes**, and the click **OK**.

Task 6: Examining the Behavior when a User Logins on Client.
1. Try to Sign in to **CLIENT1** with the MCSALAB\Marsh account.
2. A message displays stating that **The trust relationship between this workstation and the primary domain failed**, as shown in the following figure.

89

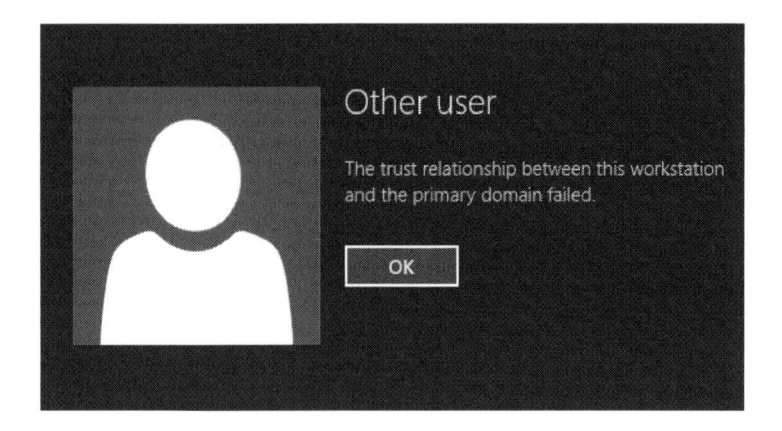

Task 7: Rejoining the Domain to Reconnect the Computer Account

1. Sign in to **CLIENT** as CLIENT1\Administrator with the password as **Password@123**.
2. Open the **System Properties** dialog box, click **Network ID**.
3. On the **Select the option that describes your network** page, as shown in the following figure, click **Next**.

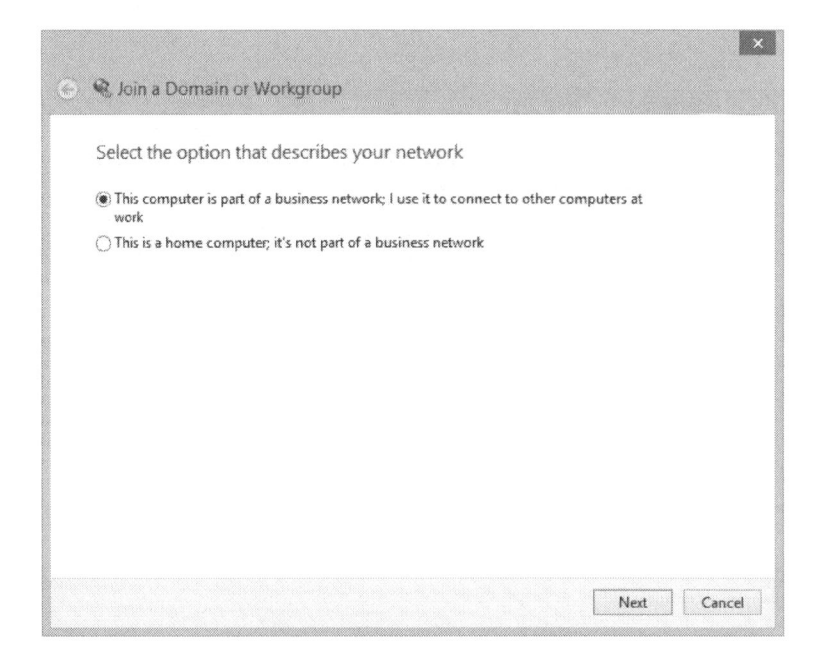

4. On the **Is your company network on a domain?** page, click **Next**.
5. On the **You will need the following information** page, click **Next**.
6. On the **Type your user name, password, and domain name for your domain account** page, in the **User name** text box, type Administrator.
7. In the **Password** text box, type **Password@123**.
8. In the **Domain name** text box, type **MCSALAB.LOCAL**, as shown in the following figure, and then click **Next**.

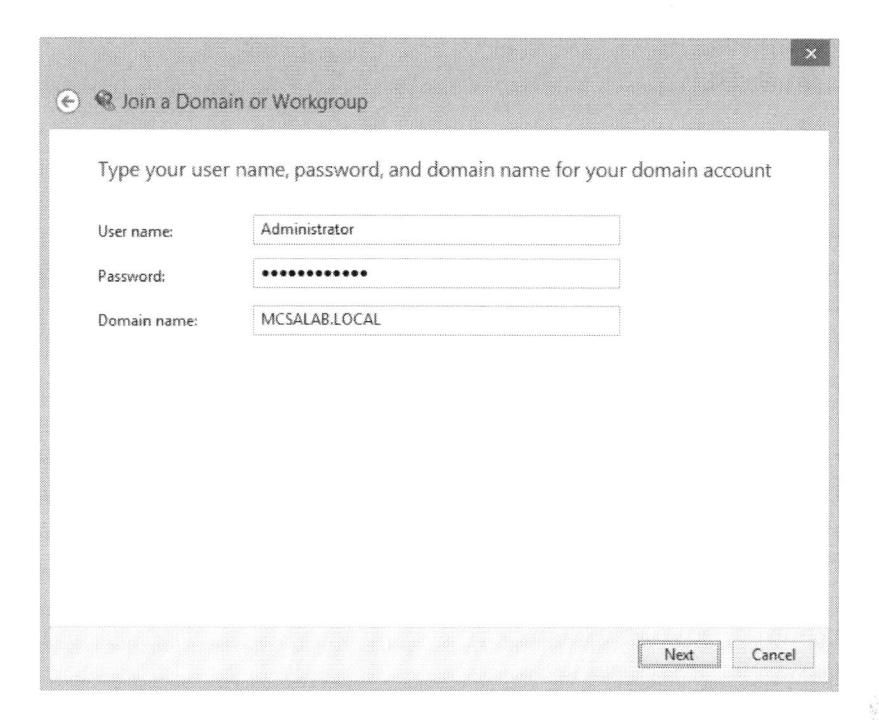

9. On the **User Account and Domain Information** dialog box, click **Yes**.
10. On the **Do you want to enable a domain user account on this computer?** page, select the **Do not add a domain user account** radio button, and then click **Next**.
11. Click **Finish**, and then click **OK**.
12. On the **Microsoft Windows** dialog box, click **Restart Now**. Wait for system to restart.
13. Sign in as **MCSALAB\Marsh** with the password as **Password@123**.
14. Make sure that you are able to sign in.

Results: After this exercise, you have successfully created and tested Organizational Units, Groups, Users, Home Folders, and the Delegation of Control Wizard. In addition, you should also have successfully reset a trust relationship.

Shut down and revert the DC1 and CLIENT1 virtual machines to prepare for the next exercise.

Exercise 8: Using Windows PowerShell to Create User Accounts and Groups

As discussed earlier, Window PowerShell is a command-line interface used to manage Windows servers and clients. You can also use Windows PowerShell to manage the Active Directory objects.

In this exercise, you will learn how to manage Active Directory objects using Window PowerShell. In addition, you will also learn how to export and import the Active Directory objects using Window PowerShell.

Start the DC1 and CLIENT1 virtual machines to perform this exercise.

Task 1: Creating a User Account Using Windows PowerShell

1. Sign in to **DC1** with the MCSALAB\Administrator account.
2. On the taskbar, click the **Windows PowerShell** icon.
3. At the **Windows PowerShell** prompt, type **cd** and then press Enter.
4. To create an **Organizational Unit** named **BranchOffice**, type the following command, and then press Enter:
   ```
   New-ADOrganizationalUnit BranchOffice
   ```
5. To create a user named **Peter** under the **BranchOffice** OU, type the following command, and then press Enter:
   ```
   New-ADUser -Name Peter -DisplayName "Peter Mark" -Path "ou=BranchOffice,dc=mcsalab,dc=local"
   ```
6. To set the password for **Peter** user, type the following command, and then press **Enter**:
   ```
   Set-ADAccountPassword Peter
   ```
   When prompted for the current password, press **Enter**.
   When prompted for the desired password, type **Password@123**, and then press **Enter**.
   When prompted to repeat the password, type **Password@123**, and then press **Enter**.
7. To enable the **Peter** user, type the following command, and then press **Enter**.
   ```
   Enable-ADAccount Peter
   ```
8. Switch to the **CLIENT1** virtual machine and sign in as **Peter** with the password as **Password@123**.
9. Verify that sign in is successful and then sign out of **CLIENT1**.

Task 2: Creating Groups Using Windows PowerShell

1. Switch back to **DC1**.
2. At the **Windows PowerShell** prompt, type the following command to create a new security (global) group named **BranchUsers**, and then press **Enter**.
   ```
   New-ADGroup BranchUsers -Path "ou=BranchOffice,dc=mcsalab,dc=local"
   ```
3. At the **GroupScope** prompt: type **Global** and then press **Enter**, as shown in the following figure.

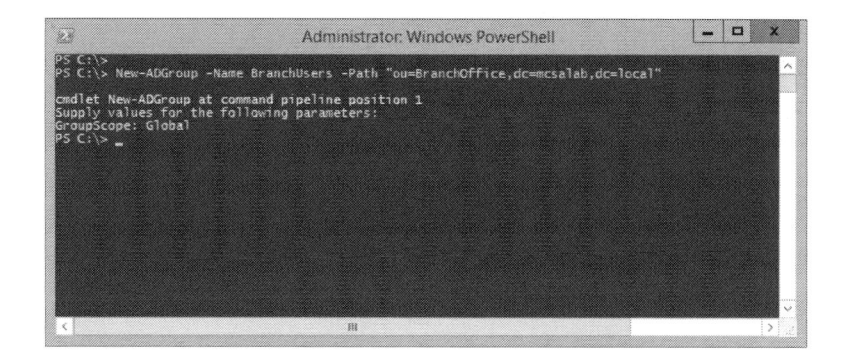

4. To add the **Peter** user as member of the **BranchUsers** group, type the following command, and then press **Enter**.
   ```
   Add-ADGroupMember BranchUsers -Members Peter
   ```
5. To view the members of the **BranchUsers** group, type the following command, and then press **Enter**.
   ```
   Get-ADGroupMember BranchUsers
   ```

Task 3: Exporting User Accounts Using the ldifde Tool

1. At the **Windows PowerShell** prompt, type the following command, and then press **Enter**, as shown in the following figure.
   ```
   ldifde -f MyUsers
   ```
2. At the **Windows PowerShell** prompt, type notepad **MyUsers** and then press **Enter**.
3. Review the **MyUsers** file and close the **Notepad**.

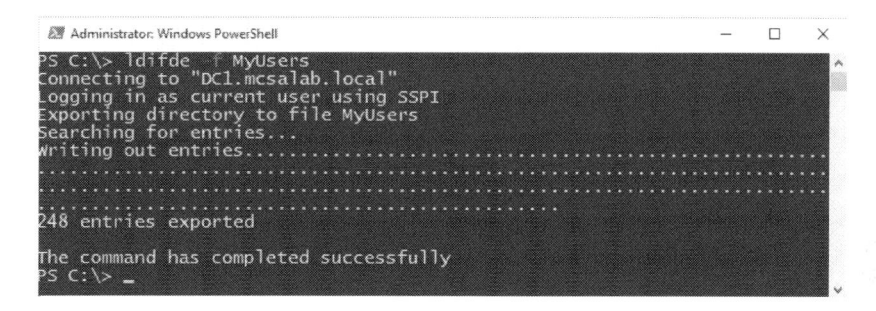

Results: After completing this exercise, you have managed AD DS objects using Windows PowerShell.

Shut down and revert the DC1 and CLIENT1 virtual machines to prepare for the next exercise.

Exercise 9: Installing and Configuring the DHCP Server Role

Dynamic Host Configuration Protocol (DHCP) is as service that is used to provide TCP/IP settings, such as IP address, subnet mask, default gateway, and DNS server to the clients, automatically. In a large enterprise network, it is difficult to manage IP addresses manually. Hence, DHCP can be a useful feature to manage the IP addresses in a large enterprise network.

In this exercise, you will learn how to install the DHCP server role and how to configure the DHCP scope. In addition, you will also learn how to use the DHCP reservation feature to reserve a specific IP address for a specific client.

Start the DC1 and CLIENT1 virtual machines to perform this exercise.

Task 1: Installing the DHCP Server Role

1. Sign in to **DC1** with MCSALAB\Administrator account.
2. Open the **Server Manager** console, if required.
3. On the **Server Manager** console, click the **Add roles and features** link.
4. On the **Add Roles and Features Wizard**, click **Next**.
5. On the **Select installation type** page, make sure that the **Role-based or feature-based installation** radio button is selected, and then click **Next**.
6. On the **Select destination server** page, click **Next**.
7. On the **Select server roles** page, select the **DHCP Server** check box.
8. On the **Add Roles and Features Wizard** dialog box, click **Add Features**.
9. The **Select server roles** page is returned, as shown in the following figure, click **Next**.

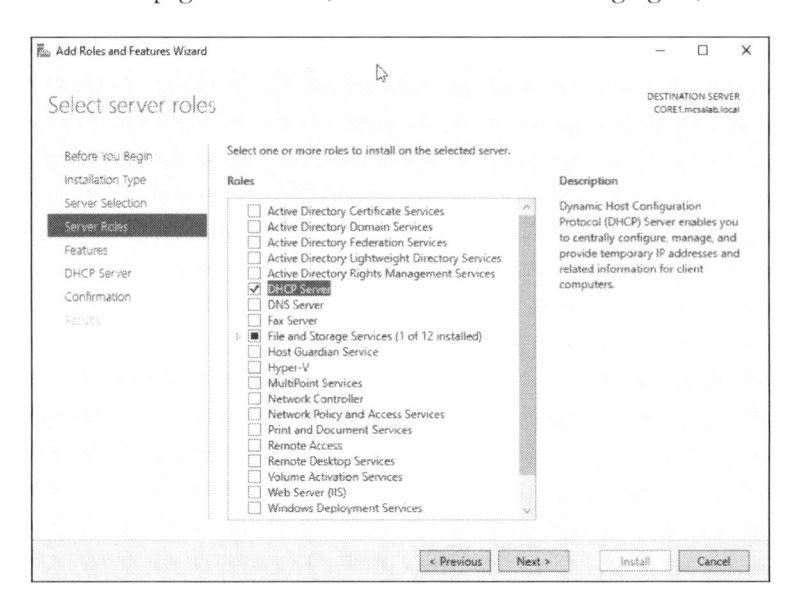

10. Complete the installation process.

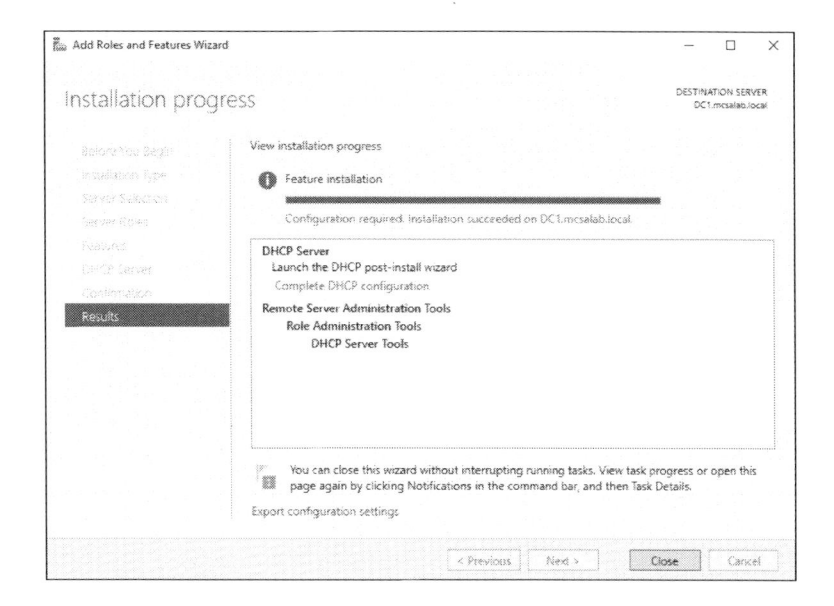

Task 2: Configuring the DHCP Scope
1. On the **Server Manager** console, click **Tools**, and then click **DHCP**.
2. On the **DHCP** console, in the left pane, expand **dc1.mcsalab.local**.
3. Select and right-click **dc1.mcsalab.local**, and then select **Authorize**.

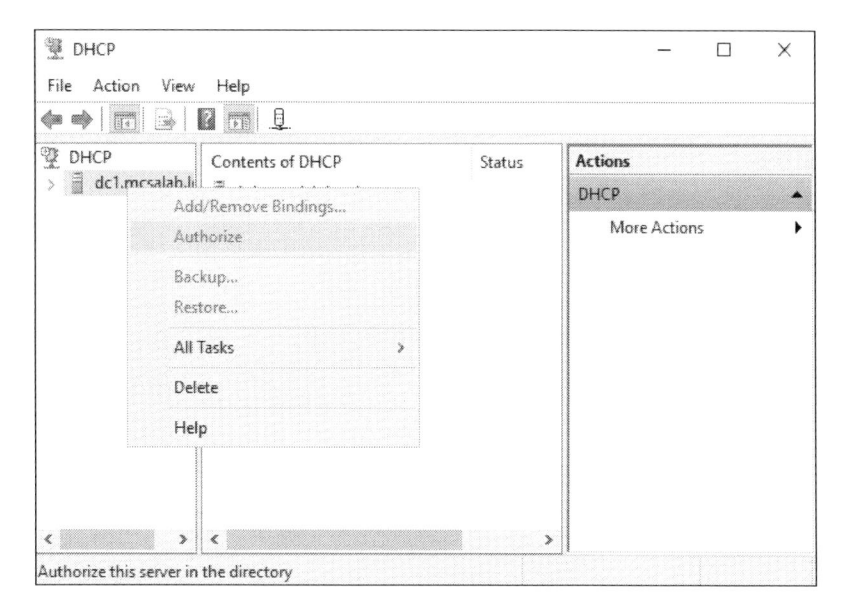

4. Select and right-click **dc1.mcsalab.local**, and then click **Refresh**. Notice that the icons next to IPv4 IPv6 changes color from red to green, as shown in the following figure.

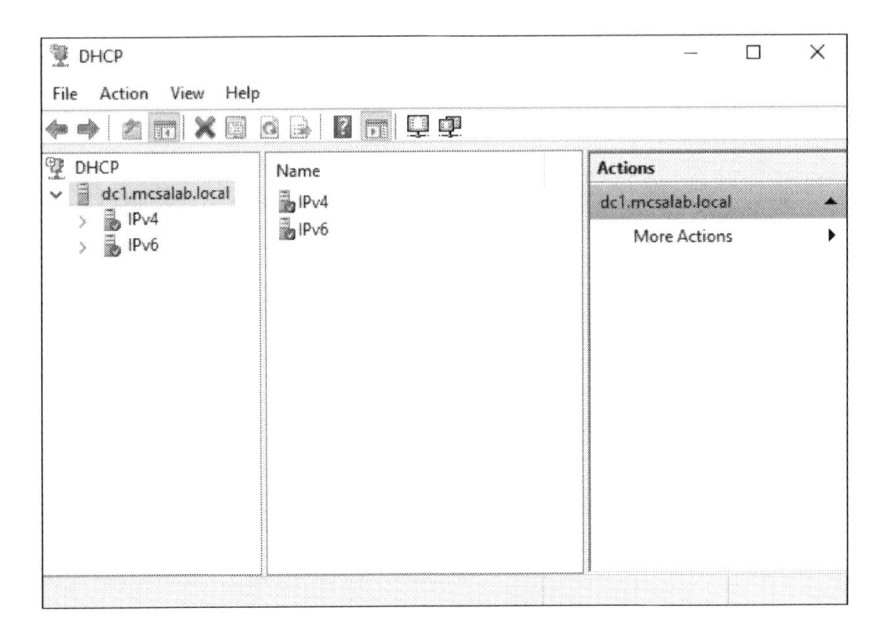

5. On the **DHCP** console, select and right-click **IPv4**, and then select **New Scope**.
6. On the welcome page of the **New Scope Wizard**, click **Next**.
7. On the **Scope Name** page, in the **Name** text box, type **DHCPScope1**, as shown in the following figure, and then click **Next**.

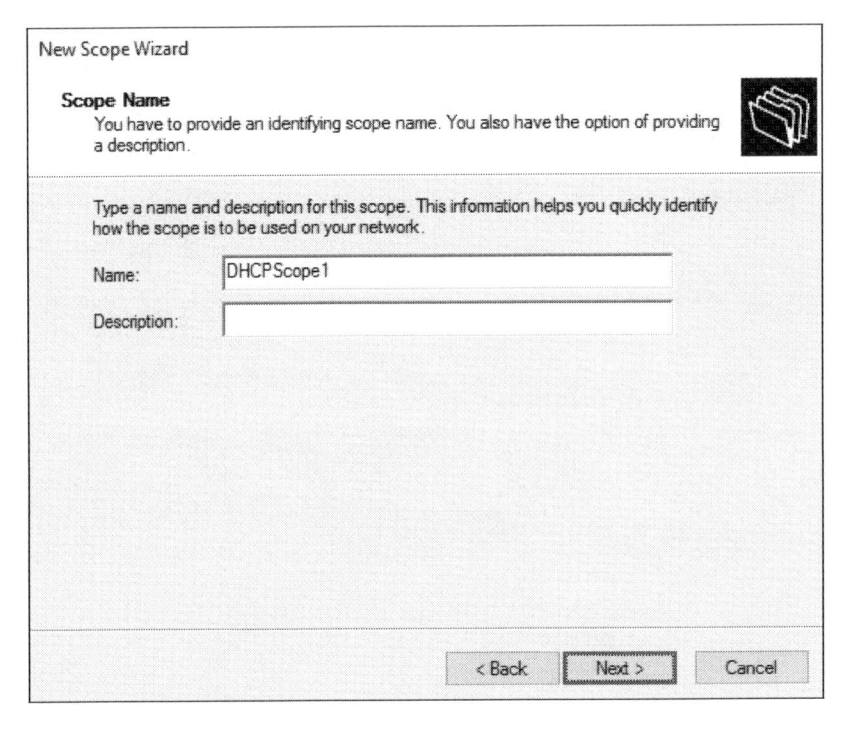

8. On the **IP Address Range** page, provide the following information, as shown in the following figure, and then click **Next**.
    - Start IP address: **10.0.0.225**
    - End IP address: **10.0.0.250**
    - Length: **8**
    - Subnet mask: **255.0.0.0**

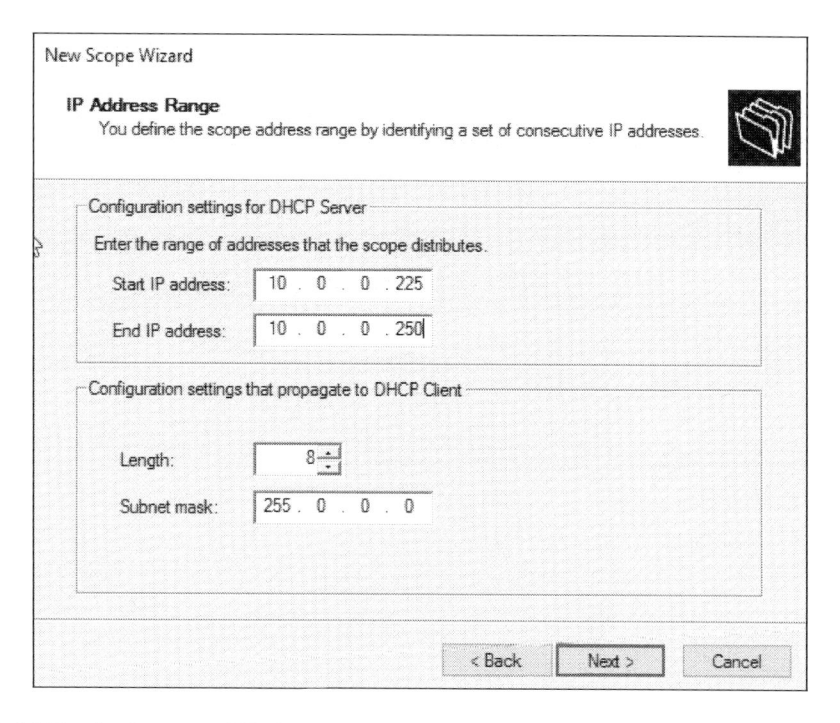

9. On the **Add Exclusions and Delay** page, exclude the following IP address range, as shown in the following figure.
    - Start IP address: **10.0.0.225**
    - End IP address: **10.0.0.230**

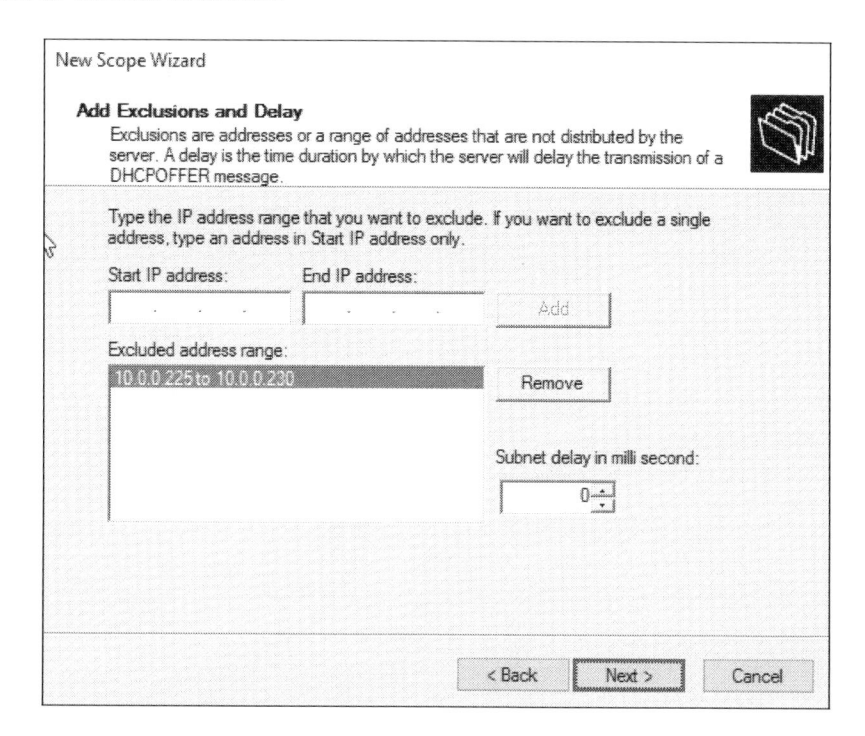

10. Click **Add**, and then click **Next**.
11. On the **Lease Duration** page, review the default lease duration limit, and then click **Next**.
12. On the **Configure DHCP Options** page, make sure that the **Yes, I want to configure**

these option now radio button is selected, as shown in the following figure, and then click **Next**.

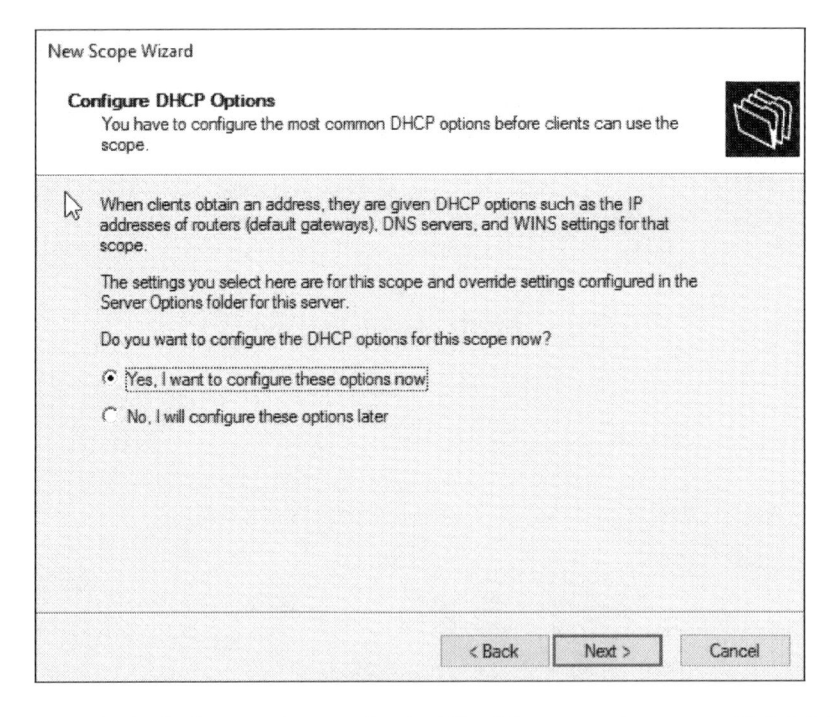

13. On the **Router (Default Gateway)** page, in the **IP address** text box, type **10.0.0.0.1**, as shown in the following figure.

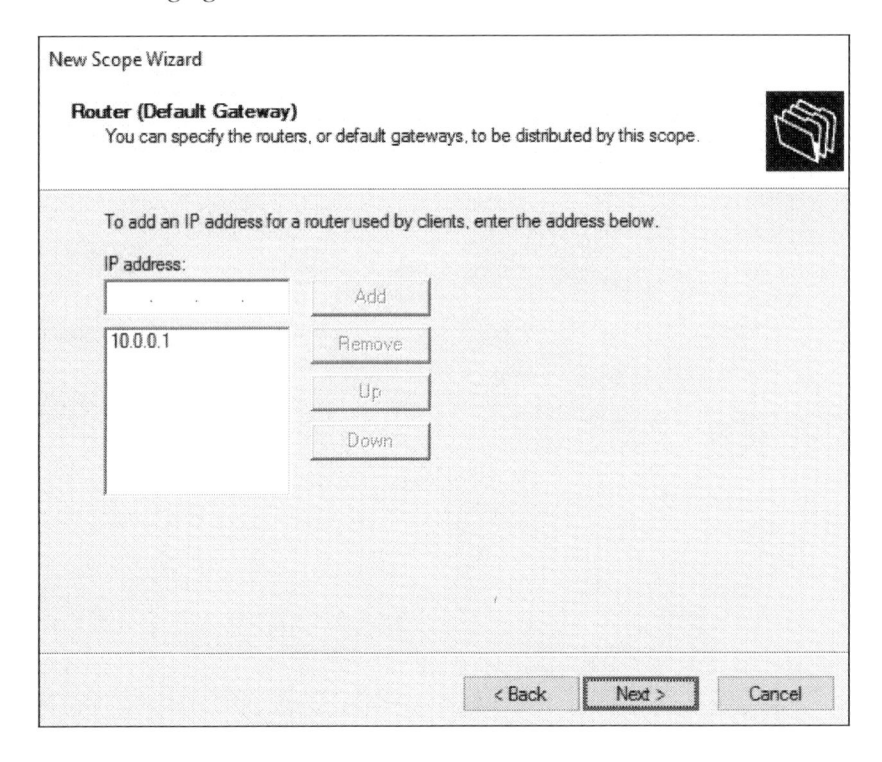

14. Click **Add**, and then click **Next**.
15. On the **Domain Name and DNS Servers** page, make sure that **10.0.0.100** is written under the **IP address** column, as shown in the following figure, and then click **Next**.

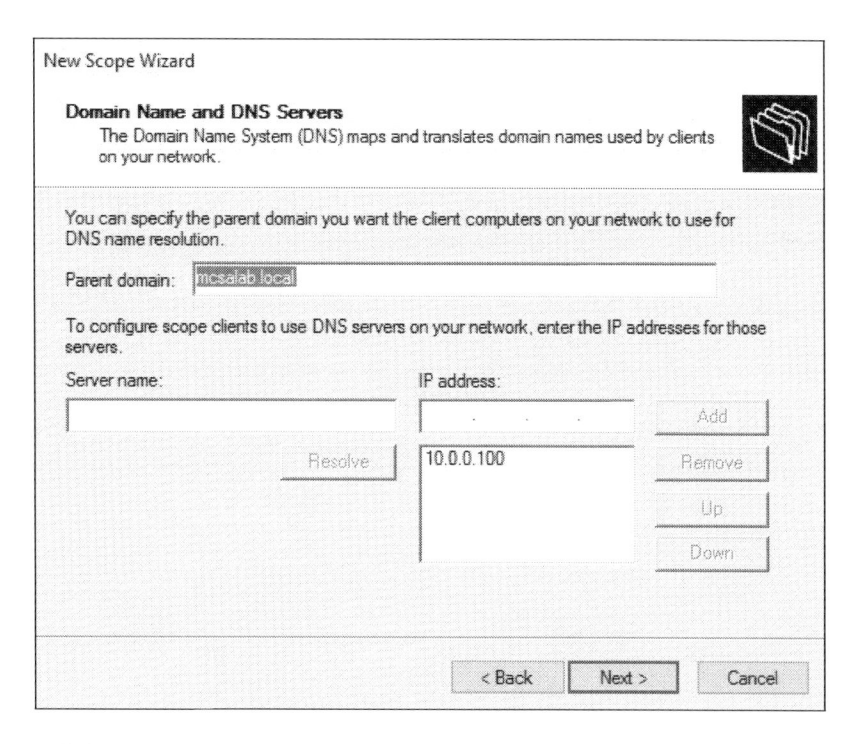

16. On the **WINS Servers** page, click **Next**.
17. On the **Activate Scope** page, make sure that the **Yes, I want to activate this scope now** radio button is selected, as shown in the following figure, and then click **Next**.

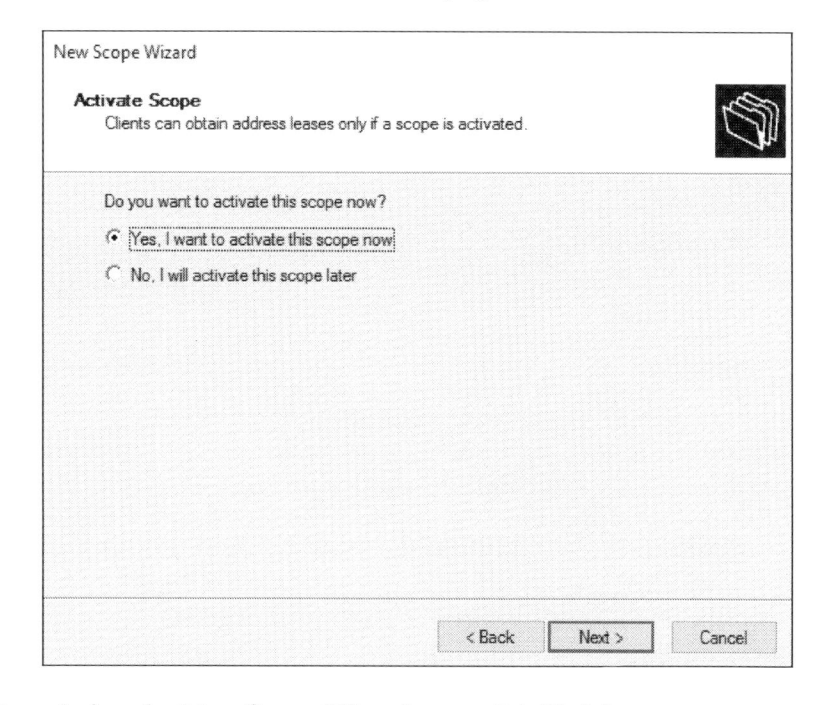

18. On the **Completing the New Scope Wizard** page, click **Finish**.
19. Select and right-click **IPv4**, and then select **Refresh**.
20. Make sure that the IPv4 node is marked with the green color, as shown in the following figure.

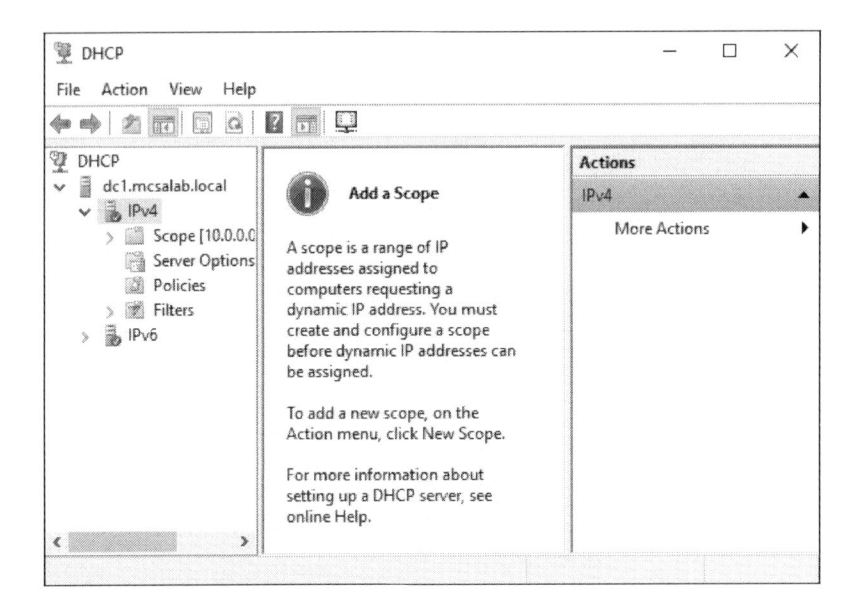

Task 3: Configuring DHCP Client

1. Open the **Network Connections** window, select and right-click the active network adapter and then select **Properties**.
2. On the **Properties** dialog box, scroll down, select **Internet Protocol Version 4 (TCP/IPv4)**, and then click **Properties**.
3. On the **Internet Protocol Version 4 (TCP/IPv4) Properties** dialog box, select the **Obtain an IP address automatically** radio button, select the **Obtain DNS server address automatically** radio button, as shown in the following figure.

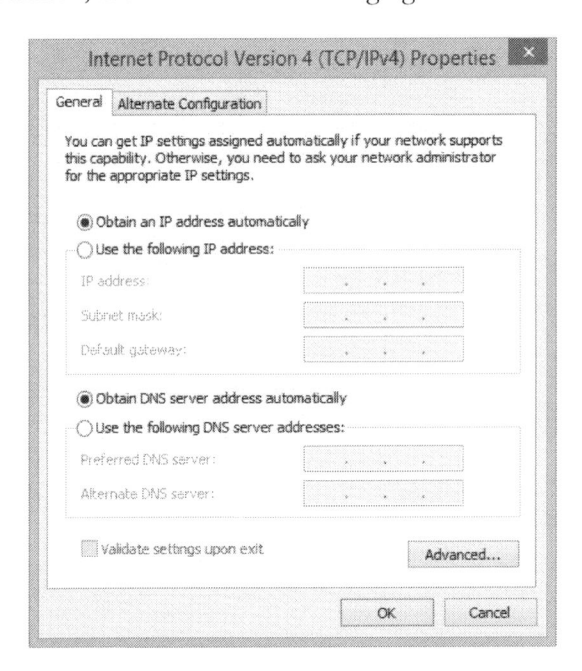

4. Click **OK**, and then click **Close**.
5. Open the **Run** dialog box, type **cmd**, and then press **Enter**.
6. On the **Command Prompt** window, type `ipconfig /renew`, as shown in the following figure, and then press **Enter**.

7. Type the `ipconfig /all` command and verify that **CLIENT1** has received TCP/IP settings, such as IP address, subnet mask, default gateway, and DNS server's IP address, as shown in the following figure.

Task 4: Configuring DHCP Reservation

1. On **CLIENT1**, on the **Command Prompt** window, type `ipconfig /all`, and then press **Enter**.
2. Find and write down the **Physical Address** of the **CLIENT1** network adapter, in this case it is **00-15-5D-77-D6-0B**, as shown in the following figure.

Note: The physical address is a unique 48 bit address, which is assigned by IEEE and network adapter's vendor.

3. Switch and sign in (if required) to **DC1** with the MCSALAB\Administrator account.
4. Make sure that the **DHCP** console is active. If not, open the **DHCP** console.
5. On the **DHCP** console, expand **dc1.mcsalab.local**, and then click **IPv4**.
6. Select and right-click **Reservations**, and then select **New Reservation**, as shown in the following figure.

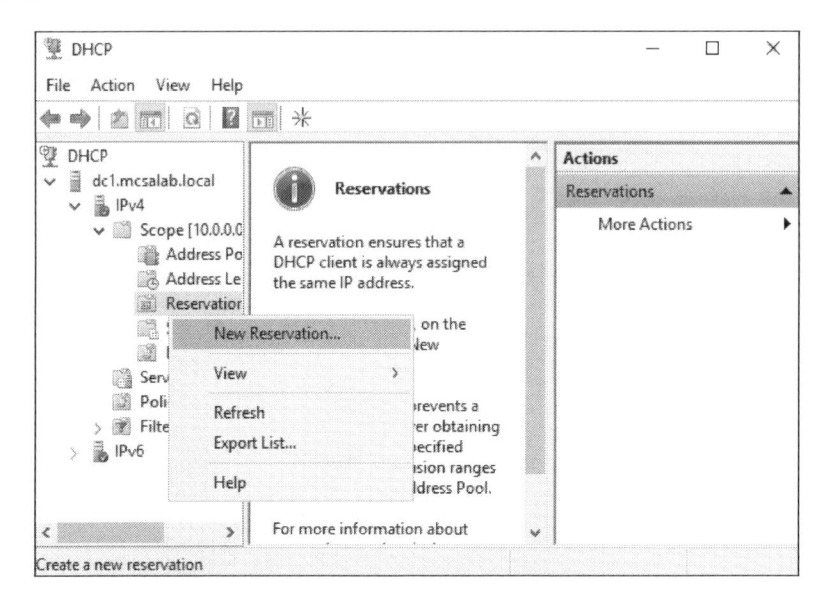

7. On the **New Reservation** dialog box, in the **Reservation Name** text box, type **CLIENT1**.
8. In the **IP address** text box, type **10.0.0.240**.
9. In the **MAC address** text box, type the physical address of the **CLIENT1** machine (00-15-5D-77-D6-0B), as shown in the following figure.

Note: Replace the physical address text with the actual physical address of your CLIENT1 machine.

10. Click **Add**, and then click **Close**.
11. Switch back and sign in to **CLIENT1**.
12. On the **Command Prompt** window, type `ipconfig /release`, and then press **Enter** to release the existing IP address.
13. On the **Command Prompt** window, type `ipconfig /renew`, and then press **Enter** to obtain a new IP address.
14. On the **Command Prompt** window, verify that IP address of **CLIENT1** is now **10.0.0.240**, as shown in the following figure.

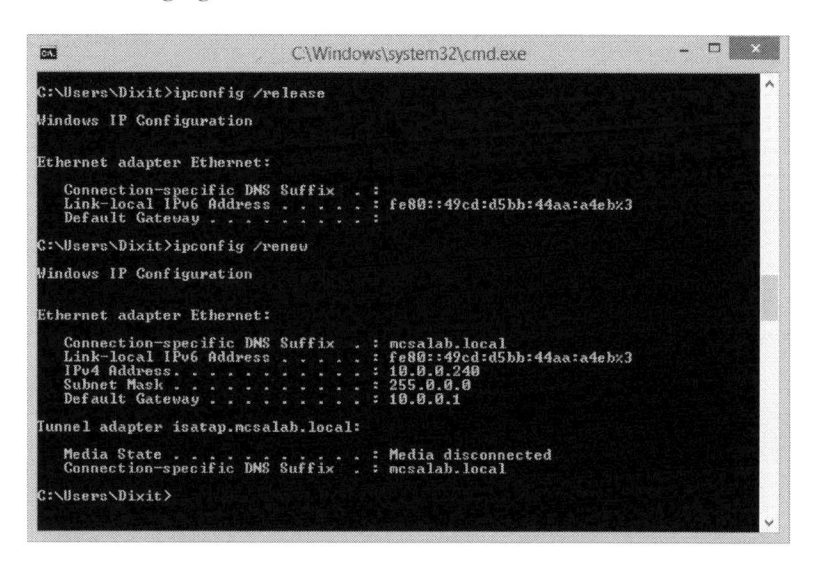

15. Close the **Command Prompt** window.

Results: *After completing this exercise, you should have configured DHCP scope, DHCP options, and DHCP reservation.*

Shut down and revert the CLEINT1 virtual machine. However, do not shut down and revert the DC1 virtual machines as we required preconfigured DHCP server to perform the next lab exercise.

Exercise 10: Configuring IPAM with DHCP

IP Address Management (IPAM) is a feature that allows you to manage infrastructure servers such as DHCP, DNS, NPS, and DC servers from a centralized location. IPAM also supports the automatic discovery of infrastructure servers of your Active Directory forest. Since it supports the DHCP server management, hence you can manage and track your dynamic and static IPv4 and IPv6 address space centrally. In this lab exercise, we will install and configure IPAM in Windows Server 2016.

To perform this lab exercise, we will use two servers named DC1.mcsalab.local and Server1.mcsalab.local. DC1 server has a pre-configured DHCP server that we will add and manage through the IPAM server.

Task 1: Installing IPAM Feature on SERVER1

To install the IPAM feature on the **SERVER1,** you need to perform the following steps:

1. Launch the **Add Roles and Features Wizard** using the **Server Manager** tool.
2. Navigate to the **Select features** page and select the **IP Address Management (IPAM) Server** role.

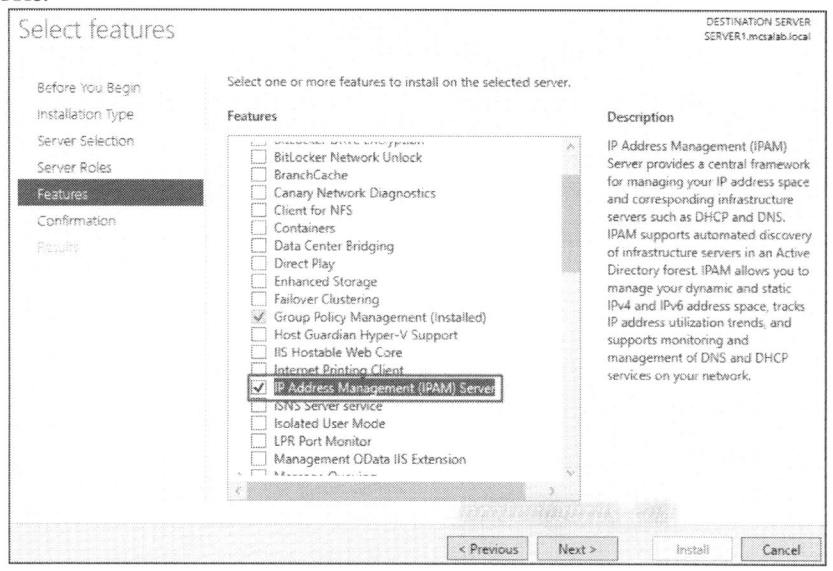

3. On the rest of the pages, click **Next** and complete the installation process.

Task 2: Configuring IPAM Server

Once you have installed IPAM feature on your server, the next step is to configure the IPAM server. As discussed earlier, the IPAM server can manage DHCP, DNS, and DC servers. However, in this post, we will manage DHCP server through the IPAM server.

To configure IPAM in Windows Server 2016, you need to perform the following steps:

1. Select the **IPAM** in the left pane and then click the **Connect to IPAM** server. Select **SERVER1.MCSALAB.local** if not selected already and then click **OK**.

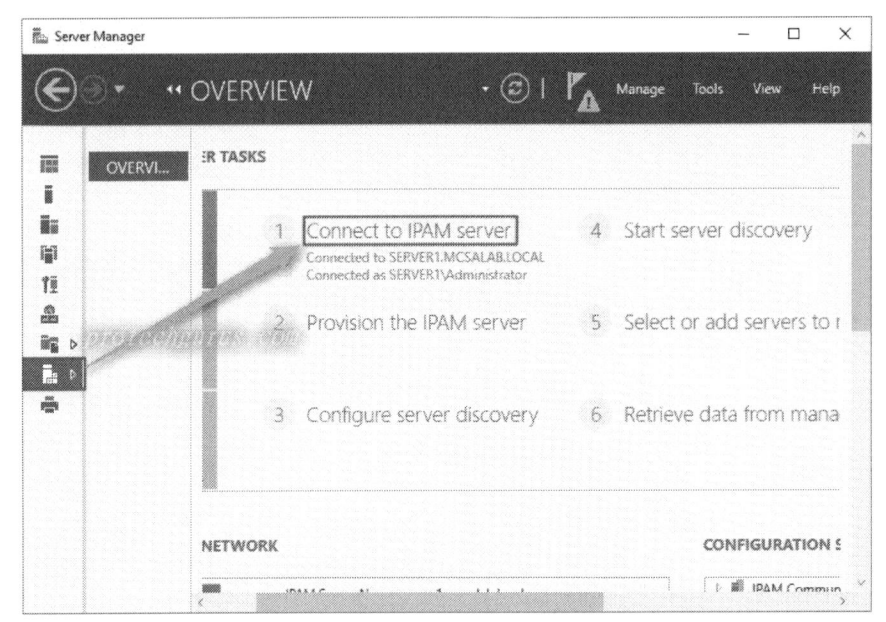

2. The next task is to Provision the IPAM server. For this, click **Provision the IPAM server** and navigate to the **Configure database** page. Here you need to specify the type of IPAM database.

3. You can either select SQL server or Windows Internal Database. For the testing lab, select the **Windows Internal Database (WID)** option and proceed to the next.

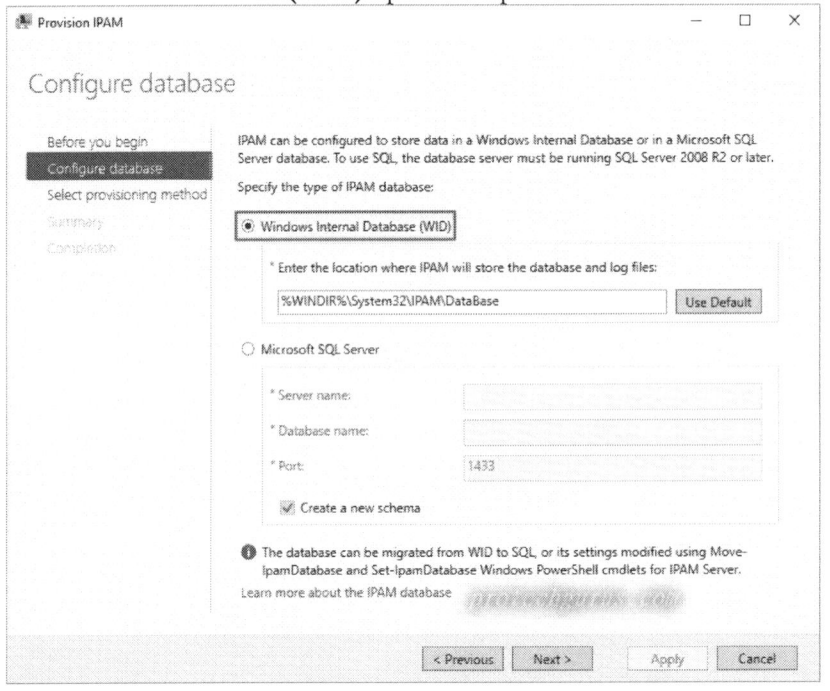

4. On the **Select provisioning method** page, select the provision method for the managed server. You can either select the manual provisioning method or the Group Policy Based provisioning method.

5. For the testing purpose, select the **Group Policy Based** provisioning method as manual provisioning required the additional configurations. Specify a GPO prefix name and proceed to the next.

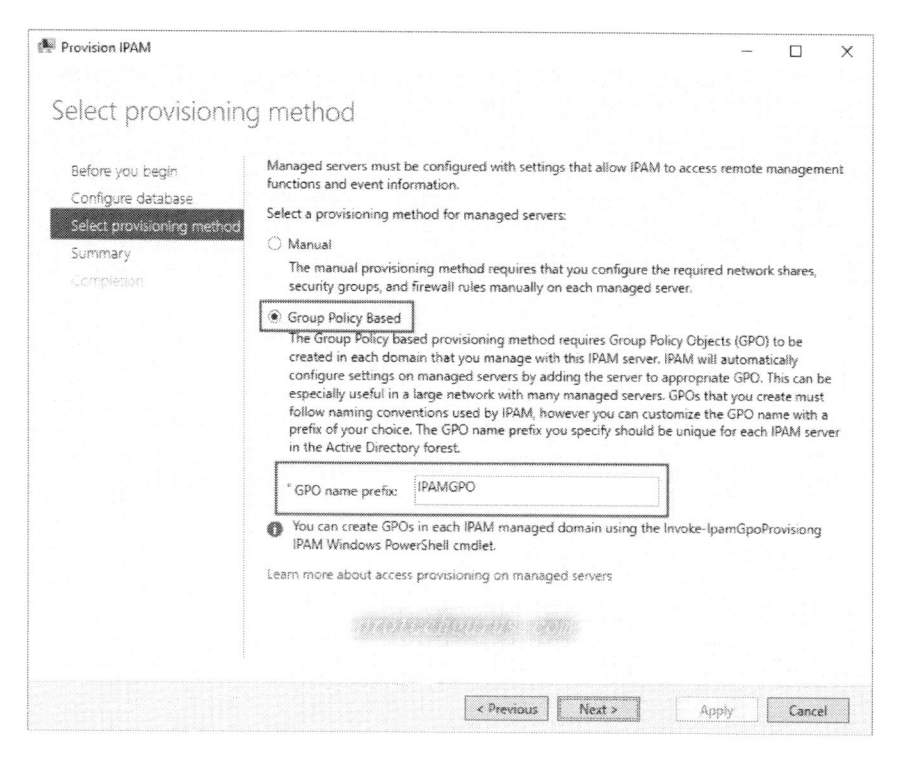

6. Click **Next** and finish the wizard.

7. After provisioning IPAM server, the next step is to configure server discovery. For this, click **Configure server discovery** link.
8. On the **Configure Server Discovery** dialog box, click **Get forests** and wait until the forest name discovered.
9. Click **Add** to add the discovered domain and then click **OK**.

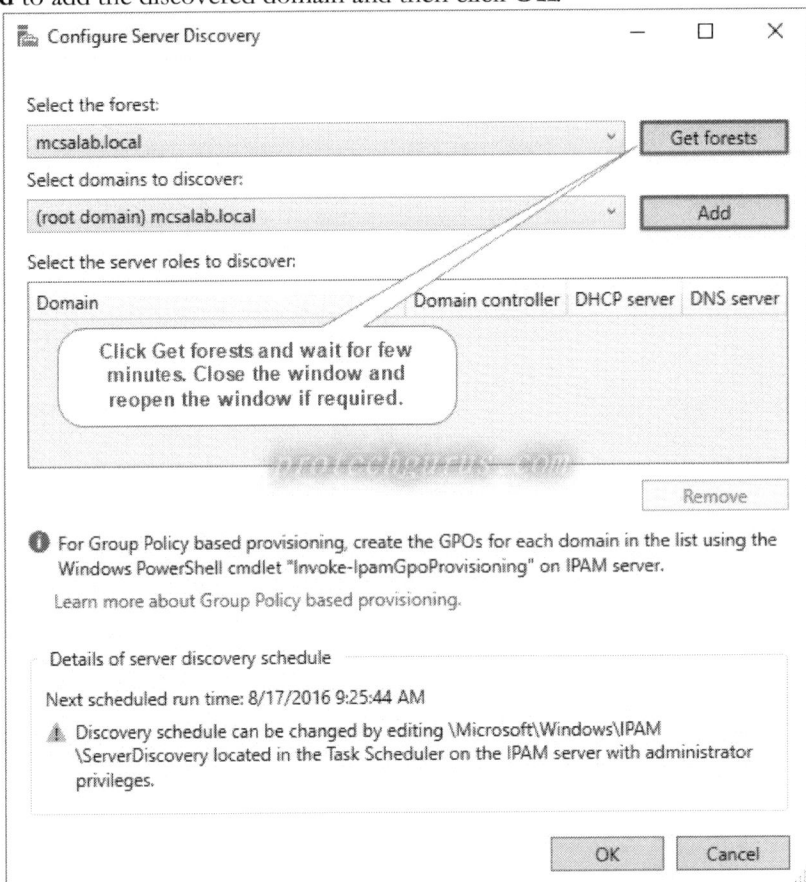

![Configure Server Discovery dialog box showing Select the forest: mcsalab.local, Get forests button, Select domains to discover: (root domain) mcsalab.local, Add button, Select the server roles to discover table with Domain, Domain controller, DHCP server, DNS server columns. Callout: "Click Get forests and wait for few minutes. Close the window and reopen the window if required." Note about Group Policy based provisioning using Invoke-IpamGpoProvisioning cmdlet. Details of server discovery schedule: Next scheduled run time: 8/17/2016 9:25:44 AM. OK and Cancel buttons.]

10. After adding domain, the next step is to start the server discovery process. For this, click the **Start server discovery link**. Discovery may take 5 to 10 minutes to complete.
11. After the discovery process, the next step is to add servers that you want to manage. For this, click the **Select or add servers to manage and verify IPAM access** link.

12. Notice that **IPAM Access Status** is **Blocked** for both servers, as shown in the following figure.

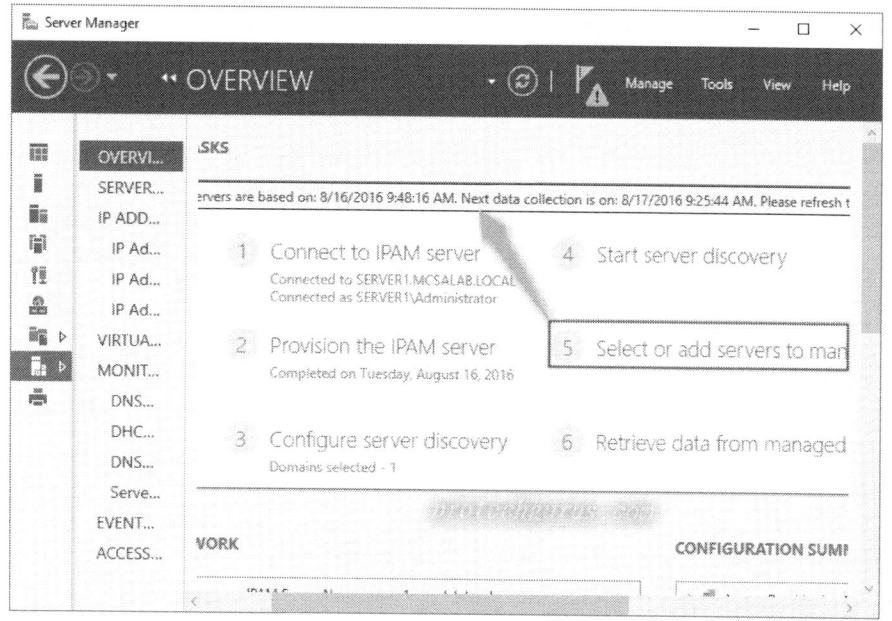

13. Leave the **Server Manager** console active and execute the following command at the Windows PowerShell prompt.

```
Invoke-IpamGpoProvisioning -Domain mcsalab.local -GpoPrefixName IPAMGPO
-IpamServerFqdn SERVER1.mcsalab.local -DelegatedGpoUser Administrator
```

14. If you get the following error as shown in the below figure. To resolve this, switch to other user and sign in to as **MCSALAB\Administrator** user and try again to execute the command.

15. Switch to the **Server Manager** tool. Select **SERVER INVENTORY**, right-click **DC1** and then select **Edit Server**.

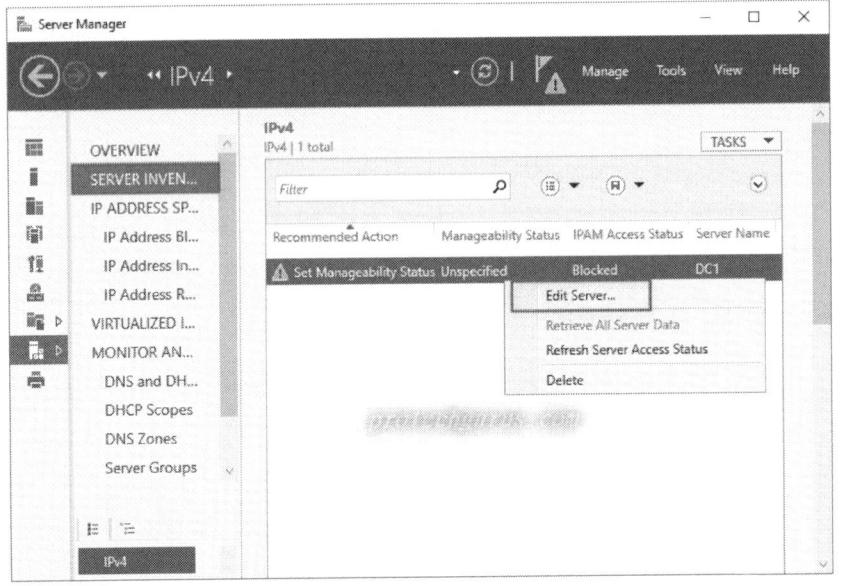

16. On the **Add or Edit Server** dialog box, select the server types that you want manage. For example, select DC, DNS and DHCP options. In the **Manageability status** drop-down list, select **Managed** and then click **OK**.

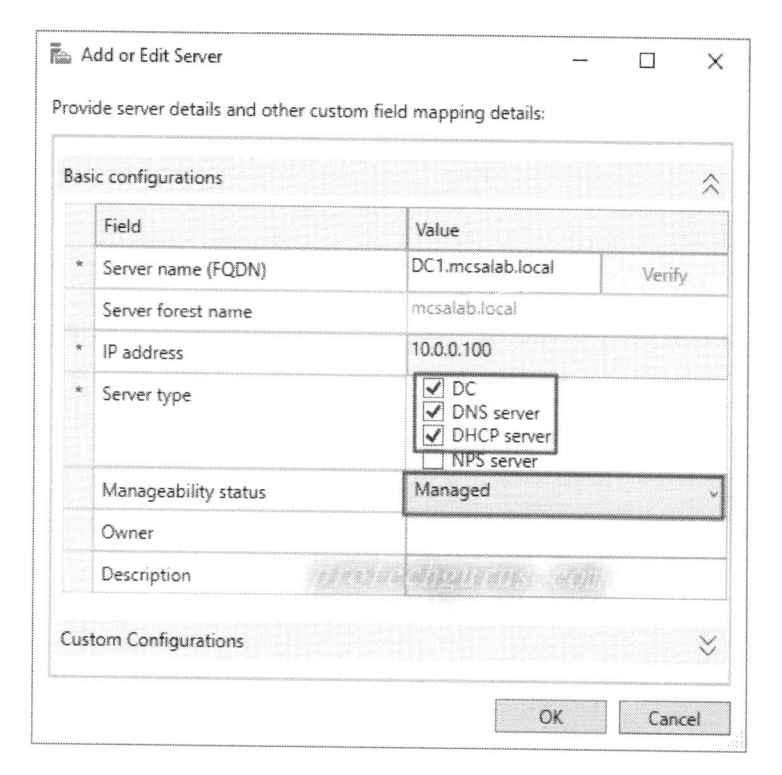

Task 3: Verifying IPAM Configuration

To verify IPAM configuration, following steps need to be followed:

1. Switch and sign in to the **DC1** server and execute the following Windows PowerShell cmdlet to update the group policy.

   `Gpupdate /force`

2. Switch back to the **SERVER1,** **r**ight-click **DC1** in the IPAM window and then select **Refresh Server Access Status**.

3. Refresh the **Server Manager** console. Wait for 10-15 minutes. Refresh again until the status changes to unblocked. Keep try to do this for a while, sometimes it may take up to an hour to change the status. But, that's all you need to do to deploy and test IPAM configuration with DHCP.

Results: In this lab exercise, we have explained how to install and configure IPAM with DHCP in Windows Server 2016. Shut down and revert the DC1 and SERVER1 virtual machines to prepare for the next exercise.

Exercise 11: Installing and Configuring DNS

Domain Name System (DNS) is a service that is used to perform the name resolution. Name resolution is a process to map domain names in to IP addresses and vice versa. The systems communicate to each other using the IP addresses, however it is difficult to remember the IP addresses of each client in a large enterprise network. DNS service allows you to communicate with the systems using the domain names, which is easier to remember than IP addresses.

In this exercise, you will learn how to install and configure the DNS server role. In addition, you will also learn how configure DNS forwarder and how to manage DNS cache.

Start the DC1, SERVER1, and CLIENT1 virtual machines to perform this exercise.

Task 1: Configuring SERVER1 as a Domain Controller without Installing the DNS Server Role

1. Sign in to **SERVER1** with the Administrator account.
2. On the **Server Manager** console, click the **Add roles and features** link.
3. On the **Before you begin page** of the **Add Roles and Features Wizard**, click **Next**.
4. On the **Select installation type** page, click **Next**.
5. On the **Select destination server** page, make sure that **SERVER1.mcsalab.local** is selected, and then click **Next**.
6. On the **Select server roles** page, select the **Active Directory Domain Services** check box.
7. On the **Add Roles and Features Wizard** dialog box, click **Add Features**, and then click **Next**.
8. On the **Select features** page, click **Next**.
9. On the **Active Directory Domain Services** page, click **Next**.
10. On the **Confirm installation selections** page, click **Install**.
11. The installation process will start. Click **Close**, once the installation succeeded.
12. On the **Server Manager** console, click the **Notifications** icon, and then click the **Promote this server to a domain controller** link, as shown in the following figure.

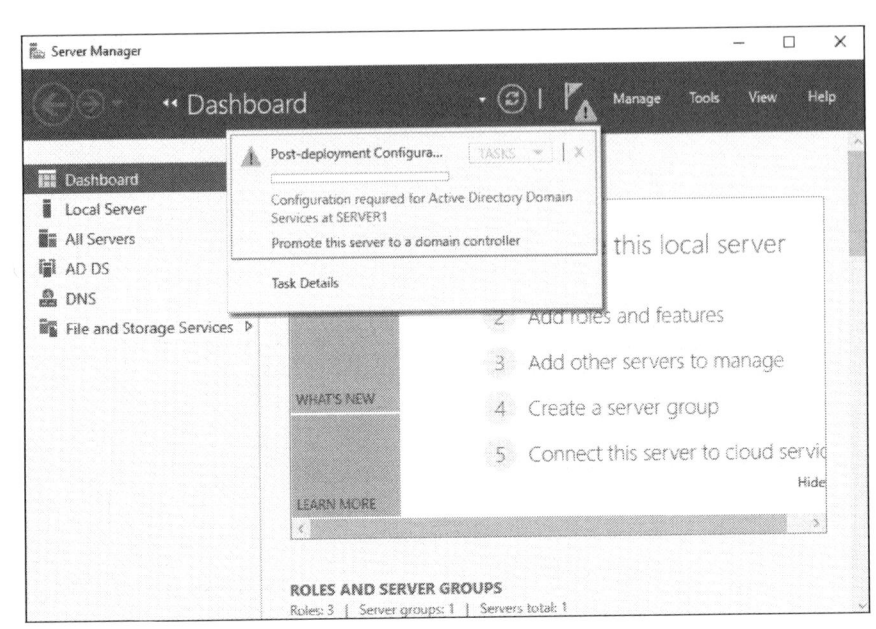

13. On the **Deployment Configuration** page of the **Active Directory Domain Services**

Configuration Wizard, make sure that the **Add a domain controller to an existing domain** radio button is selected.

14. Under the **Supply the credentials to perform this operation** section, click **Change**.
15. On the **Windows Security** dialog box, in the **User name** text box, type **MCSALAB\Administrator**. In the **Password** text box, type **Password@123**.
16. The **Deployment Configuration** page is returned, as shown in the following figure. Review the selected options, and then click **Next**.

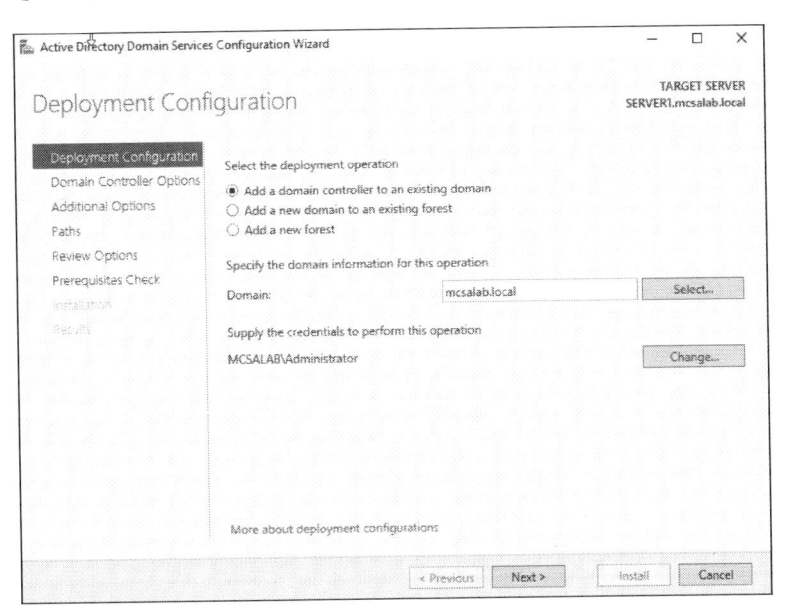

17. On the **Domain Controller Options** page, clear the **Domain Name System (DNS) server** check box.
18. Under the DSRM password section, type **Password@123** in the **Password** and **Confirm password** text boxes, as shown in the following figure, and then click **Next**.

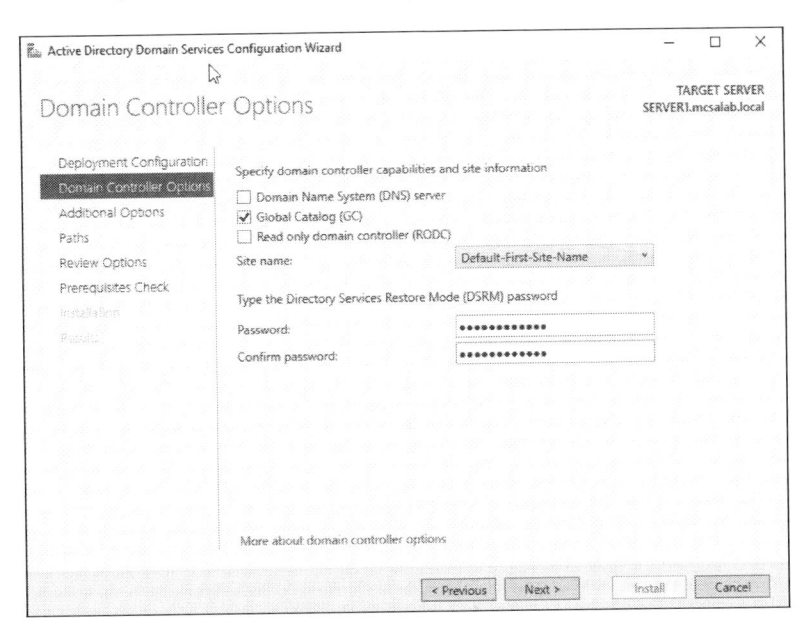

19. Click **Next**, until the **Prerequisites Check** page is displayed.
20. On the **Prerequisites Check** page, click **Install**.

21. The installation process will start and the server will restart automatically. After **SERVER1** restarts, sign in to **SERVER1** with the MCSALAB\Administrator account.

Task 2: Creating and Configuring the Myzone.local Zone on DC1

1. Sign in to **DC1** with the MCSALAB\Administrator account.
2. On the **Server Manager** console, click **Tools**, and then click **DNS**.
3. On the **DNS Manager** console, expand **DC1**, select and right-click **Forward Lookup Zones**, and then select **New Zone**, as shown in the following figure.

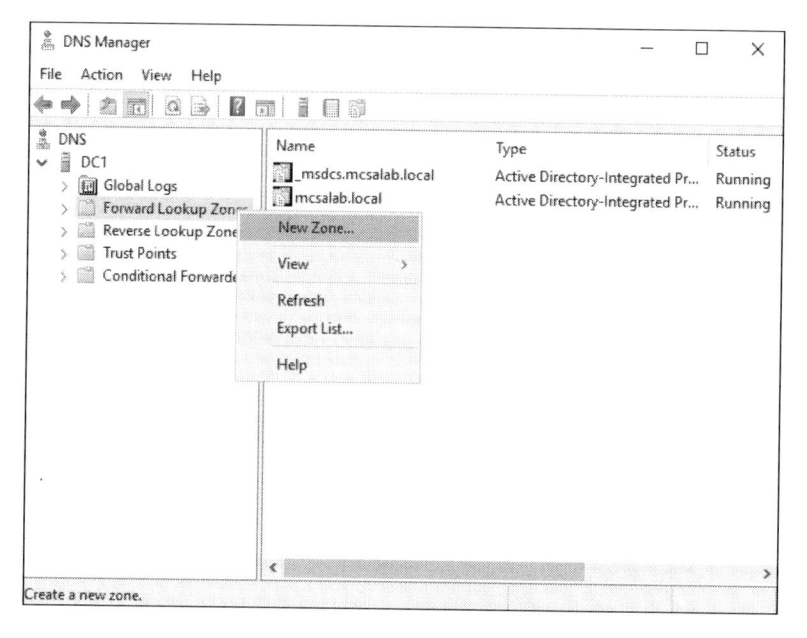

4. On the welcome page of the **New Zone Wizard**, click **Next**.
5. On the **Zone Type** page, make sure that the **Primary zone** radio button is selected.
6. Clear the **Store the zone in Active Directory** check box, as shown in the following figure, and then click **Next**.

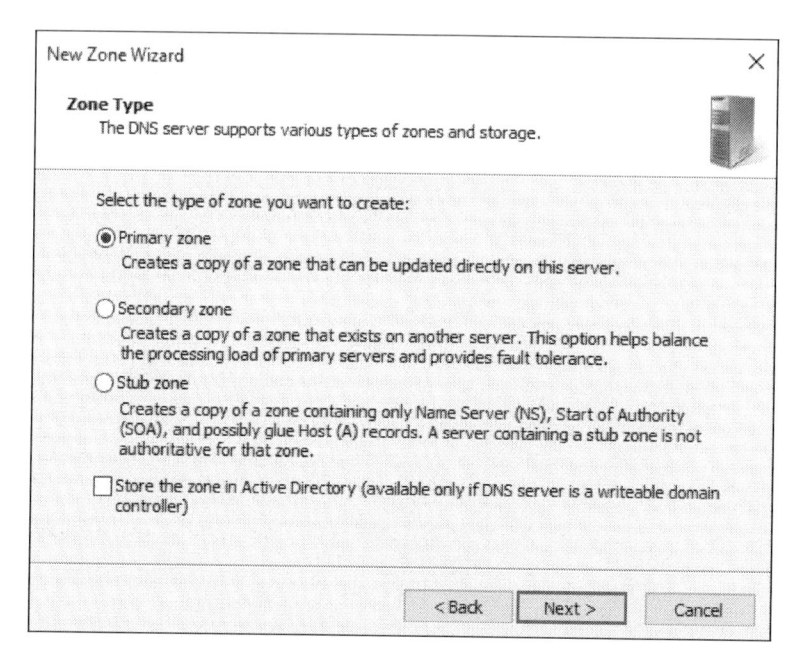

7. On the **Zone Name** page, in the **Zone name** text box, type **Myzone.local**, as shown in the following figure, and then click **Next**.

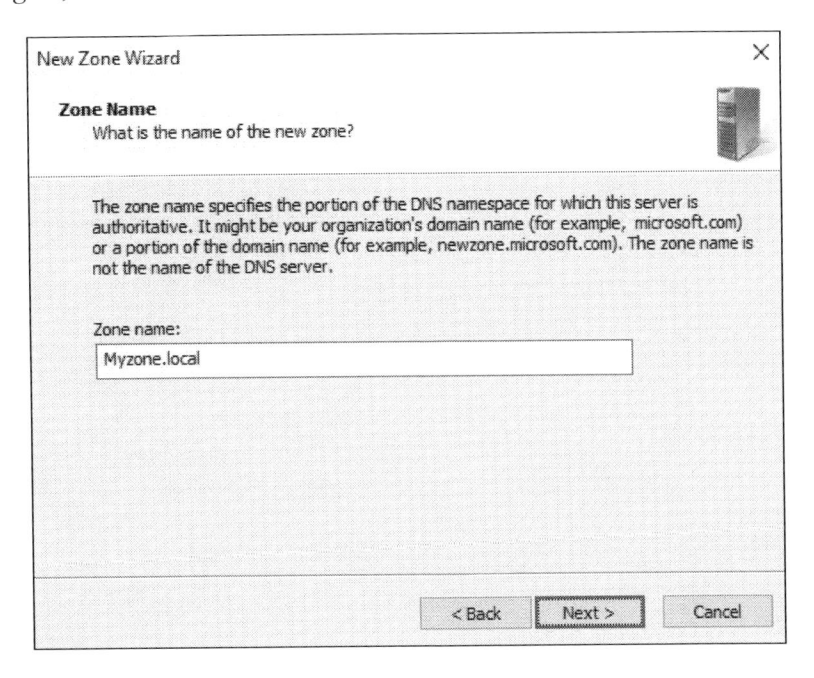

8. On the **Zone File** page, click **Next**.
9. On the **Dynamic Update** page, make sure that the **Do not allow dynamic updates** radio button is selected, as shown in the following figure, and then click **Next**.

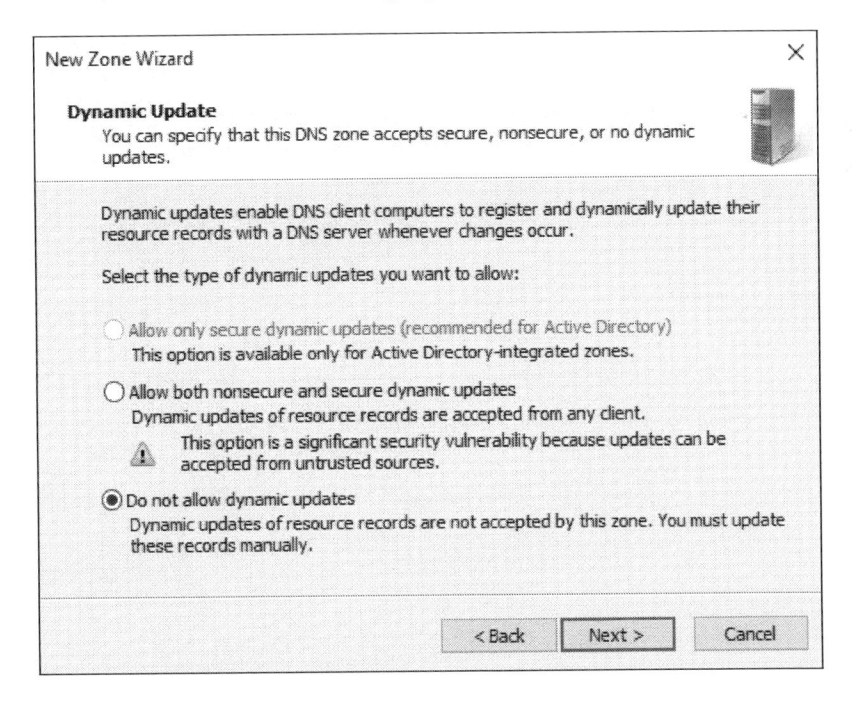

10. On the **Completing the New Zone Wizard** page, as shown in the following figure, review the zone configuration options, and then click **Finish**.

[Screenshot: Completing the New Zone Wizard dialog showing Name: Myzone.local, Type: Standard Primary, Lookup type: Forward, File name: Myzone.local.dns]

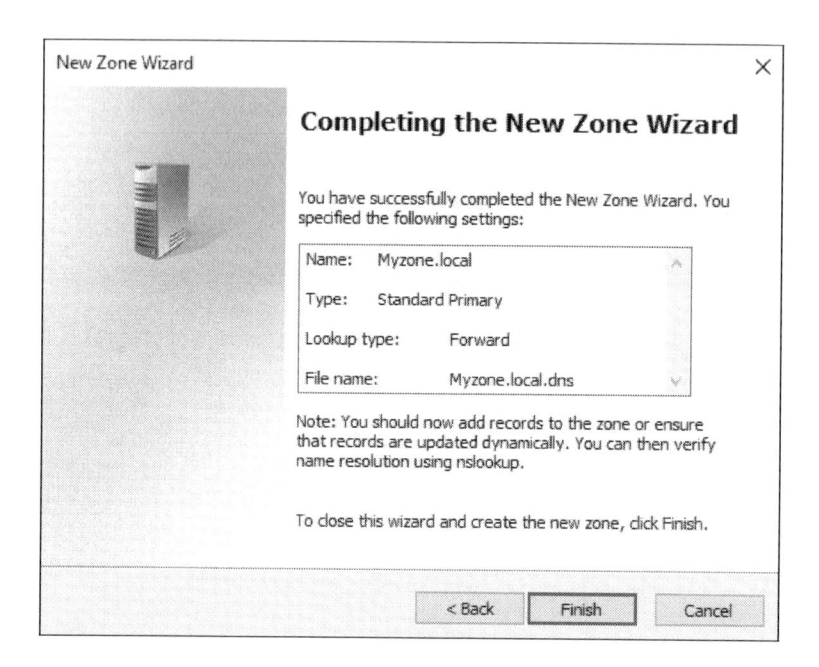

11. On the **DNS Manager** console, expand **Forward Lookup Zones**.
12. Select and right-click the **Myzone.local** zone, and then select **New Host (A or AAAA)**, as shown in the following figure.

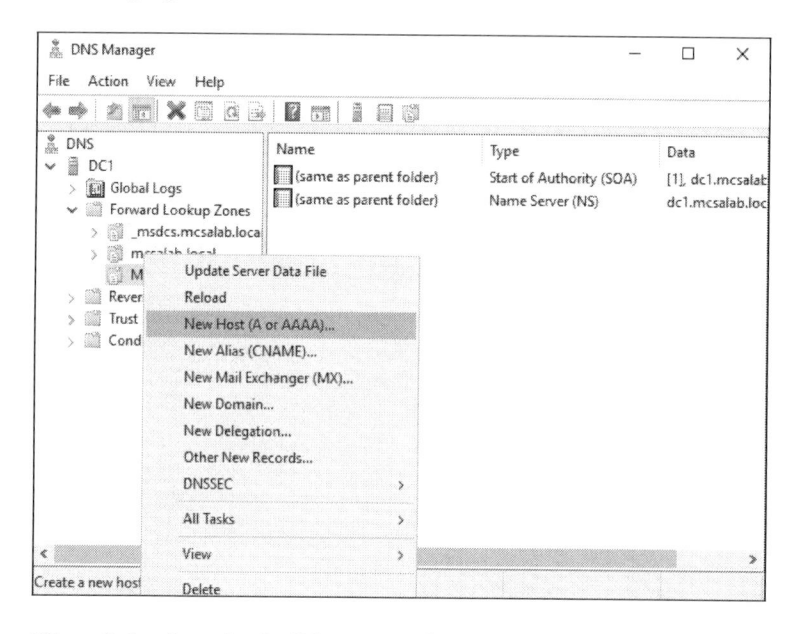

[Screenshot: DNS Manager console with right-click context menu showing New Host (A or AAAA) option highlighted]

13. On the **New Host** dialog box, in the **Name** text box, type **www**. In the **IP address** text box, type **10.0.0.101**, as shown in the following figure, and then click **Add Host**.

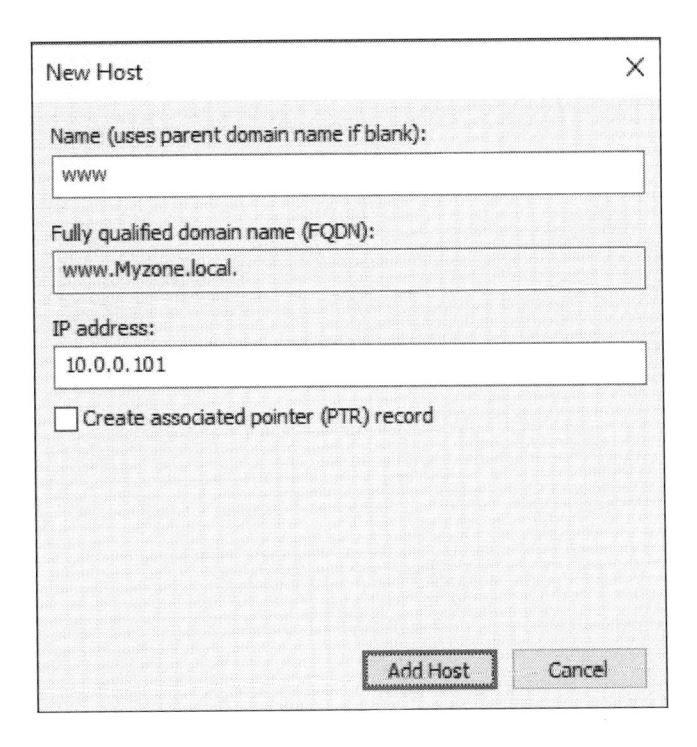

[Screenshot of New Host dialog box showing:
- Name: www
- FQDN: www.Myzone.local.
- IP address: 10.0.0.101
- Create associated pointer (PTR) record checkbox unchecked
- Add Host and Cancel buttons]

14. On the **DNS** message box, click **OK**.
15. On the **New Host** dialog box, click **Done**.
16. Leave the **DNS Manager** console active.

Task 3: Adding the DNS Server Role on the SERVER1

1. Switch and Sign in to **SERVER1** with the MCSALAB\Administrator account.
2. On the **Server Manager** console, click the **Add roles and features** link.
3. On the **Before you begin** page of the **Add Roles and Features Wizard**, click **Next**.
4. On the **Select installation type** page, click **Next**.
5. On the **Select destination server** page, make sure that **SERVER1.mcsalab.local** is selected, and then click **Next**.
6. On the **Select server roles** page, select the **DNS Server** check box.
7. On the **Add Roles and Features Wizard** dialog box, click **Add Features**.
8. The **Select Server roles** page is returned, as shown in the following, click **Next**.

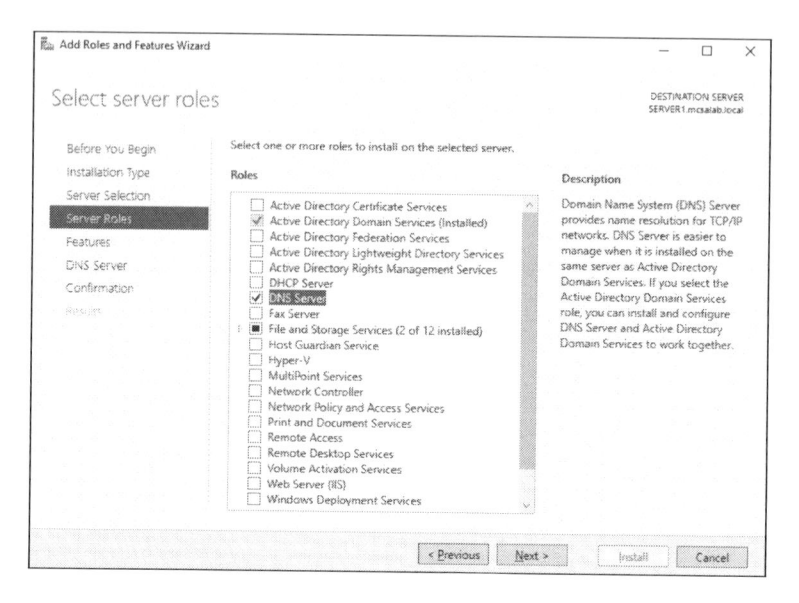

9. On the **Select Features** page, click **Next**.
10. On the **DNS Server** page, click **Next**.
11. On the **Confirm installation selections** page, click **Install**.
12. The installation process will start. Click **Close**, once the installation succeeded.

Task 4: Verifying Replication of the mcsalab.local Zone

1. On **SERVER1**, on the **Server Manager** console, click **Tools**, and then click **DNS**.
2. On the **DNS Manager** console, expand **SERVER1**, and then expand **Forward Lookup Zones**.
3. Right-click **Forward Lookup Zone** and then select **Refresh**.
4. Make sure that the **_msdcs.mcsalab.local** and **mcsalab.local** zones are displayed.

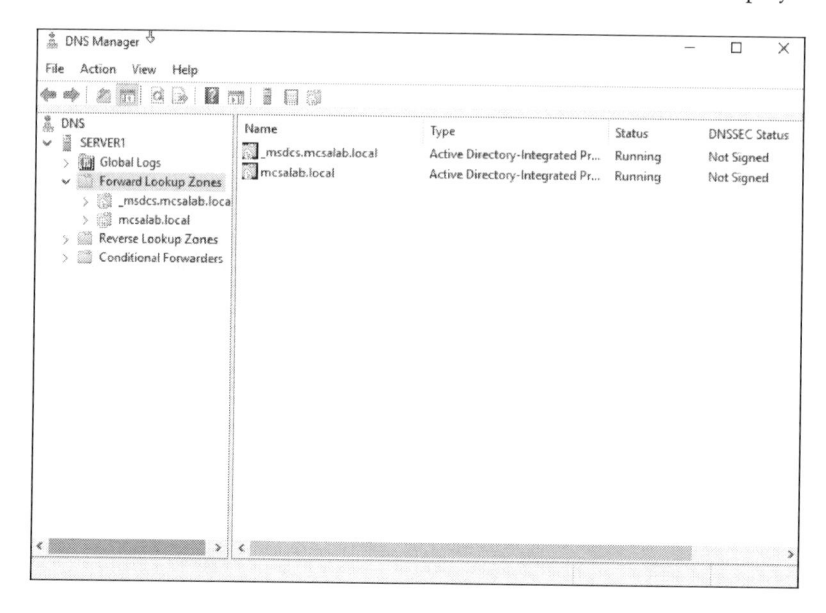

Note: If the zone list is empty, proceed to the next step, otherwise close the

DNS Manager console.

5. On **SERVER1**, switch back to the **Server Manager** console, click **Tools**, and then click **Active Directory Sites and Services**.
6. On the **Active Directory Sites and Services** console, expand **Sites**, and then click **Default-First-Site-Name**, and then click **Servers**, and then click **DC1**.
7. Select **NTDS Settings**, in the right pane, select and right-click the SERVER1 replication connection, and select **Replicate Now**, as shown in the following figure.

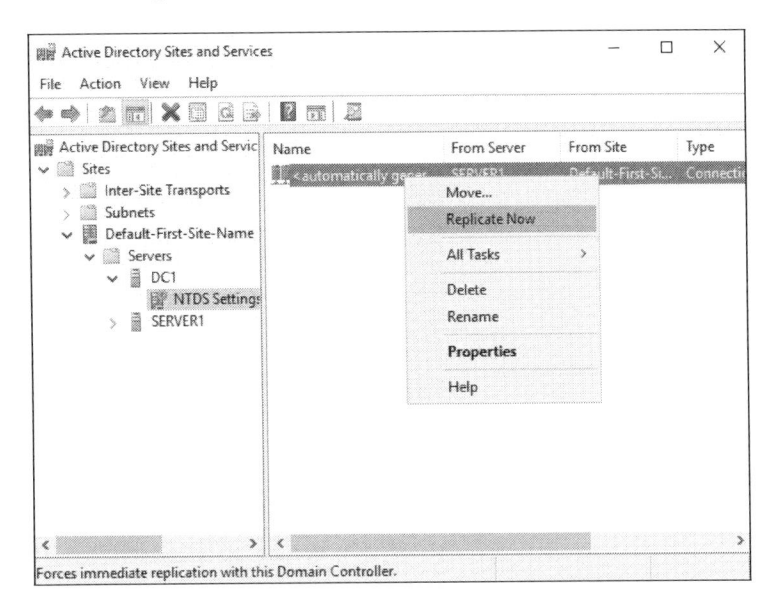

Note: If you receive an error message, proceed to the next step, and then retry this step after 5 minutes.

8. In the left pane, expand **SERVER1**, and then select **NTDS Settings**.
9. In the right pane, select and right-click the DC1 replication connection, select **Replicate Now**, and then click **OK**.
10. Switch back to the **DNS Manager** console, select and right-click **Forward Lookup Zones**, and then click **Refresh**.
11. Make sure that **the _msdcs.mcsalab.local** and **mcsalab.local** zones are displayed.
12. Close the **DNS Manager** console.

Task 5: Configuring DNS Forwarder

1. Switch and sign in to **DC1**.
2. Open the **DNS Manager** console.
3. On the **DNS Manager** console, select and right-click **DC1**, and then select **Properties**, as shown in the following figure.

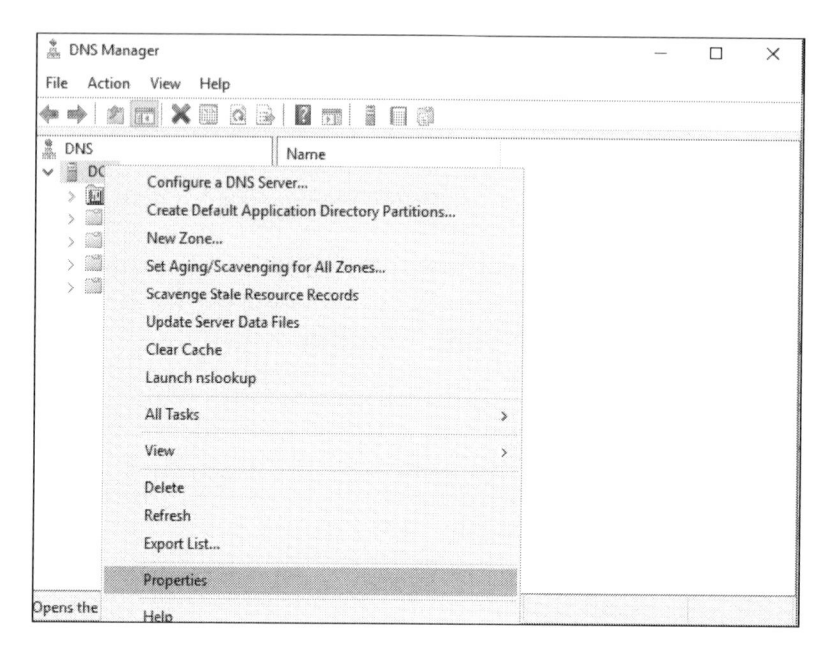

4. On the **DC1 Properties** dialog box, select the **Forwarders** tab, as shown in the following figure.

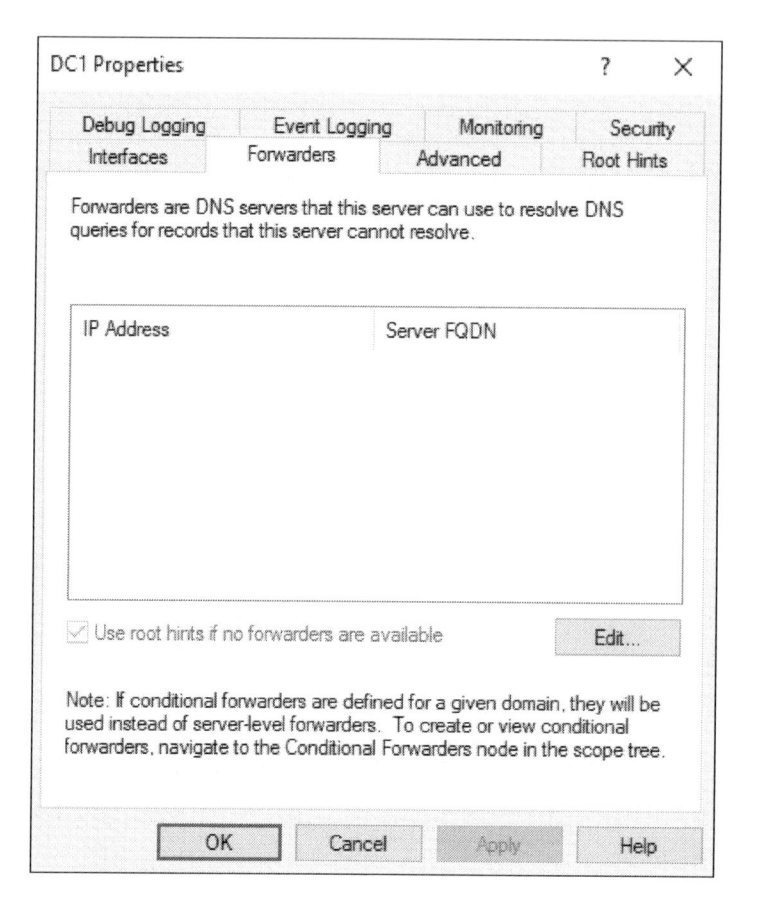

5. On the **Forwarders** tab, click **Edit**.
6. On the **Edit Forwarders** dialog box, type **10.0.0.101**, as shown in the following figure, and then click **OK**.

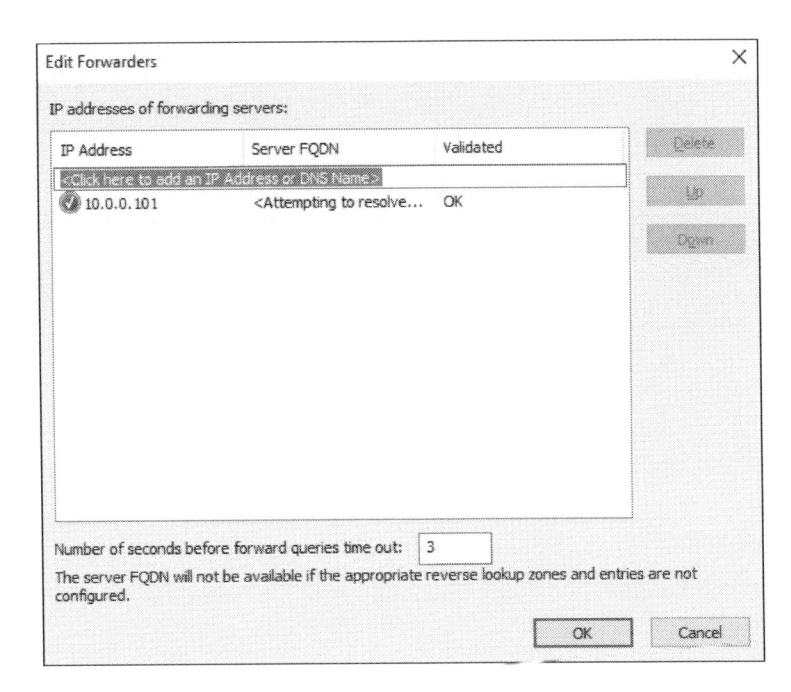

7. On the **DC1** dialog box, click **OK**.
8. On the **DNS Manager** console, select and right-click **DC1**, and then click **All Tasks**, and then click **Restart**.
9. Switch and sign in to **CLIENT1**.
10. Open the **Command Prompt** window.
11. On the **Command Prompt** window, type **ping www.myzone.local**, and the press **Enter**.
12. Make sure that you are able to resolve the **www.myzone.local** FQDN successfully, as shown in the following figure.

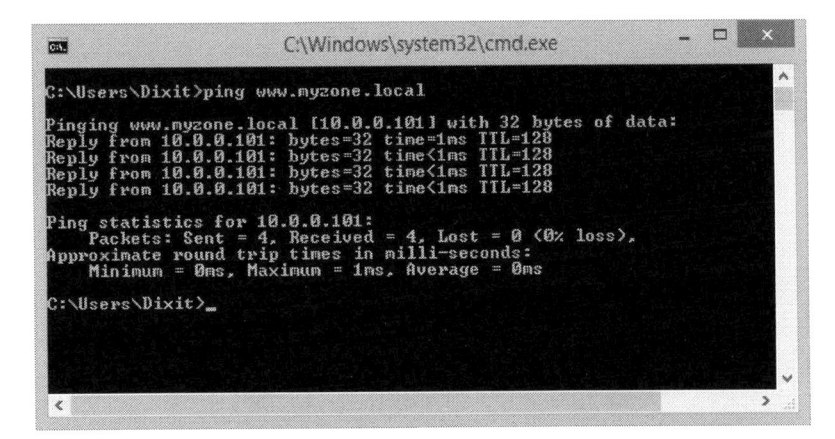

13. On the **Command Prompt** window, type **nslookup**, and then press **Enter**.
14. At the **nslookup** prompt, type **www.myzone.local**, and then press **Enter**.
15. Make sure that you receive an IP address for this host, as shown in the following figure.

16. Leave the **Command Prompt** window active.

Task 6: Managing the DNS Cache

1. On CLIENT1, on the **Command Prompt** window, type the following command and then press **Enter**, as shown in the following figure.
   ```
   ipconfig /displaydns
   ```

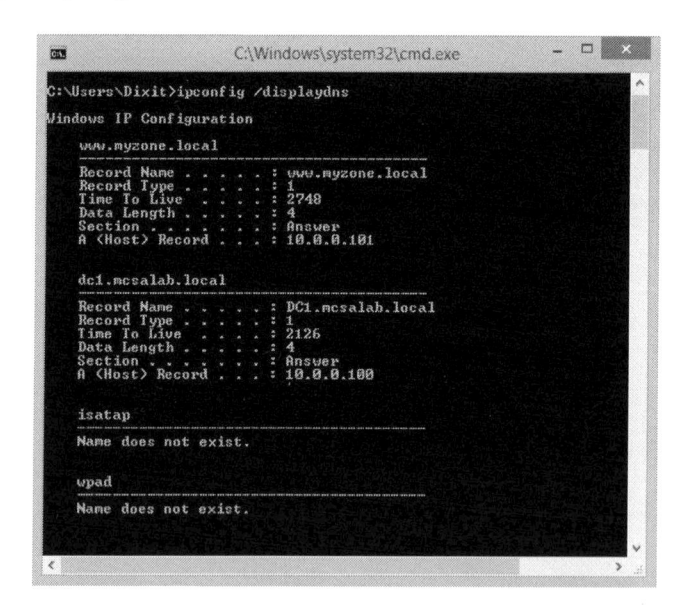

2. Examine the output and close the **Command Prompt** window.
3. Press the **Windows** key, and then type **cmd**.
4. Select and right-click **Command Prompt**, and then select **Run as administrator** as shown in the following figure.

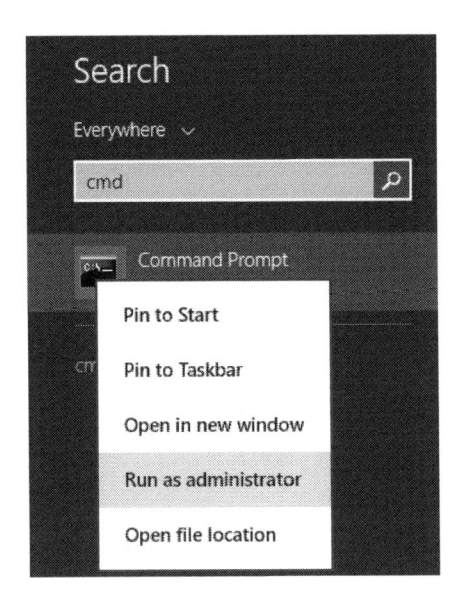

5. On the **User Account Control** dialog box, click **Yes**.
6. On the **Command Prompt** window, type the following command to clear the DNS cache, and then press **Enter**.
   `ipconfig /flushdns`
7. On the **Command Prompt** window, type the following command and verify that the DNS cache has been cleared, and then press **Enter**.
   `ipconfig /displaydns`
8. Close the **Command Prompt** window.

Results: After completing this exercise, you should have deployed DNS server, DNS zone, DNS forwarder, and DNS cache.

Shut down and revert the DC1, SERVER1, and CLIENT1 virtual machines to prepare for the next exercise.

Exercise 12: Installing and Configuring Windows Deployment Services (WDS)

Windows Deployment Services (WDS) is a service role that allows you to deploy Windows operating systems to the PXE supported clients. You can install Windows operating systems on the PXE-enabled clients without the need of physical media. Further, it allows you to deploy Windows operating systems on multiple clients simultaneously. Thus, reducing the overall installation time. here, we will explain how to install and configure WDS in Windows Server 2016. You can use either a physical server or a virtual machine running on a virtualized platform such as Hyper-V, VMware, or VirtualBox.

Prerequisites to Configure WDS Server

Before to configure WDS server, first you need to ensure that your server meets the following requirements:

1. A Domain Controller or a Domain Member server.
2. A properly configured DNS server to provide name resolution.
3. A DHCP server with the appropriate DHCP pool to provide IP address to the PXE clients.
4. An NTFS shared folder to store the WDS image files.
5. An installation media such as DVD or ISO image for the clients that you intend to install.
6. Clients with the PXE-enabled LAN adapter.

We assume that your server meets the above-mentioned prerequisites. If required, you can visit the following links to prepare your WDS server.

Note: Our DC1 server is already configured as DHCP server, so we will start WDS configuration directly.

Task 01: Installing WDS Server Role

To install **Windows Deployment Services (WDS)** server role, you need to perform the following steps:

1. On the **Server Manager** tool, click **Manage**, and then click **Add Roles and Features**.
2. Accept the default selections and click **Next** until you get the Select server roles page.
3. On the **Select server roles** page, as shown in the following figure, select the **Windows Deployment Services** check box.

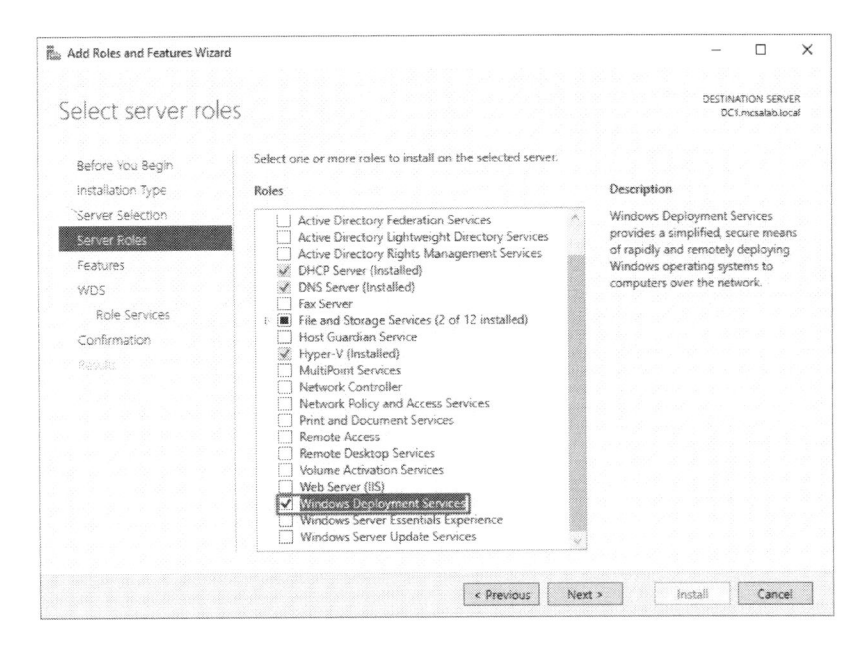

4. On the **Add Roles and Features Wizard** window, click **Add Features**.
5. Accept the default selections and click **Next**, until you get the Confirm installation selections page.
6. Click **Install** and complete the installation process.

Task 02: Configure WDS Server

After installing WDS server role, next you need to configure WDS server. To do so, you need to perform the following steps:
1. On the Server **Manager** tool, click **Tools** and then select **Windows Deployment Services**.
2. On the **Windows Deployment Services** console, expand **Servers**.
3. Select and right-click your WDS server name and select **Configure Server**.

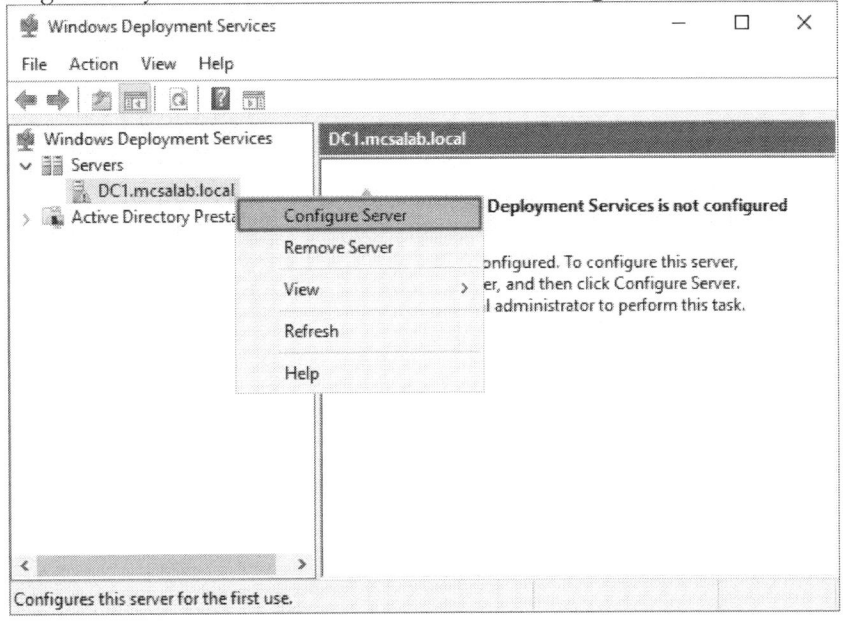

4. Navigate to the **Install Options** page, ensure that the **Integrated with Active Directory** radio button is selected and then click **Next**.
5. On the **Remote Installation Folder Location** page, select the shared folder or click **Next**

to accept the default value. This folder will hold the WDS images.
6. On the **DHCP Server** page, if your WDS server also hosts the DHCP server role, select the **Do not listen on DHCP and DHCPv6** option. If your DHCP server is running on a different server, remove **Do not listen on DHCP Port** option.

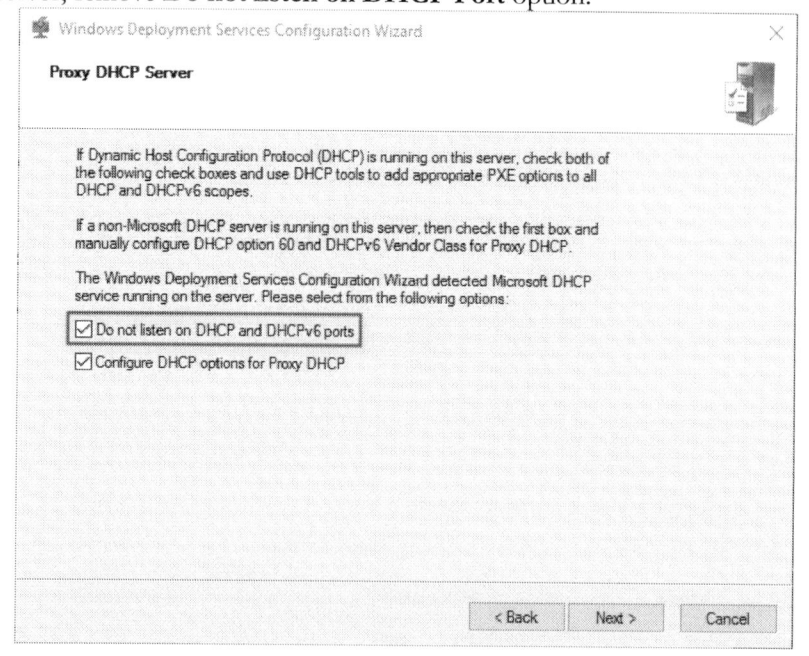

7. On the **PXE Server Initial Settings** page, there are three options: All the options are self-explanatory. Select the **Respond to all client computers (known and unknown)** radio button and then click **Next**. This option will allow all the PXE-enabled clients to start the installation process. Further, the **Admin Approval** check box allows an administrator to manually approve each client before they can start the installation process.

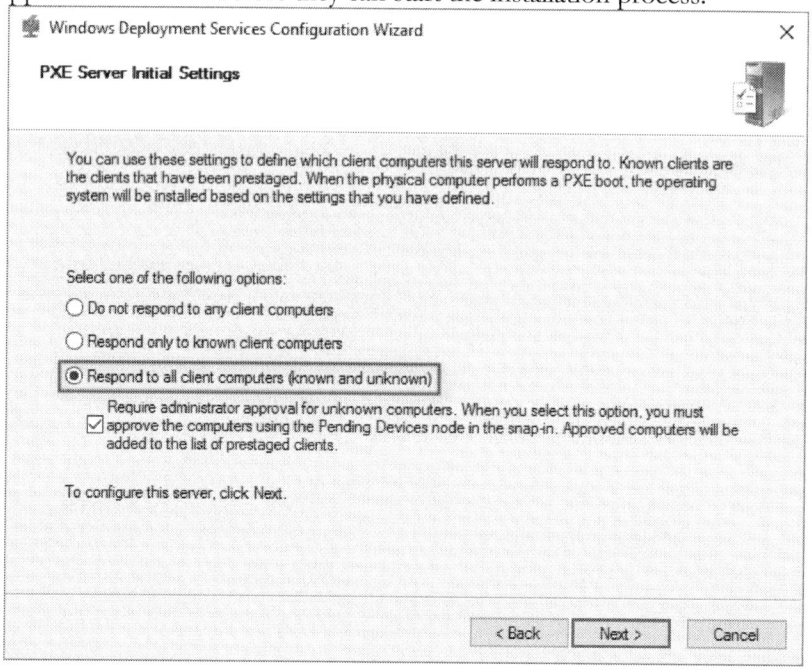

8. On the **Operation Complete** page, clear the **Add images to the server now** check box and click **Finish**. If you get "*The service did not respond to the start or control request in a timely*

fashion" error, right-click WDS server and then start the WDS service manually to troubleshoot it. If the WDS service still failed to start, check the WDS server properties and ensure that the **Do not listen on DHCP port** option is selected.

Task 03: Adding Install Image to WDS Server

Now, you have installed and configured WDS in Windows Server 2016. The next step is to add the WDS images that you want to deploy on your network. To add the WDS images, you need to add the Boot images and Install images files for the supported Windows operating systems. To add an install.wim image file to WDS server, you need to perform the following steps:

1. Select and right-click **Install Images** and then click **Add Install Image**.
2. On the **Image Group** page, select an existing image group name or type a name to create a new one.
3. On the **Image File** page, click **Browse** and navigate to the Sources directory of the installation media and select the Install.wim file.

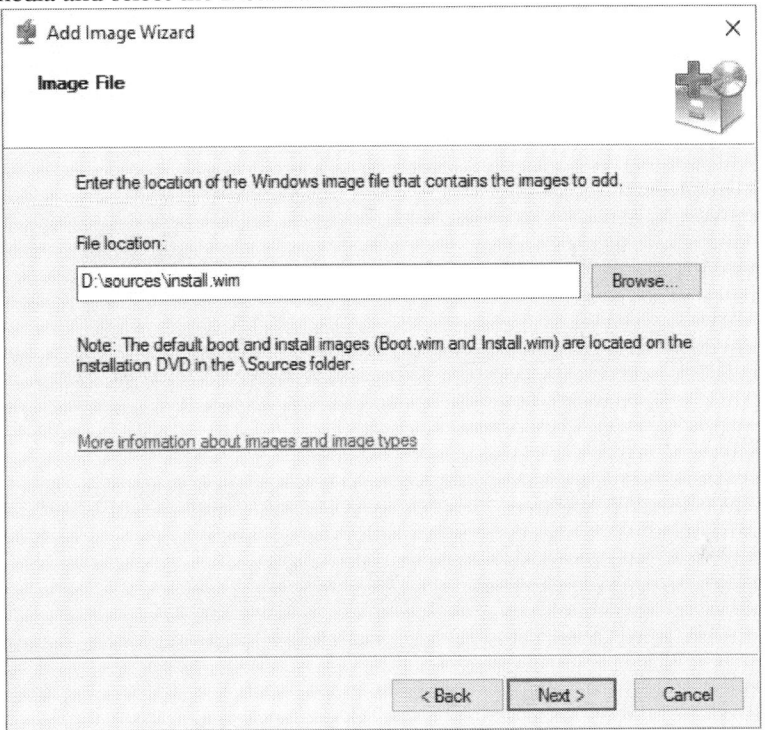

4. On the **Available Images** page, select the editions that you intend to deploy for your network.

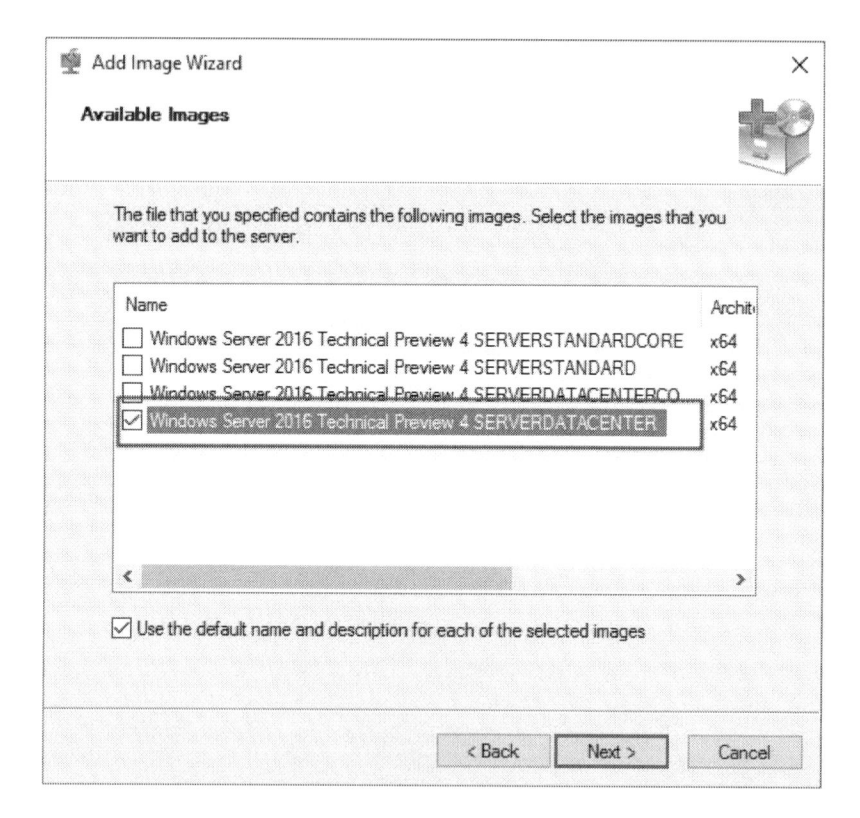

5. Accept the default selections through the rest of the pages and click **Finish** to complete the task.

Note: The process may take several minutes.

Task 04: Adding Boot Image to WDS Server

Along with the install.wim file that contains the Windows OS files you also need to add a boot image. The boot image is used to initiate the boot process for a Windows OS.

To add a boot image file (boot.wim) to WDS server, you need to perform the following steps:

1. Select and right-click **Boot Images** and then click **Add Boot Image**.
2. Click **Browse** and navigate to installation media and select the boot.wim file.

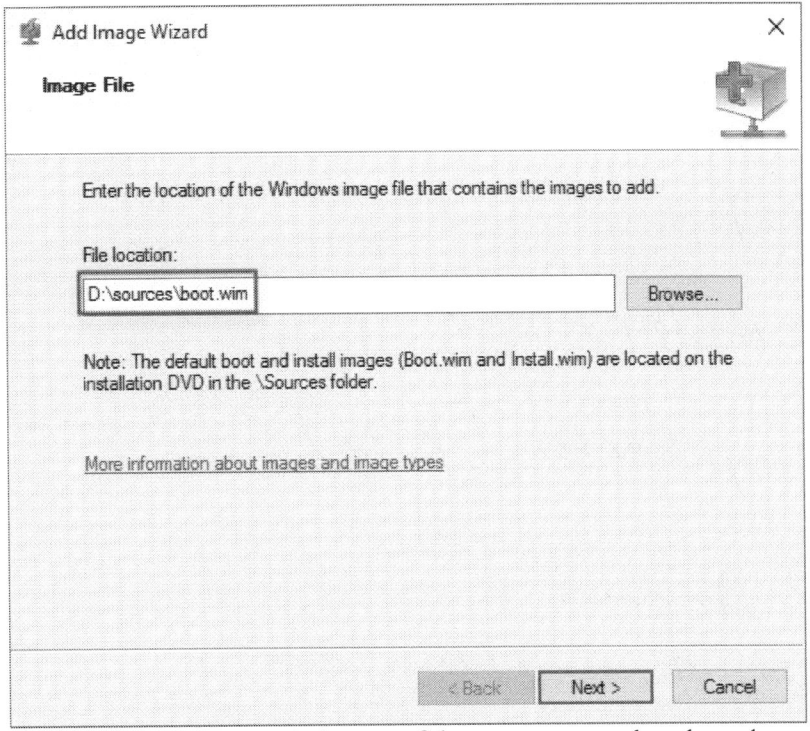

3. Accept the default selections through the rest of the pages to complete the task.

Task 05: Installing Windows OS using WDS

Now, your WDS server is ready to be used. To test your WDS configuration, perform the following steps:

1. Create a new virtual machine and use the I will install operating system later option.
2. On the client machine that has the PXE–enabled LAN adapter, reboot the machine and select the **Network Boot** option.
3. When the system reboots, press **F12** for network service boot. After a few minutes, the **Windows Setup** screen will display.

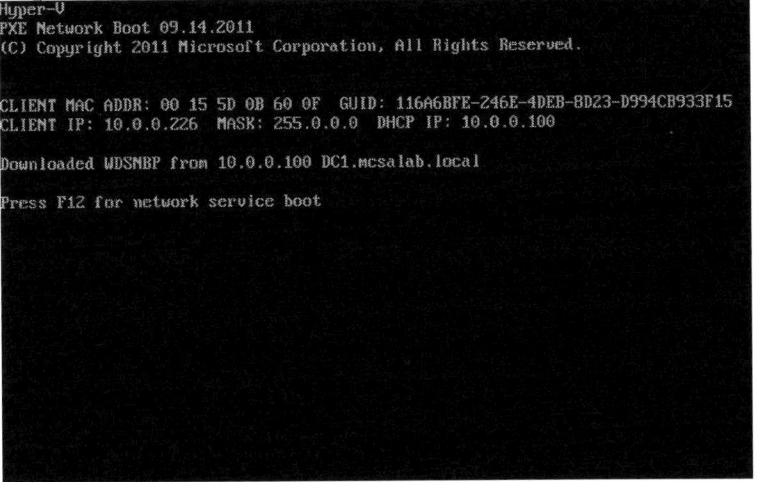

4. Follow the on-screen instructions and complete the installation process.

Note: If you face any issue, visit the following link.

Create a virtual machine using PXE client.

Routing
NAT
DHCP Relay Agent

- dial-up server (VPN)

  R R Access
  Remote Access Managment -

Exercise 13: Implementing LAN Routing

LAN routing is a Window feature that enables you to communicate between different subnets. To communicate between different subnets, typically a device called router is used, but you can also use a Windows server, such as Windows Server 2016 server to perform the LAN routing. However, Windows Server 2016 does not support all the features supported by a router. It is typically helpful for a small network with the limited number of subnets.

In this exercise, you will learn how to use a Windows Server 2016 server as a software router to enable LAN routing between two or more subnets.

Start the DC1, ROUTER, and SERVER2 virtual machines to perform this exercise.

Task 1: Installing the LAN Routing Feature on ROUTER

1. Sign in to **ROUTER** with the Administrator account.
2. On the **Server Manager** console, click the **Add roles and features** link.
3. On the **Before you began page** of the **Add Roles and Features Wizard**, click **Next**.
4. On the **Select installation type** page, click **Next**.
5. On the **Select destination server** page, click **Next**.
6. On the **Select Server roles** page, select the **Remote Access** check box, as shown in the following figure, and then click **Next**.

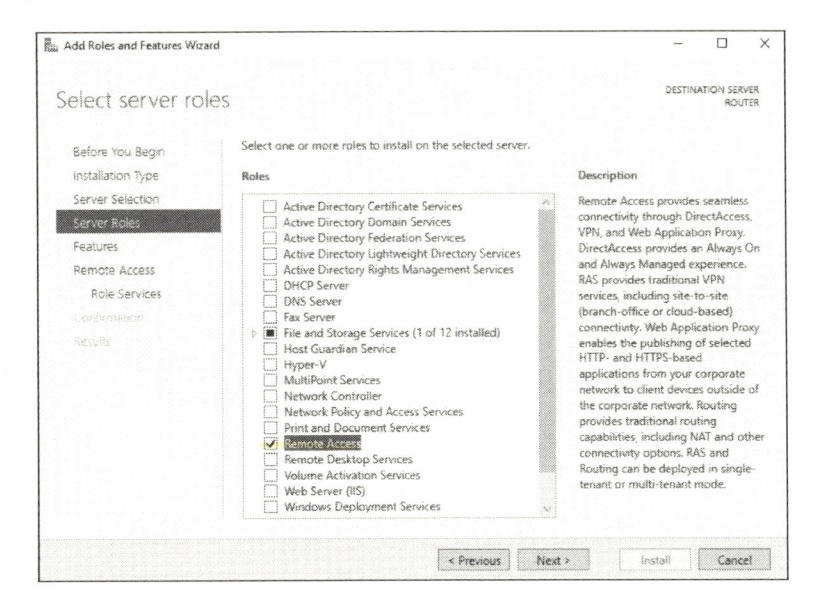

7. On the **Select features** page, click **Next**.
8. On the **Remote Access** page, click **Next**.
9. On the **Select roles services** page, select the **Routing** check box.
10. On the **Add Roles and Features Wizard** dialog box, click **Add Features**.
11. The **Select role services** page is returned, as shown in the following figure, click **Next**.

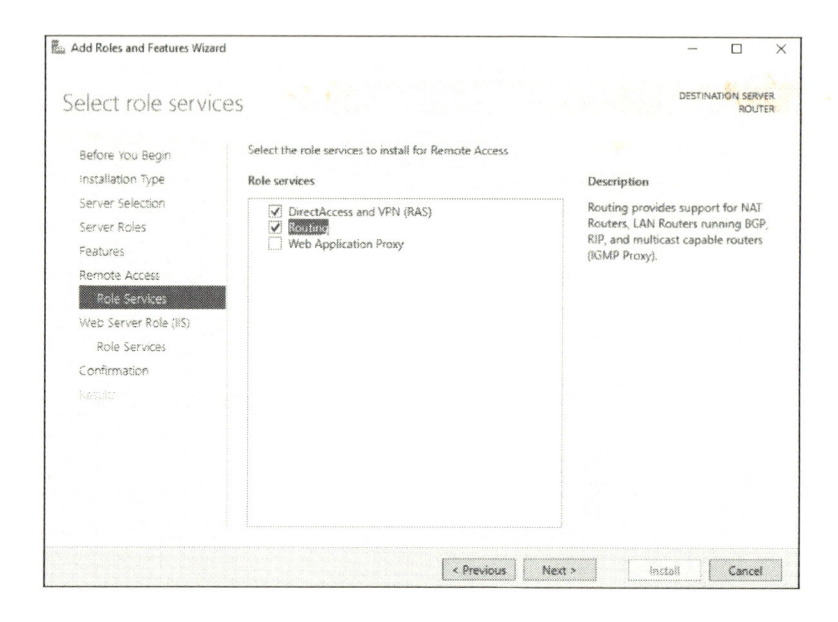

Note: The DirectAccess and VPN (RAS) check box will be selected automatically.

12. On the **Web Server Role (IIS)** page, click **Next**.
13. On the **Select role services** page, click **Next**.
14. On the **Confirm installation selection** page, click **Install**.
15. Click **Close**, once the installation succeeded.

Task 2: Configuring the LAN Routing Service on ROUTER

1. On the **Server Manager** console, click **Tools**, and then click **Remote and Routing Access**.
2. On the **Routing and Remote Access** console, select and right-click **ROUTER (local)**, and then select **Configure and Enable Routing and Remote Access**, as shown in the following figure.

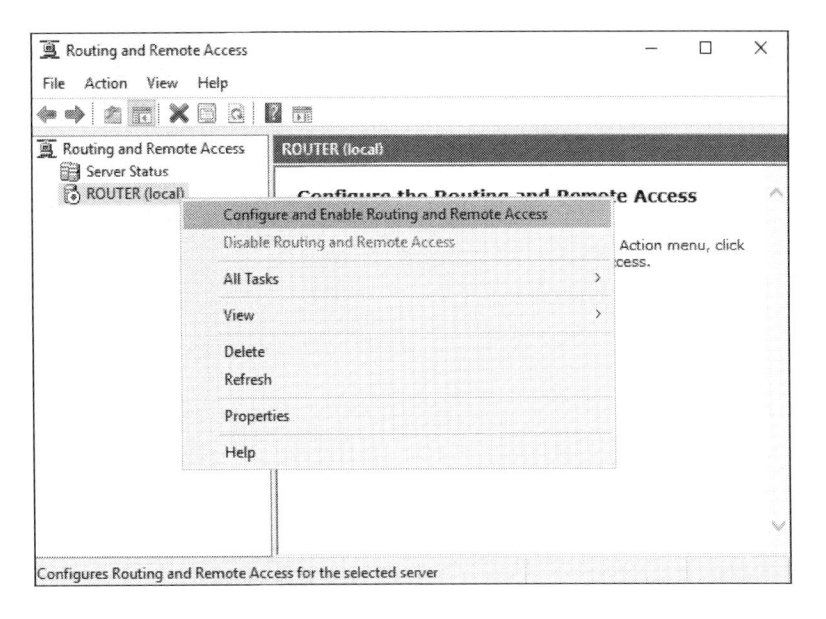

3. On the welcome page of the **Routing and Remote Access Server Setup Wizard**, click **Next**.
4. On the **Configuration** page, select the **Custom configuration** radio button, as shown in the following figure, and then click **Next**.

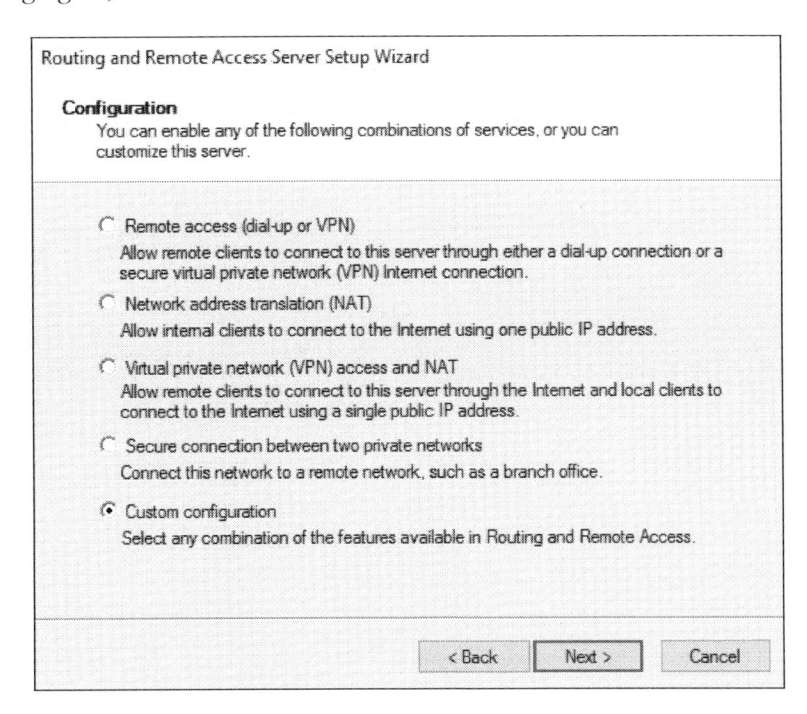

5. On the **Custom Configuration** page, select the **LAN routing** check box, as shown in the following figure.

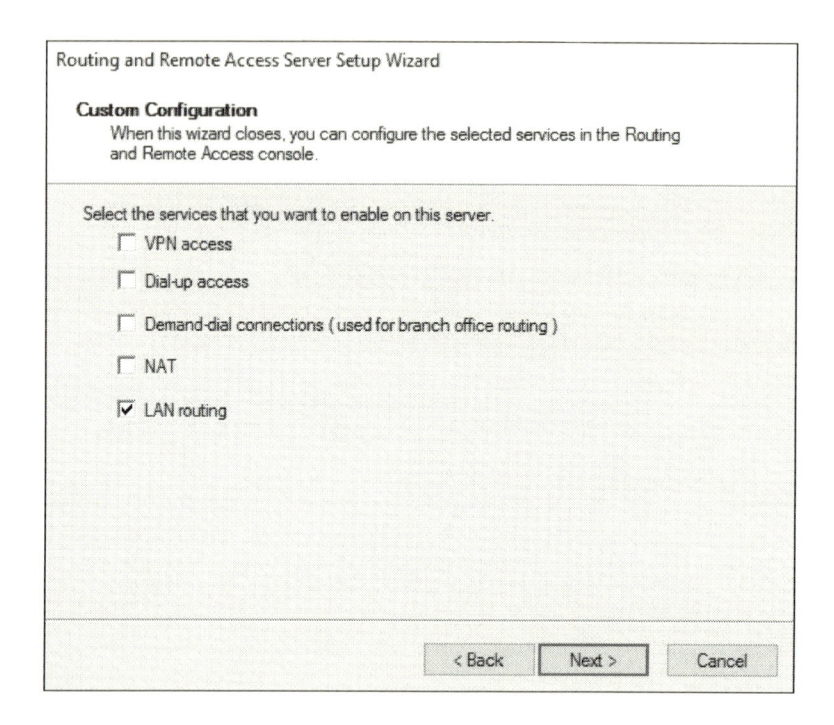

![Routing and Remote Access Server Setup Wizard - Custom Configuration with LAN routing checked]

6. Click **Next**, and then click **Finish**.
7. On the service message box, click **Start Service**.
8. Make sure that the **ROUTER (local)** node's color changes red to green, as shown in the following figure.

![Routing and Remote Access console showing ROUTER (local) configured]

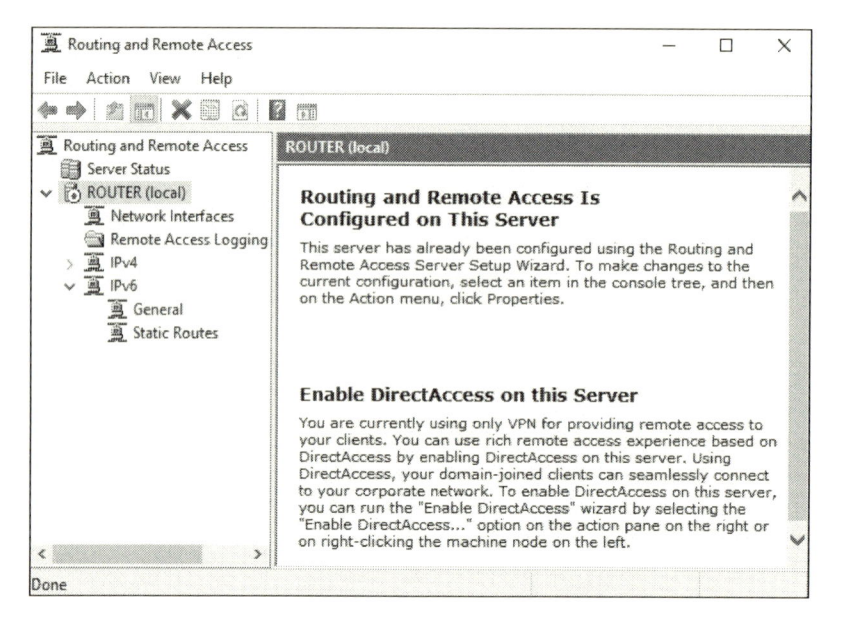

9. Close the **Routing and Remote Access** console.
10. On the **ROUTER** virtual machine, open the **Run** dialog box, type **firewall.cpl** in the **Open** text box, and then press **Enter**.
11. On the **Windows Firewall** window, in the left pane, click the **Turn Windows Firewall on or off** link.
12. On the **Customize Settings** window, select the **Turn off Windows Firewall (not recommended)** radio button for each profile, as shown in the following figure.

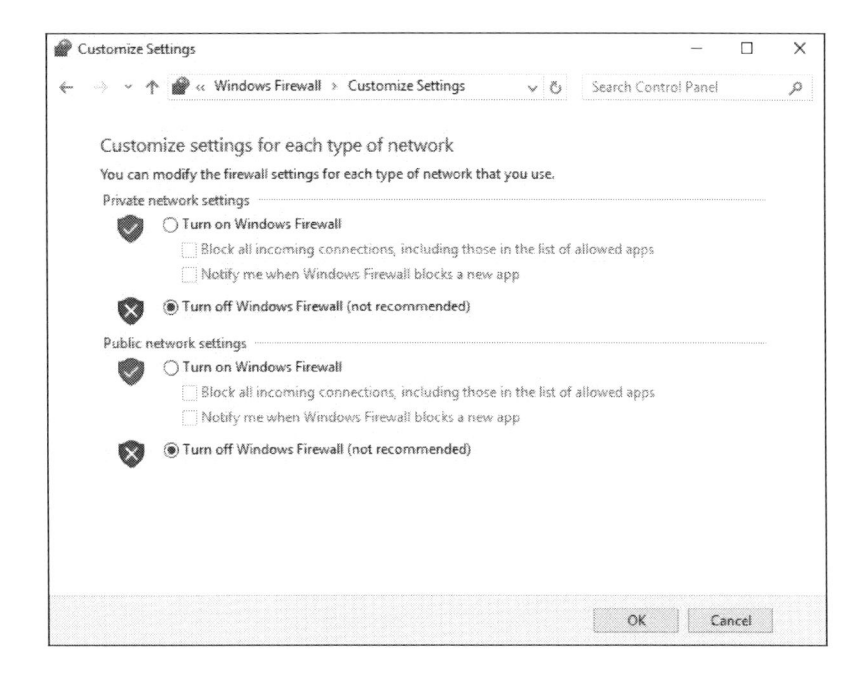

13. Close the **Customize Settings** window.

Task 3: Testing the Connectivity between DC1 and SERVER2 Servers

1. Switch and sign in to **SERVER2** with the Administrator account.
2. Open the **Run** dialog box, type **firewall.cpl**, in the **Open** text box, and then press **Enter**.
3. On the **Windows Firewall** window, in the left pane, click the **Turn Windows Firewall on or off** link.
4. On the **Customize Settings** window, select the **Turn off Windows Firewall (not recommended)** radio button for each firewall profiles
5. Close the **Customize Settings** window.
6. Switch and sign in to **DC1** with MCSALAB\Administrator account.
7. Open the **Command Prompt** window, on the **Command Prompt** window, type the following commands and then press **Enter** after each one.
    - **Ping 10.0.0.1**
    - **Ping 192.168.0.1**
    - **Ping 192.168.0.2**
8. You should be able to communicate to all systems successfully, as shown in the following figure.

```
Administrator: C:\Windows\system32\cmd.exe

C:\Users\Administrator>ping 10.0.0.1

Pinging 10.0.0.1 with 32 bytes of data:
Reply from 10.0.0.1: bytes=32 time<1ms TTL=128
Reply from 10.0.0.1: bytes=32 time=1ms TTL=128
Reply from 10.0.0.1: bytes=32 time=1ms TTL=128
Reply from 10.0.0.1: bytes=32 time=1ms TTL=128

Ping statistics for 10.0.0.1:
    Packets: Sent = 4, Received = 4, Lost = 0 (0% loss),
Approximate round trip times in milli-seconds:
    Minimum = 0ms, Maximum = 1ms, Average = 0ms

C:\Users\Administrator>ping 192.168.0.1

Pinging 192.168.0.1 with 32 bytes of data:
Reply from 192.168.0.1: bytes=32 time=1ms TTL=127
Reply from 192.168.0.1: bytes=32 time=1ms TTL=127
Reply from 192.168.0.1: bytes=32 time=1ms TTL=127

Ping statistics for 192.168.0.1:
    Packets: Sent = 3, Received = 3, Lost = 0 (0% loss),
Approximate round trip times in milli-seconds:
    Minimum = 1ms, Maximum = 1ms, Average = 1ms
Control-C
^C
C:\Users\Administrator>ping 192.168.0.2

Pinging 192.168.0.2 with 32 bytes of data:
Reply from 192.168.0.2: bytes=32 time=3ms TTL=127
Reply from 192.168.0.2: bytes=32 time=1ms TTL=127
Reply from 192.168.0.2: bytes=32 time=1ms TTL=127
Reply from 192.168.0.2: bytes=32 time=1ms TTL=127

Ping statistics for 192.168.0.2:
    Packets: Sent = 4, Received = 4, Lost = 0 (0% loss),
Approximate round trip times in milli-seconds:
    Minimum = 1ms, Maximum = 3ms, Average = 1ms
```

9. Close the **Command Prompt** window.

Results: After completing this exercise, you will have configured LAN routing between DC1 and SERVER2 servers.

Do not shut down or revert any virtual machine, as these will be used in the next exercise.

Exercise 14: Configuring IPv6 Addressing

IPv6 addressing scheme provides more unique addresses and is more secure than traditional IPv4 addressing scheme. An IPv6 address comprises of eight blocks and each block can contain 16 (bit) hexadecimal digits. You can enable communication between IPv4 and IPv6 nodes using the various techniques, such as Teredo, ISATAP, and 6to4 tunneling.

In this exercise, you will learn how to configure IPv6 addresses on Window-based systems.

Make sure that the DC1, ROUTER, and SERVER2 virtual machines are running before start this exercise.

Task 1: Disabling IPv6 Address on DC1
1. Switch and Sign in to **SERVER2** with the Administrator account.
2. On the taskbar, click the **Windows PowerShell** icon.
3. At the **Windows PowerShell** prompt, type **ping 10.0.0.100**, and then press **Enter**.
4. Verify that you are able communicate with the DC1 (10.0.0.100) server, as shown in the following figure.

5. Switch and Sign in to **DC1** with the MCSALAB\Administrator account.
6. On the **Server Manager** console, in the left pane, click **Local Server**.
7. In the **Properties** pane, click the **10.0.0.100, IPv6 enabled** link, as shown in the following figure.

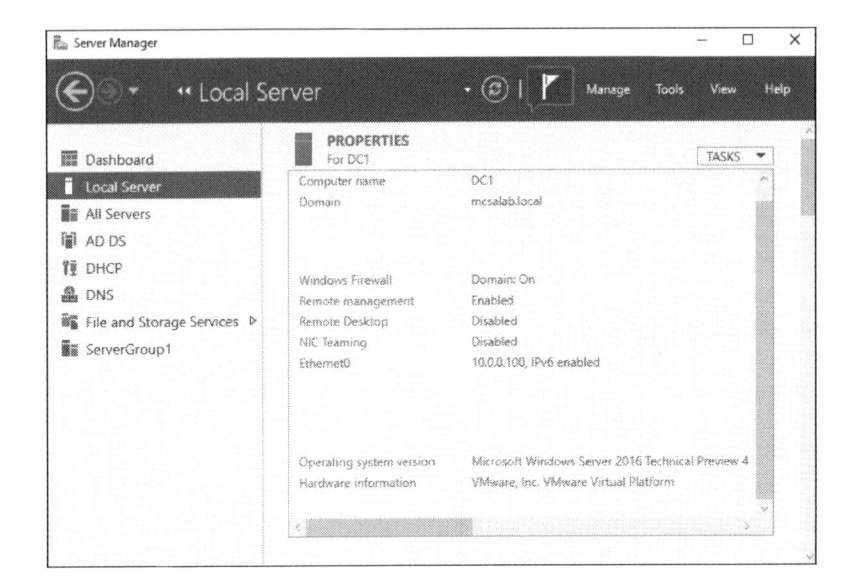

8. On the **Network Connections** window, select and right-click your network adapter, and then select **Properties**, as shown in the following figure.

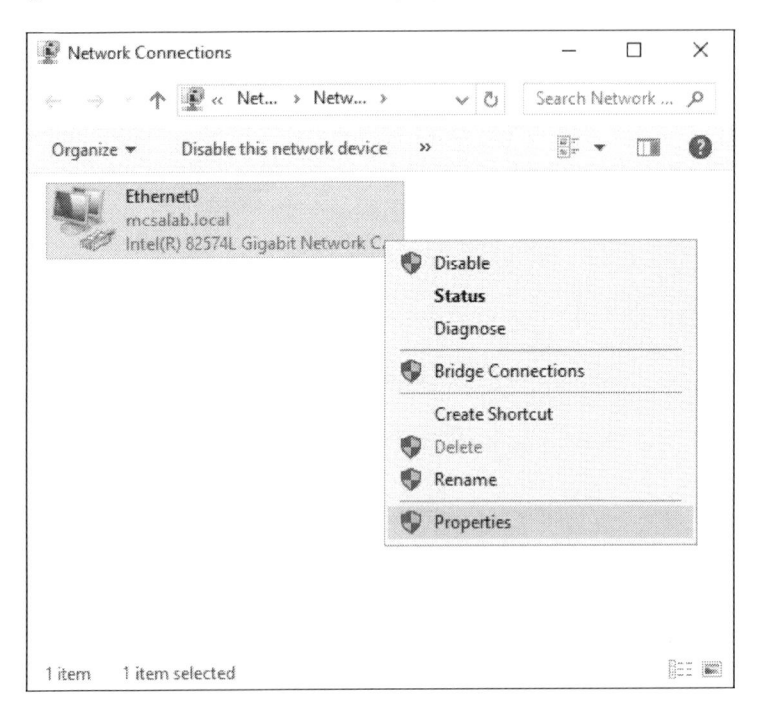

9. On the network adapter's properties dialog box, clear the **Internet Protocol Version 6 (TCP/IPv6)** check box, as shown in the following figure, and then click **OK**.

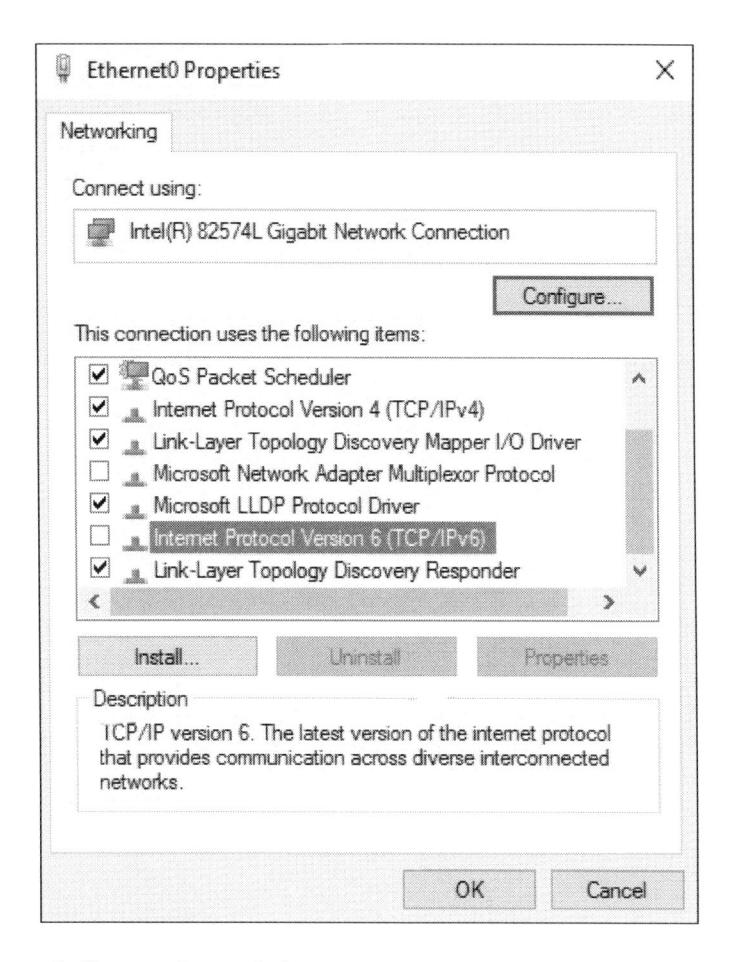

10. Close the **Network Connections** window.
11. On the **Server Manager** console, verify that your network adapter lists only **10.0.0.100**, as shown in the following figure. You may need to refresh the **Server Manager** console. Notice that DC1 is now an IPv4-only host.

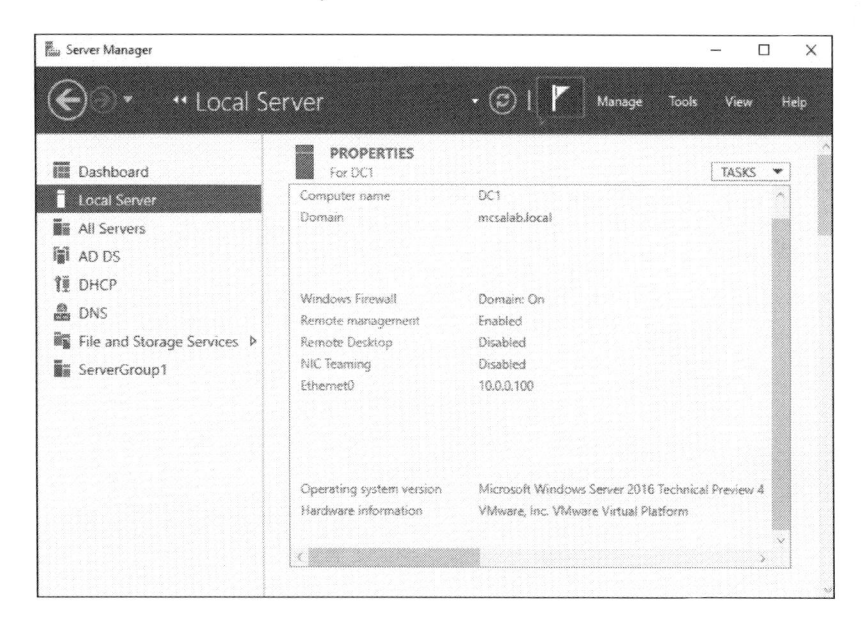

Task 2: Disabling IPv4 Address on SERVER2

1. Switch and Sign in to **SERVER2** with the Administrator account.
2. On the **Server Manager** console, in the left pane, click **Local Server**.
3. In the **Properties** pane, click the **192.168.0.2, IPv6 enabled** link.
4. On the **Network Connections** window, select and right-click active network adapter, and then select **Properties**.
5. On the network adapter's properties dialog box, clear the **Internet Protocol Version 4 (TCP/IPv4)** check box, as shown in the following figure, and then click **OK**.

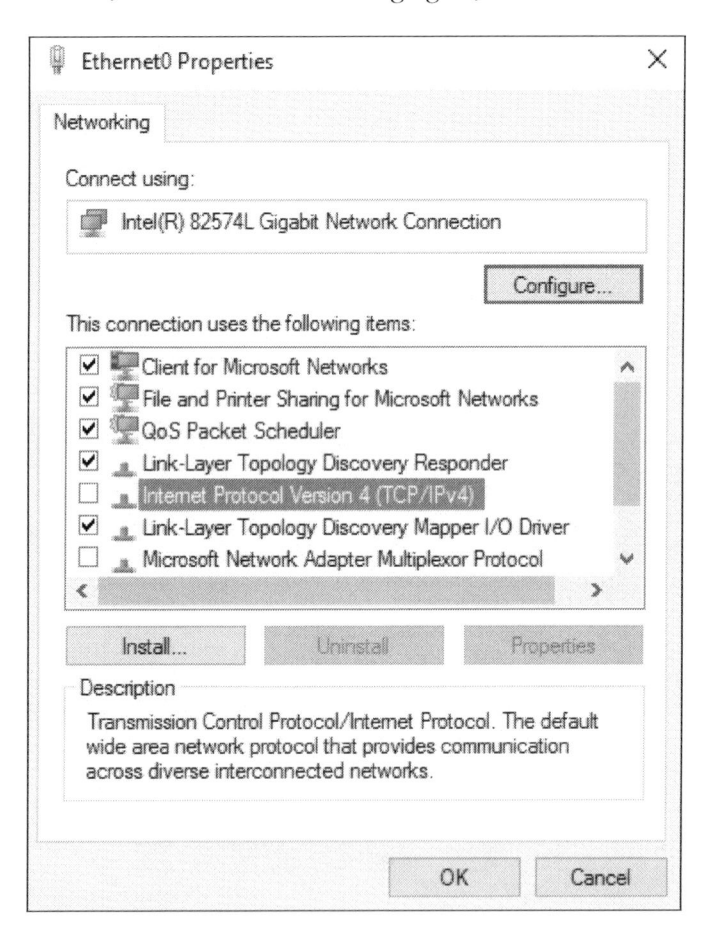

6. Close the **Network Connections** window.
7. On the **Server Manager** console, verify that network adapter now lists only IPv6 enabled, as shown in the following figure. You may need to refresh the **Server Manager console**. Notice that **SERVER2** is now an IPv6-only host.

Task 3: Configuring an IPv6 Network on ROUTER

1. Switch and Sign in to **ROUTER** with the Administrator account.
2. On the taskbar, click the **Windows PowerShell** icon.
3. To configure a network address that will be used on the IPv6 network, at the **Windows PowerShell** prompt, type the following cmdlet, and then press **Enter**, as shown in the following figure.
   ```
   New-NetRoute -InterfaceAlias "Ethernet1" -DestinationPrefix
   2001:AABB:0:1::/64 -Publish Yes
   ```

Note: Ethernet1 is the name of the network adapter connected to the external subnet.

4. To allow clients to obtain the IPv6 network address automatically from **ROUTER**, at the **Windows PowerShell** prompt, type the following cmdlet, and then press **Enter**, as shown in the following figure.
   ```
   Set-NetIPInterface -InterfaceAlias "Ethernet1" -
   AddressFamily IPv6 -Advertising Enabled
   ```

5. At the **Windows PowerShell** prompt, type **ipconfig.exe**, and then press **Enter**. Notice that **Ethernet1** now has an IPv6 address on the **2001:AABB:0:1::/64** network, as shown in the

following figure. This address will be used for communication on the IPv6-only network.

```
PS C:\> ipconfig.exe
Windows IP Configuration

Ethernet adapter Ethernet1:

   Connection-specific DNS Suffix  . :
   IPv6 Address. . . . . . . . . . . : 2000:aabb:0:1:c49f:2e71:b9c9:3fd3
   Link-local IPv6 Address . . . . . : fe80::c49f:2e71:b9c9:3fd3%2
   IPv4 Address. . . . . . . . . . . : 192.168.0.1
   Subnet Mask . . . . . . . . . . . : 255.255.255.0
   Default Gateway . . . . . . . . . :

Ethernet adapter Ethernet0:

   Connection-specific DNS Suffix  . :
   Link-local IPv6 Address . . . . . : fe80::ccf3:82f9:d491:820%6
   IPv4 Address. . . . . . . . . . . : 10.0.0.1
   Subnet Mask . . . . . . . . . . . : 255.0.0.0
   Default Gateway . . . . . . . . . :

Tunnel adapter isatap.{987A90B1-CB3B-4140-985E-9349EF31246F}:

   Media State . . . . . . . . . . . : Media disconnected
   Connection-specific DNS Suffix  . :

Tunnel adapter isatap.{E1B8BD09-43CB-48F3-BC92-0228C9A9493C}:

   Media State . . . . . . . . . . . : Media disconnected
   Connection-specific DNS Suffix  . :
PS C:\>
```

Task 4: Verifying IPv6 Address on SERVER2

1. Switch and Sign in to **SERVER2** with the Administrator account.
2. On the taskbar, click the **Windows PowerShell** icon.
3. At the **Windows PowerShell** prompt, type **ipconfig.exe**, and then press **Enter**. Notice that your network adapter now has an IPv6 address on the on the **2001:AABB:0:1::/64** network, as shown in the following figure.

```
PS C:\Users\Administrator> ipconfig.exe
Windows IP Configuration

Ethernet adapter Ethernet0:

   Connection-specific DNS Suffix  . :
   IPv6 Address. . . . . . . . . . . : 2000:aabb:0:1:bc99:223:3a82:8f06
   Link-local IPv6 Address . . . . . : fe80::bc99:223:3a82:8f06%3
   Default Gateway . . . . . . . . . :
PS C:\Users\Administrator>
```

4. The network address was obtained from the router through the stateless configuration.

Results: After completing the exercise, you will have configured an IPv6-based network.

Shut down and revert the DC1, SERVER2 and ROUTER virtual machines to prepare for the next exercise.

Exercise 15: Installing and Configuring Remote Access VPN Server

In this lab exercise, we will explain how to setup Remote Access VPN using Windows Server 2016 server and Windows 10 client. To complete this lab exercise, first of all understand the lab topology we are going to use.

We will use the following virtual machines to complete this lab exercise:

1. ROUTER1
   - Hosts the Remote Access Server role.
   - Connected to CLIENT1 using 10.0.0.1/8 IP address.
   - Connected to the SERVER2 using 192.168.1.1/24 IP address.
   - Acts as VPN Server.
2. SERVER2:
   - Acts as an internal (private) client and is connected to ROUTER1 using 192.168.1.2/24 IP address and 192.168.1.1 as the Default gateway.
3. CLIENT1:
   - Acts as a remote (Public) client and is connected to ROUTER1 using 10.0.0.101/8 IP address and 10.0.0.1 as the Default gateway.

Ensure that you have reverted all the virtual machines in the previous state. Start the SERVER2, ROUTER1, and CLIENT1 virtual machines. Ensure that the Windows Firewall is turned off on all the virtual machines to avoid any network connectivity issues.

It is recommended that all of your participating systems of this lab exercise should belong either to the same Domain network or should belong to a Workgroup network. Mixed type of network may create some issues to complete the lab exercise. Here, all systems are based on the Workgroup-based network.

Task 1: Installing Remote Access Service Role

On **ROUTER1**, perform the following steps to install the **Routing and Remote Access Server** role.

1. Launch the **Add Roles and Features Wizard**. Click **Next** and accept the default selections until the **Select server roles** page displays.
2. Select the **Remote Access** server role and click **Next**.

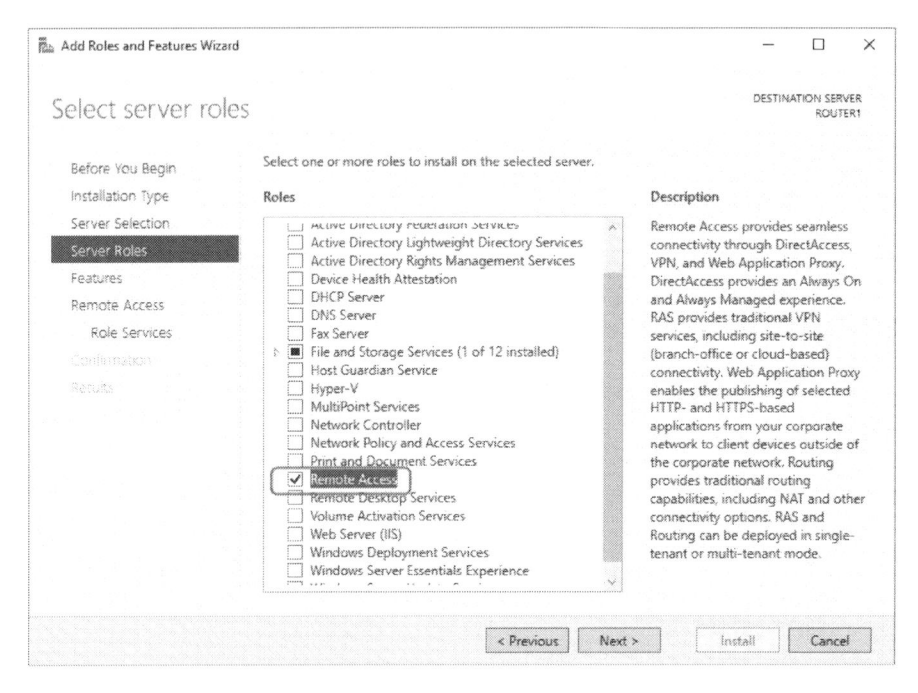

3. Click **Next** until the **Select role services** page displays.
4. Select the **DirectAccess and VPN (RAS)** and **Routing** role services and then click **Next**.

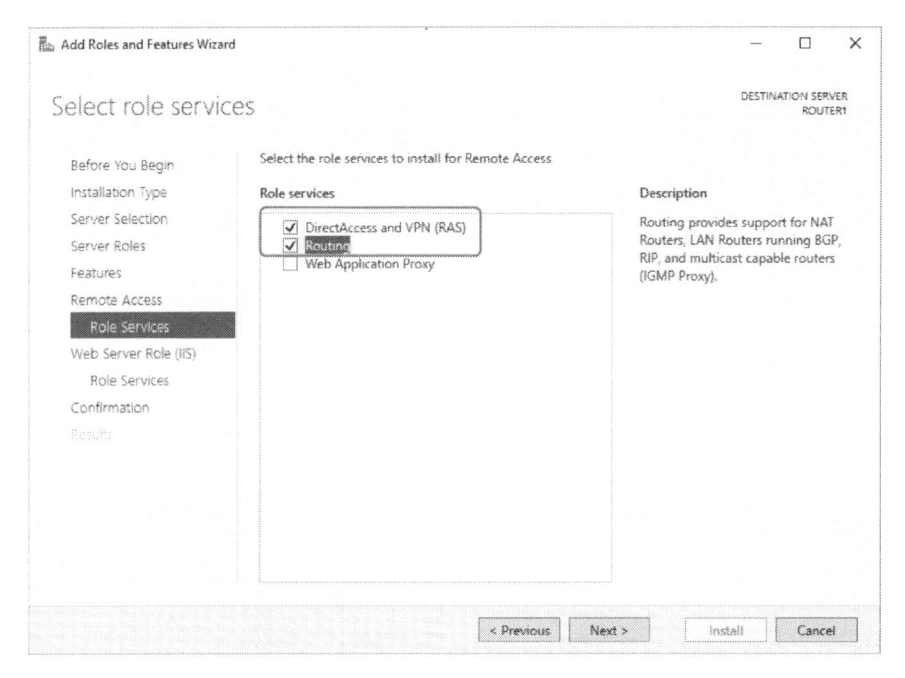

5. On the rest of the pages, accept the default selections by clicking **Next**.
6. Wait until the installation process completes.

Task 2: Configure VPN

In order to configure VPN on Windows Server 2016, you need to perform the following steps on ROUTER1.

1. Open the **Routing and Remote Access** console by using the **Server Manager** console.

2. Click **Tools** and selecting the **Routing and Remote Access** option.

3. Select and right-click **Server name (ROUTER1)** and then select **Configure and Enable Routing and Remote Access**.

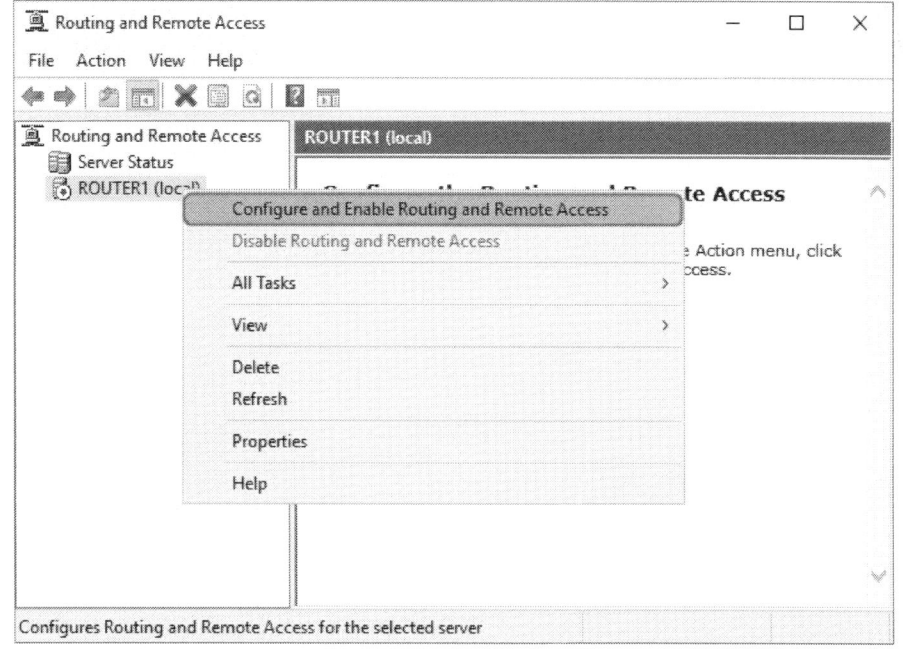

4. On the **Welcome** page, click **Next**.

5. On the **Configuration** page, ensure that the **Remote access (dial-up or VPN)** option is selected and then click **Next**.

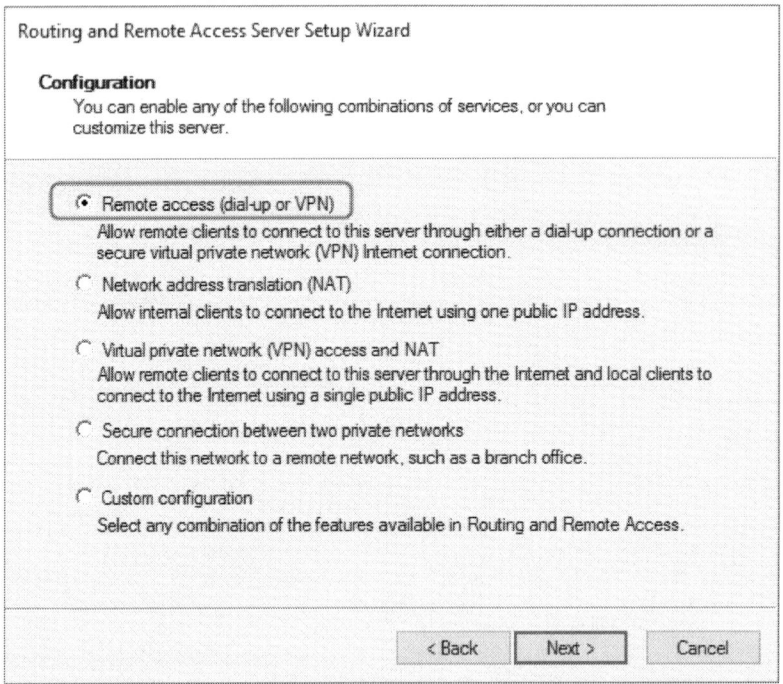

6. On the **Remote Access** page, select the **VPN** option and then click **Next**.

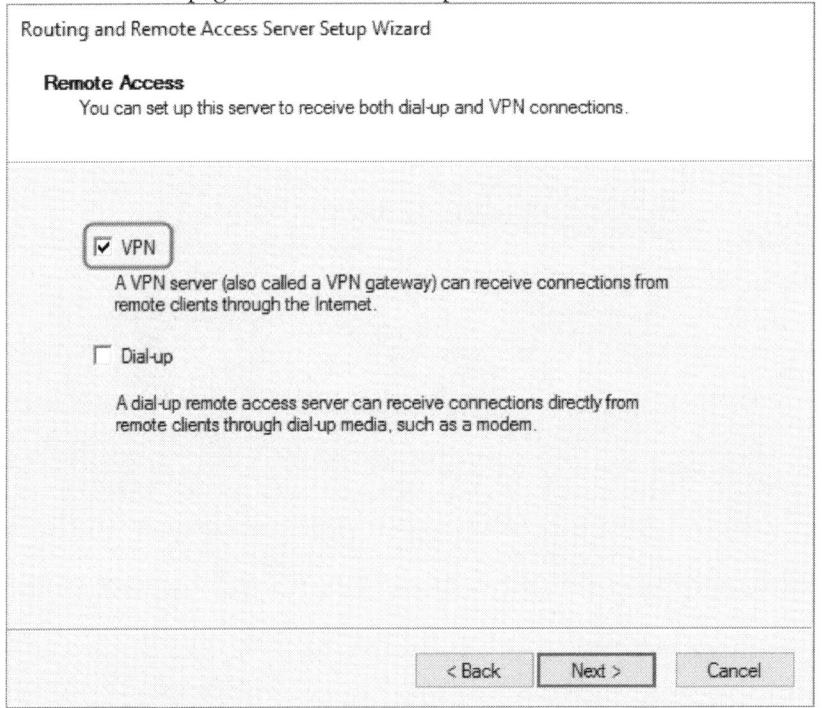

7. On the **VPN Connections** page, select the network adapter that is connected to the **Public** network (Internet) and proceed to next. In this case, **Ethernet0** network adapter is connected to the Public system **CLIENT1**.

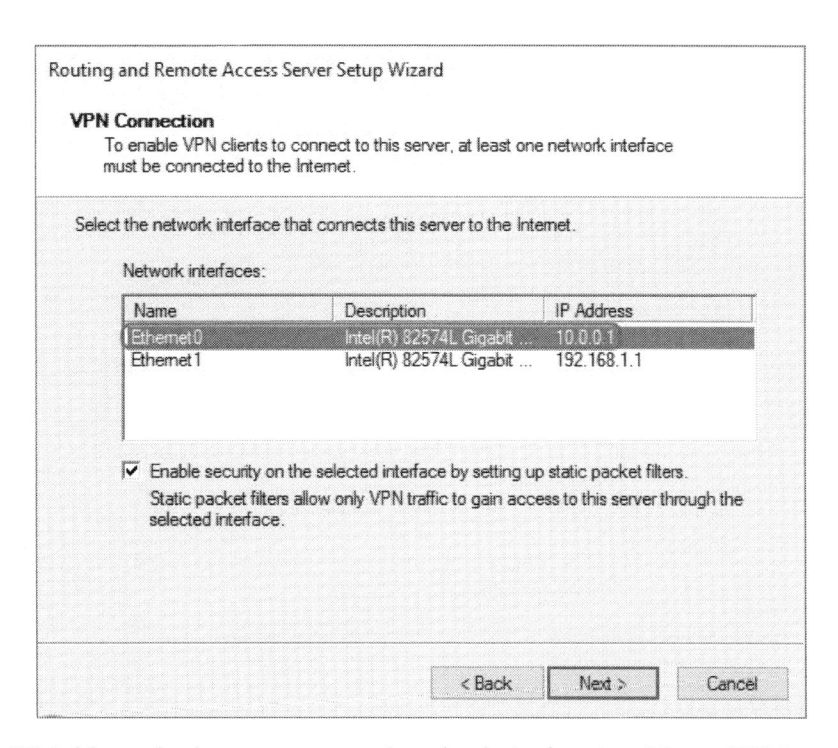

8. On the **IP Address Assignment** page, select the desired option. If your VPN server is also configured as active DHCP server, select **Automatically**. If you want to assign IP addresses to the VPN clients using the VPN server, select the **From a specified range of addresses** option and then click **Next**.

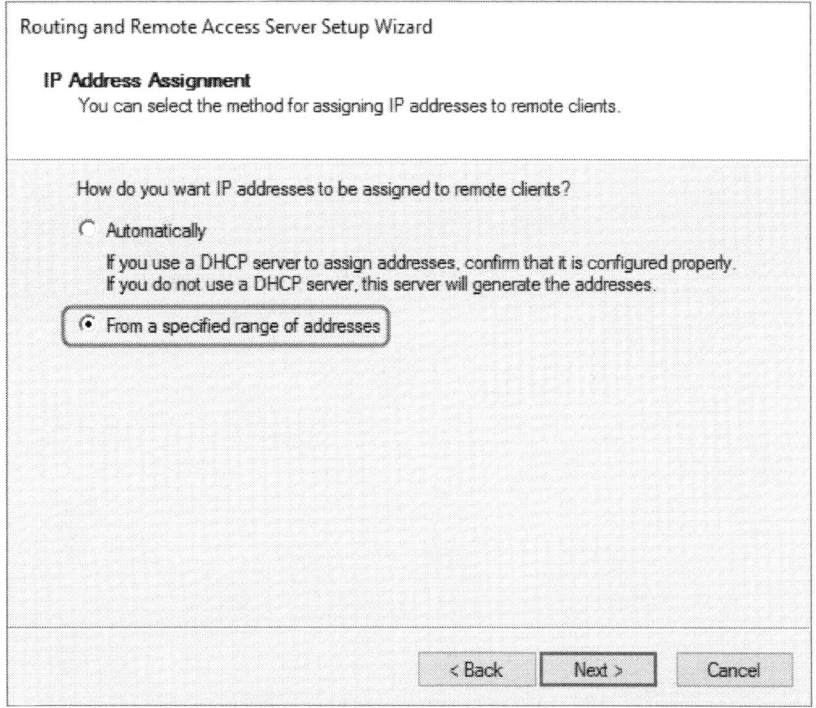

9. On the **IP Address Assignment** page, click **New** and set the **Start** and **End** IP ranges depending on the number of VPN clients your network contains. For example, set the **10.0.0.240** to **10.0.0.245** range for the testing purpose and proceed to **Next**.

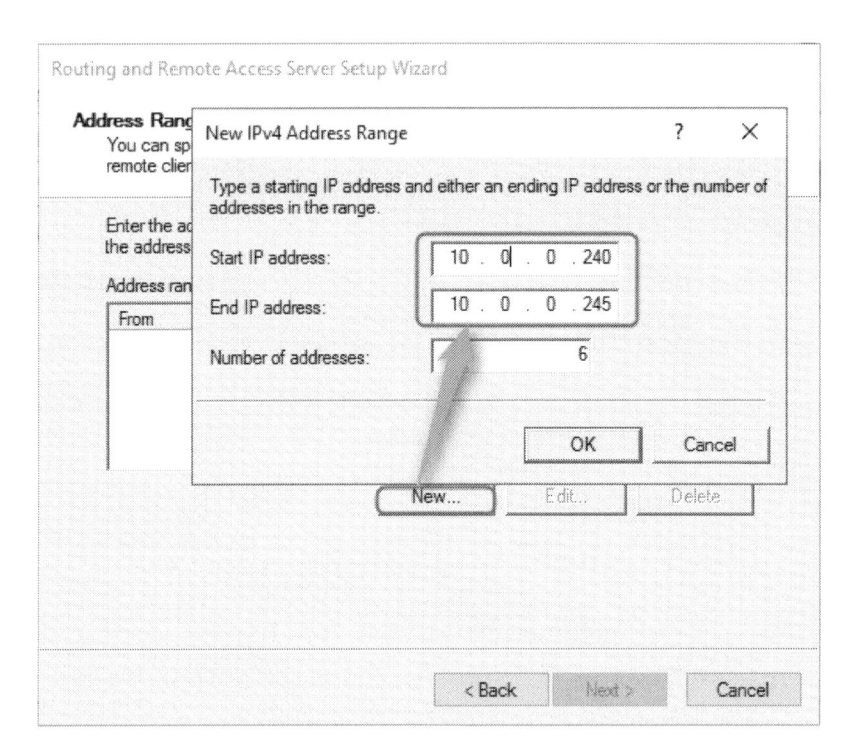

10. On the **Manage Multiple Remote Access Servers** page, select the **No** option as we will configure RADIUS server in a separate article. Click **Next** and finish the wizard.

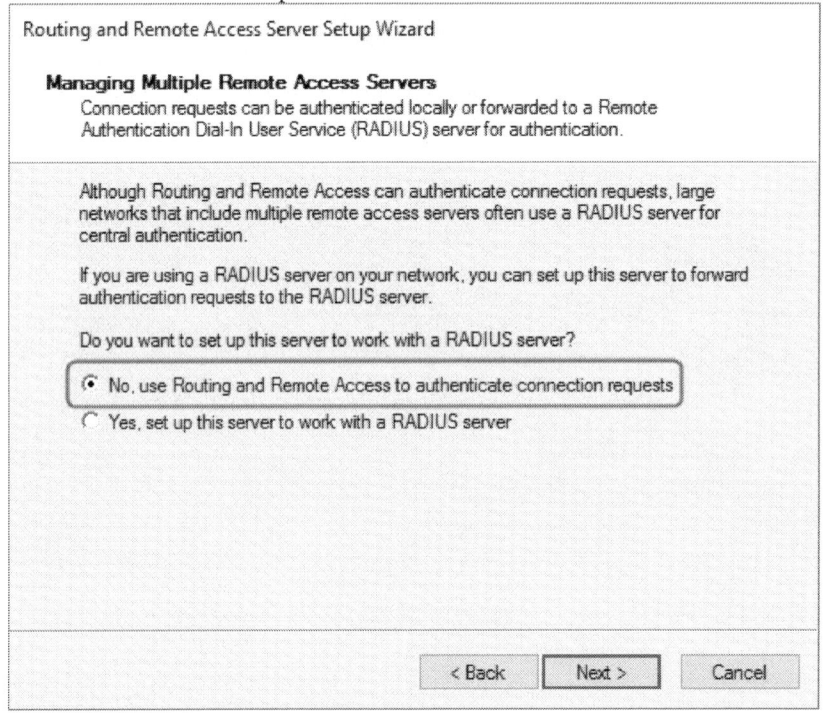

11. On the **Service** message box click **OK** to start the **Remote Access** service.

Task 3: Creating VPN User

In order to connect and authenticate to VPN server, VPN clients require a user credentials. For this, you need to perform the following steps.

1. Execute the following command on VPN server **ROUTER1** to create a test user named as **VPNUser1**. It will be used by remote users to connect to VPN server.

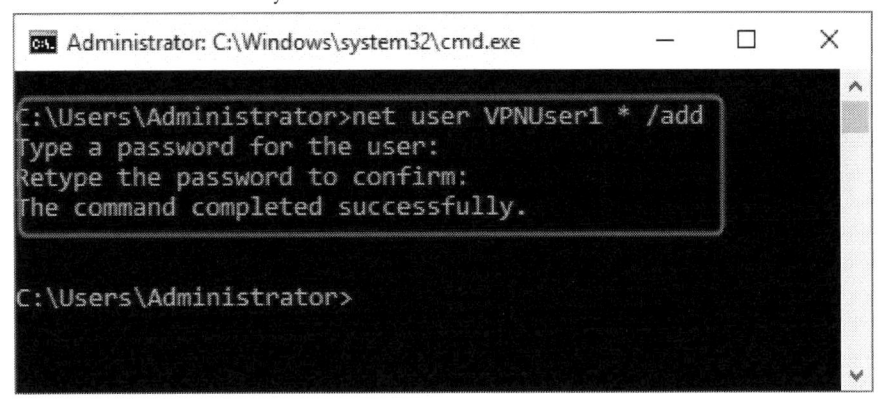

```
C:\Users\Administrator>net user VPNUser1 * /add
Type a password for the user:
Retype the password to confirm:
The command completed successfully.

C:\Users\Administrator>
```

2. Now, type **lusrmgr.msc** in the **Run** dialog box and open the **Properties** of VPNUser1.
3. Select the **Dial-in** tab and then select the **Allow access** option for the selected user.

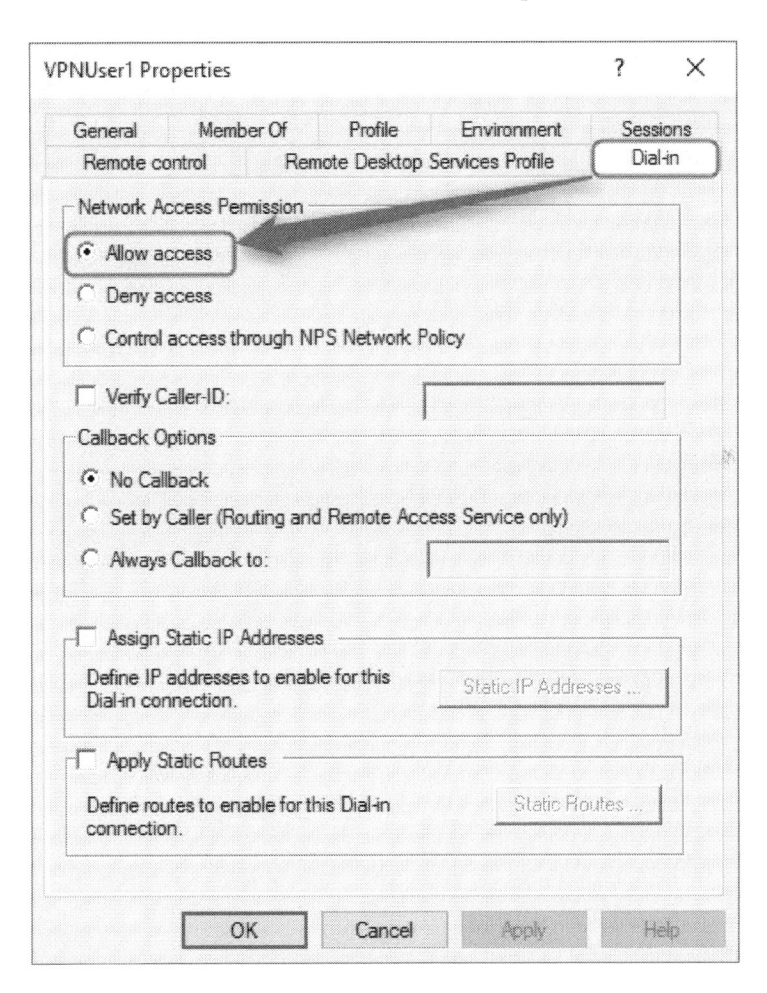

Task 4: Connecting VPN Client to VPN Server

Now, you have successfully configured VPN server. The next step is to test your VPN configuration. For this, you need to perform the following steps on VPN client that is CLIENT1.

149

1. Move on to **CLIENT1**, open the **Network and Sharing Center Wizard**, and select **Set up a new connection or network** to create a new VPN connection.

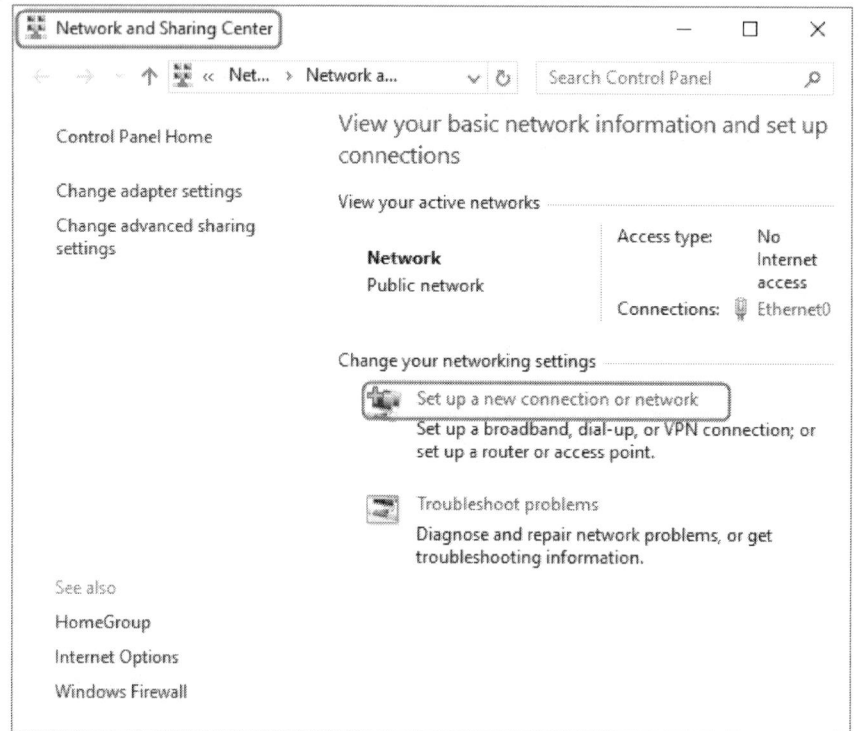

2. Select the **Connect to a workplace** option and then click **Next**.

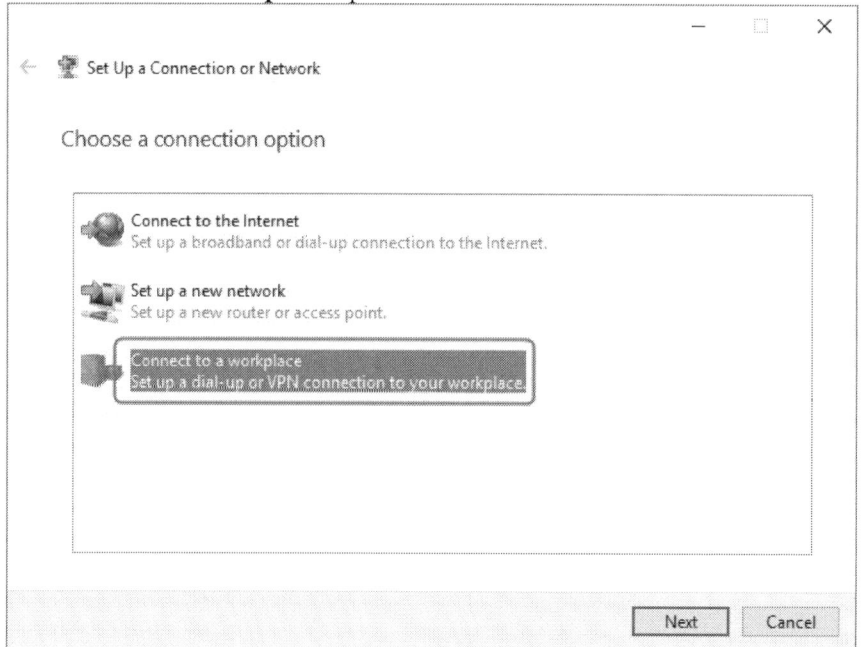

3. On the **How do you connect to VPN** page, select **Use my Internet Connection (VPN)** option and then click **Next**.

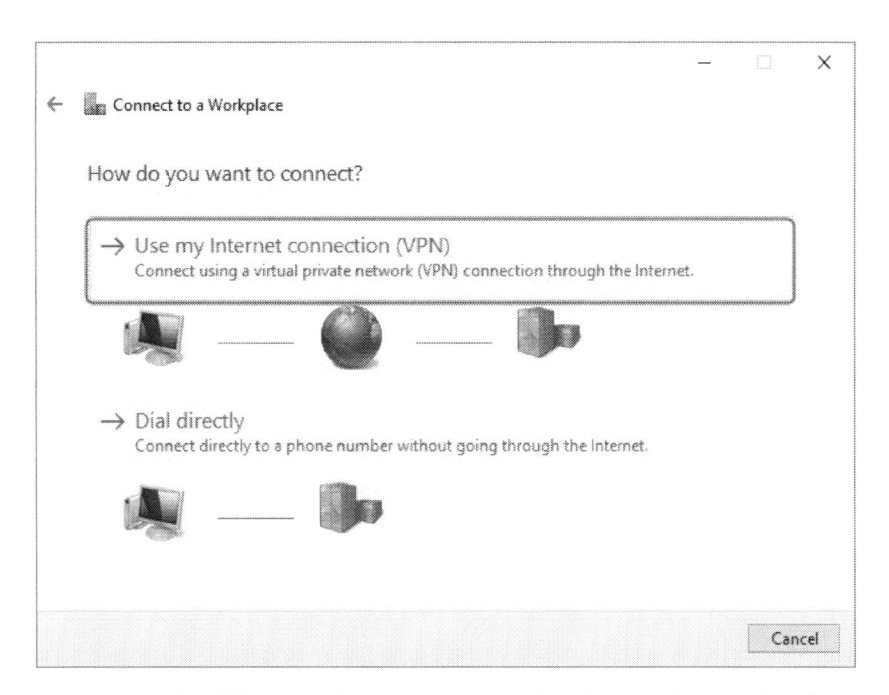

4. On the next page, select **I'll setup Internet connection later** and then click **Next**.

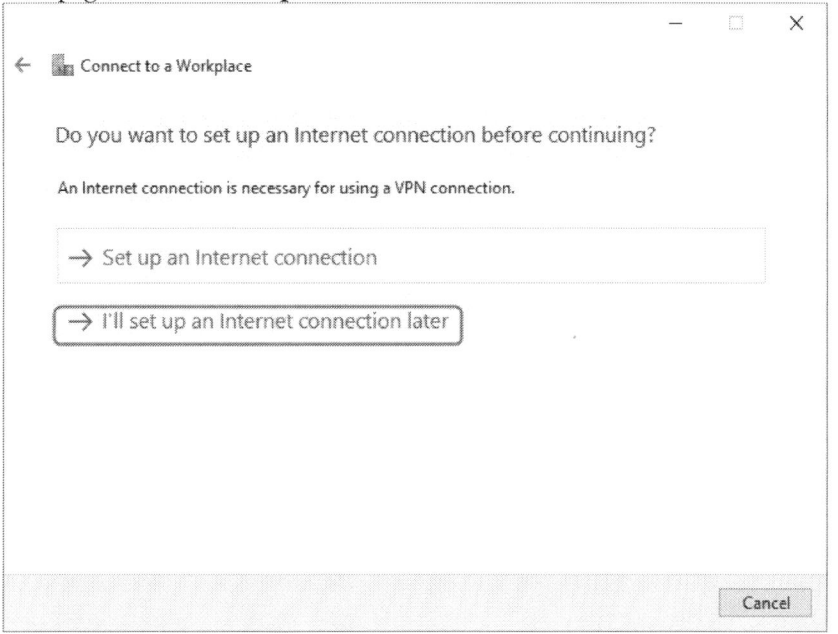

5. On the **Type the Internet address to connect to** page, type hostname (if the DNS server is already configured) or simply type the **Public IP address of VPN server**, in this case **10.0.0.1** and then click **Create**.

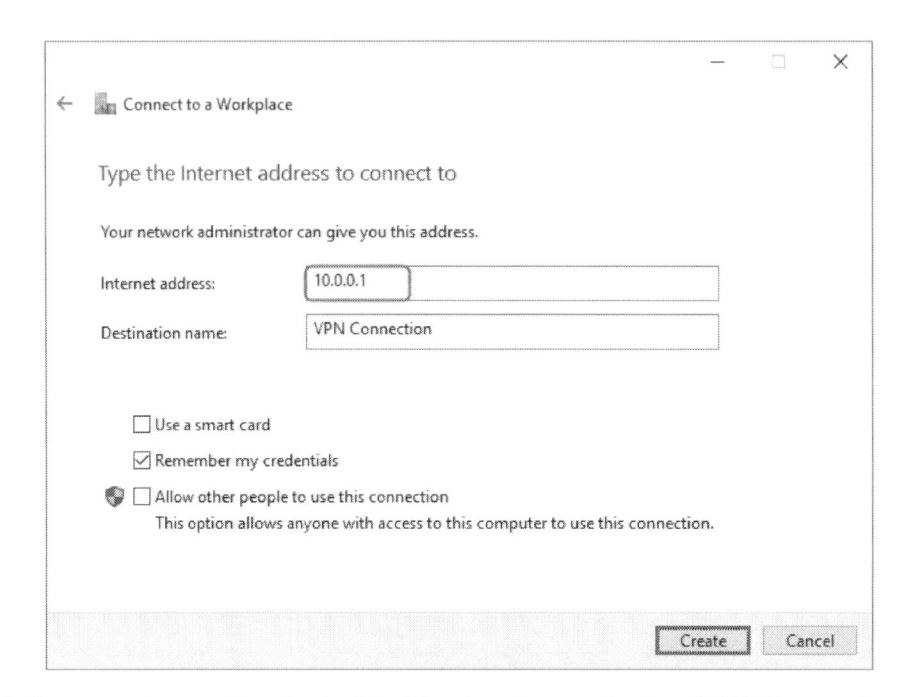

6. Click the network status icon in the **Notification Area** and select **VPN Connection**.

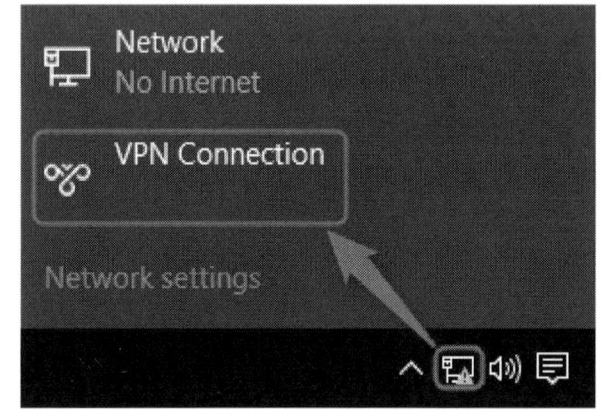

7. On the **NETWORK & INTERNET** screen, select **VPN Connection** and then click **Connect**.

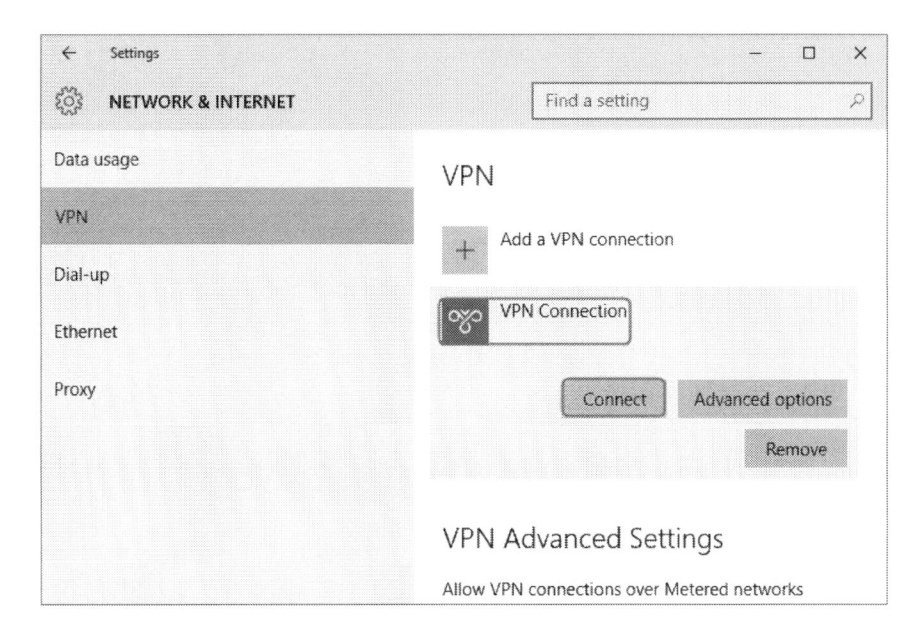

8. On the **Sign In** screen, type the username and password of VPN server that you have previously created or use an existing one and click **OK** to connect.

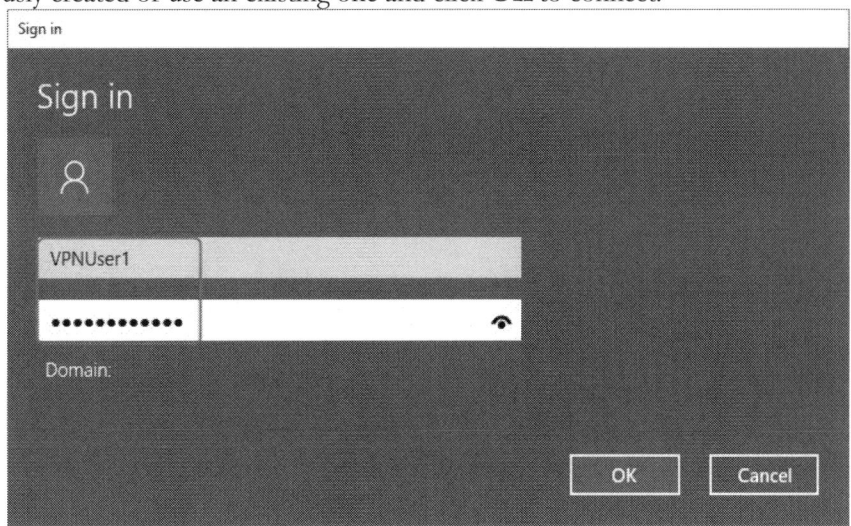

9. Ensure that you are successfully connected to VPN server.

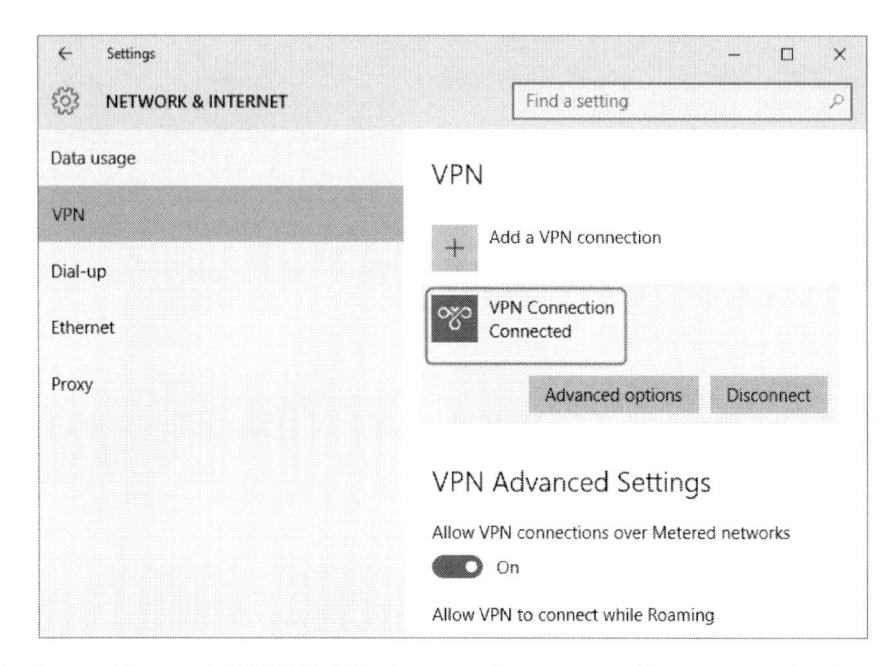

10. To further verify, type **\\192.168.1.2\c$** to test that you are able to access the data of the Private client that is **SERVER2**.

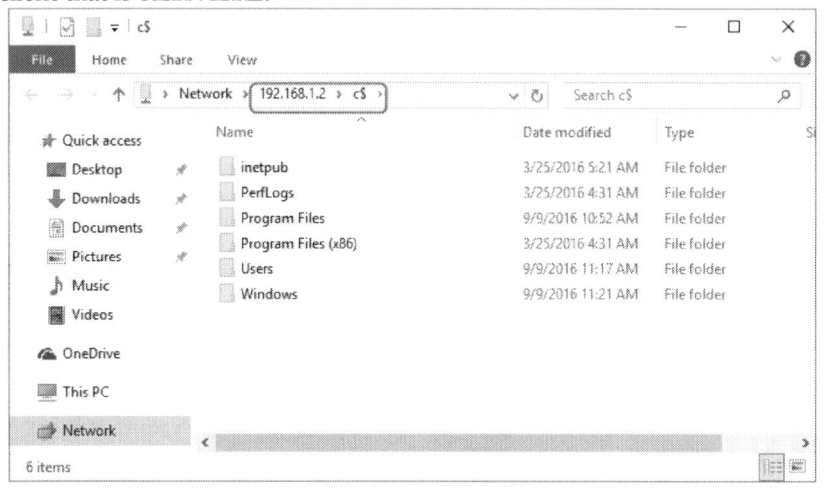

Note: Use the Administrator user if you are unable to access SERVER2 using VPNUser1.

Results: Now, you have successfully configured VPN. Now revert the SERVER2, CLIENT1, and ROUTER1 virtual machines to prepare for the next lab exercise.

Exercise 16: Installing and Configuring Disk Storage

Disks are used to store the system data as well as personnel data. There are various storage technologies, such as SATA, IDE, iSCSI, and Fibre Channel that can be used to store the data. In a virtualized environment, you can add additional virtual hard disks to the virtual machines, and then you can create additional volumes on these disks.

In this exercise, you will learn how to manage disks on a Window server. Further, you will learn how to shrink and extend volumes.

Task 1: Adding New Virtual Disks to DC1

1. Make sure that the **DC1** virtual machine is powered off.
2. On your host machine, on the **VMware** console, select and right-click the **DC1** virtual machine, and then select **Settings**.
3. On the virtual machine's setting dialog box, ensure that **Hard Disk** is selected, and then click **Next**.

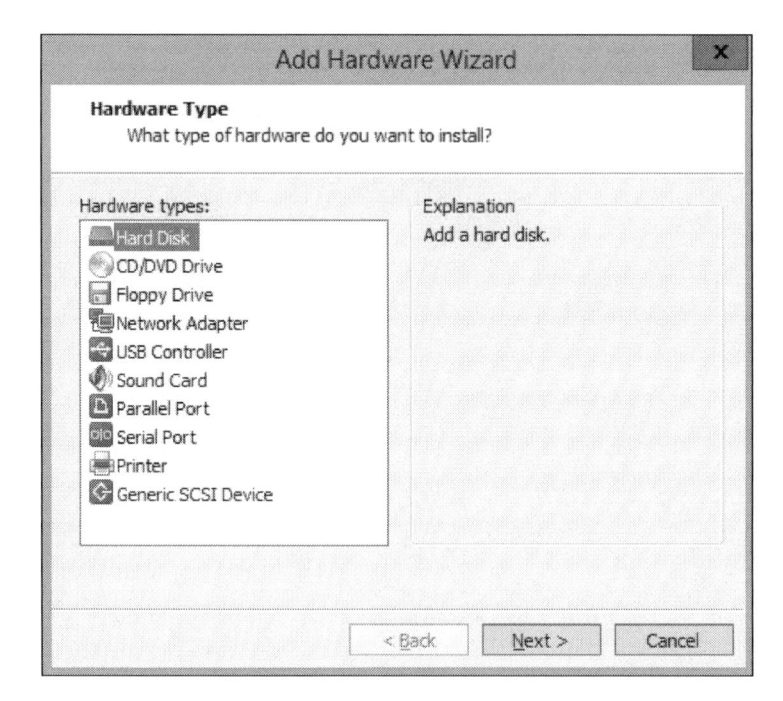

4. On the **Select a Disk Type** page, accept the default selection (**SCSI**), and then click **Next**.
5. On the **Select a Disk** page, make sure that the **Create a new virtual disk** radio button is selected, and then click **Next**.

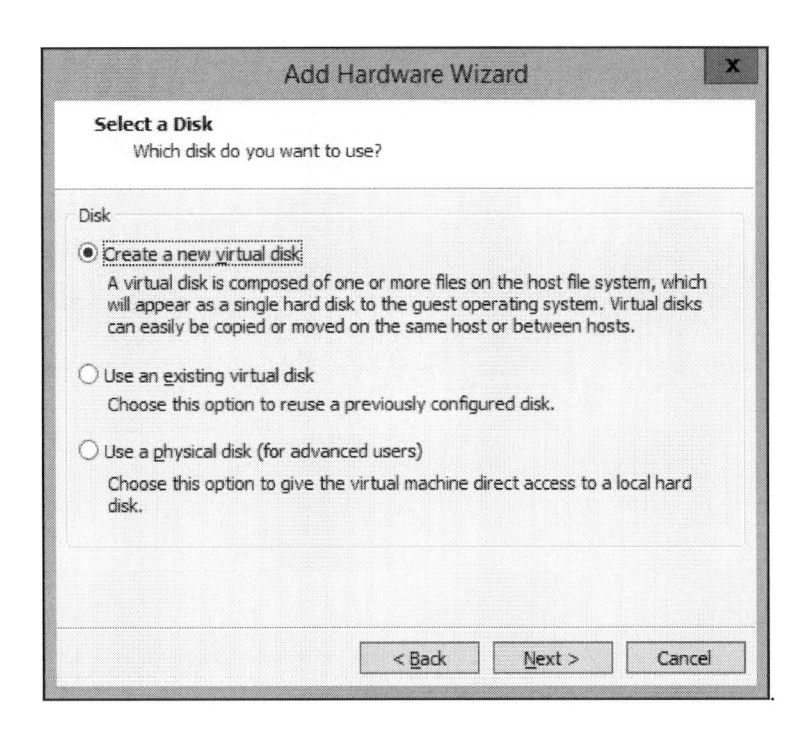

6. On the **Specify Disk Capacity** page, set the disk size as **10** GB, select the **Store virtual disk as a single file** radio button, and then click **Next**.

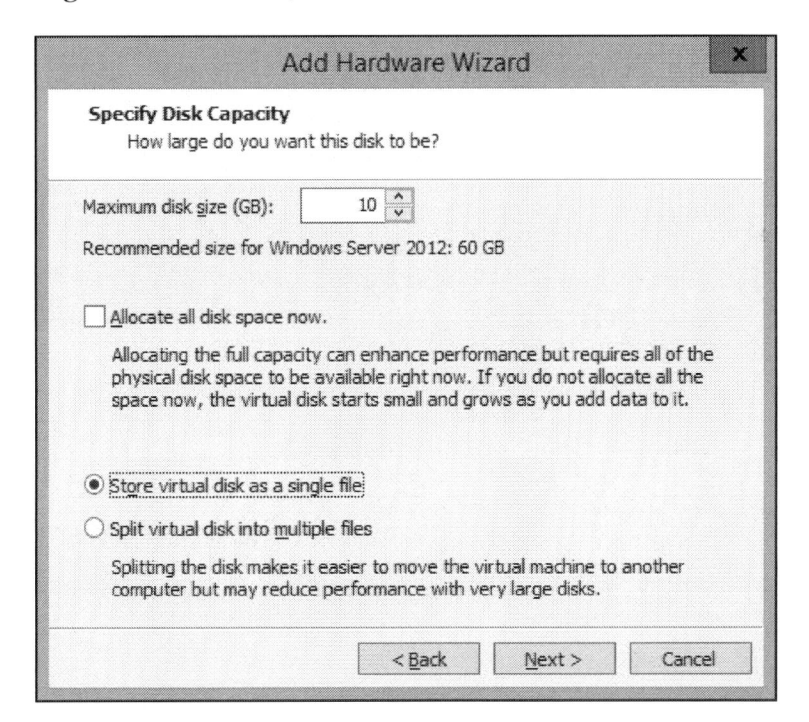

7. On the **Specify Disk File** page, accept the default file name, and then click **Finish**.

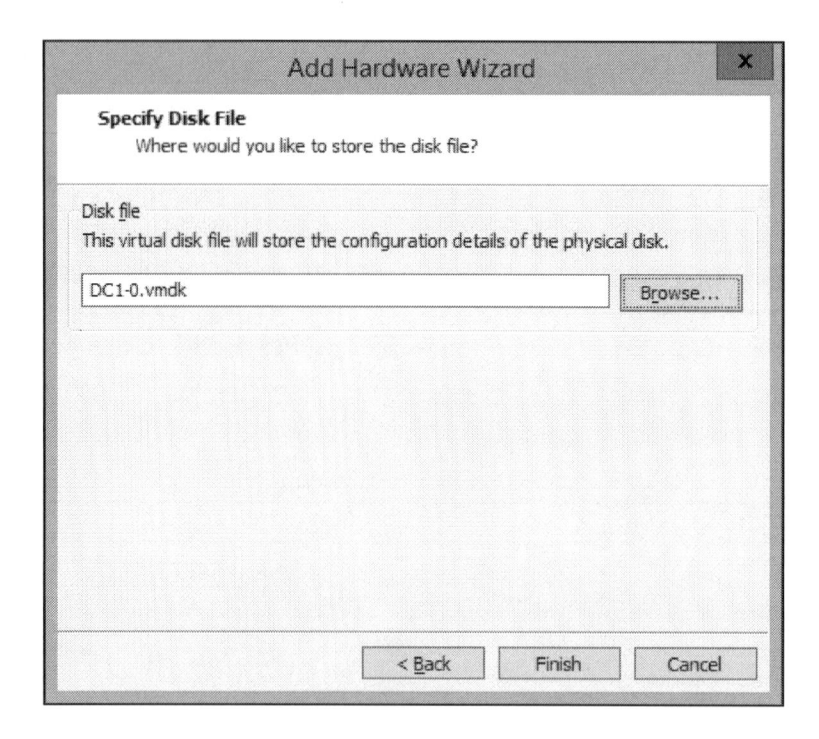

8. Add one more new virtual disk with following settings:
    - Store virtual disk as a single file.
    - Size: **10** GB.
    - File name : **Accept default**.

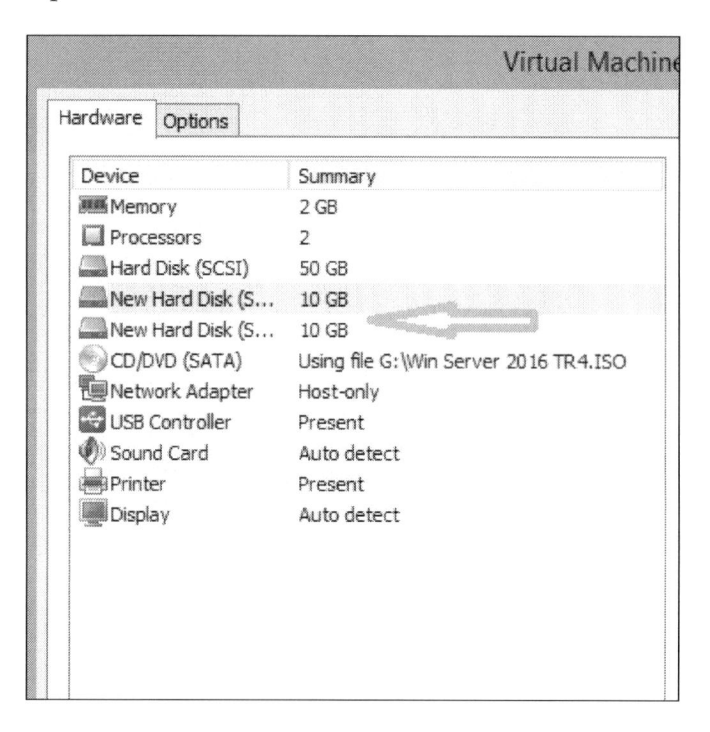

Task 2: Initializing the Added Disks
1. Power on the **DC1** virtual machine.
2. Open the **Server Manager** console.

3. On the **Server Manager** console, click **Tools**, and then click **Computer Management**.
4. On the **Computer Management** console, under the **Storage** node, select **Disk Management**.
5. In the **Disks** pane, select and right-click **Disk 1**, and then select **Online**, as shown in the following figure.

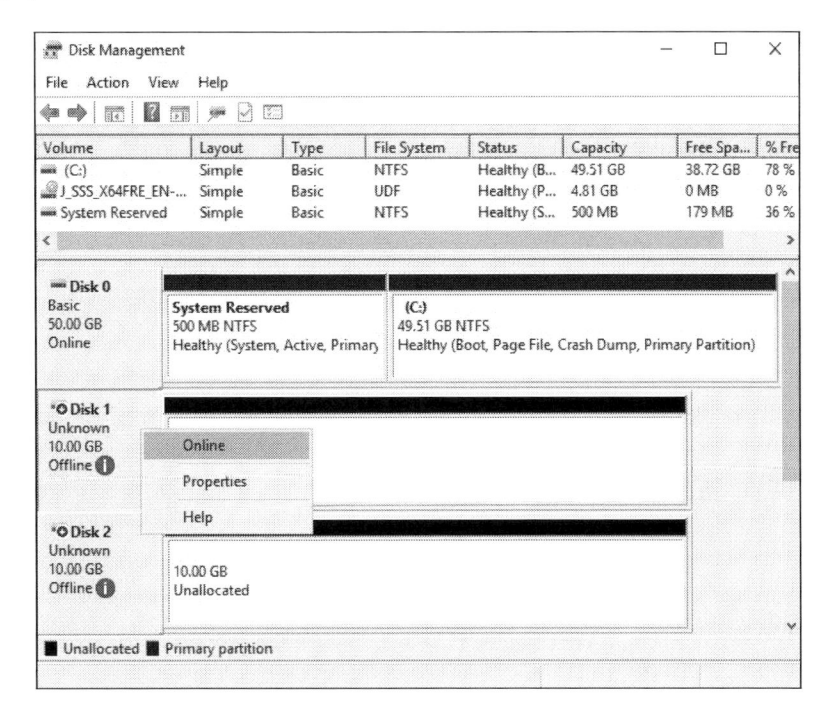

6. Select and right-click **Disk 1**, and then select **Initialize Disk**.
7. On the **Initialize Disk** dialog box, make sure that the **Disk 1** check box is selected, select the **GPT (GUID Partition Table)** radio button, and then click **OK**.

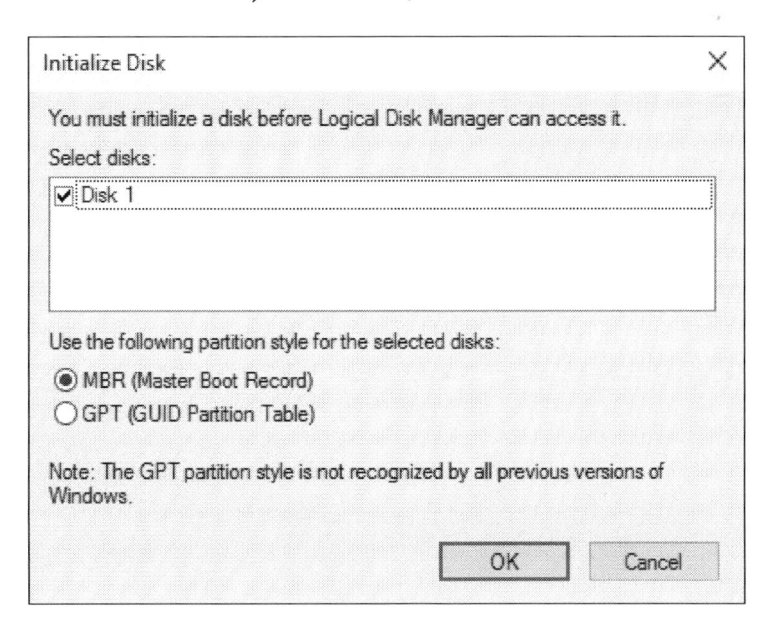

Note: The GPT partition table supports more features than the traditional MBR partition table.

8. In the **Disks** pane, select and right-click **Disk 2**, and then select **Online**.
9. Select and right-click **Disk 2**, and then select **Initialize Disk**.
10. On the **Initialize Disk** dialog box, make sure that the **Disk 2** check box is selected, select the **GPT (GUID Partition Table)** radio button, and then click **OK**.

Task 3: Creating and Formatting Simple Volumes

1. On the **Computer Management** console, under the **Disk Management** node, select and right-click the **Unallocated** space of **Disk 1**, and then select **New Simple Volume**, as shown in the following figure.

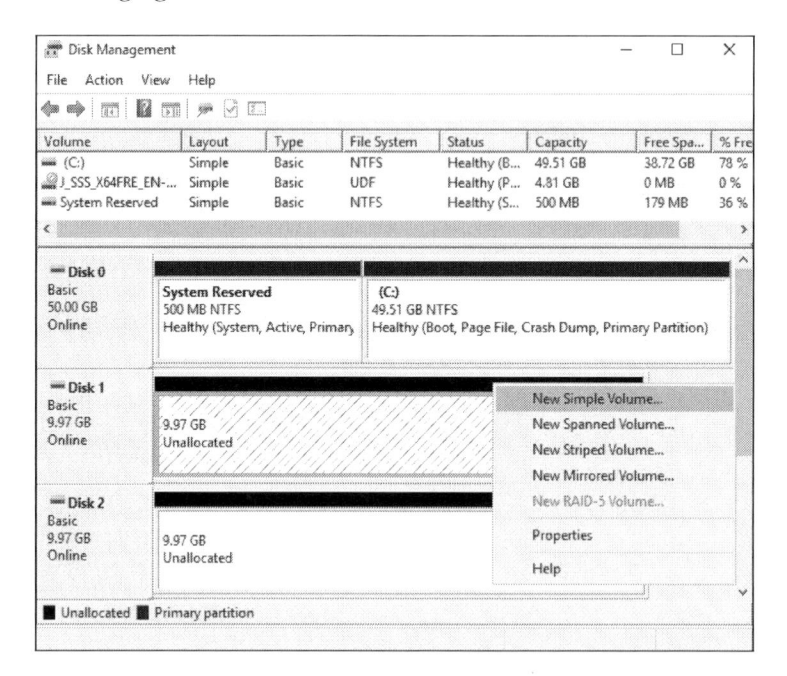

2. On the **Welcome to the New Simple Volume Wizard** page, click **Next**.
3. On the **Specify Volume Size** page, in the **Simple volume size MB** value box, type **5000**, as shown in the following figure, and then click **Next**.

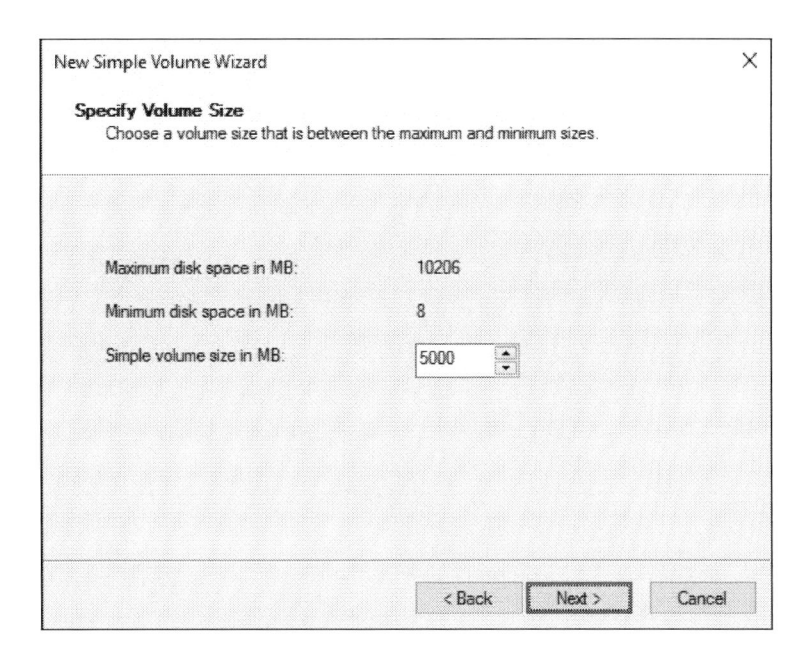

4. On the **Assign Drive Letter or Path** page, make sure that the **Assign the following drive letter** check box is selected, accept the default drive letter, as shown in the following figure, and then click **Next**.

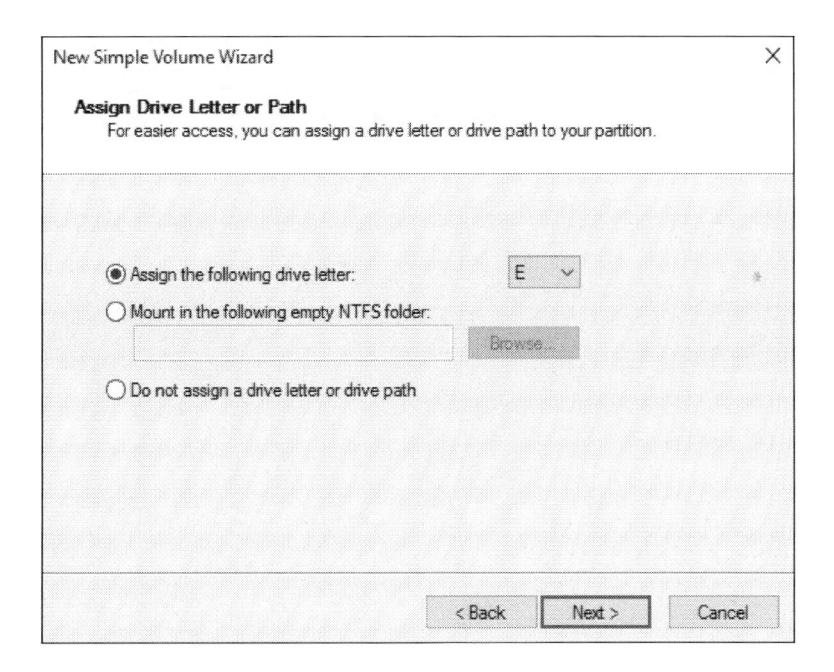

5. On the **Format Partition** page, in the **Volume label** text box, type **Volume1**, as shown in the following figure, and then click **Next**.

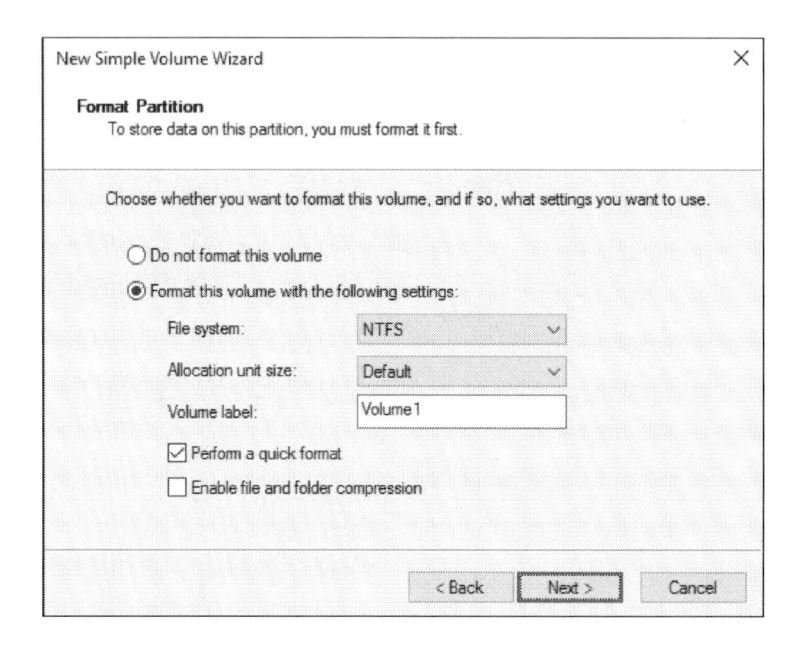

6. On the **Completing the New Simple Volume Wizard** page, click **Finish**.
7. On the **Disk Management** console, select and right-click the **Unallocated** space of **Disk 2**, and then select **New Simple Volume**.
8. On the **Welcome to the New Simple Volume Wizard** page, click **Next**.
9. On the **Specify Volume Size** page, in the **Simple volume size in MB** value box, type **5000**, and then click **Next**.
10. On the **Assign Drive Letter or Path** page, make sure that the **Assign the following drive letter** check box is selected, accept the default drive letter, and then click **Next**.
11. On the **Format Partition** page, in the **Volume label** text box, type **Volume2**, and then click **Next**.
12. On the **Completing the New Simple Volume Wizard** page, click **Finish**.
13. Leave the **Computer Management** console active.
14. Press the **Windows+E** keys to open the **Windows Explorer** window.
15. Verify that the **Volume1** and **Volume2** are created, as shown in the following figure.

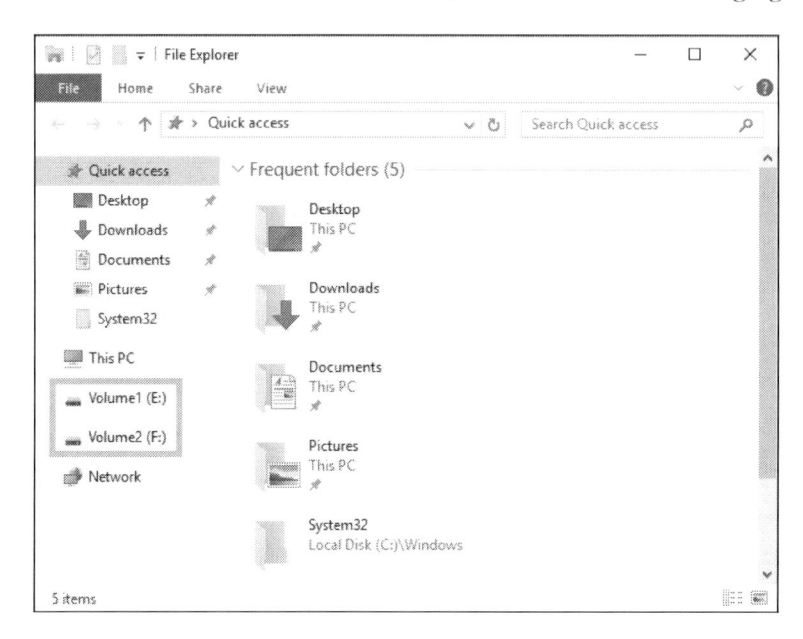

16. Close the **Windows Explorer** window.

Task 4: Shrinking the Volumes

1. On **DC1**, switch to the **Computer Management** console.
2. On the **Computer Management** console, under the **Disk Management** node, select and right-click **Volume1**, and then select **Shrink Volume**, as shown in the following figure.

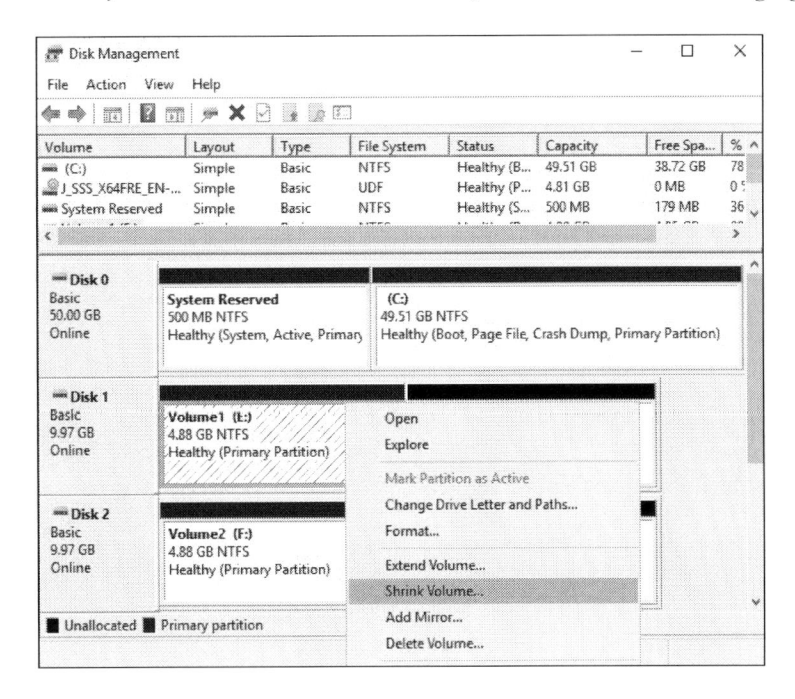

3. On the shrink dialog box, in the **Enter the amount of space to shrink in MB** value box, type **1000**, as shown in the following figure, and then click **Shrink**.

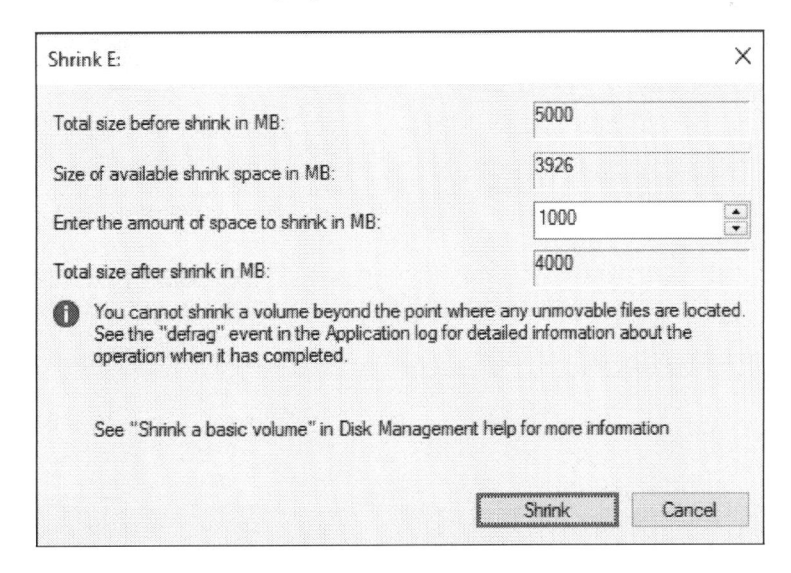

Task 5: Extending the Volumes

1. On the **Computer Management** console, under the **Disk Management** node, select and right-click **Volume2**, and then select **Extend Volume**.
2. On the **Welcome to the Extended Volume Wizard** page, click **Next**.

3. On the **Select Disks** page, in the **Select the amount of space in MB** value box, type **3000**, as shown in the following figure, and then click **Next**.

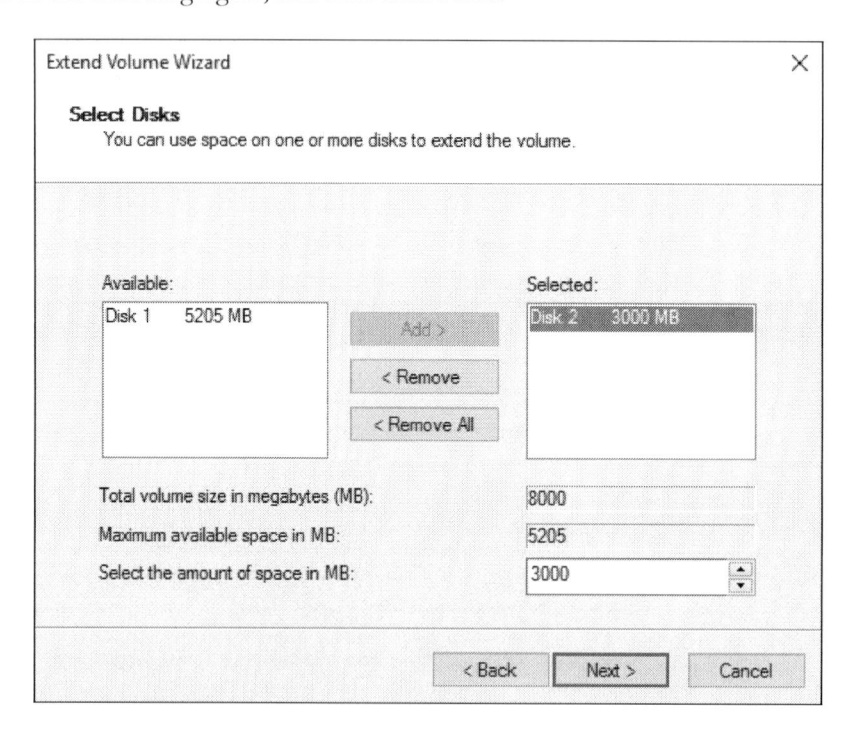

4. On the **Completing the Extended Volume Wizard** page, click **Finish**.
5. Press the **Windows+E** keys to open the **Windows Explorer** window, verify that the volumes' sizes are reflected.

Results: After completing this exercise, you should have initialized new disks, and created and formatted simple volumes. In addition, you should also have shrink and extended the volumes.

Do not shut down or revert the DC1 virtual machine, as it will be used in the next exercise.

Exercise 17: Configuring a Redundant Storage Space

Redundant Array of Inexpensive Disk (RAID) is a storage technology that allows you to combine multiple hard disks in a single large hard disk. It also provides redundancy and fault tolerance in the event of a disk failure. RAID can be configured either as a hardware RAID (which requires a hardware controller device) or as a software RAID (which does not require any specific hardware device). RAID can be divided in to various RAID levels and each RAID level supports various features and limitations.

In this exercise, you will learn how to create storage pools, how to create and test a mirrored volume.

Ensure that the DC1 virtual machine is running and you have not reverted it in the previous state.

Task 1: Creating a Storage Pool

1. Sign in to **DC1** and open the **Server Manager** console.
2. Open the **Disk Management** console, select and right-click **Disk 1**, and then delete the created volume. Also delete the volume for **Disk 2**, as shown in the following figure.

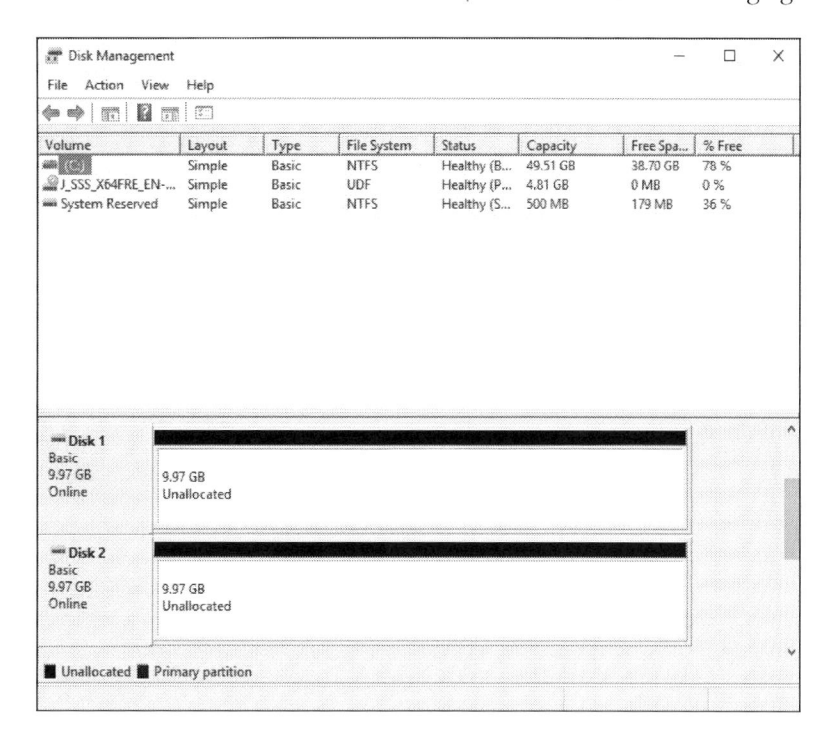

3. On the **Server Manager** console, in the left pane, select **File and Storage Services**, and then select **Storage Pools.**
4. In the **STORAGE POOLS** pane, click **TASKS**, and then click **Rescan Storage**.
5. Click again **TASKS**, and then click **New Storage Pool**, as shown in the following figure.

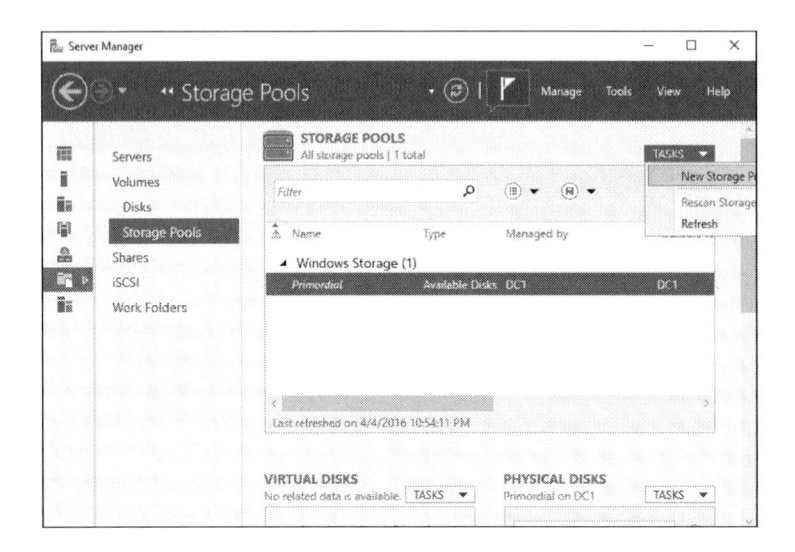

6. On the **Before you begin** page, click **Next**.
7. On the **Specify a storage pool name and subsystem** page, in the **Name** text box, type **MyStoragePool1**, as shown in the following figure, and then click **Next**.

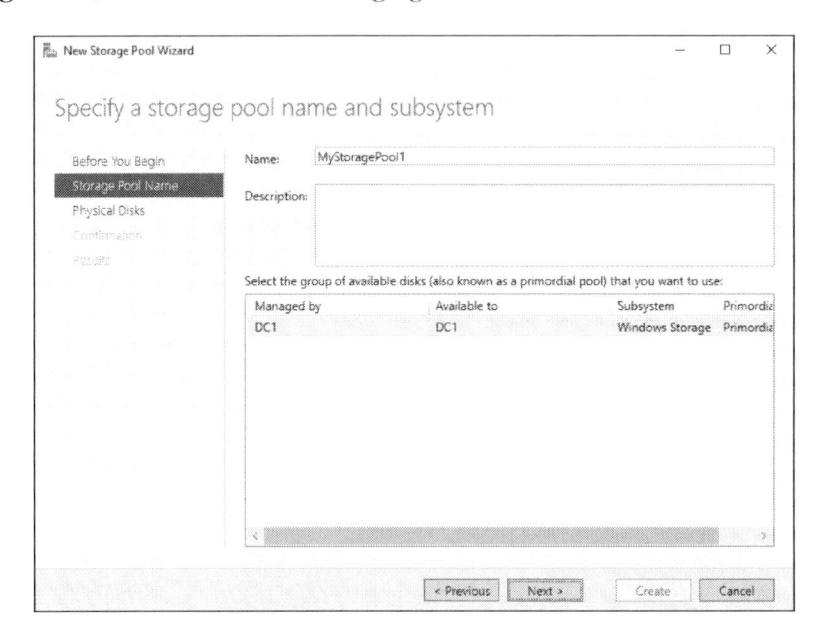

8. On the **Select physical disks for the storage pool** page, select the all available disk check boxes, as shown in the following figure, and then click **Next**.

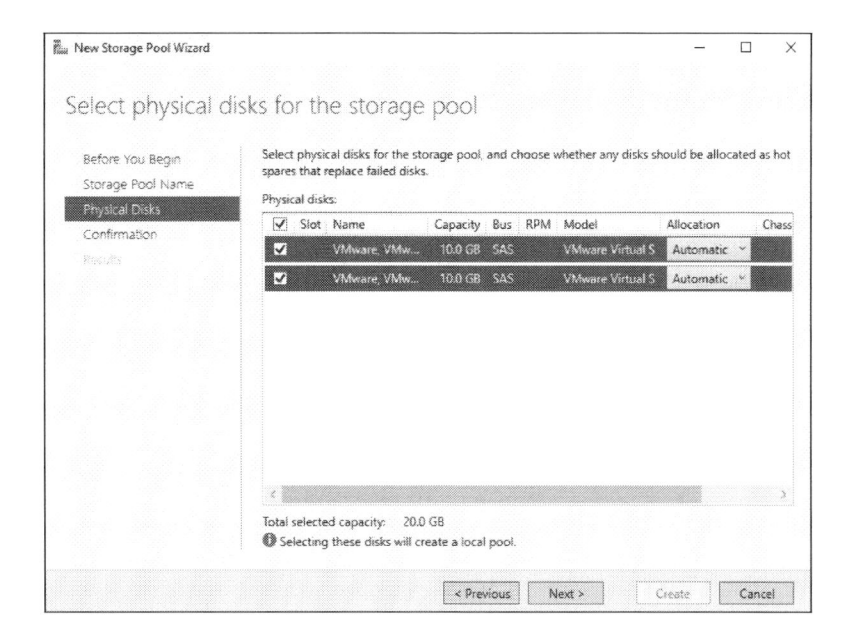

9. On the **Confirm selections** page, click **Create**.
10. On the **View results** page, click **Close**, once the task is competed.

Task 2: Creating a Mirrored Virtual Disk

1. On **DC1**, on the **Server Manager** console, in the **Storage Spaces** pane, select **MyStoragePool1**.
2. On the **VIRTUAL DISKS** pane, click **TASKS**, and then click **New Virtual Disk**, as shown in the following figure.

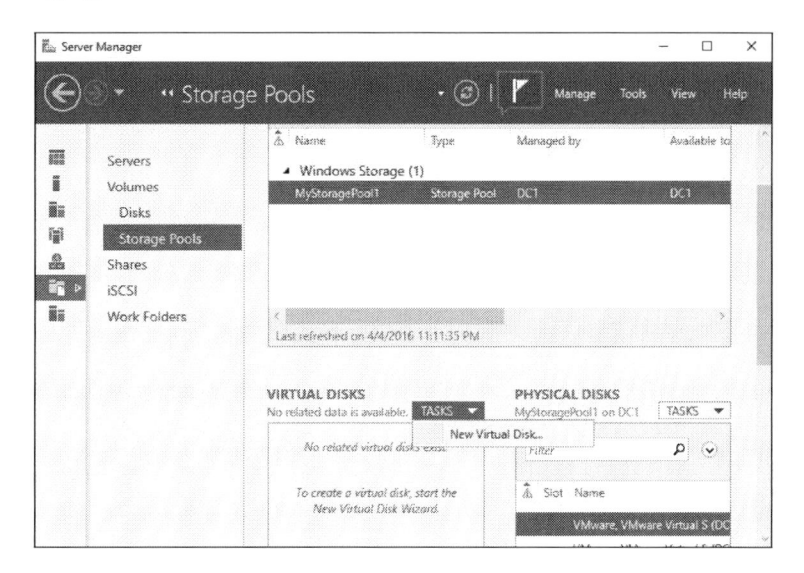

3. On the **Before you begin** page, click **Next**.
4. On the **Select the storage pool** page, make sure that **MyStoragePool1** is selected, and then click **Next**.
5. On the **Specify the virtual disk name** page, in the **Name** text box, type **Mirrored Disk1**, as shown in the following figure, and then click **Next**.

167

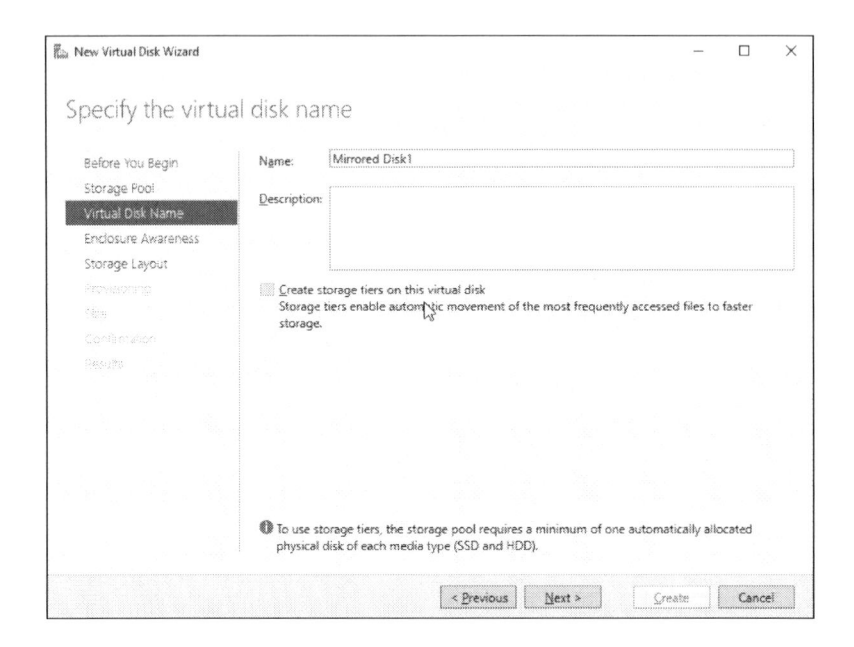

6. On the **Select the storage layout** page, in the **Layout** section, select **Mirror**, as shown in the following figure, and then click **Next**.

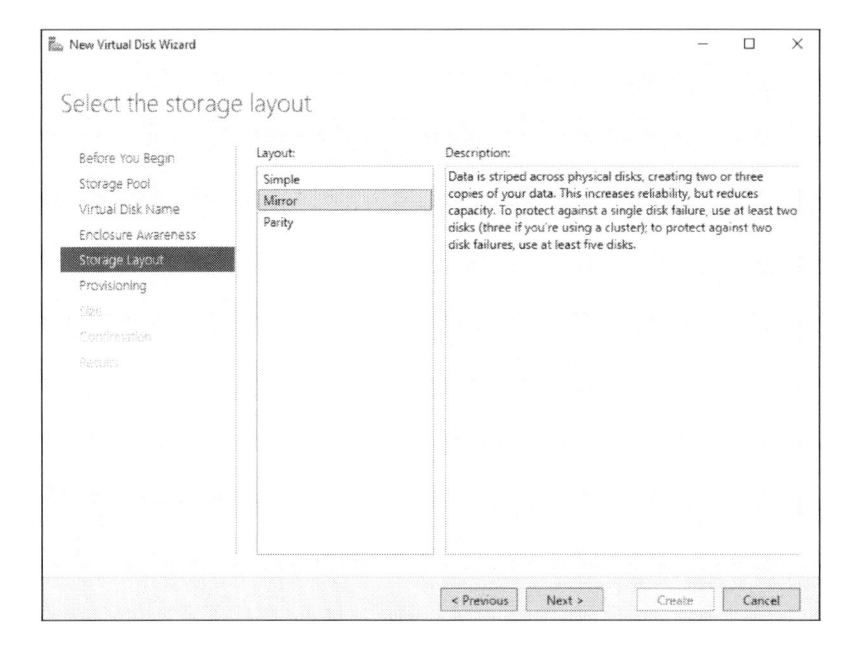

7. On the **Specify the provisioning type** page, select the **Thin** radio button, as shown in the following figure, and then click **Next**.

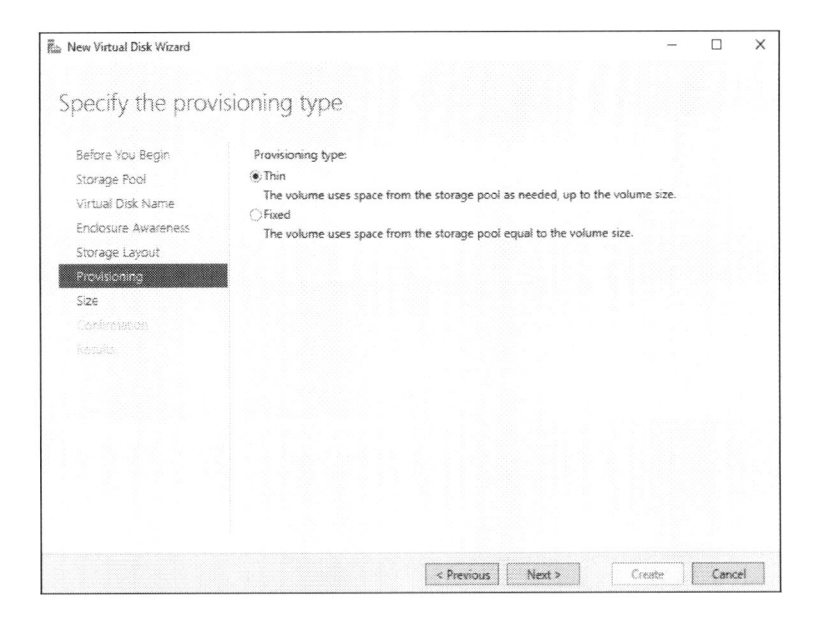

[Screenshot: New Virtual Disk Wizard — Specify the provisioning type, with Thin selected.]

8. On the **Specify the size of the virtual disk** page, in the **Virtual disk size** box, type **5**, as shown in the following figure, and then click **Next**.

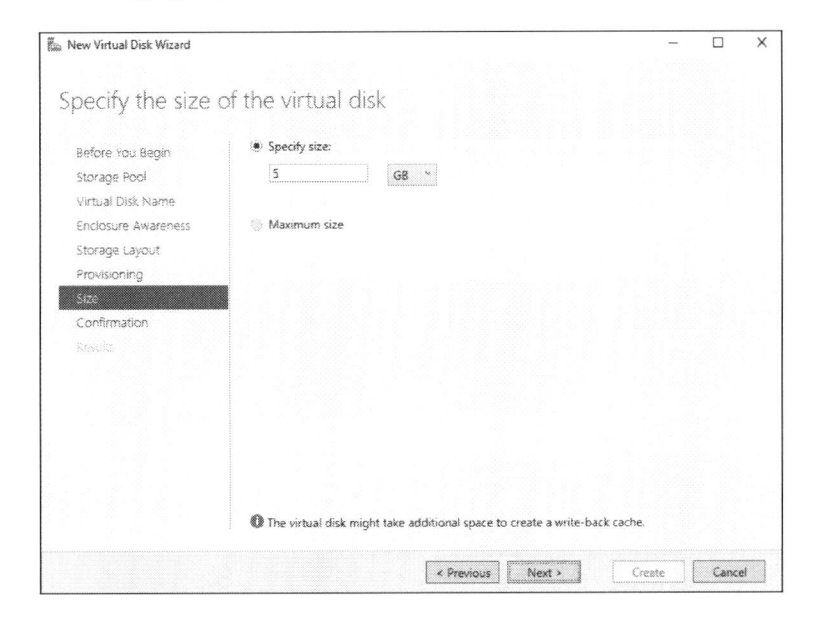

[Screenshot: New Virtual Disk Wizard — Specify the size of the virtual disk, with 5 GB entered.]

9. On the **Confirm selections** page, click **Create**.
10. On the **View results** page, wait until the task completes.
11. Make sure that the **Create a volume when this wizard closes** check box is selected, and then click **Close**.
12. On the **Before you begin page of the New Volume Wizard**, click **Next**.
13. On the **Select the server and disk** page, in the **Disk** section, select the **Mirrored Disk1** virtual disk, as shown in the following figure, and then click **Next**.

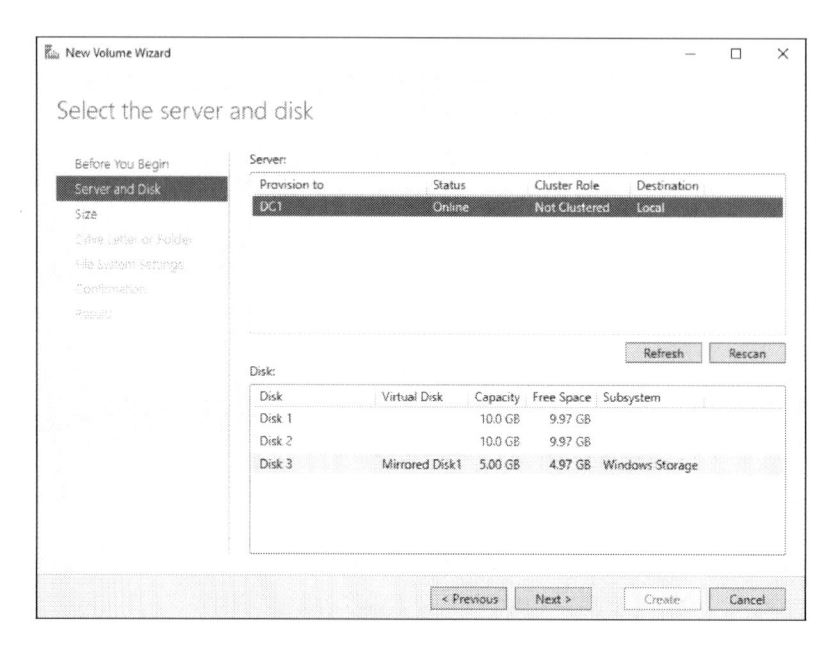

14. On the **Specify the size of the volume** page, click **Next**.
15. On the **Assign to a drive letter or folder** page, notice the Drive letter, as shown in the following figure, and then click **Next**.

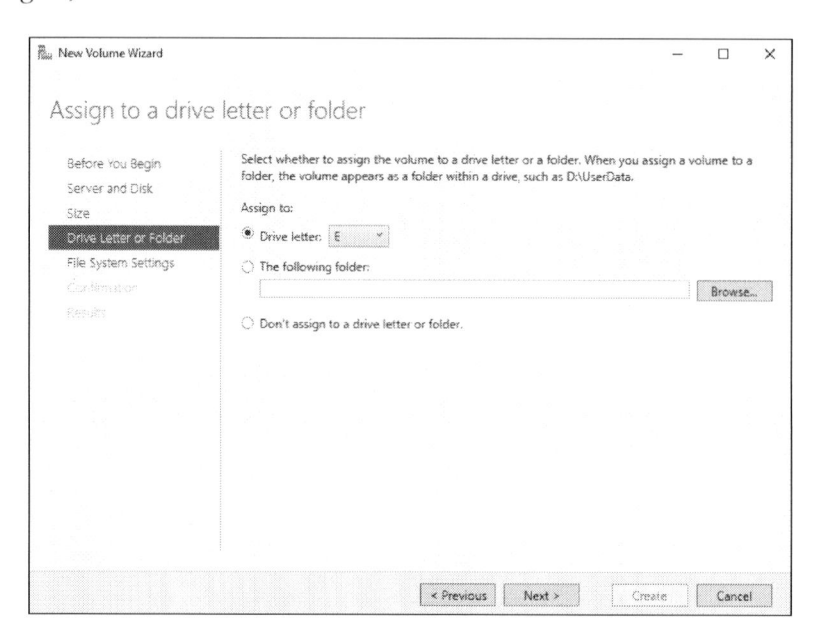

16. On the **Select file system settings** page, in the **File system** drop-down menu, ensure that **ReFS** is selected.
17. In the **Volume** label text box, type **Mirrored Volume1**, as shown in the following figure, and then click **Next**.

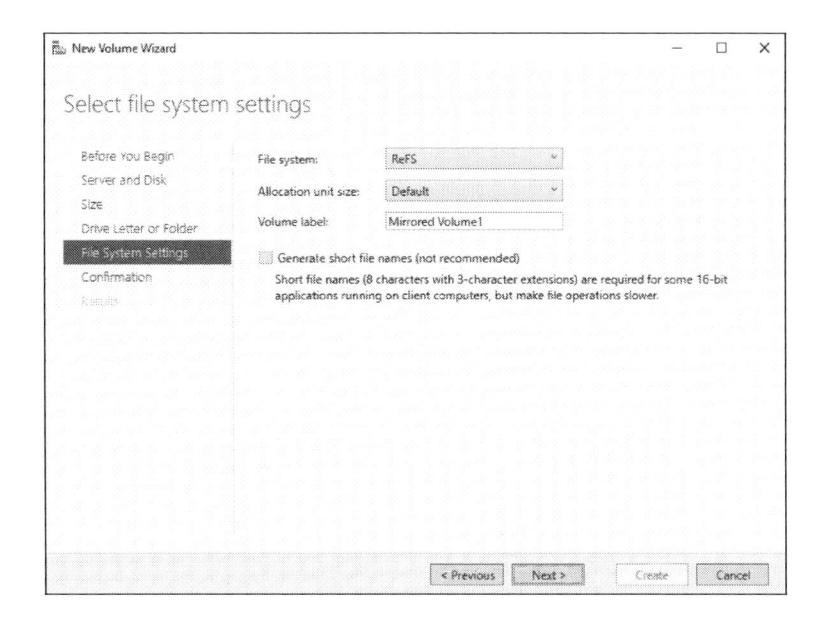

Note: ReFS is a new file system that supports more features than NTFS file system.

18. On the **Confirm selections** page, click **Create**.
19. On the **Completion** page, click **Close**, once the task completes.

Task 3: Creating a File in to Mirrored Volume1

1. Open the **Windows Explorer** window, double-click **Mirrored Volume1**.
2. Create the **MyTextFile1** file under **Mirrored Volume1,** as shown in the following figure.

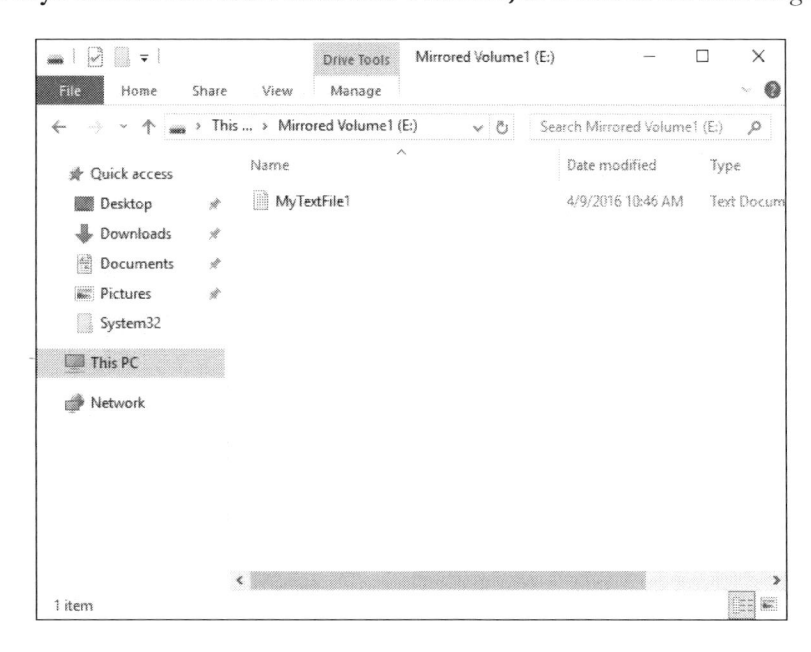

171

3. Close the **Windows Explorer** window.

Task 4: Removing a Physical Drive

1. On your host machine, on the **VMware** console, select and right-click **DC1**, and then select **Settings**.
2. On the **Virtual Machine Settings** dialog box, select **Hard Disk 2** hard drive, as shown in the following figure.

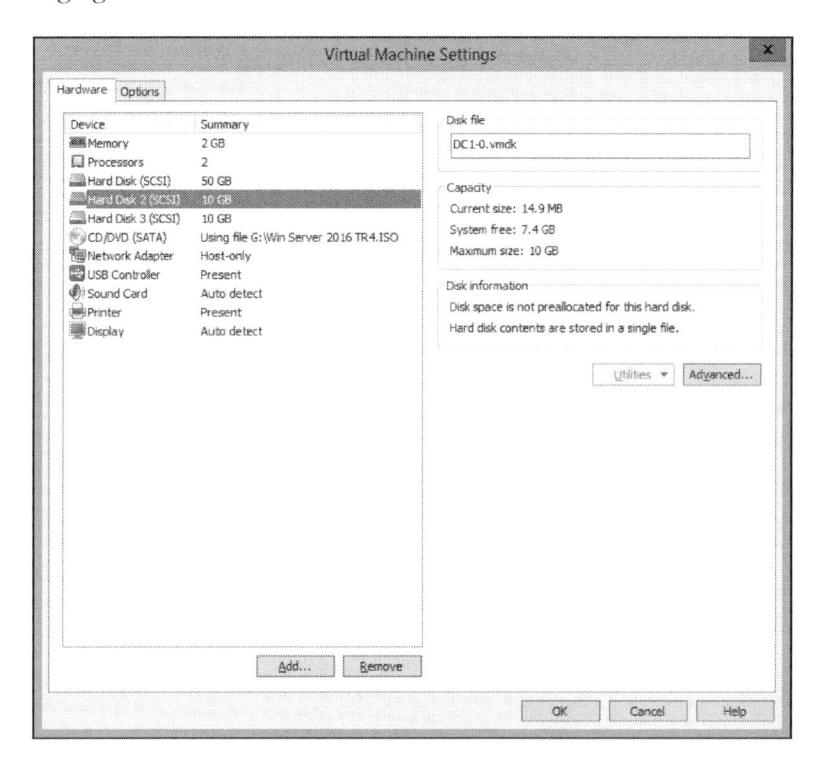

3. In the right pane, click **Remove**, and then click **OK**.

Task 5: Verifying the File Availability

1. On **DC1**, switch to the **Computer Management** console or open it if required.
2. Make sure that the **Disk Management** node is selected, verify that the **Disk 2** is disappeared from the disk list, as shown in the following figure.

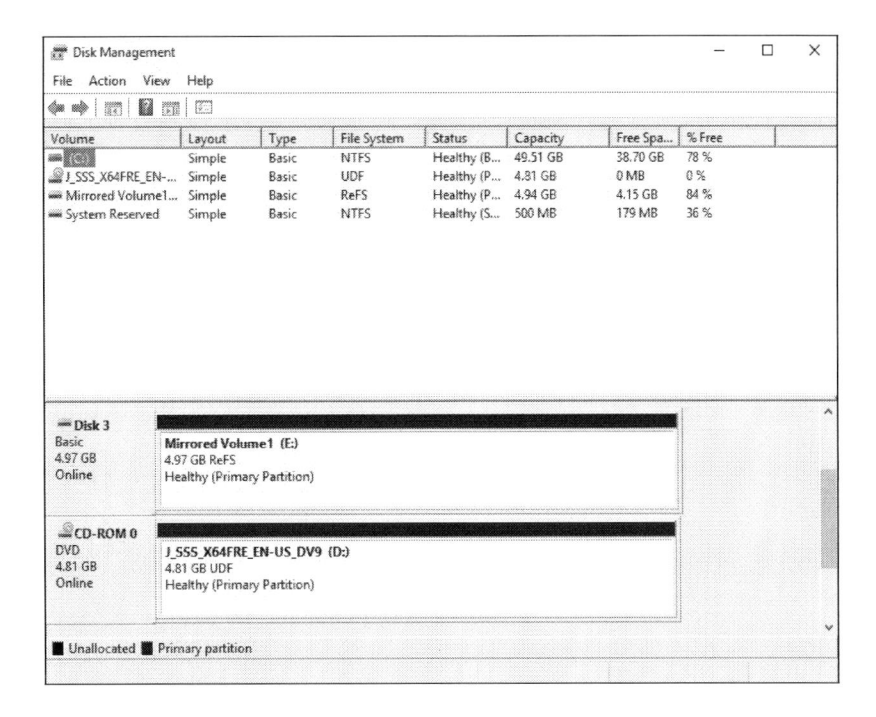

[Screenshot of Disk Management window showing volumes including (C:), J_SSS_X64FRE_EN-..., Mirrored Volume1..., and System Reserved, along with Disk 3 (Basic, 4.97 GB, Online) containing Mirrored Volume1 (E:) and CD-ROM 0 containing J_SSS_X64FRE_EN-US_DV9 (D:)]

3. Open the **Windows Explorer** window.
4. On the **Windows Explorer** window, double-click **Mirrored Volume1**.
5. Verify that the **MyTextFile1** file is still available.
6. Close the **Windows Explorer** window.

Results: After completing this exercise, you should have created a storage pool and added some disks to it. Then you should have created a mirrored virtual disk from the storage pool. In addition, after removing a physical drive, you should have verified that the virtual disk was still available and accessible.

Shut down and revert the DC1 virtual machine to prepare for the net exercise.

Exercise 18: Implementing File Sharing

File sharing allows you to share and access the files on a network. You can also set the desired permissions (NTFS and shared permissions) on a file share for the various users. In addition, you can enable the access-based enumeration feature on a file share, which allows users to access only those shared files for which they have the access permission.

Start the DC1, SERVER1, and CLIENT1 virtual machines to perform this exercise.

Task 1: Creating the Folder Structure for the New Share

Before start to this exercise, you need to create **Peter** and **Shawn** user accounts on the **DC1** virtual machine. To do this, you need to perform the following steps:

1. Sign in to **DC1** with the MCSALAB\Administrator account.
2. Open the **Active Directory Users and Computers** console, and then expand the **mcsalab.local** node.
3. Select and right-click **Users** in the left pane, select **New**, and then click **User**.
4. Follow the simple steps to create the **Peter** and **Shawn** user accounts.
5. The following figure displays the **Active Directory Users and Computers** console. **Peter** and **Shawn** user accounts are listed under the **Users** node.

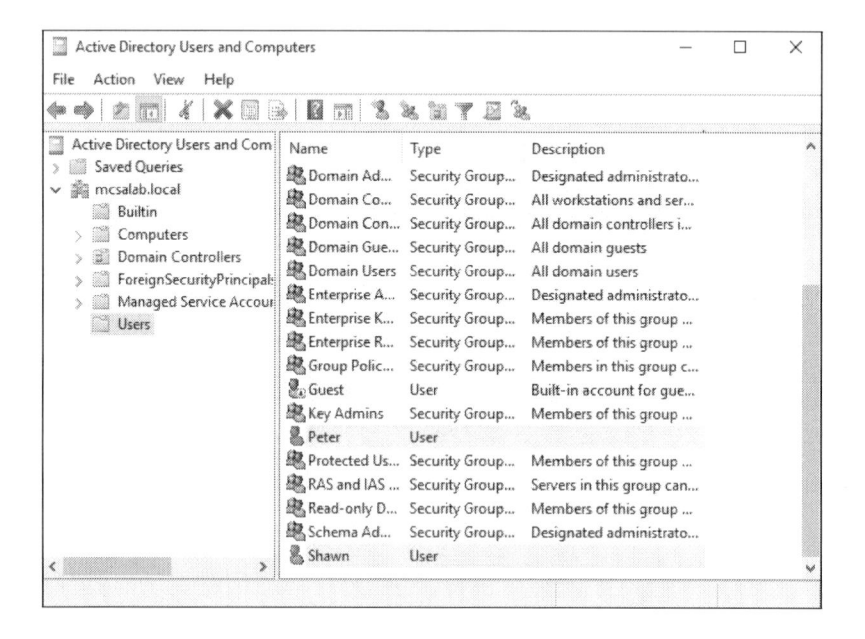

Note: If you face problems to create user accounts, you may refer the exercise 6 and 7.

6. Switch and Sign in to **SERVER1** with the MCSALAB\Administrator account.
7. Create a folder named **MyData**.
8. Double-click the **MyData** folder.
9. Create the **Marketing** and **Sales** folders under it, as shown in the following figure.

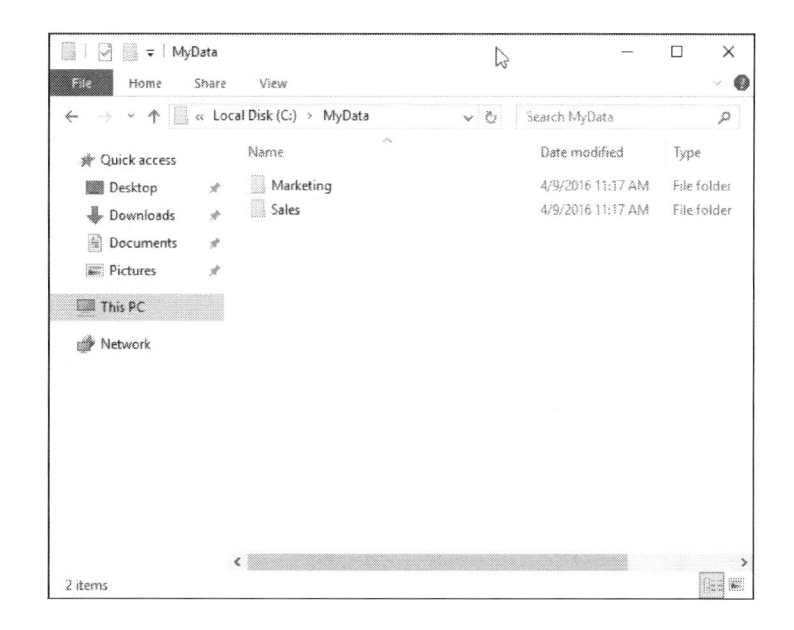

Task 2: Configuring NTFS Permissions on the Folder Structure

1. On SERVER1, on the **Windows Explorer** window, navigate to drive **Local Drive (C:)**.
2. Select and right-click the **MyData** folder, and then select **Properties**.
3. On the **MyData Properties** dialog box, select **Security**, and then click **Advanced**, as shown in the following figure.

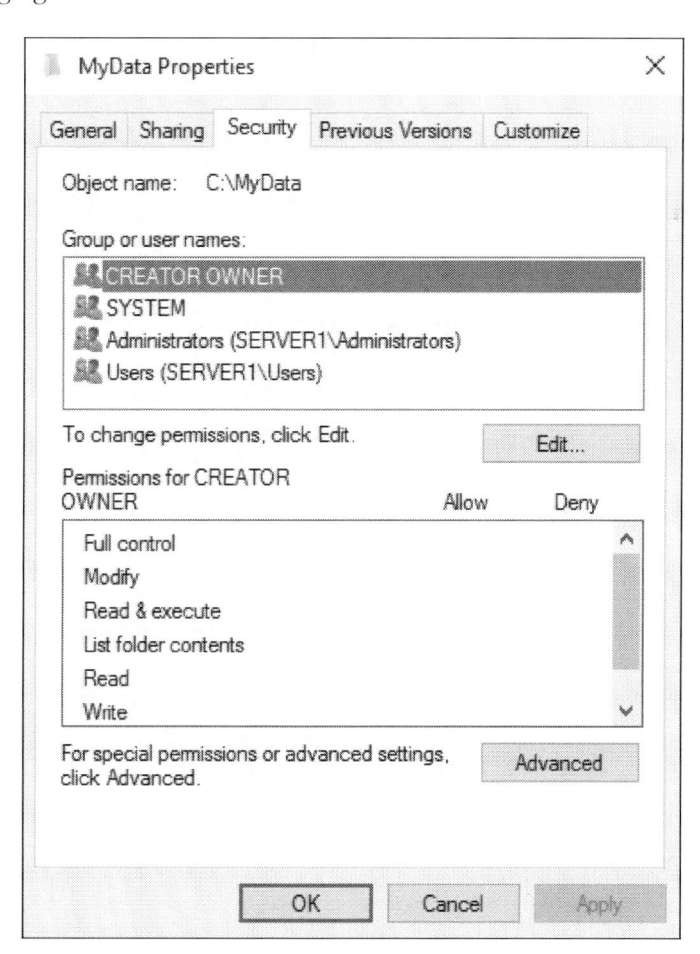

4. On the **Advanced Security Settings** for **MyData** dialog box, click **Disable Inheritance**.
5. On the **Block Inheritance** dialog box, as shown in the following figure, select the **Convert inherited permissions into explicit permissions on this object** option, and then click **OK**.

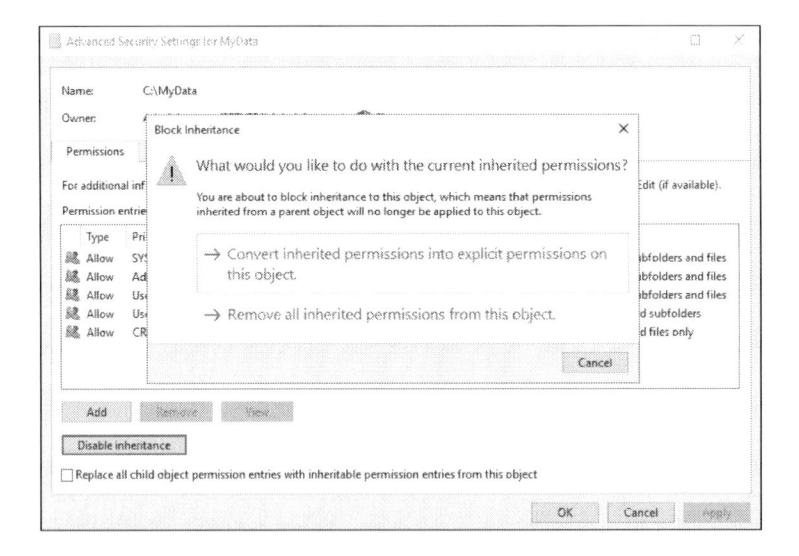

6. Click **OK** twice to close the **MyData Properties** dialog box.
7. On the **Windows Explorer** window, double-click the **MyData** folder.
8. Select and right-click the **Marketing** folder, and then select **Properties**.
9. On the **Marketing Properties** dialog box, click **Security**, and then click **Advanced**.
10. On the **Advanced Security Settings for Marketing** dialog box, click **Disable Inheritance**.
11. On the **Block Inheritance** dialog box, select the **Convert inherited permissions into explicit permissions on this object** option.
12. **Remove** the **Read & Execute** and **Special permissions** for **Users (SERVER1\Users)**, as shown in the following figure, and then click **OK**.

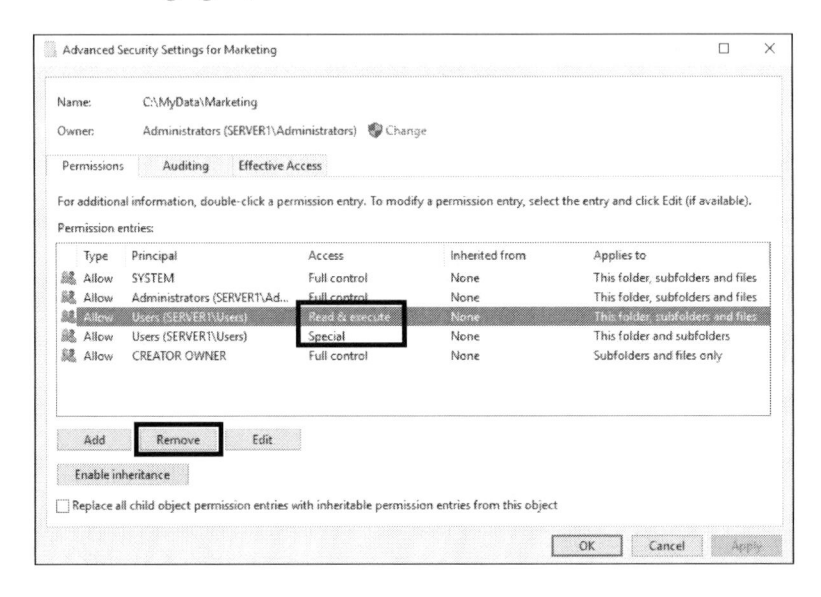

13. On the **Security** tab, click **Edit**.
14. On the **Permissions for Marketing** dialog box, click **Add**.

15. On the **Select Users, Computers, Service Accounts, and Groups** dialog box, type **Peter**, click **Check Names**, as shown in the following figure, and then click **OK**.

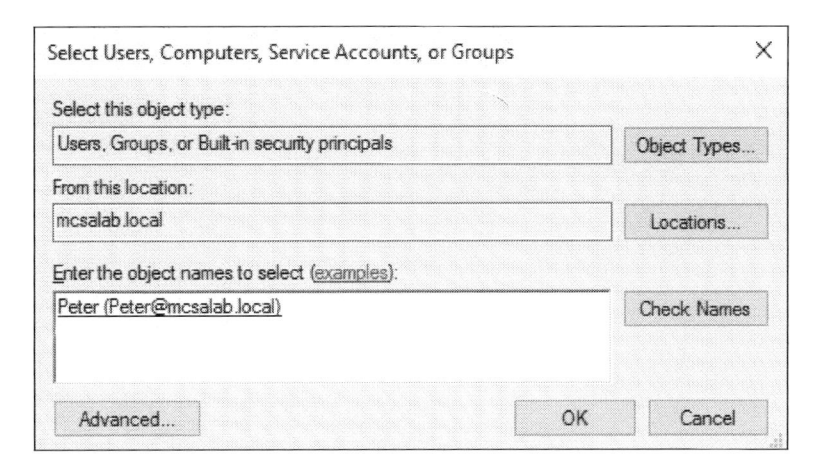

Note: You may be asked to provide Domain administrator credentials.

16. On the **Permissions for Marketing** dialog box, select the **Modify** check box under the **Allow** section, as shown in the following figure.

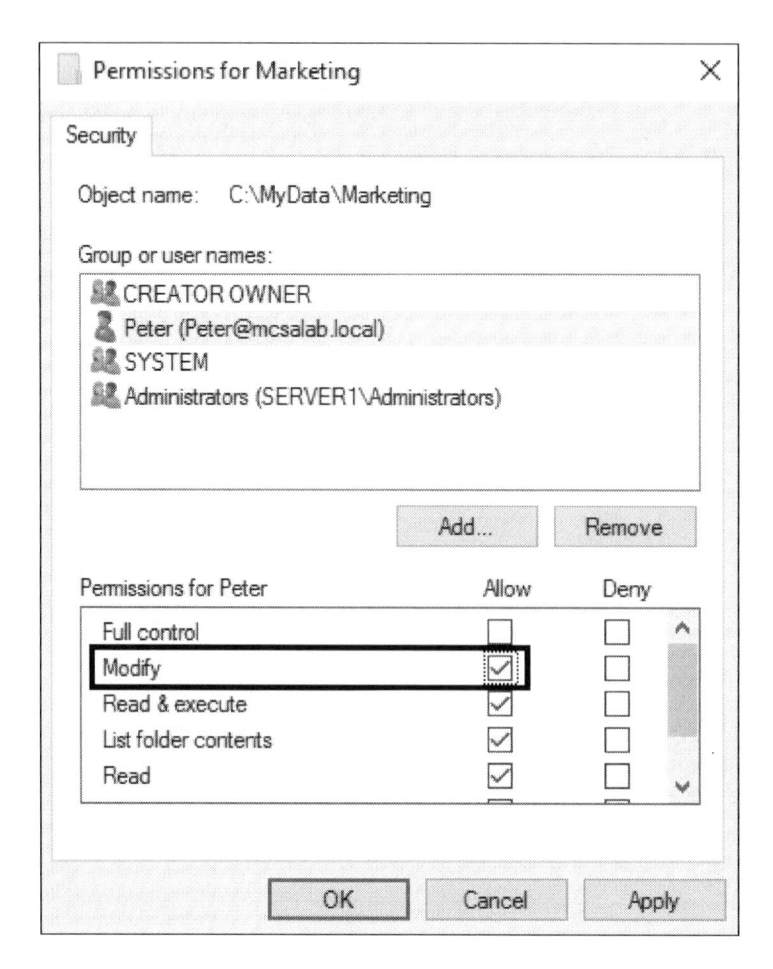

[Screenshot: Permissions for Marketing dialog box — Object name: C:\MyData\Marketing. Group or user names: CREATOR OWNER, Peter (Peter@mcsalab.local), SYSTEM, Administrators (SERVER1\Administrators). Permissions for Peter: Modify is checked (Allow), Read & execute, List folder contents, and Read are also checked under Allow.]

17. Click **OK** to close the **Permissions for Marketing** dialog box.
18. Click **OK** to close the **Marketing Properties** dialog box.

Task 3: Sharing the Folder

1. On **SERVER1**, select and right-click the **MyData** folder, and then select **Properties**.
2. On the **MyData Properties** dialog box, select the **Sharing** tab, and then click **Advanced Sharing**.
3. On the **Advanced Sharing** dialog box, select the **Share this folder** check box, as shown in the following figure, and then click **Permissions**.

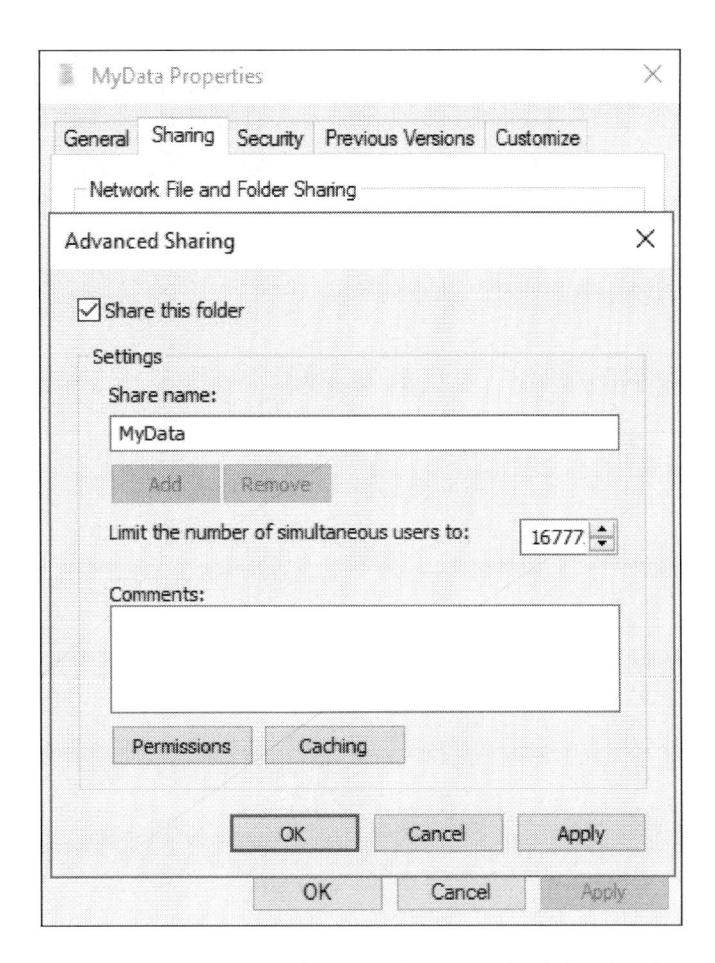

4. On the **Permissions for MyData** dialog box, as shown in the following figure, and then click **Add**.

![Permissions for MyData dialog box showing Share Permissions tab with Everyone group selected and Read permission allowed]

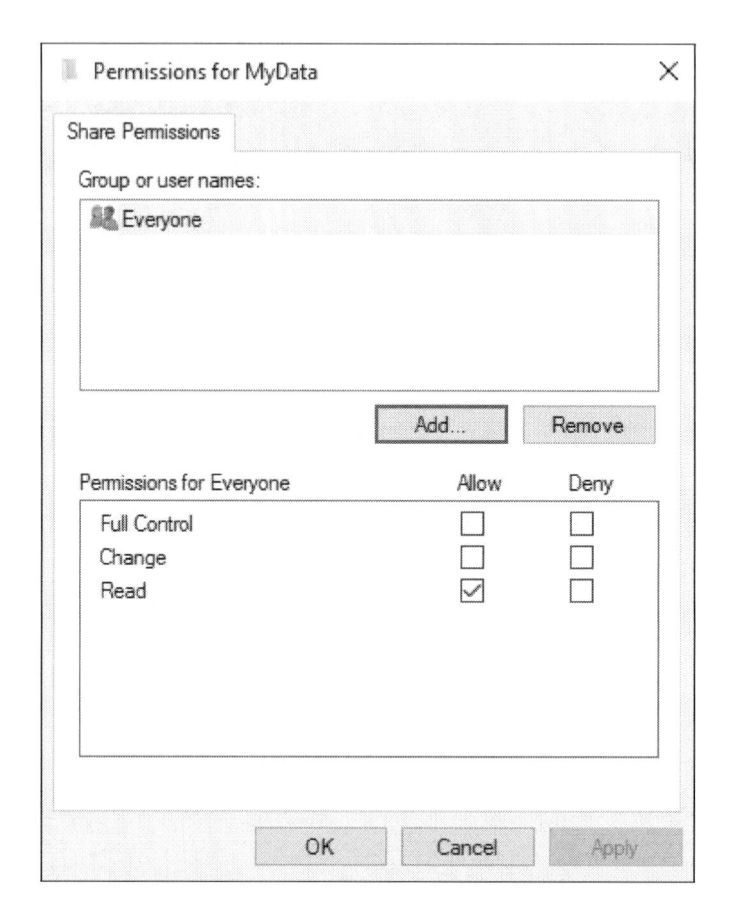

5. On the **Select Users, Computers, Service Accounts, or Groups** dialog box, in the **Enter the object names to select (examples):** text area, type **Authenticated Users**.
6. Click **Check Names**, and then click **OK**.
7. On the **Permissions for MyData** dialog box, make sure that the **Authenticated Users** is selected in the **Share Permissions** section, and then select the **Change** check box under the **Allow** section, as shown in the following figure.

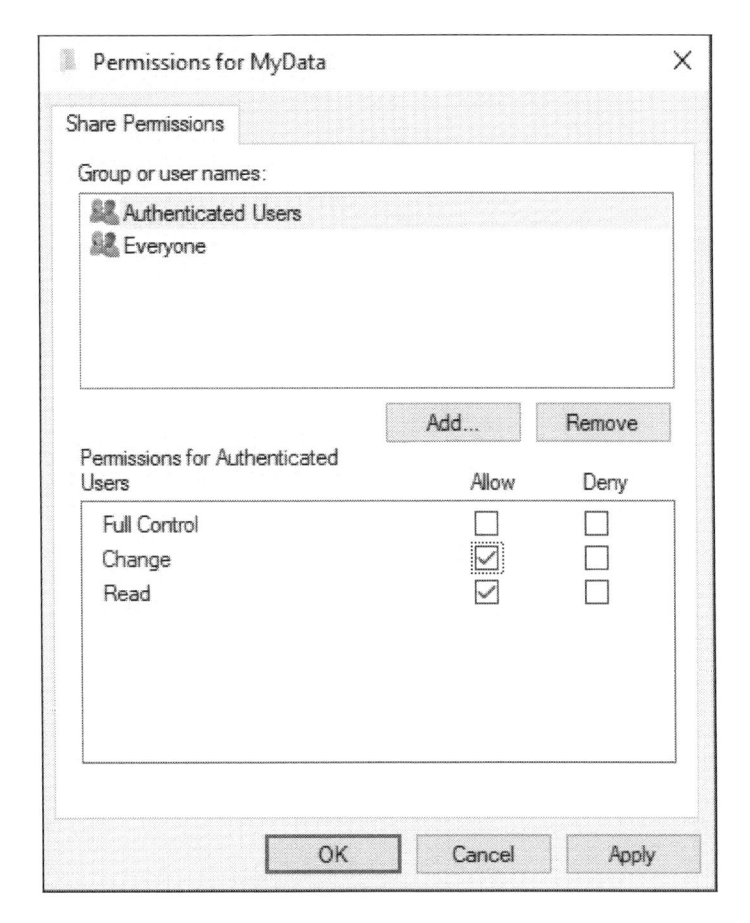

8. Click **OK** to close the **Permissions for MyData** dialog box.
9. Click **OK** to close the **Advanced Sharing** window.
10. Click **Close** to close the **MyData Properties** dialog box.

Task 4: Accessing the Shared Folder
1. Switch and Sign in to **CLIENT1** with the MCSALAB\Peter account.
2. Open the **Run** dialog box, type **\\SERVER1\MyData**, and then press **Enter**.
3. Double-click the **Marketing** folder.

Note: Peter should be able to access to the Marketing folder.

4. Sign out of **CLIENT1**.

Task 5: Enabling Access-based Enumeration
1. Switch back and Sign in to **SERVER1** with the MCSALAB\Administrator account.
2. Open the **Server Manager** console, on the **Server Manager** console, in the left pane, select **File and Storage Services**.
3. On the **File and Storage Services** page, click **Shares**.
4. In the **Shares** pane, select and right-click **MyData**, and then click **Properties**, as shown in

the following figure.

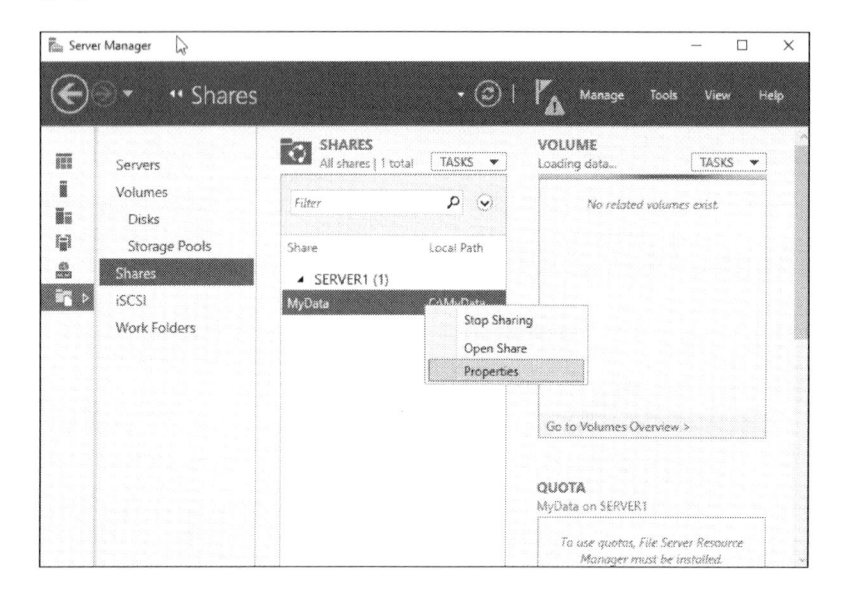

5. On the **MyData Properties** dialog box, in the left pane, select **Settings**, and then select the **Enable access-based enumeration** check box, as shown in the following figure.

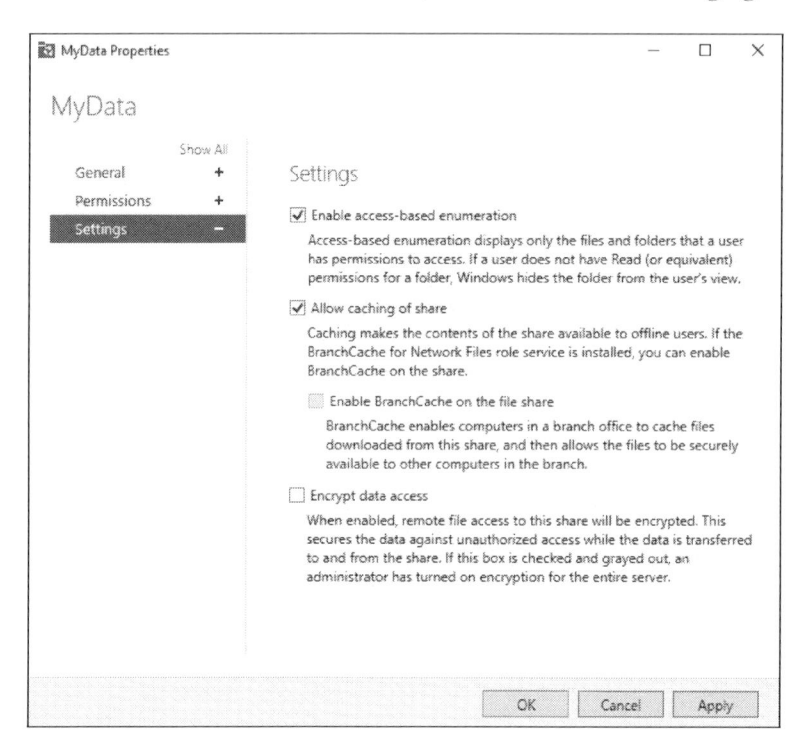

6. Click **OK** to close the **MyData Properties** dialog box.
7. Close the **Server Manager** console.

Task 6: Testing the Access-based Enumeration Configuration

1. Switch back and sign in to **CLIENT1** with the **MCSALAB\Shawn** account.
2. Click the **Desktop** tile.
3. Open the **Run** dialog box, in the **Open** text box, type **\\SERVER1\MyData**, and then press **Enter**.

Note: *Shawn should only be able to view the Sales folder, the folder for which he has been assigned permissions.*

4. Sign out of **CLINET1**.

Results: *After completing this exercise, you should have created and tested a file share. In addition, you should also have tested the access-based enumeration feature for the shared folder.*

Shut down and revert the DC1, SERVER1, and CLIENT1 virtual machines to prepare for the next exercise.

Exercise 19: Implementing Shadow Copies

Shadow copy is a feature that allows you to recover the files (including the shared files) which are accidently overwritten or deleted. First, you need to enable this feature (on a desired disk) then you can create multiple shadow copy versions on a disk. However, shadow copy cannot be considered as an alternate of the Window backup feature, because it only works until the system is working on which you have enabled it. If the system goes down or crashed accidently, shadow copy cannot be used to recover the system or system's data.

In this exercise, you will learn how to use the shadow copy feature to recover the accidently deleted files.

Start the DC1 and SERVER1 virtual machines to perform this exercise.

Task 1: Configuring Shadow Copies

1. Sign in to **SERVER1** with the MCSALAB\Administrator account.
2. Open the **Windows Explorer** window.
3. Select and right-click **Local Disk (C:),** and then click **Configure Shadow Copies**.
4. On the **Shadow Copies** dialog box, make sure that **C:** volume is selected, and then click **Enable**.
5. On the **Enable Shadow Copies** message box, click **Yes**.
6. On the **Shadow Copies** dialog box, click **Settings**.
7. On the **Settings** dialog box, as shown in the following figure, click **Schedule**.

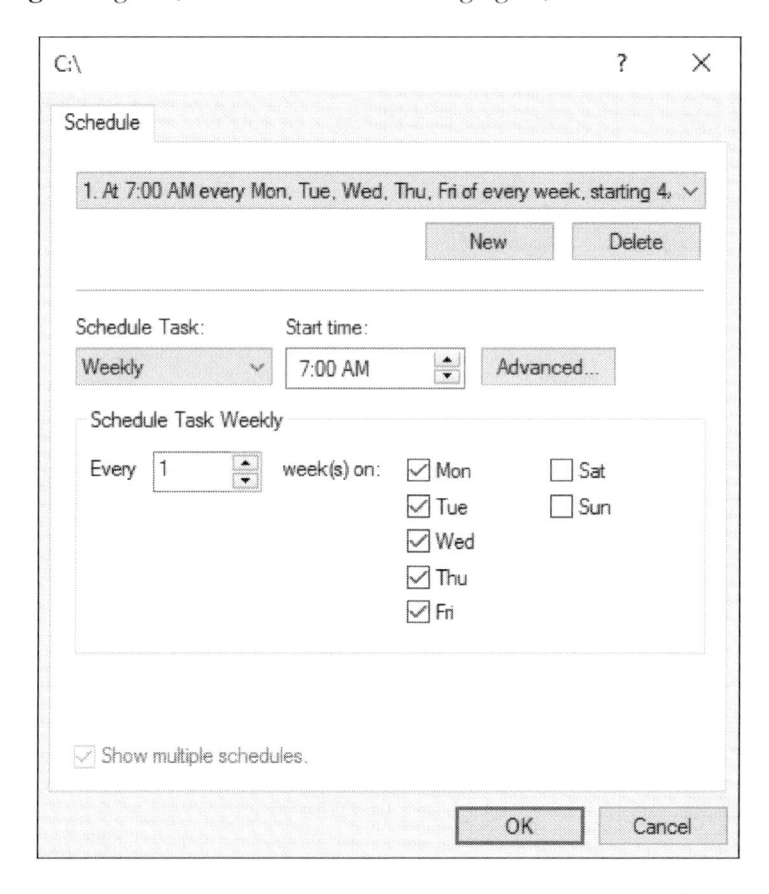

8. On the **C:** schedule dialog box, review the various schedule options, and then click **OK**.

9. On the **Settings** dialog box, click **OK**.
10. Click **OK** to close the **Settings** dialog box.
11. On the **Shadow Copies** dialog box, click **OK**.

Task 2: Recovering a Deleted File Using Shadow Copy

1. On **SERVER1**, switch to the **Windows Explorer** window.
2. Navigate to **Local Disk (C:)**, and then click **Users**.
3. Select and right-click **Public**, and then click **Delete**.
4. Also delete the **Public** folder from **Recycle Bin**.
5. On the **Windows Explorer** window, select and right-click the **Users** folder, and then click **Properties**.
6. On the **Users Properties** dialog box, click the **Previous Versions** tab, as shown in the following figure.

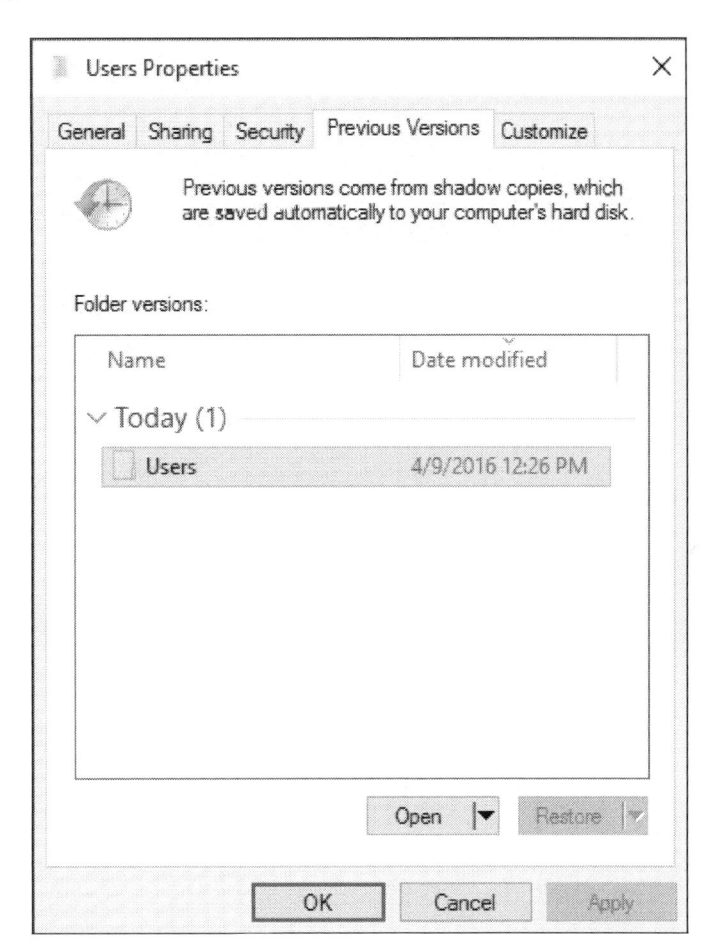

7. Select the folder version for the **Users** folder, and then click **Open**.
8. Verify that the **Public** is listed in the folder, select and right-click **Public**, and then click **Copy**.
9. On the other **Windows Explorer** window, navigate to the **Local Disk (C:)\Users** folder, and then click **Paste**.
10. Close the **Windows Explorer** window.
11. Click **OK** and close all open windows.

Results: *After completing this exercise, you should have configured the Shadow Copies feature to recover the accidently deleted file.*

12. Shut down and revert the DC1 and SERVER1 virtual machines to prepare for the next exercise.

Exercise 20: Implementing Network Printing

A printer is a hardware device which translate the soft copies in to hard copies. A single printer can be shared on a network and then it can be accessed by multiple clients to send the print jobs. Once you shared a printer on a network, you need to connect it on each clients in order to send the print jobs. However, in a large enterprise network, where multiple printers are used to handle a number of thousand print jobs, you may need to configure the printer pool for ease print management.

In this exercise, you will learn how to install, share, and manage a network printer on a Windows-based network.

Start the DC1, SERVER1, and CLIENT1 virtual machines to perform this exercise.

Task 1: Installing the Print and Document Services Server Role

1. Sign in to **SERVER1** as MCSALAB\Administrator.
2. On the **Server Manager** console, click **Manage**, and then click **Add Roles and Features**.
3. On the **Before you begin** page of the **Add Roles and Features Wizard**, click **Next**.
4. On the **Select installation type** page, make sure that the **Role-based or feature-based installation** radio button is selected, and then click **Next**.
5. On the **Select destination server** page, click **Next**.
6. On the **Select Server Roles** page, as shown in the following figure, select the **Print and Document Services** check box. If the **Add Roles and Features Wizard** dialog box displays, click **Add Features**, and then click **Next**.

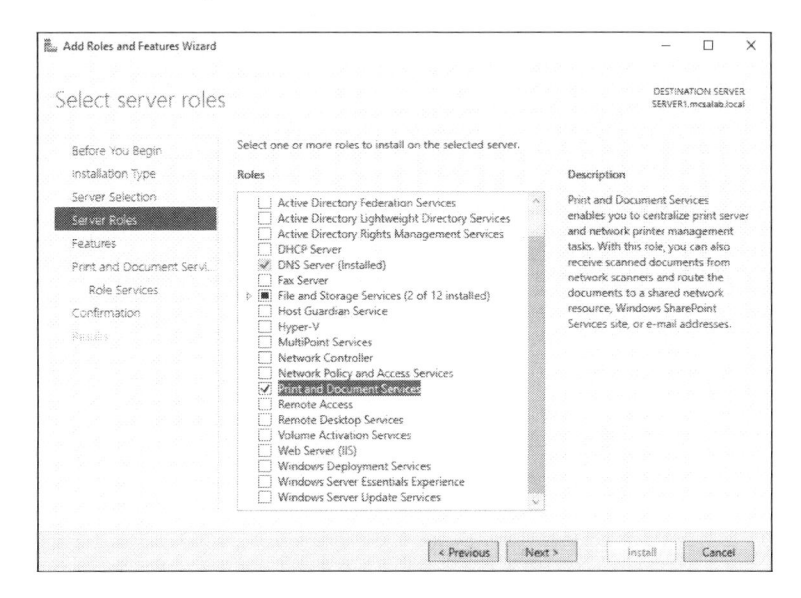

7. On the rest of the pages, click **Next** until the **Confirm Installation Selections** page displays.
8. Click **Install** to install the required role services, and then click **Close** once the installation succeeded.

Task 2: Installing a New Printer

1. On the **Server Manager** console, click **Tools**, and then click **Print Management**.
2. On the **Print Management** console, expand **Printer Servers**, and then click **SERVER1**

(Local).
3. Select and right-click **Printers**, and then click **Add Printer**, as shown in the following figure.

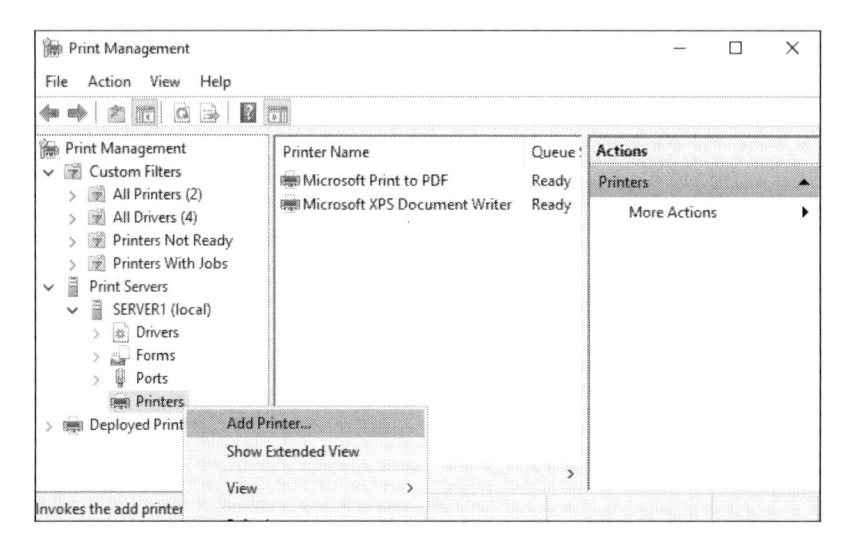

4. On the **Network Printer Installation Wizard** page, select the **Add a new printer using an existing port** radio button, as shown in the following figure, and then click **Next**.

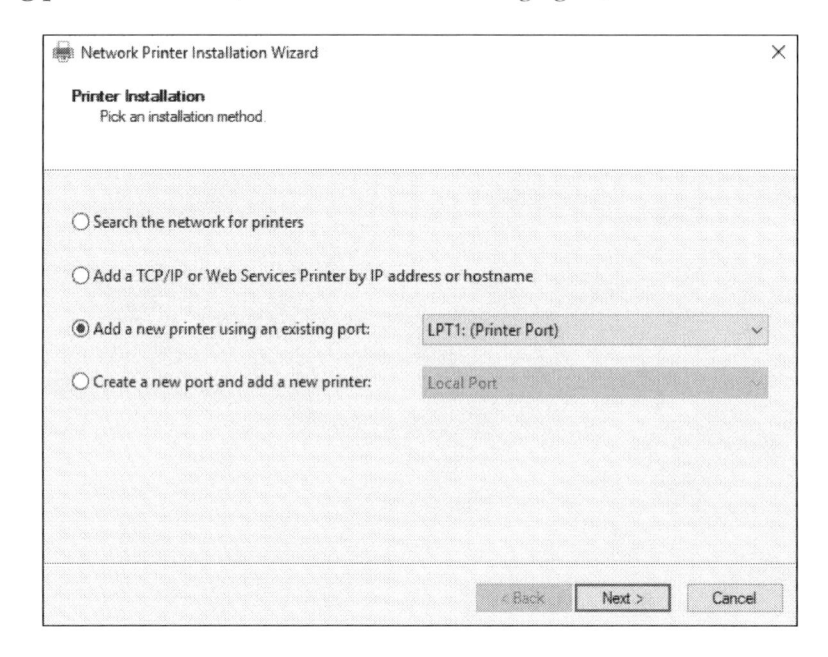

5. On the **Printer Driver** page, make sure that the **Install a new printer** radio button is selected, and then click **Next**.
6. On the **Printer Installation** page, select **Canon** in the **Manufacture** list.
7. Select any of the printer model in the **Printers** list in the right pane, as shown in the following figure, and then click **Next**.

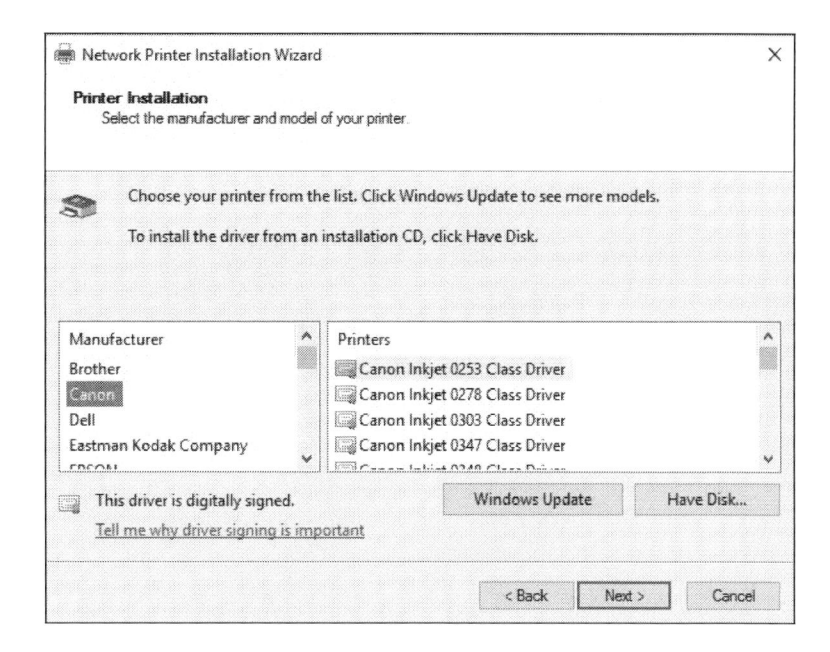

8. On the **Printer Name and Sharing Settings** page, click **Next**.
9. On the **Printer Found** page, click **Next**, and then click **Finish**.

Task 3: Configuring Printer Pooling

1. On the **Print Management** console, select and right-click the recently added printer, and then click **Properties**.
2. On the printer properties dialog box, click the **Sharing** tab, select the **List in the directory** check box, as shown in the following figure, and then click **Apply**.

![Canon Inkjet 0253 Class Driver Properties - Sharing tab screenshot]

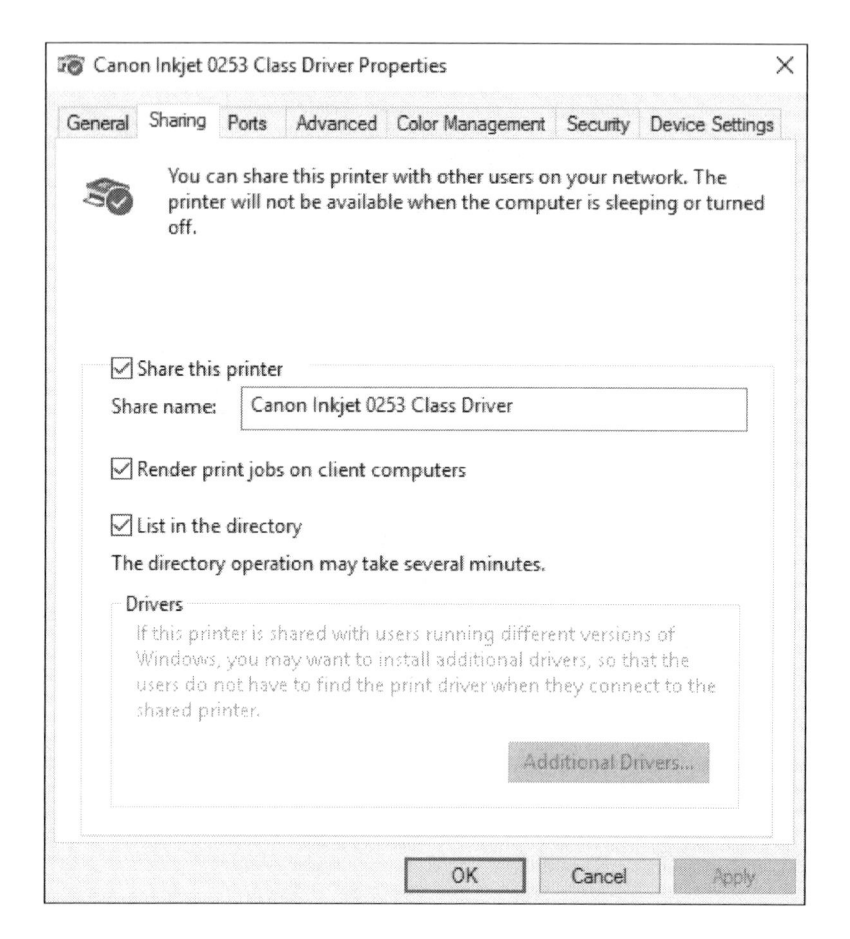

3. On the printer properties dialog box, click the **Ports** tab, select the **Enable printer pooling** check box, and then select the **LPT2**: check box to select it as an additional port, as shown in the following figure.

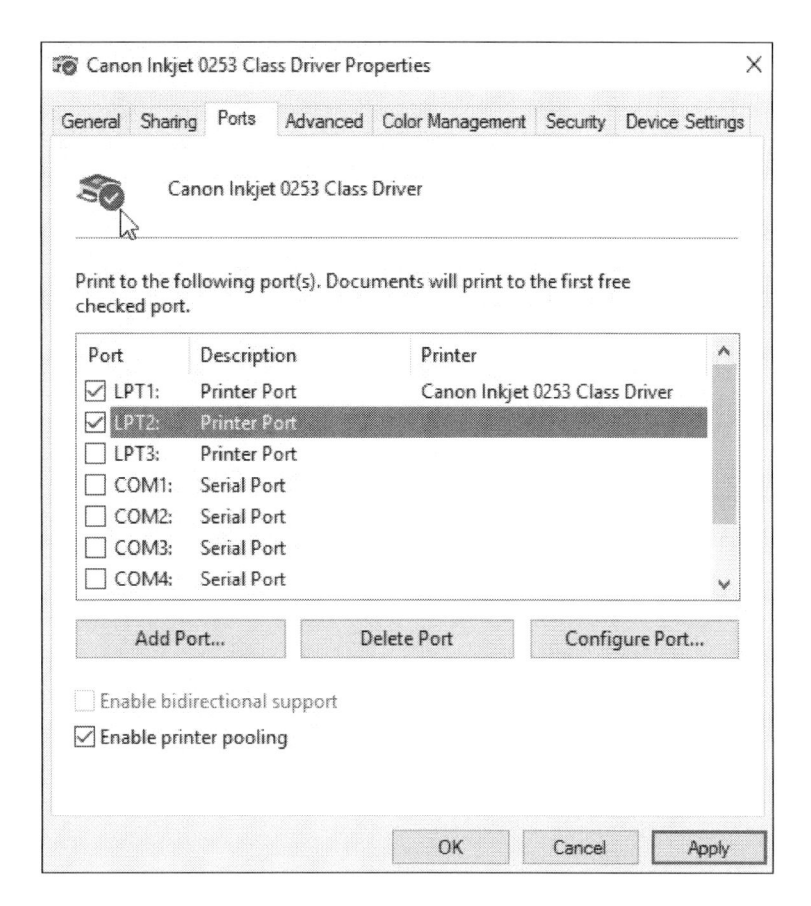

4. Click **OK** to close the printer properties dialog box.
5. Close the **Print Management** console.

Task 4: Connecting a Printer on a Client

1. Switch and Sign in to **CLIENT1** as MCSALAB\Administrator with the password as **Password@123**.
2. Open **Control Panel**, on the **Control Panel** window, click the **Add a device** link under **Hardware and Sound**.
3. On the **Add a device** window, select the discovered printer, as shown in the following figure, and then click **Next**.

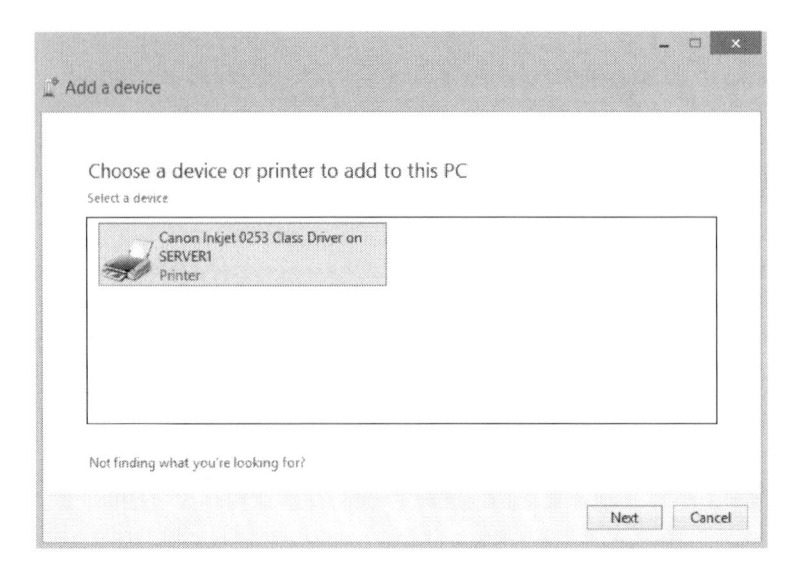

4. On the **Control Panel** window, click the **View devices and printers** link, under **Hardware and Sound**.
5. Make sure that the recently added printer is listed.

> *Results: After completing this exercise, you should have installed and configured a network printer. In addition, you should also have configured the printer pooling.*

Shut down and revert the DC1, SERVER1, and CLIENT1 virtual machines to prepare for the next exercise.

Exercise 21: Implementing Group Policy Objects

A Group Policy Object (GPO) is a collection of security policies and settings that are used to control the users' and computers' behavior on a network. You can use various security policies to restrict the Active Directory objects from accessing the unwanted resources, such as features, services, files, or tools. Once you promote a server as a domain controller, the Default Domain Policy and Default Domain Controller Policy GPOs are created by default on the domain controller. These GPOs contain various preconfigured policies that are applied on the domain controllers and computers. However, you can create a new GPO with the custom security policies and settings using the Group Policy Management console.

In this exercise, you will learn how to create a GPO and how to configure a GPO to prevent Active Directory objects from accessing the resources on a Windows-based domain network.

Start the DC1 and CLIENT1 virtual machines to perform this exercise.

Task 1: Creating a New GPO

1. Sign in to **DC1** with the MCSALAB\Administrator.
2. Open the **Server Manager** console, if required.
3. On the **Server Manager** console, click **Tools**, and then click **Group Policy Management**.
4. On the **Group Policy Management** console, expand **Forest: mcsalab.local**, and then click **Domains**.
5. Select and right-click **mcsalab.local**, and then select **Create a GPO in this domain**, as shown in the following figure.

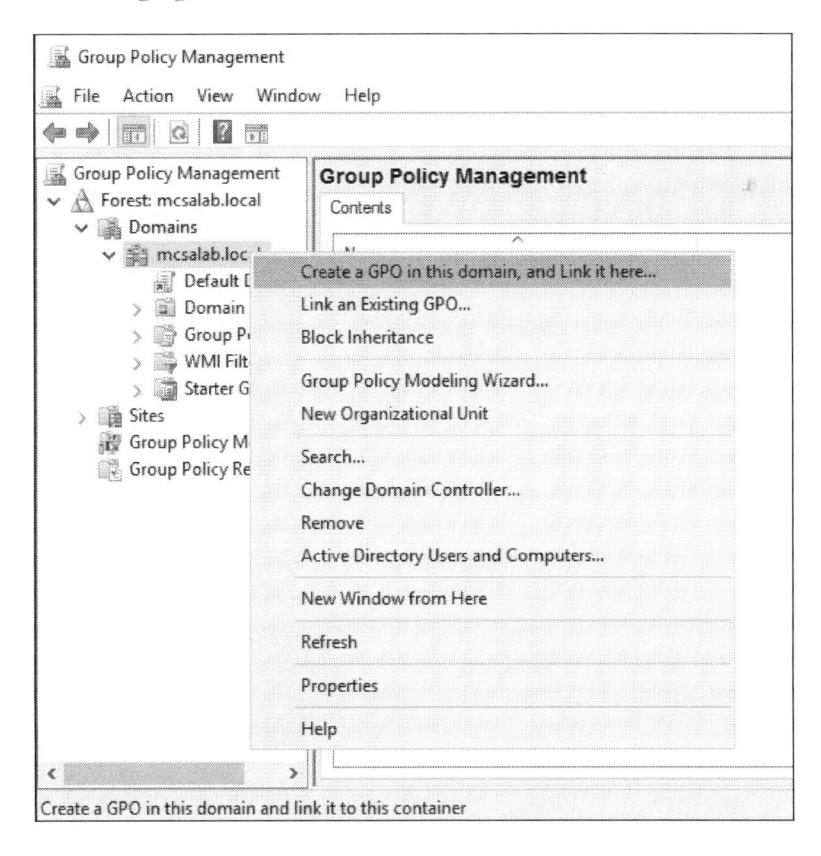

6. On the **New GPO** dialog box, in the **Name** text box, type **Internet Explorer GPO**, and

then click **OK**.

Task 2: Configuring the Internet Explorer GPO

1. On **DC1**, on the **Group Policy Management** console, select and right-click **Internet Explorer GPO**, and then click **Edit**.
2. On the **Group Policy Management Editor** console, navigate to **User Configuration\Policies\Administrative Templates**.
3. Select and right-click **All Settings**, and then select **Filter Options**, as shown in the following figure.

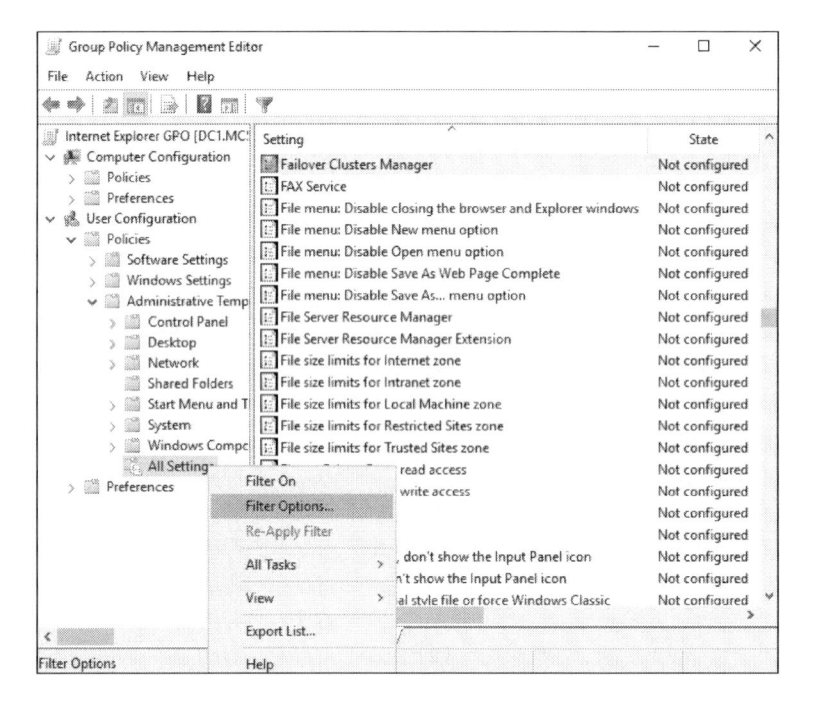

4. On the **Filter Options** dialog box, select the **Enable Keyword Filters** check box.
5. In the **Filter for word(s):** text box, type **General**, as shown in the following figure, and then click **OK**.

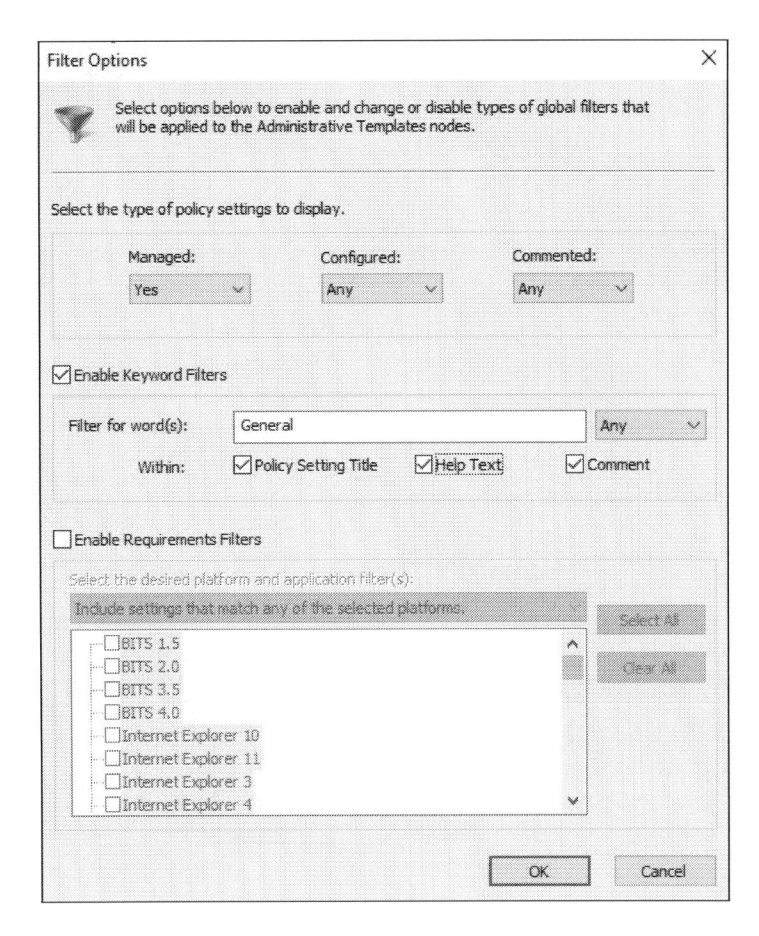

6. In the **Settings** pane in the right hand, select and right-click **Disable the General page**, and then select **Edit**, as shown in the following figure.

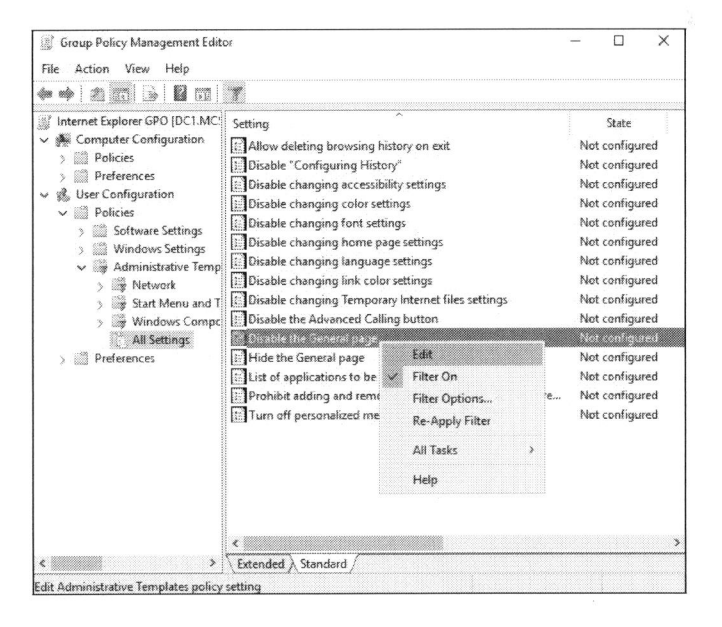

7. On the **Disable the General** page dialog box, select the **Enabled** radio button, and then click **OK**.
8. Close the **Group Policy Management Editor** console.

Task 3: Creating a Domain User to Test the GPO

1. On **DC1**, open the **Command Prompt** window.
2. Execute the following command, as shown in the following figure (type Password@123 when you are prompted for password).
   ```
   dsadd user cn=User1,"cn=users,dc=mcsalab,dc=local" -disabled no -pwd *
   ```

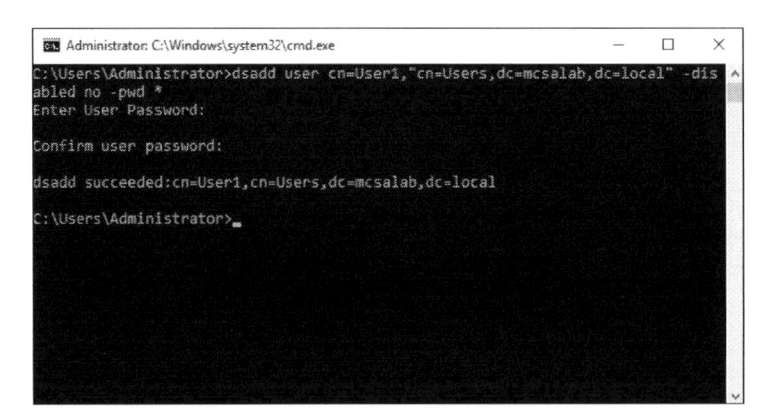

3. Close the **Command Prompt** window.

Task 4: Testing the Internet Explorer GPO

1. Switch and Sign in to **CLIENT1** as MCSALAB\User1 with the password as Password@123.
2. Open the **Run** dialog box, type **control** in the **Open** text box, and then press **Enter**.
3. On the **Control Panel** window, click **Network and Internet**.
4. On the **Network and Internet** window, as shown in the following figure, click **Change your homepage**.

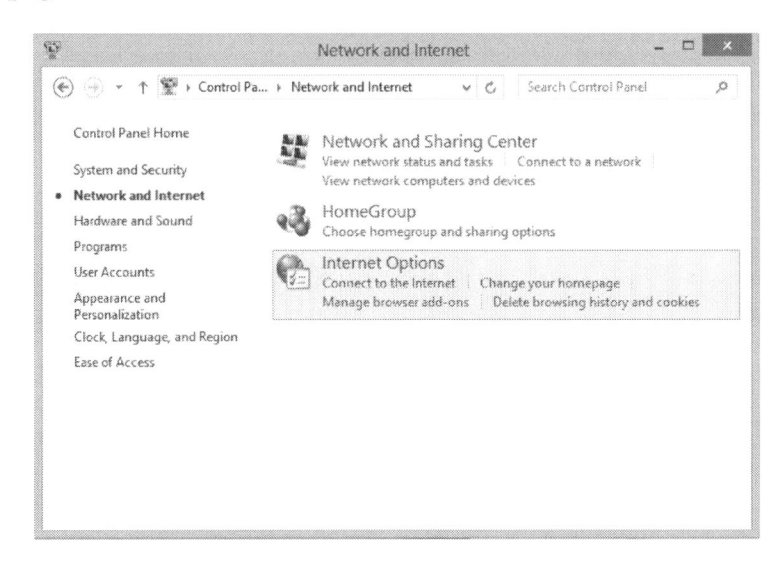

5. When you click the **Change your home** page link, you will get a message, as shown in the following figure.

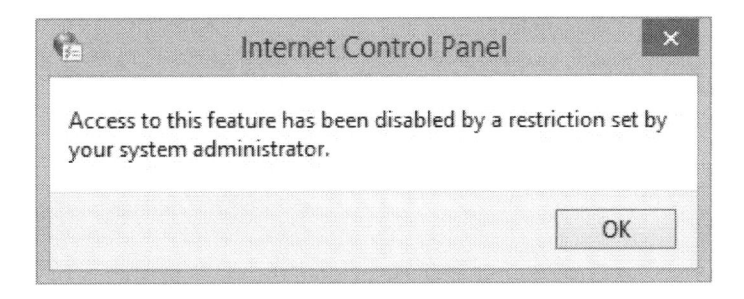

6. Click **OK** to close the **Internet Control Panel** message box.
7. On the **Control Panel** window, click **Internet Options**. Notice that, in the **Internet Properties** dialog box, the **General** tab is not available, as shown in the following figure.

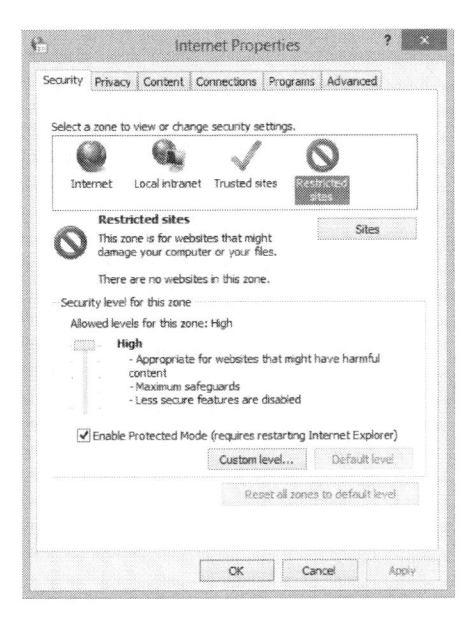

8. Close all open windows and sign out.

Task 5: Configuring Security Filtering to Exempt a User from the Internet Explorer GPO

1. Switch and sign to **DC1**.
2. Open the **Group Policy Management** console, if required.
3. On the **Group Policy Management** console, select and right-click **Internet Explorer GPO**.
4. In the right pane, click the **Delegation** tab.
5. On the **Delegation** tab, click the **Advanced** button.
6. On the **Internet Explorer GPO Security Settings** dialog box, click **Add**.
7. On the **Select Users, Computers, Service Accounts, or Groups** text box, type **User1**, as shown in the following figure, and then click **OK**.

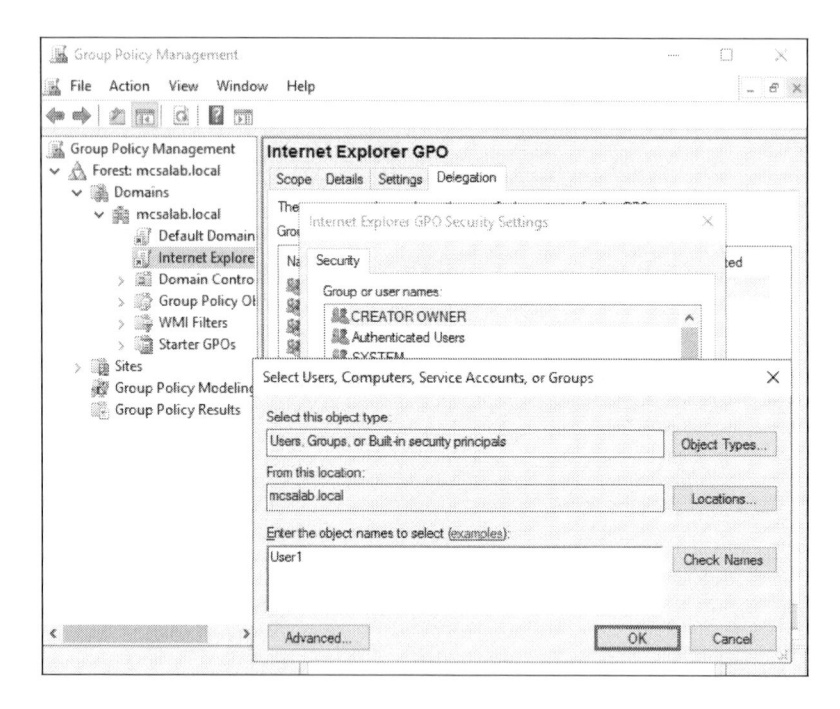

8. On the **Internet Explorer GPO Security Settings** dialog box, in the **Security** section, select **User1**.
9. In the **Permissions for User1** section, select the **Deny** check box, as shown in the following figure, and then click **OK**.

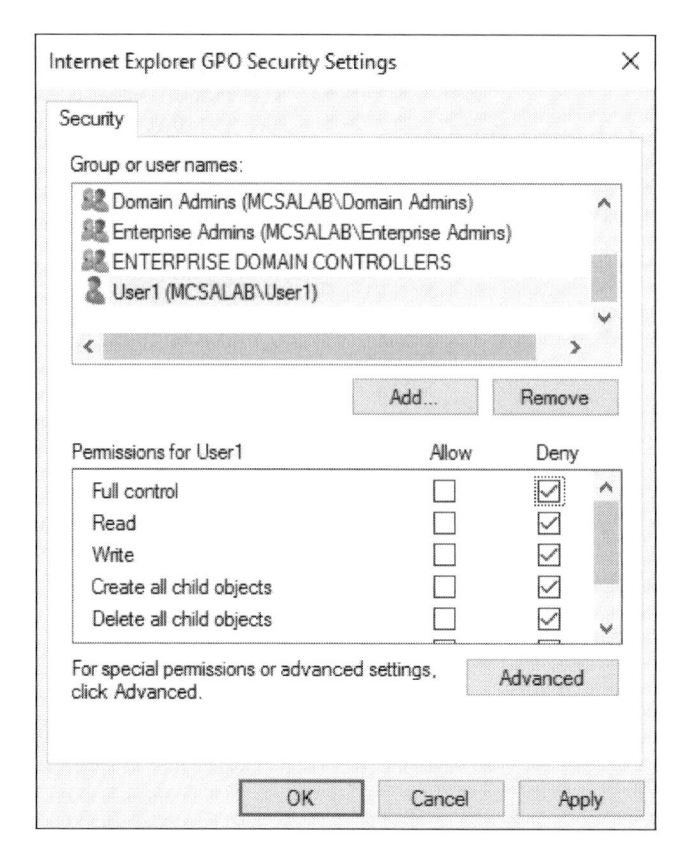

10. On the **Windows Security** dialog box, click **Yes**.

11. Close the **Group Policy Management** console.

Task 6: Testing the Internet Explorer GPO

1. Switch and Sign in to **CLIENT1** as MCSALAB\User1 with the password as Password@123.
2. Open the **Run** dialog box, type **control** in the **Open** text box, and then press **Enter**.
3. On the **Control Panel** window, click **Network and Internet**.
4. On the **Network and Internet** dialog box, click **Change your homepage**. Notice that the **General** tab is available on the **Internet Properties** dialog box.
5. Close all open windows, and sign out.

Results: After completing this exercise, you should have configured and tested a GPO.

Shut down and revert the DC1 and CLIENT1 virtual machines.

Exercise 22: Implementing AppLocker and Firewall Using Group Policy

AppLocker is a security feature that allows you to restrict specific applications for specific groups or users.

In the exercise, you will learn how to control an application using the AppLocker feature. Further, you will also learn how to manage Windows Firewall using the Group Policy Management console.

Start the DC1 virtual machine to perform this exercise.

Task 1: Restricting an Application Using AppLocker

1. Sign in to **DC1** as MCSALAB\Administrator with the password as Password@123.
2. Open the **Group Policy Management** console.
3. Navigate to **Forest: mcsalab.local\Domains\mcsalab.local**.
4. Select and right-click **Group Policy Objects**, and then select **New**.
5. On the **New GPO** dialog box, in the **Name** text box, type **Software Policy**, and then click **OK**.
6. Right-click **Software Policy**, and then select **Edit**.
7. On the **Group Policy Management Editor** console, navigate to **Computer Configuration\Policies\Windows Settings\Security Settings\Application Control Policies\AppLocker**, as shown in the following figure.

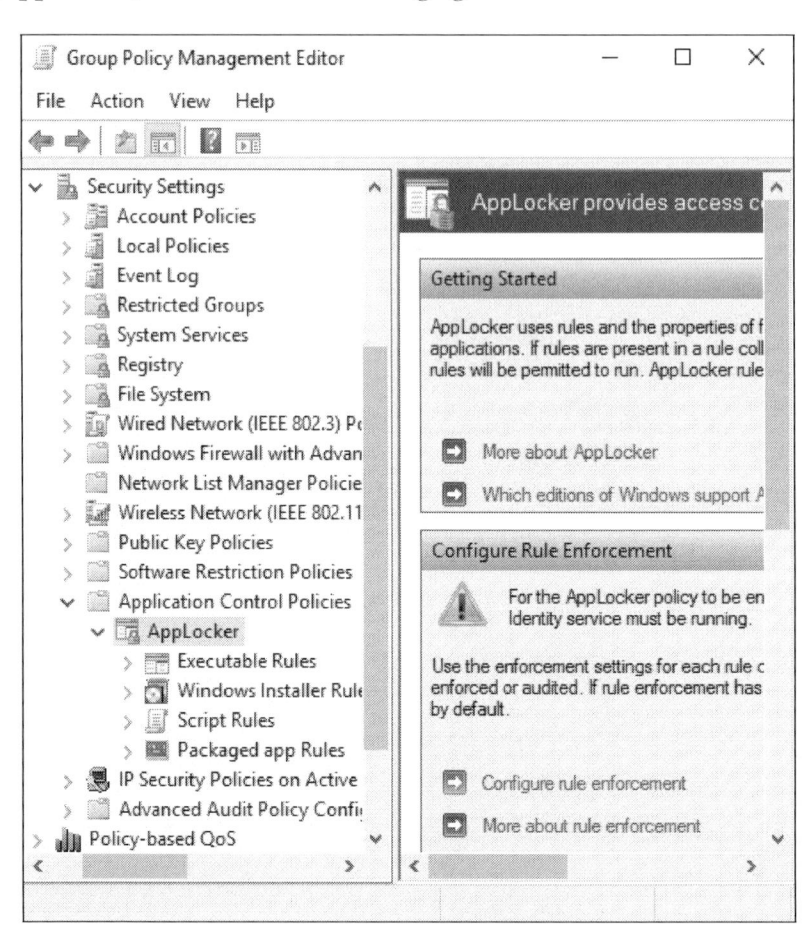

8. Expand **AppLocker**, right-click **Executable Rules**, and then select **Create New Rule**.
9. On the **Before You Begin** page, select **Next**.
10. On the **Permissions** page, under the **Users or Groups** box, select **Deny**, and then select **Next**.
11. On the **Conditions** page, select the **Path** radio button, as shown in the following figure, and then click **Next**.

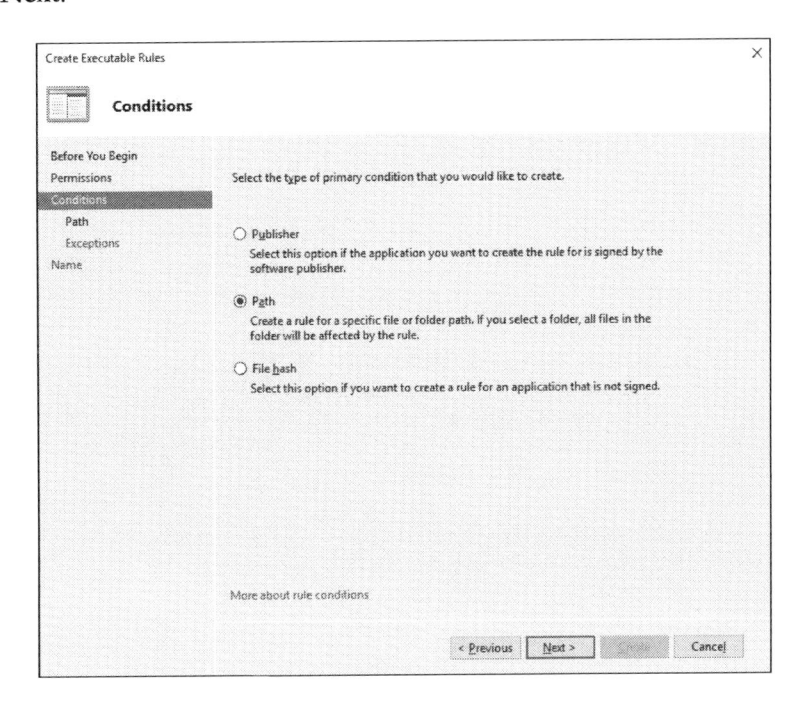

12. On the **Path** page, click **Browse Files**, browse to **C:\Windows\System32\calc.exe**, click **Open**, as shown in the following figure, and then select **Next**.

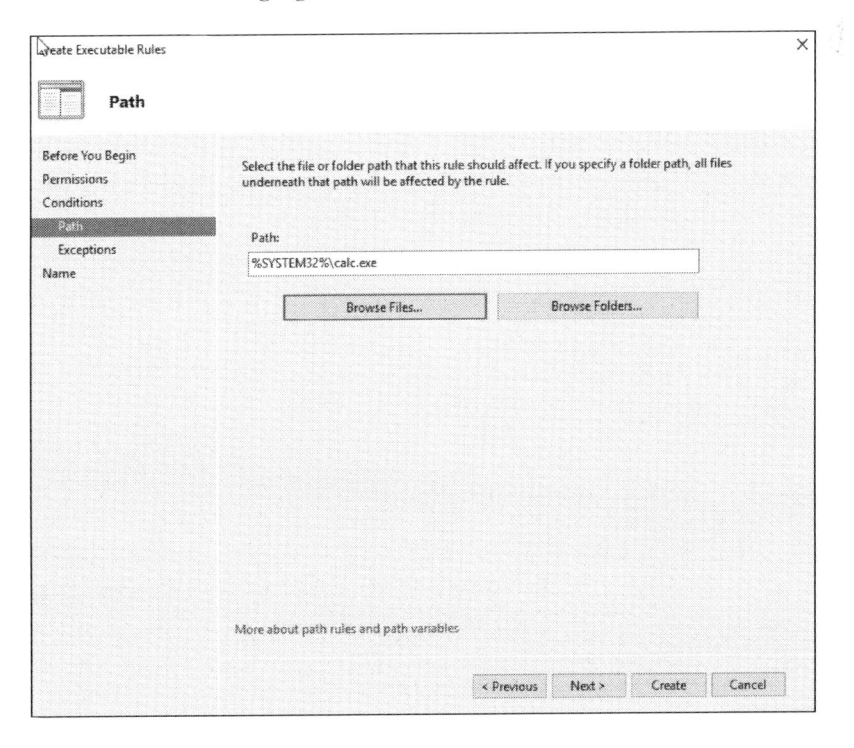

13. On the **Exceptions** page, select **Next**.
14. On the **Name and Description** page, in the **Name** text box, type **Block Calculator**, and then click **Create**.
15. If the **AppLocker** dialog box appears and prompts to create default rules, click **Yes**.
16. On the **Group Policy Management Editor** console, as shown in the following figure, notice the default executables rules.

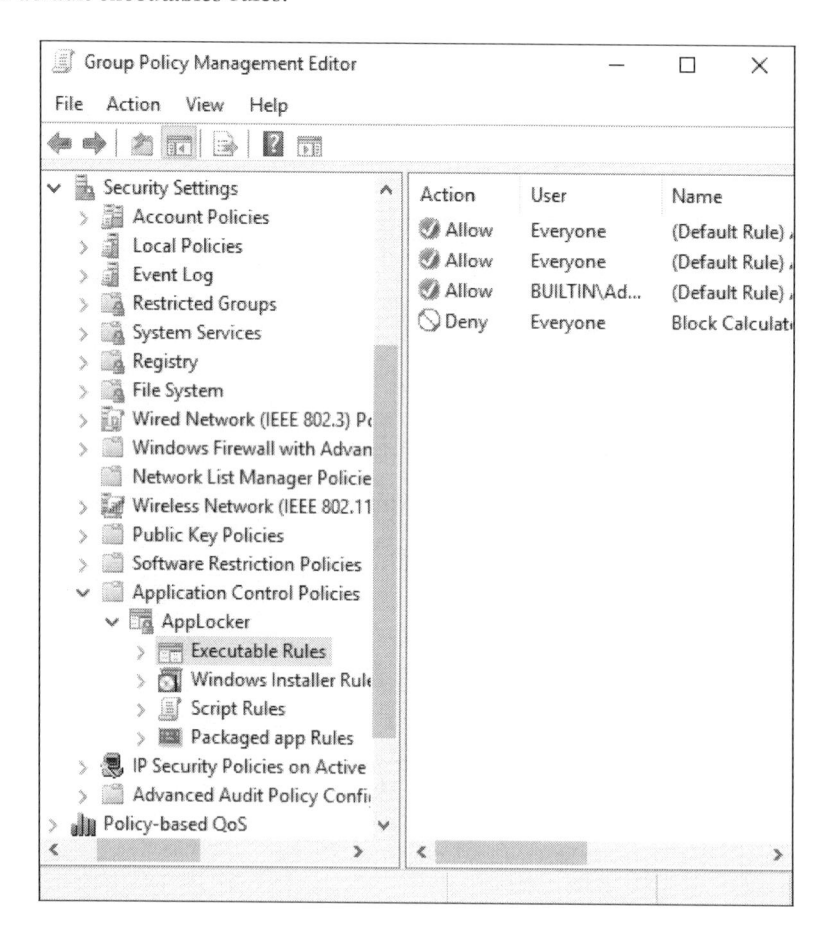

17. Select the **AppLocker** node in the left pane, and then click the **Configure rule enforcement** link, as shown in the following figure.

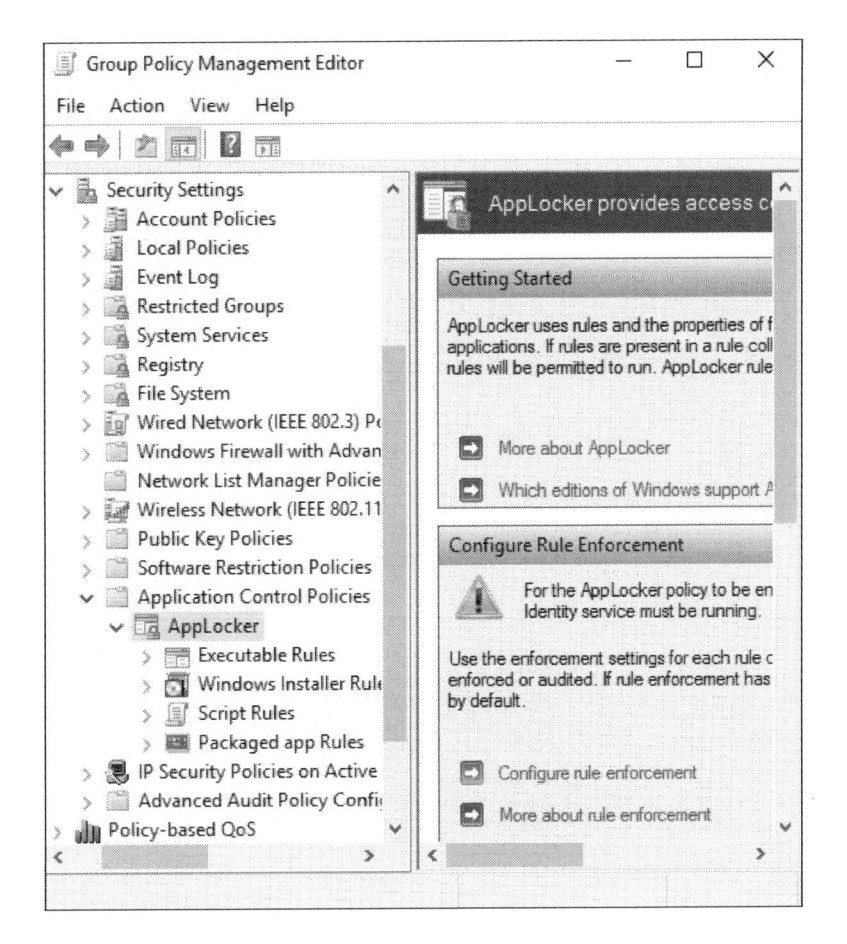

18. On the **Enforcement** tab of the **AppLocker Properties** dialog box, under **Executable** rules, select the **Configured** check box.
19. Make sure that the **Enforce rules** option is selected in the drop-down list, as shown in the following figure, and then click **OK**.

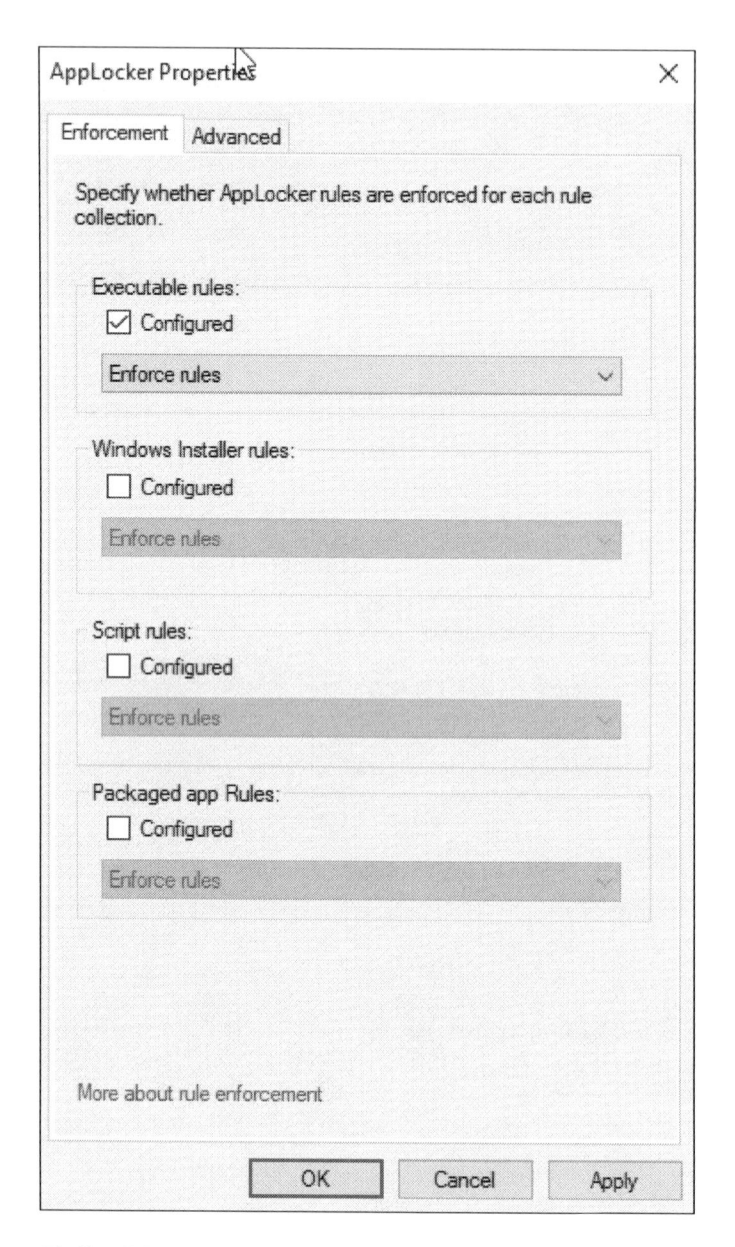

20. Close the **Group Policy Management Editor** console.
21. On the **Group Policy Management** console, select and right-click **Domain Controllers,** and then select **Link an Existing GPO**.
22. On the **Select GPO** dialog box, select **Software Policy**, and then click **OK**.

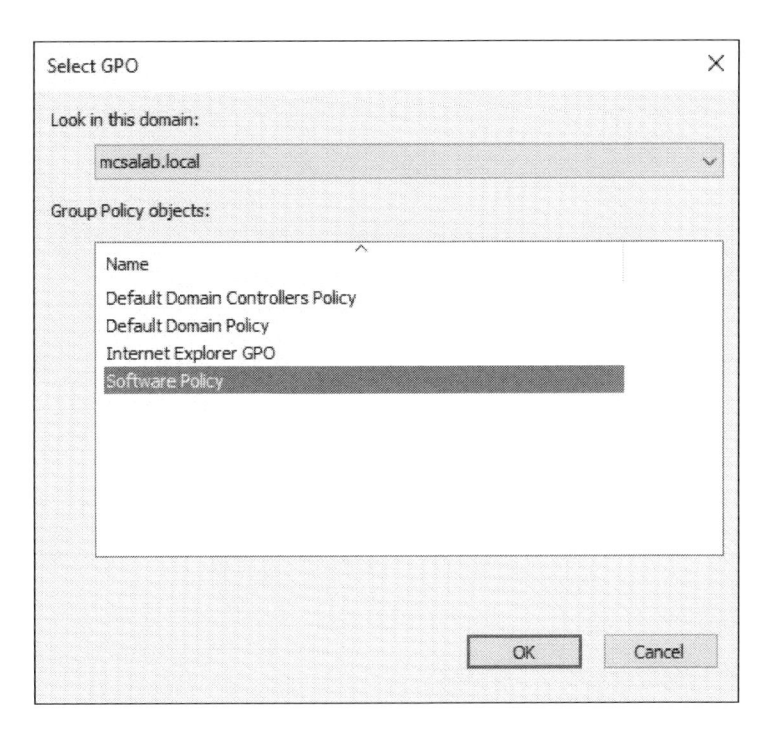

23. Under the **Link Group Policy Objects** tab, select **Software Policy**, and then click **Link Order** to move this policy to top.

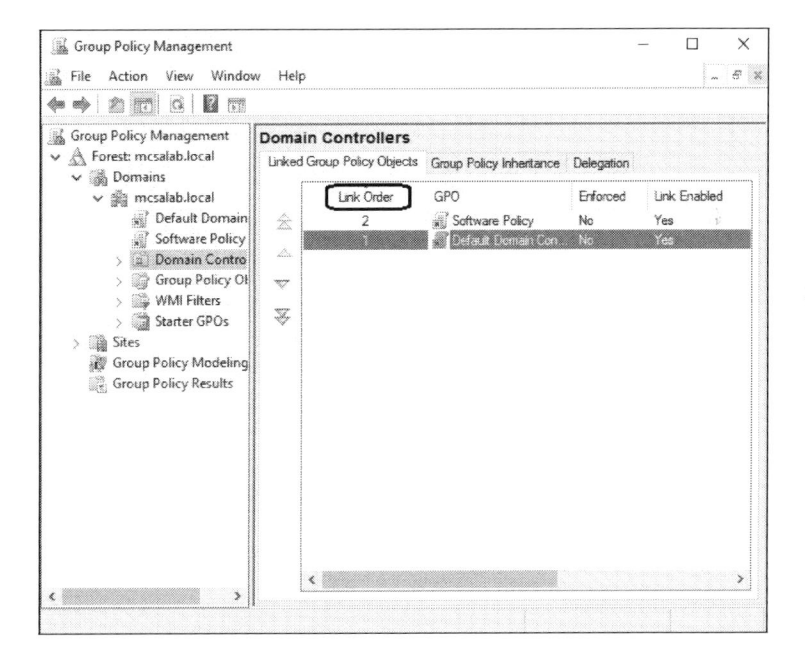

24. Open the **Run** dialog box, type **services.msc**, and then press **Enter**.
25. On the **Services** console, select and right-click **Application Identity**, and then select **Properties**.
26. On the **Application Identity Properties (Local Computer)** dialog box, set the **Startup type** as **Automatic**, click **Start**, as shown in the following figure, and then click **OK**.

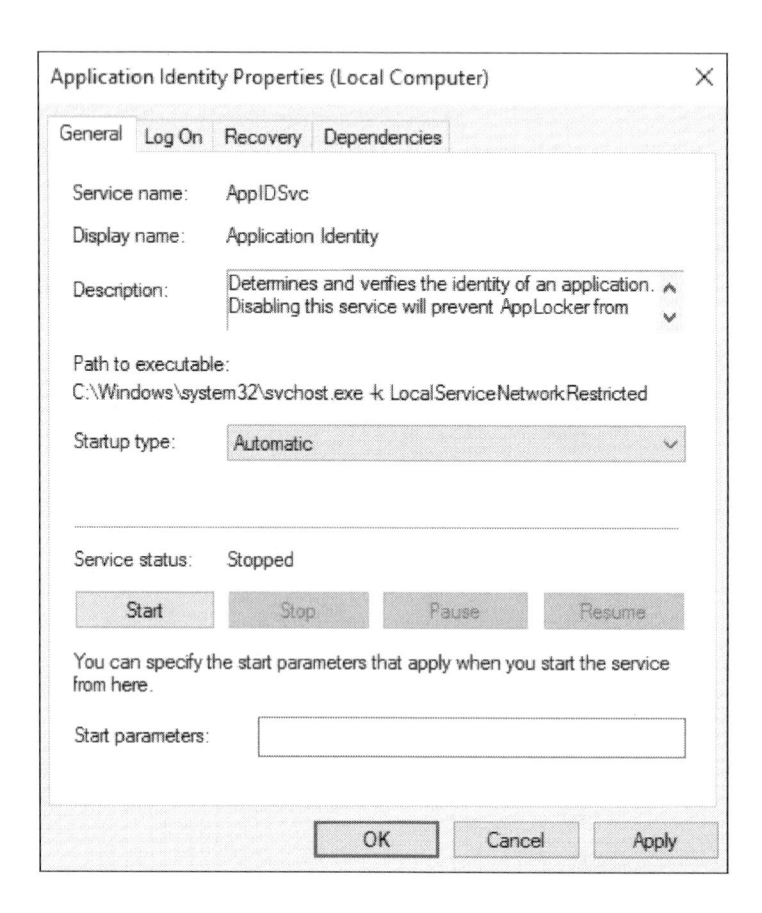

Note: If you get an error, just close the Service Manager window.

27. Open the **Command Prompt** window, type **gpupdate /force**, and then press **Enter**.
28. Sign out from to **DC1** and Sign in back to **DC1** as MCSALAB\Administrator.
29. Open the **Run** dialog box, type **calc.exe** in the Open text box, and then press **Enter**.
30. You should get an error as shown in the following figure.

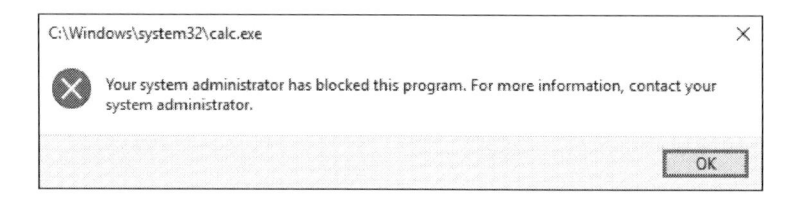

Note: If you are still able to open the Calculator application, restart the DC1 server, and then try again.

Task 2: Configuring Windows Firewall Rules Using Group Policy

1. Sign in to **DC1** and open the **Group Policy Management** console, if required.
2. Navigate to **Forest: mcsalab.local\Domains\mcsalab.local\Group Policy Objects**.
3. Right-click the **Group Policy Objects** node, and then select **New**, as shown in the following figure.

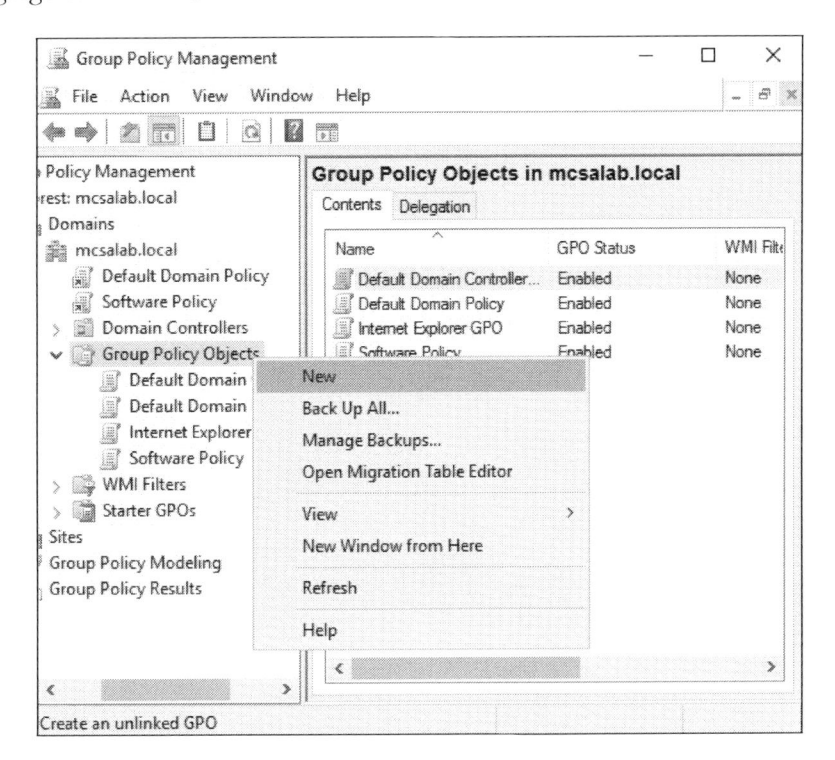

4. In the **Name** text box type **Firewall GPO**, and then click **OK**.

5. Expand **Group Policy Objects**, right-click **Firewall GPO**, and then select **Edit**.
6. On the **Group Policy Management Editor** console, navigate to **Computer Configuration\Policies\Windows Settings\Security Settings**.
7. Under the **Security Settings** node, expand **Windows Firewall with Advanced Security**, and then expand the **Windows Firewall with Advanced Security – LDAP** node, as shown in the following figure.

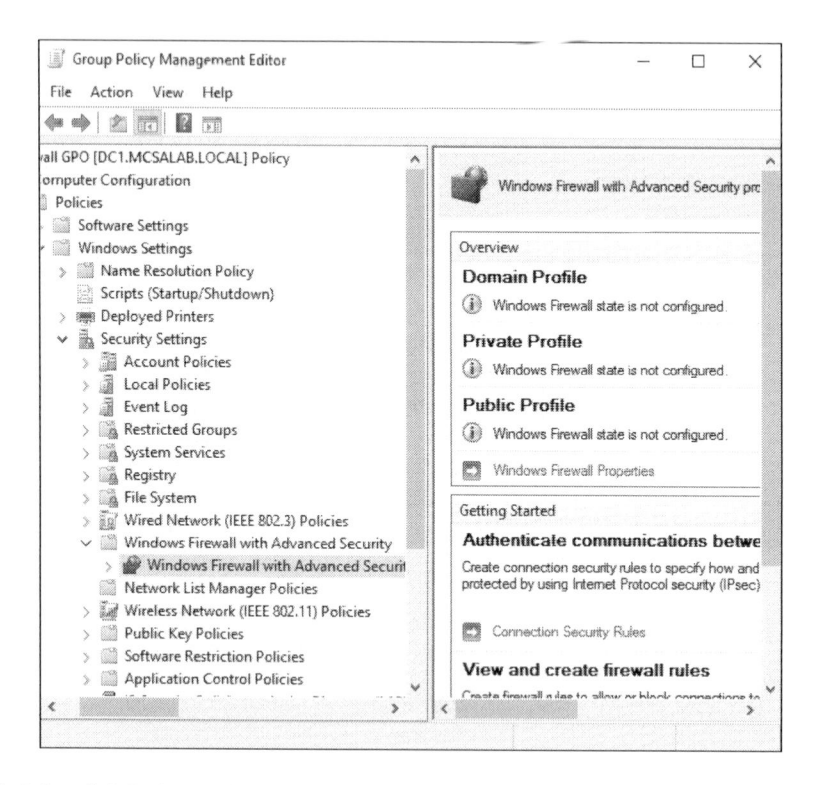

8. Select and right-click **Inbound Rules**, and then select **New Rule**, as shown in the following figure.

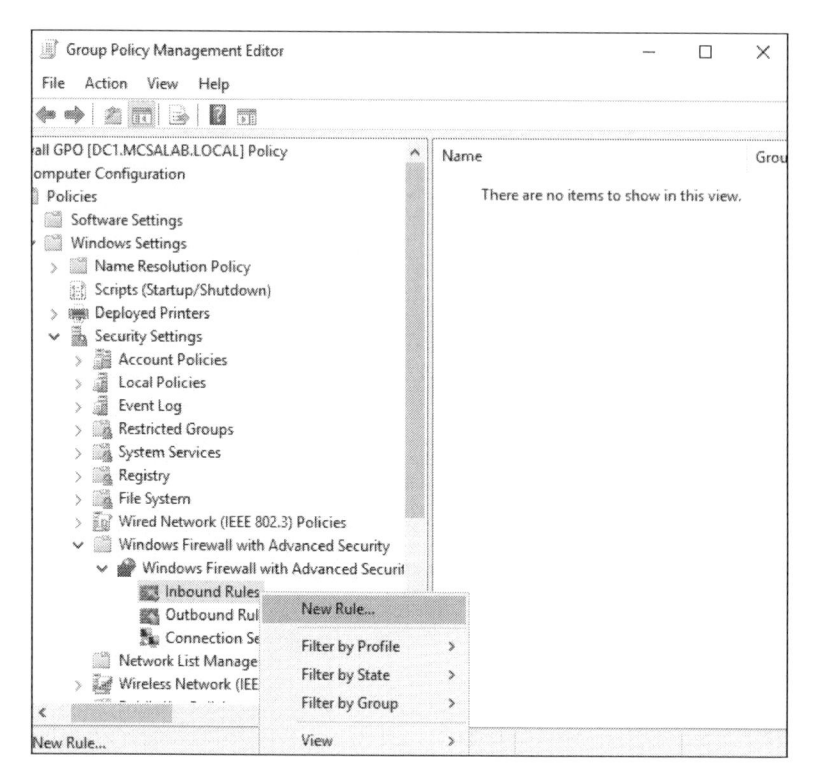

9. On the **New Inbound Rule Wizard**, on the **Rule Type** page, the select **Predefined** radio button.
10. In the drop-down list, select **Remote Desktop**, as shown in the following figure, and then

click **Next**.

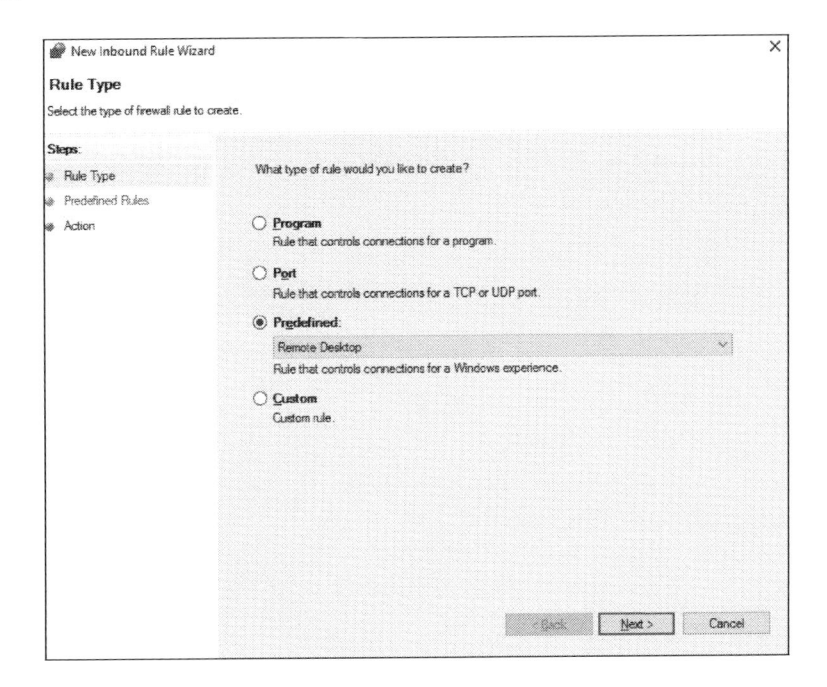

11. On the **Predefined Rules** page, click **Next**.
12. On the **Action** page, select the **Block the connection** radio button, as shown in the following figure, and then click **Finish** to close **New Inbound Rule Wizard**.

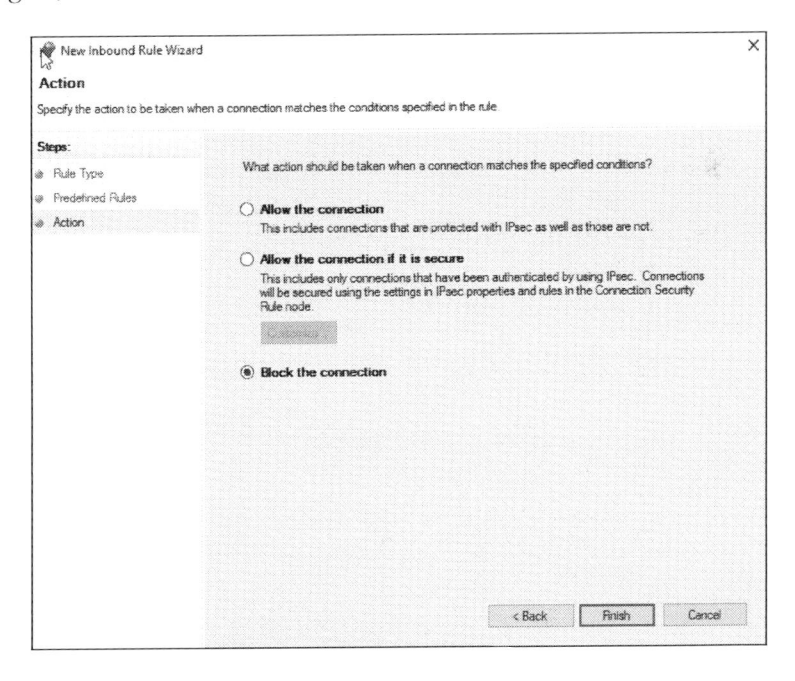

13. Close the **Group Policy Management Editor** console.
14. Open the **Command Prompt** window and type **gpupdate /force**, and then press **Enter**.
15. On the **Group Policy Management** console, select **Firewall GPO** in the left pane.
16. If displayed, on the **Internet Explorer** dialog box click **Close**
17. In the right pane, select the **Settings** tab and verify that the **Inbound Rules** are configured, as shown in the following figure.

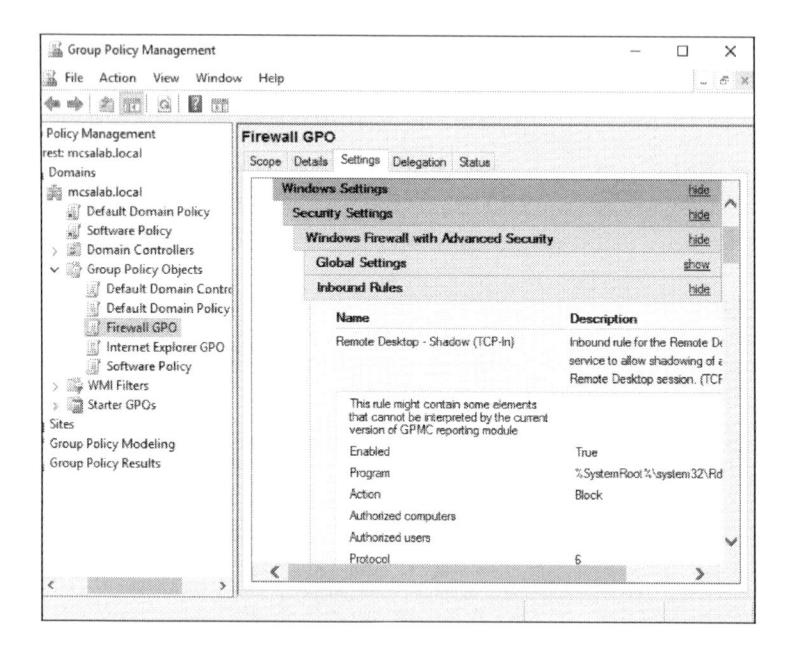

18. Close the **Group Policy Management** console.

Results: After completing this exercise, you should have configured AppLocker and Windows Firewall rules using the Group Policy Management console.

Shut down and revert the DC1 virtual machine.

Hope, you have enjoyed a great learning experience with this learning guide and hope you will provide great rating to this lab guide.

Exercise 23: Installing and Configuring Network Load Balancing

Many organization implement load balancing techniques to provide high availability for specific applications and services. Network Load Balancing (NLB) is one of the most popular load balancing techniques for Windows-based network. In this exercise, we will explain how to implement and test NLB in Windows Server 2016.

In order to do this exercise, you need to perform the following tasks:

1. Install the Network Load Balancing feature on **NLB Nodes.**
2. Configure NLB cluster.
3. Configure Default Website to Test NLB Cluster
4. Verify NLB Configuration.

To perform this lab exercise, we will use the DC1 and SERVER1 virtual machines as NLB nodes and CLIENT1 as Web client to test the NLB configuration.

Task 1: Installing the Network Load Balancing Feature on NLB nodes

Perform the following steps on the NLB nodes that are going to participate in the NLB cluster to install the **Network Load Balancing** feature.

1. Using the **Server Manager** console, launch the **Add Roles and Features Wizard**.
2. Click **Next** until the **Select server roles** page is displayed and then select the **Web Server (IIS)** server role.

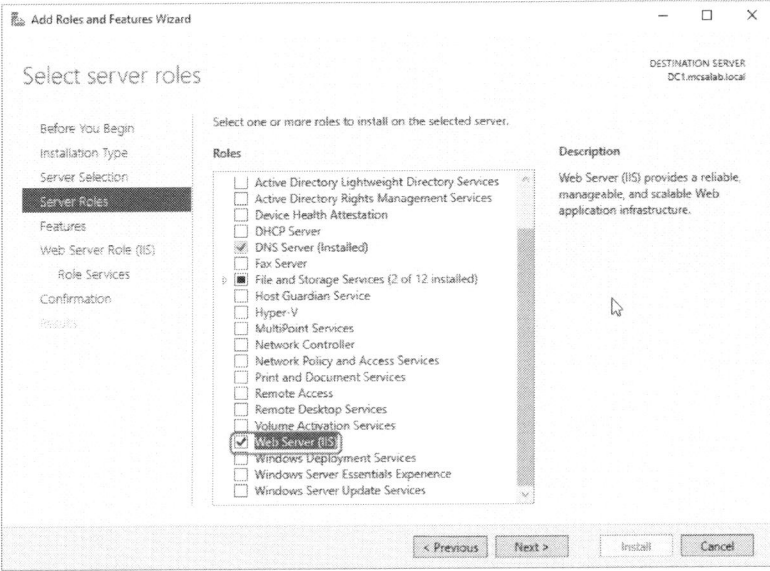

3. On the **Select features** page, select the **Network Load Balancing** feature and proceed to next.

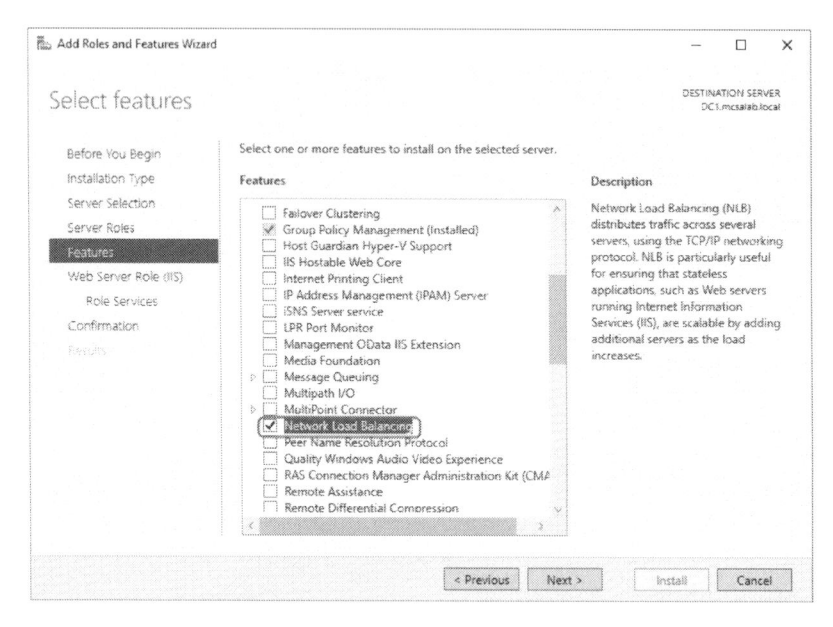

4. On the rest of the pages, accept the default selections and complete the installation process.
5. Using the similar steps, install the **Web Server (IIS)** server role and **Network Load Balancing** feature on the second NLB node that is **SERVER1**.

Task 2: Configuring A Network Load Balance Cluster

After installing **Network Load Balancing** feature on DC1 and SERVER1 nodes, the next step is to configure **Network Load Balance Cluster**. For this, you need to perform the following steps:

1. On the **Server Manager** console of the **DC1** NLB node, click **Tools** and select **Network Load Balancing Manager**.
2. Select and right-click **Network Load Balancing Clusters** and then click **New Cluster**.

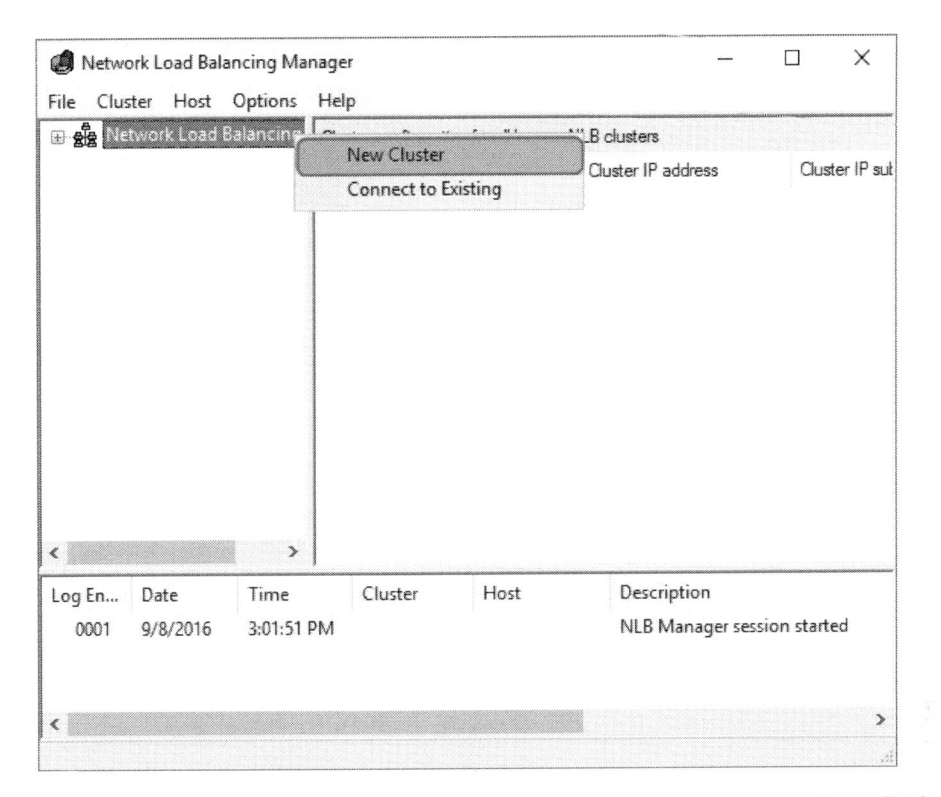

3. On the **New Cluster: Connect** dialog box, type **DC1.mcsalab.local** in the **Host** field and then click **Connect.** Verify that the **Interface name** is listed and then proceed to next.

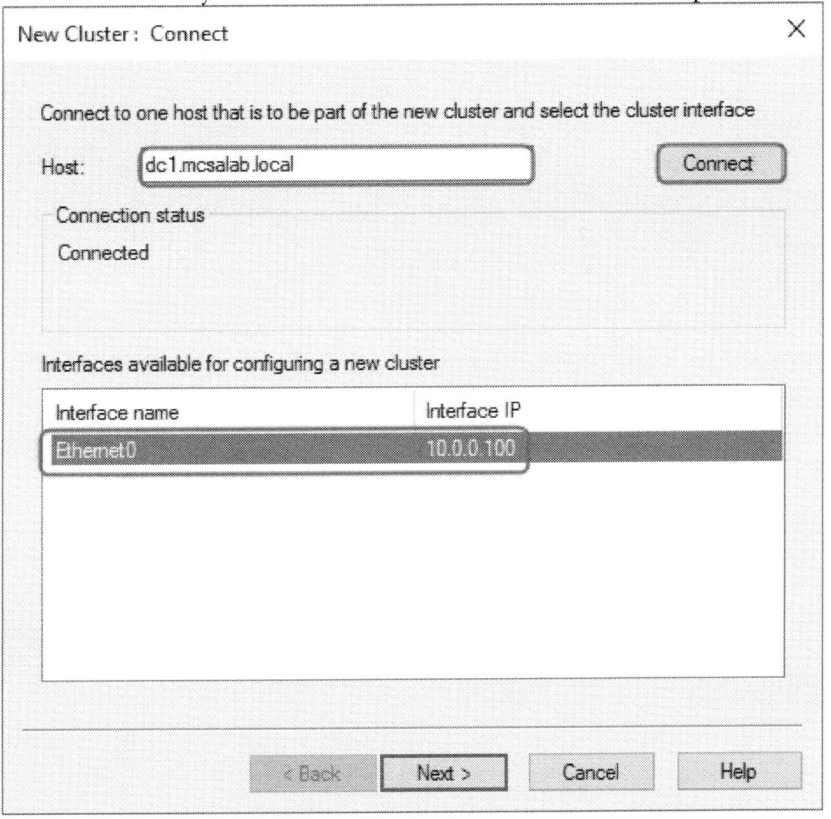

4. On the **New Cluster: Host Parameters** dialog box, set the priority value as **1**. This NLB node will reply the clients' queries, first. Before clicking **Next**, also ensure that the default status has set as **Started**.

5. On the **New Cluster: Cluster IP Addresses** dialog box, click **Add** to add a new **Cluster IP address**.

   Note: The Cluster IP address is the new virtual IP address on which the host service, in this case, IIS will run.

6. On the **Add IP Address** dialog box, specify a Cluster IP Address such as 10.0.0.250, and click **OK**.

New Cluster: Cluster IP Addresses

The cluster IP addresses are shared by every member of the cluster for load balancing. The first IP address listed is considered the primary cluster IP address and used for cluster heartbeats.

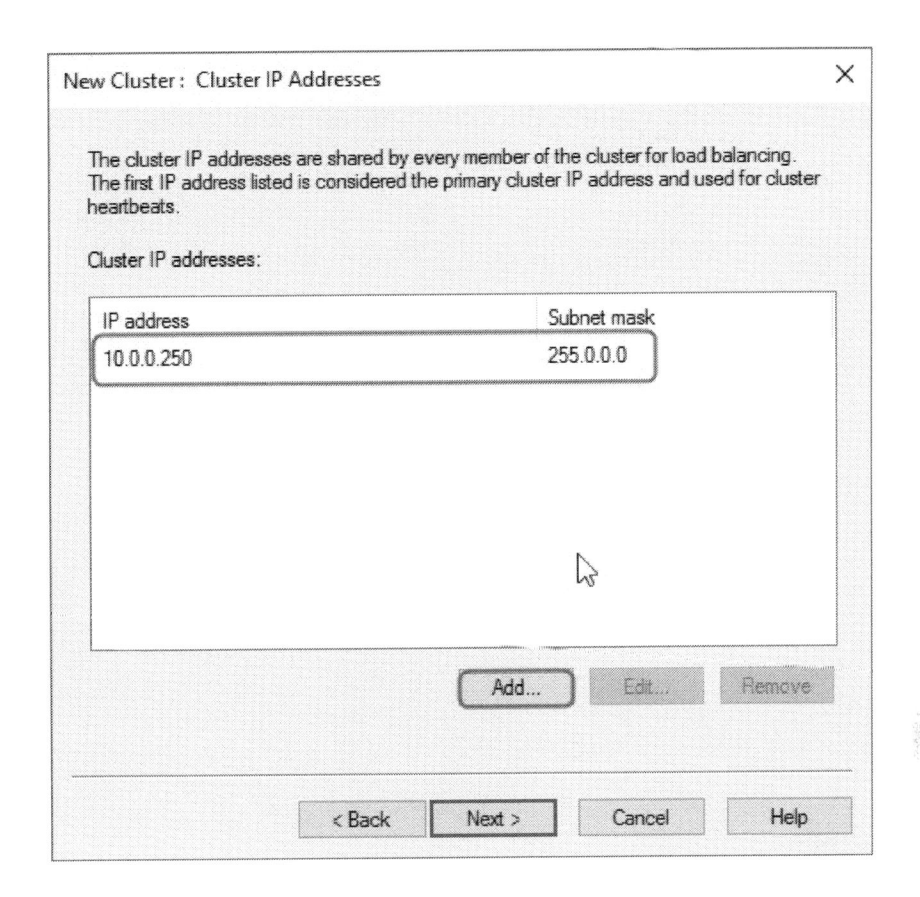

Cluster IP addresses:

IP address	Subnet mask
10.0.0.250	255.0.0.0

[Add...] [Edit...] [Remove]

[< Back] [Next >] [Cancel] [Help]

7. Click **Next** to proceed on the **New Cluster: Cluster Parameters** dialog box, select a cluster operation mode. For example, **Unicast** and then click **Next**.

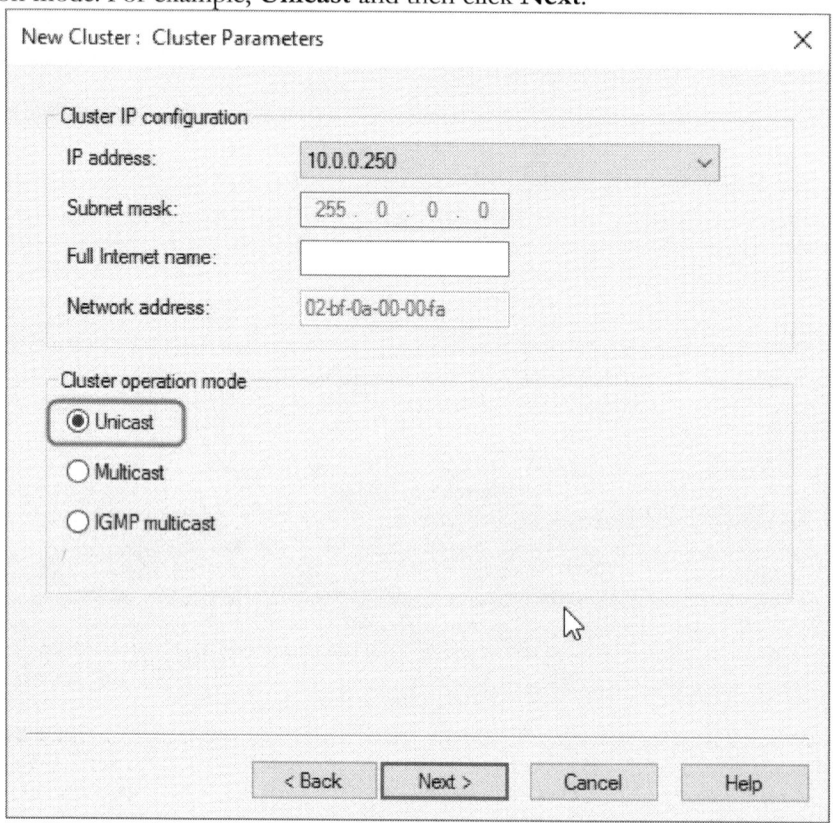

8. On the **New Cluster: Port Rules** dialog box, click **Finish** and wait until the DC1 NLB node is added successfully. The Icon Color of the added NLB node should be green.

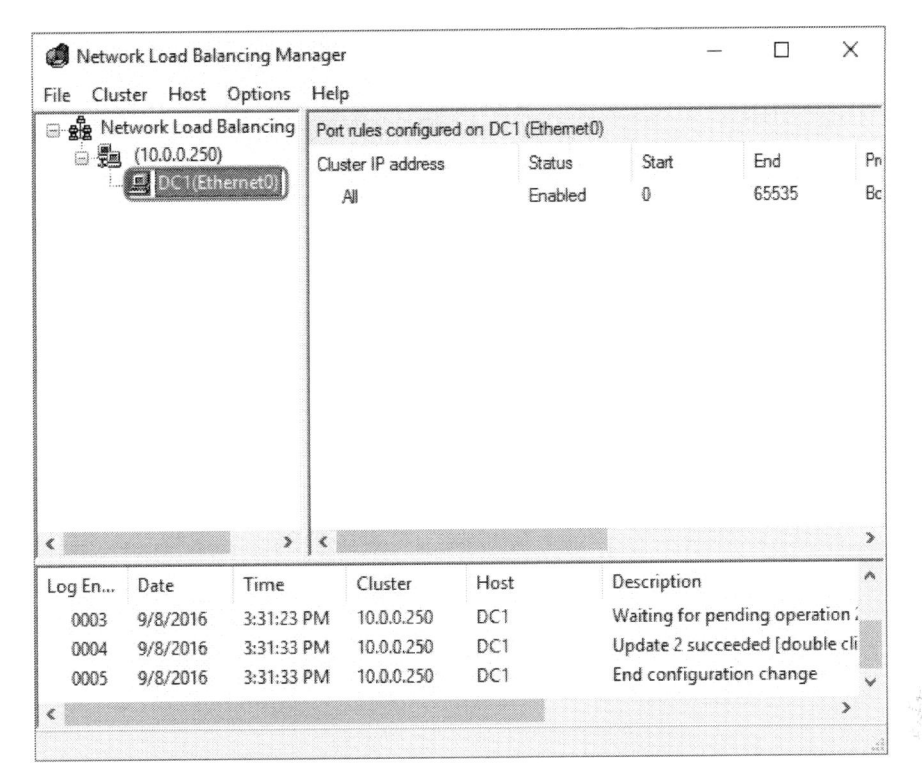

9. Select and right-click the added cluster and then select **Add Host To Cluster**.

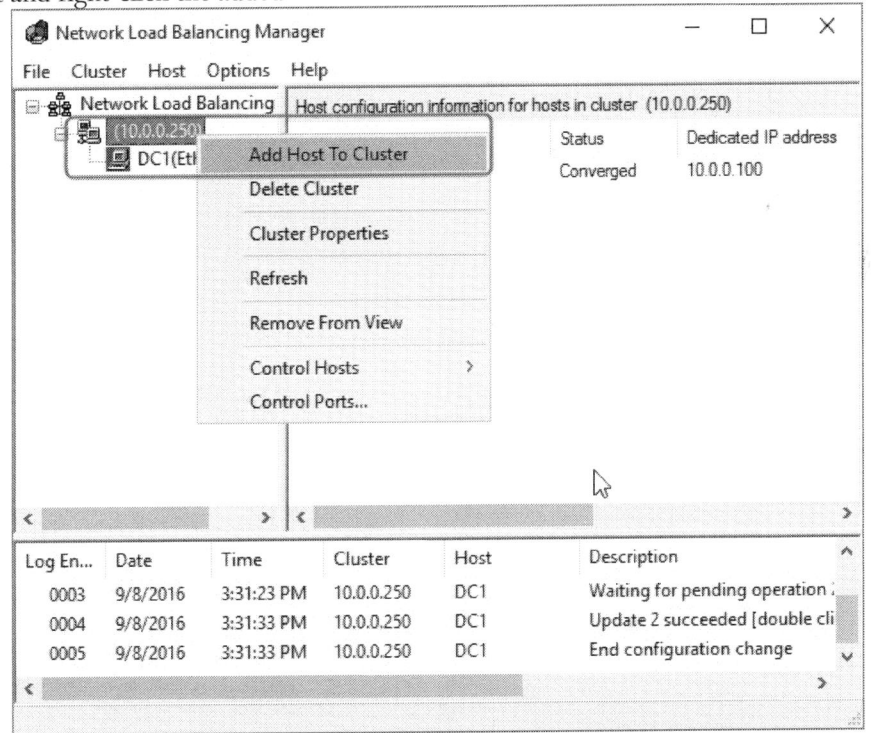

10. On the **Add Host to Cluster: Connect** dialog box, type **SERVER1,** and then click **Connect** to add one more NLB node.

*Important: If you get the **Host unreachable** error while connecting SERVER1 as the NLB node, move on to SERVER1 and open the Network Load Balancing Manager console. Repeat the same steps as you used to add the DC1 NLB node.*

11. On the **Add Host to Cluster: Host Parameters** dialog box, set the priority value as **2** and proceed to next.
12. Accept the default selections on the rest of the pages and complete the wizard.
13. Finally, verify that the second NLB nodes DC1 is added successfully.

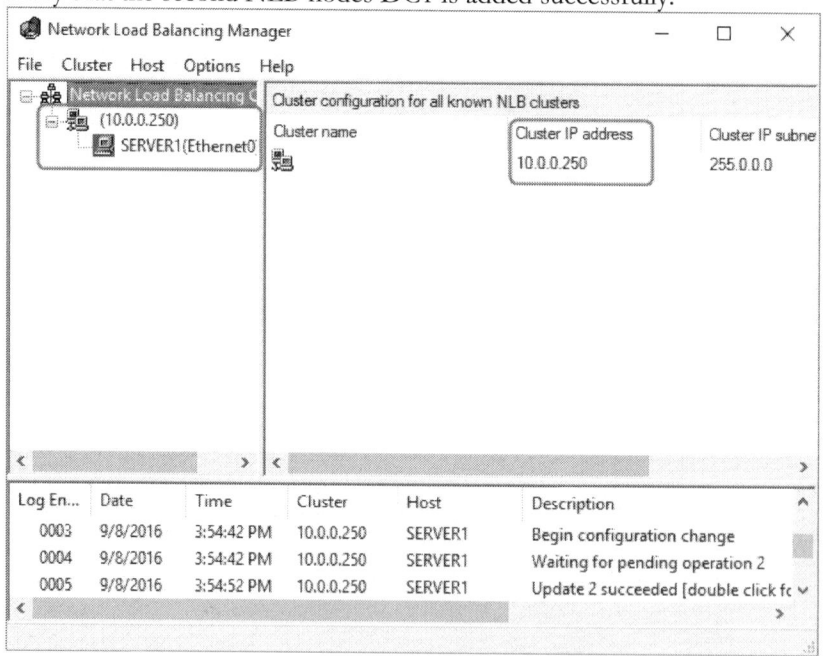

Task 3: Configuring Default Website to Test the NLB Configuration

To test the NLB cluster, we will use the Default Website on NLB node1 and NLB node2. The Website will be mapped with the cluster IP address "10.0.0.250".

To do so, first, you need to perform the following steps on DC1 (NLB node1).

1. Open the **Internet Information Services (IIS) Manager console.**
2. Expand the **Sites** node, select and right-click the **Default Web Site**.
3. Select **Add the Virtual Directory**. In the **Alias** box, type a name. In the **Physical path** box, type **\\DC1\C$\Intetpub\wwwroot** and then click **OK**.
4. Double-click **Directory Browsing** and click **Enable**.
5. Right-click **Default Web Site**, select **Manage Website** and then select **Restart**.

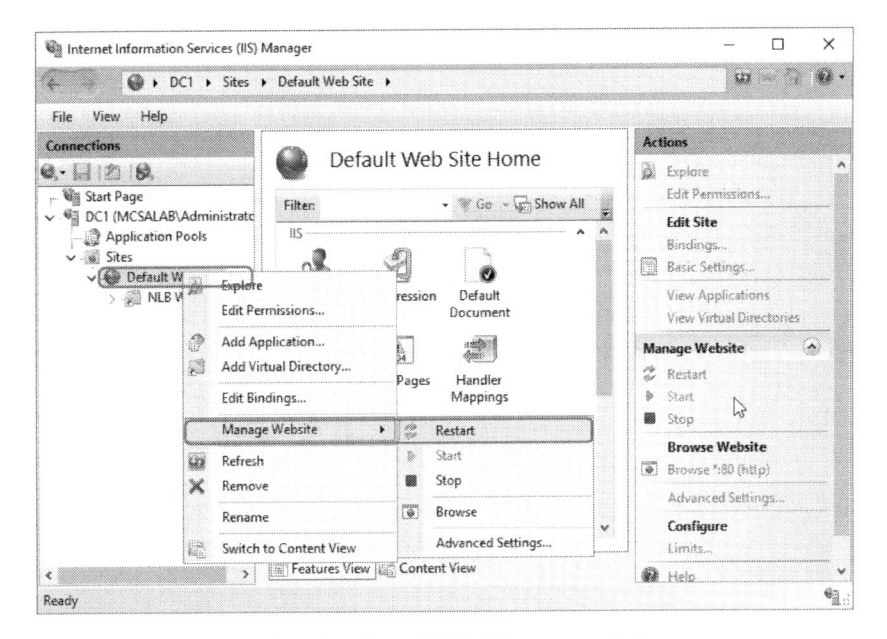

6. Close the **Internet Information Services (IIS) Manager** window.
7. Repeat the same steps to activate **Default Website** on **SERVER1** NLB node.

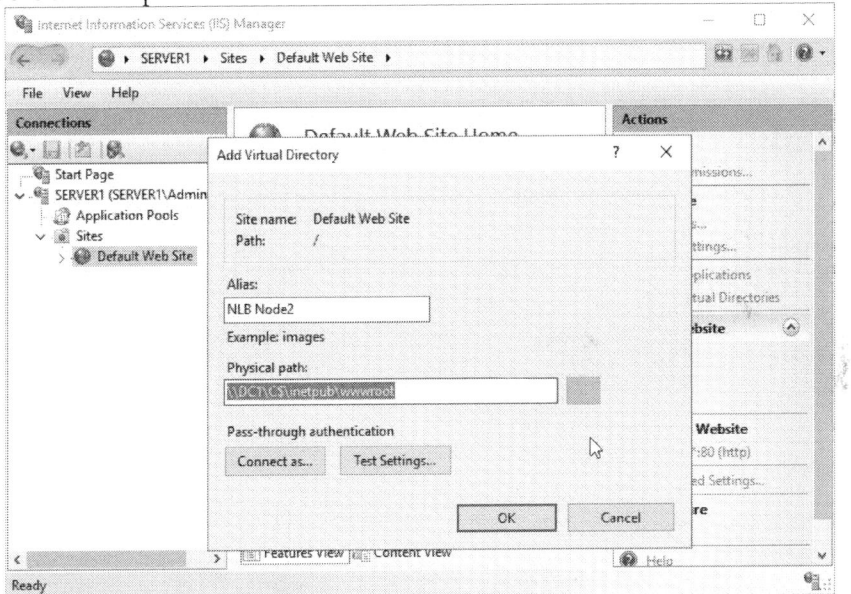

8. Optionally, if you want to access website through the hostname such as www.mcsalab.local, add the **www** DNS host record with the **10.0.0.250** IP address.

Task 4: Verifying NLB Cluster

To verify and validate NLB Cluster, you need to perform the following steps:

1. Type 10.0.0.250 in the **Internet explorer** and verify that you are able to access the **Default Website**.

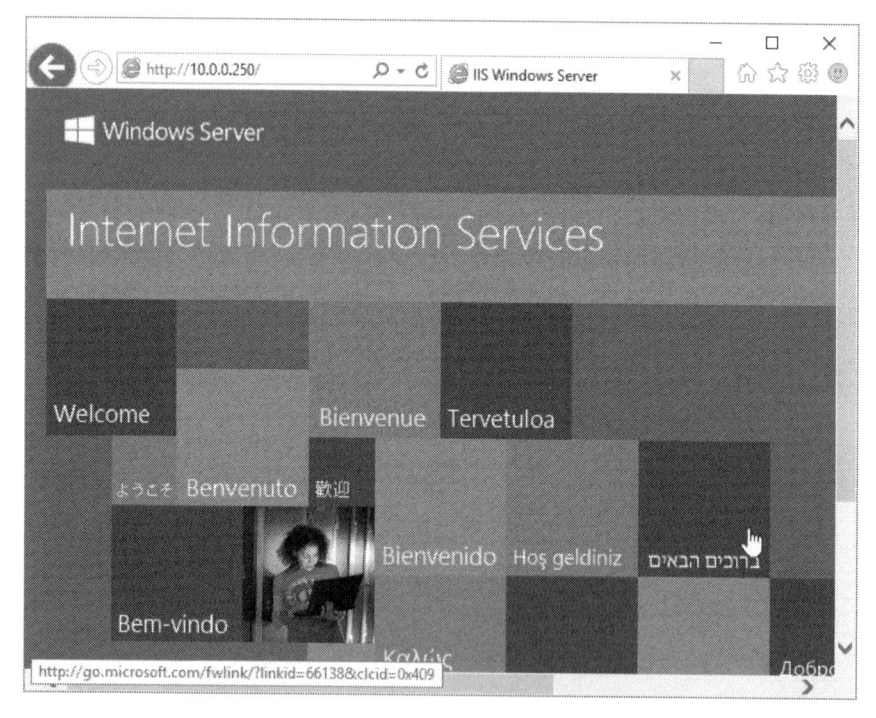

2. Close the **Internet Explorer**.
3. On the **DC1** node, open the **Network Load Balancing Manager** window, select and right-click **DC1(Ethernet)**, select **Control Host** and then select **Stop** to stop this node temporary.

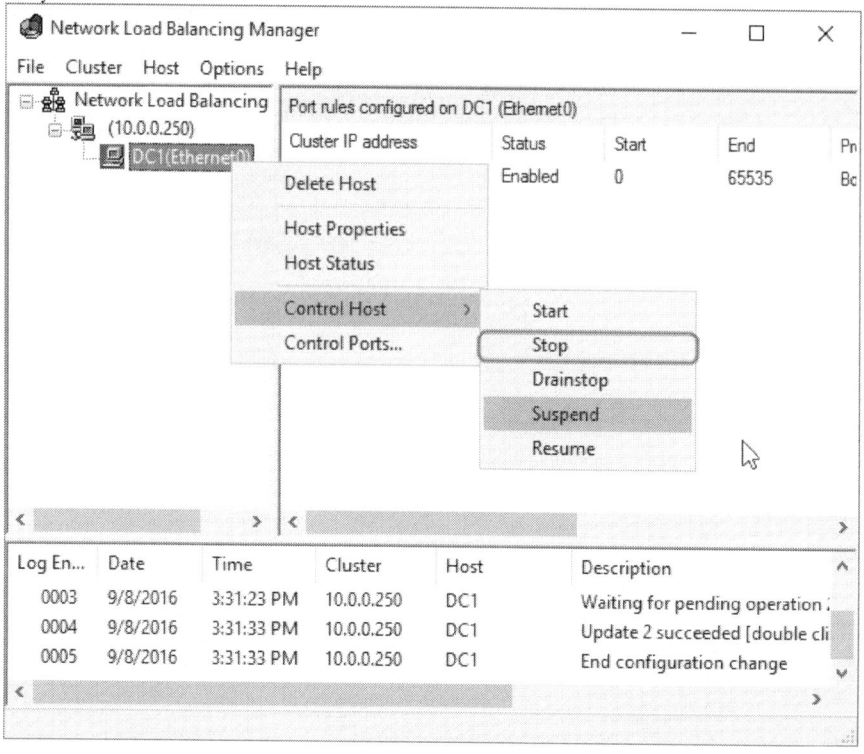

4. Switch back to **CLIENT1** and try again to open the Default Website. The Default Website should still be displayed. However, this time the SERVER1 NLB node will serve the Website.

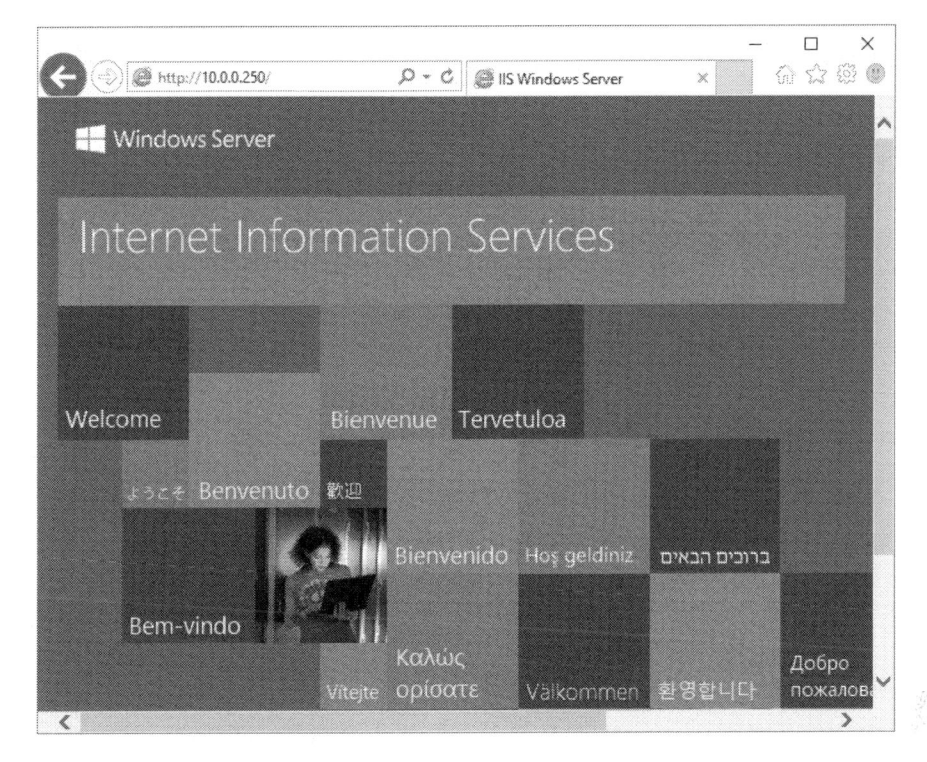

5. Now, stop the **SERVER1** NLB node also.
6. Try to reopen the Default Website on the CLEINT1. Now, it should not be displayed as both the NLB nodes are stopped. However, if you are still able to open the Default Website on CLEINT1, this might be because of cached web pages. To resolve this, reboot the CLIENT1 machine and try again.

Results: You have successfully installed and configured NLB using Windows Server 2016. Now, shutdown and revert the DC1, SERVER1, and CLIEJNT1 virtual machines to prepare for the next exercises.

Hope, you have loved thins book and enjoyed the learning. Please leave your suggestions and feedback.

Other Helpful IT eBooks

Hope, you have enjoyed this handy eBook. There are few more Books. You may be interested in the following Books:

1. Step By Step **AWS Cloud** Lab Manual/Practical Guide for Ultimate Beginners
   https://getbook.at/awslabguide
2. **Docker Container**: Concept and Hands-on Exercises
   https://getbook.at/docker-container
3. Step By Step **Azure Cloud** Lab Manual/Practical Guide for Ultimate Beginners
   https://getbook.at/azure-cloud
4. Step By Step **CCNA** Lab Manual/Practical Guide for Ultimate Beginners
   https://getbook.at/ccna-lab
5. Step By Step **Windows Server 2012 R2** Lab Manual/Practical Guide
   https://getbook.at/server-2012
6. Step By Step **Docker Container** Lab Manual/Practical Guide
   https://getbook.at/vmware-guide
7. AWS Solutions Architect: **Practice Exam** Questions
   https://getbook.at/aws-questions

For more IT Administration, concept, and step by step tutorials, please visit our blog tutorials (https://protechgurus.com)

Your Feedback

Since you are at the end of this handy guide, so we assume that you have gone through the entire Book content and it helped you to gain some knowledge and skills. We humbly request you to leave your genuine positive feedback for this guide. If you have any suggestion to improve the content quality, we would like to appreciate and welcome you at contact@protechgurus.com.

©ProTechGurus

Made in the USA
Las Vegas, NV
22 October 2020